D0762737

The New
Rivers & Wildlife
Handbook

THE NEW
RIVERS & WILDLIFE
HANDBOOK

National Rivers Authority

Edited by Diana Ward, Nigel Holmes and Paul José,

Editorial Steering Group (1993–94)
Paul Raven (NRA)
Paul José, (RSPB)
Isobel Drury (RSNC)

Citation
For bibliographic purposes this book should be referred to as *The New Rivers and Wildlife Handbook* under the authorship of the RSPB, NRA and RSNC.

The techniques *per se* referred to in this handbook do not necessarily reflect the partner organisations' policies, because each should be considered on a site specific basis and, in some instances, overriding flood defence requirements mean that to achieve the necessary protection standard, other methods and materials are used.

The partner organisations accept no liablity whatsoever for any loss or damage arising from the interpretation or use of the information, or reliance upon views contained herein.

The use of proprietary and commercial trade names in this handbook does not necessarily imply endorsement of the product by the RSPB, NRA or RSNC.

The New Rivers and Wildlife Handbook

Published by The Royal Society for the
Protection of Birds, The Lodge, Sandy,
Bedfordshire SG19 2DL.

Copyright: The Royal Society for the
Protection of Birds, The National Rivers
Authority, The Wildlife Trusts, 1994.
All rights reserved. No part of the publication
may be reproduced in any form or by any means
without the prior written permission of the RSPB.

Great care has been taken throughout this book to
ensure accuracy, but the Society cannot accept
responsibility for any error that may occur. Any
comments or corrections should be addressed to
the RSPB at the address above.

ISBN No: 0 903138 70 0

Indexed by Anne Watson

Designed by Philip Cottier

Typesetting by Amanda Sedge and
Hilary Grandon

Figures by Drawing Attention (Rob and Rhoda
Burns)

Printed by KPC Group

RSPB Ref: 24/33/93

Cover Photographs:
Top: Ford Brook, Case Study 3.1(a). Two-stage
channel incorporating creation of wetland edge
habitat. *Chris Gomersall (RSPB)*
Middle: Kingfisher. Chris Knight *(Nature
Photographers)*
Bottom: Ford Brook, Case Study 3.1(a).
Trapezoidal channel characteristic of former
improvement schemes. *Chris Gomersall (RSPB)*

Acknowledgements

The Royal Society for the Protection of Birds, the National Rivers Authority and the Royal Society for Nature Conservation acknowledge that this handbook has only been possible as a result of the prodigious efforts of a large number of individuals and organisations.

The partner organisations are particularly indebted to Nigel Holmes, who, with Paul José and Diana Ward, technically edited the text. Special thanks also go to Richard Vivash for producing the material on river engineering techniques and for compiling the case studies in liaison with Nigel Holmes.

The project managers were Diana Ward (March 1989 – September 1992) and Paul José, (December 1992 onwards). Additionally, thanks are due to steering group members Paul Raven and Isobel Drury; and project officers Stuart Mcfadzean and Martin Janes.

Financial support for the project from the NRA and RSNC is gratefully acknowledged.

Contributors

Parts 1 and 2: Wildlife, River Processes and Survey Methods

Hydrology
– Paul José

Geomorphology
– Andrew Brookes and Malcolm Newson

Plant ecology and survey
– Nigel Holmes

River corridor Survey
– Nigel Holmes

Bird ecology and survey
– John Andrews, Colin Bibby and Graham Elliott

Mammal ecology and otter survey
– James Cadbury and Isobel Drury

Fish ecology and survey
– Alwynne Wheeler, Kevin O'Grady, Peter Barham, Mark Pilcher

Amphibian and reptile ecology and survey
– Sarah Niemann and Nick Milton

Invertebrate ecology and survey
– Patrick Armitage and John Hogger

Part 3 : Management Practices to Benefit Wildlife

River engineering techniques
– Richard Vivash

Aquatic vegetation control, establishment and management
– Pip Barrett and Alistair Driver

Bank vegetation control, establishment and management
– Karen Buckley, Val Holt and Claire Redmond

Tree and scrub establishment and management
– Judith Crompton

Part 4 : Case Studies

Richard Vivash and Nigel Holmes.

In addition the following provided considerable assistance in the collation and preparation of the material in parts 3 and 4 of the handbook.

NRA Regions
Anglian Region
John Ash (now MAFF), Peter Barham, Stan Jeavons
Chris Spray (now Northumbrian Water plc)
Paul Woodcock (now Anglian Water plc), Jonathan Wortley

Northumbria and Yorkshire Region
P Bates, Ken Barton, Arlene Brookes, Liz Chalk, Tony Clarke
John Frankish, Kevin Jeynes, Peter Johnson, Simon Keys, R Parry,
John Pygott, Andy Robinson, David Rooke, P Scanlon, Godfrey Williams

North West Region
H Davidson, Steve Garner, Terry Linford, Chris Newton,
Pam Nolan, David Porter, Peter Walsh

Severn-Trent Region
Bob Bishop, Andrew Crawford, Liz Galloway, Bill Garrod,
Andrew Heaton, Val Holt, Allun Jones, Jeremy Pursglove
(now Mott MacDonald)

Southern Region
Jane Cecil, Richard Francis, P Jones, John Morgan, Brian Richomme

South Western Region
Dan Alsop, Chris Birks, Graham Bull, Chris Bown, Judith Crompton, Denise Exton, Norman Grundy,
C Hayward, Lyn Jenkins, Len Miles, Peter Nicholson, Anne Skinner, John Woods

Thames Region
Alastair Driver, John Gardiner, Vaughan Lewis, David Van Beeston, Dave Webb

Welsh Region
Catherine Beaver, Rick Brassington, Leonard Chase,
Les Harrison, Richard Howell, Teg Jones, T Lloyd, Liz Roblin,
Phil Weaver, Richard Wightman, Terry Widnall

DANI
Joe Nicholson, Noel Higginson, Andy McMullin, John Courtney,
I Boyd, A Kirkwood, David McGill

British Waterways
Jonathan Briggs

Walsall Borough Council

Medway River Project
Brian Smith

English Nature
Doug Kite

Silsoe College
Nick Haycock

Appendices

Health and safety
– John Hudson (NRA)

Statutory protection
Part I: Phil Boon (SNH) and Margaret Palmer
Part II: Roger Buisson (RSPB), Dave Pritchard (RSPB)

General Acknowledgements
Additional thanks are due to the large number of individuals who also provided considerable input to the project. This included a range of aspects, for example: review of handbook content; provision of photographic material, and general support for the project.

John Banks (NRA), Kevin Bayes (RSPB), Geoff Bayliss (NRA), Peter Borrows (NRA), Colin Bray (NRA), Dave Burgess (RSPB), Len Campbell (RSPB), Chris Catling (NRA), Leonard Chase (R Lugg IDB and R Wye LFDC), J Clarke, Tim Cleeves (RSPB), Lynne Collins (RSNC), Chris Corrigan (RSPB), John Crellin (NRA), Caroline Davies (RSPB), Chris Durdin (RSPB), Andrew Farrar (RSPB), John Fitzsimons (NRA), John Gardiner (NRA), Tony Gent (EN), Chris Gomersall (RSPB), Graham Goodall (Shuttleworth College), Roger Hanbury (BW), Andrew Hay (RSPB), Richard Hey (UEA), Barbara Hooper (RSPB), Rebecca Johnson (NRA), Mary Rose Lane (RSNC), Frank Lucas (RSPB), Jane Madgwick (Broads Authority), Deryck Major (NRA), David Martin (NRA), Clive Mason (NRA), Guy Mawle (NRA), Ian McLean (EN), Chris Mills (NRA), Chris Newbold (EN), Denise Oxton (NRA), Helen Partridge (NRA), David Pelleymounter (NRA), Lindsay Pickles (NRA), Richard Porter (RSPB), Chris Povey (NRA), T ap Reinholt, Mark Robins (RSPB), Mick Rouse (Angling Times), Sandy Rowden (NRA), Tim Sands (RSNC), Chris Sargeant (RSPB), John Sharpe (RSPB), Rebecca Sinton (RSPB), Gareth Thomas (RSPB), Lesley Sproat (NRA), Andy Swash (MAFF), Basil Tinkler (NRA), Stephanie Tyler (RSPB), Nicky Watts (RSPB), I Whittle (NRA), R Wightman (formerly NRA), David Withrington (EN).

Thanks to Natalie Pillow, Jean Dennis, Hilary Maynard and all the RSPB/NRA word processing staff for their patient work typing and retyping the draft text. Thanks to Sylvia Sullivan (general editor), who co-ordinated publication related aspects for the handbook. Finally, thanks and apologies to any individuals and organisations we have failed to mention by name for their input to the handbook.

Foreword by the Prime Minister

Britain's rivers are one of our greatest natural assets. They are home to a splendid diversity of wildlife; they give pleasure to a great many people; and they are one of the most important features of the landscape.

In a crowded island such as ours, river quality and river flows are often affected by man's activities. As a result, our rivers often have to be managed — for flood defence, for water resources, and as part of development schemes. In recent years, river management works have increasingly been carried out with close attention to their long-term impact on river ecosystems. This is reflected in a number of the Government's recent policy initiatives, notably the strategy for Flood and Coastal Defence, published in 1993 by the Ministry of Agriculture, Fisheries and Food and the Welsh Office.

There is greater recognition that the apparently conflicting pressures of nature conservation and river management can be met at one and the same time, by working *with* rather than against nature. Such an approach is a clear application of the principles of sustainable development; ensuring that the actions we take today protect the environment for tomorrow's generations.

I am pleased to be associated with this new handbook, which should help reinforce the collaboration between those concerned with nature conservation, and those such as the National Rivers Authority, who act as both river managers and as conservationists. I hope it will prove a useful reference work for all those involved in river management.

The Rt Hon John Major, MP

Contents

INTRODUCTION

Introduction

Background

This handbook is a practical guide to techniques of river management that integrate the requirements of flood defence, wildlife and other river interests. It is published 10 years after the first edition. During this time a virtual revolution in river management has occurred in the UK. There are many reasons for this:

- increased public awareness of environmental issues through the 1980s, particularly as a result of losses of wildlife throughout the country;

- significant changes in agricultural policy leading to set-aside, Environmentally Sensitive Areas (ESAs), Countryside Stewardship and other schemes which affect the way many rivers needed to be managed;

- new Environmental Assessment (EA) legislation requiring all works with the potential to have a significant effect upon the environment to be subject to formal EA. In the context of river engineering this includes new, improvement and heavy maintenance works (MAFF 1992). The Environmental Statement on the extent of the impacts (DoE/WO, 1989) is open to public scrutiny;

- the formation of the NRA in 1989; in particular the new 'stand alone' duty requiring the NRA to 'promote' conservation;

- the responsive attitude of river engineers to strive to integrate flood defence and land drainage Standards of Service with improved wildlife, fisheries, recreation and visual amenity interests;

- publication of clear guidance on integrating environmental and engineering aspects of flood defence works such as Environmental Procedures for Inland Flood Defence Works (MAFF 1992);

- better published information on river management techniques and increased training opportunities;

- experience that sympathetic 'soft' engineering can be as effective, and no more expensive, than destructive 'hard' engineering;

- the acknowledgement that river management has to be addressed in a more holistic manner, not on a site by site basis, taking account of catchment influences on the river. This has been developed by the NRA through Catchment Management Planning.

The new handbook provides an updated guide to environmentally sensitive river management practices which should be adopted by water management bodies. Many of the techniques described have now been adopted as standard practice by flood defence engineers. The new handbook is founded on the 'best practice' principles contained in the first edition. Most importantly, the second edition uses various case studies to evaluate the success of the range of techniques currently employed, in both ecological and engineering terms. The environmentally sensitive techniques presented, clearly show that flood defence works can provide not only the opportunity to conserve existing habitat but also to enhance the water environment. Indeed, partnership between engineers and conservationists utilising the pooled resources and expertise of their organisations provides the key not only to successful river management but also future rehabilitation and restoration opportunities.

The integration of hydraulic and ecological techniques is the key theme for the development of sustainable solutions to the challenges of river management. Central to this approach is to consider a river, within a catchment framework. This entails consideration of the impact of river management works not only at the site itself but also upstream, downstream, and the land adjacent to the channel; in essence, the whole hydrological unit. This is embodied in the concept of catchment management planning. This concept is fundamental in carrying forward sustainable river management, rehabilitation and ultimately restoration.

The handbook provides engineers working on flood defence, land drainage, rehabilitation and other aspects of river management with an authoritative yet accessible guide to environmentally sensitive practices. The document also provides a source of advisory material to other river management practioners including conservation staff and environmental managers within the public, private and voluntary sectors.

Three themes are crucial to bear in mind throughout the handbook:

• forward planning, whereby engineering and environmental objectives can be identified and reconciled at the earliest opportunity;

• the use of professional judgement to ensure that the techniques implemented are appropriate to the site concerned in both hydraulic and ecological terms;

• flood defence works that currently provide the major opportunities whereby the environmental improvement of river habitats can be achieved.

To this end, the handbook provides engineers and conservationists with clear guidance on opportunities for enhancing rivers for wildlife.

Structure of the handbook

The text is separated into four parts: Part 1 outlines the importance of hydrology and geomorphology in determining the nature and diversity of river habitats. The wide range of plants and animals, and those species characteristic of river habitats, are then described.

Part 2 provides an overview of ecological and geomorphological survey methods, essential precursors to engineering works on rivers. This provides background on how to assess the wildlife value of rivers and gain an understanding of the physical processes that are operating.

Part 3 describes river management practices and gives examples of the best techniques for relevant site conditions. Those that have been included have proven hydraulic performance, benefit wildlife and are usually beneficial to other river users as well.

The general text is underpinned by Part 4: comprising a series of case studies which give details of environmentally sound river management practices. The first, Ford Brook, sets the tone for effective partnership in river management. It is a prime example where a potentially damaging scheme was initially proposed. However after extensive consultation the proposal was changed to a cost effective and environmentally beneficial scheme. The change resulted from a partnership between engineers, an environmental consultant and the local urban wildlife group to satisfy all interests. The final river engineering case study is the R Avon (Warwickshire) catchment, where over several years a range of enhancements have been undertaken to rehabilitate a river corridor largely denuded of its conservation interest by previous environmentally unfriendly management practices. This illustrates the trend to integrate environmental and other interests within a catchment framework.

Key References

Department of the Environment and the Welsh Office (1989) *Environmental Assessment: A Guide to Procedures.* HMSO.

Ministry of Agriculture, Fisheries and Food, Department of the Environment and Welsh Office (1991) *Conservation Guidelines for Drainage Authorities.* PB 0743 MAFF, London.

Ministry of Agriculture, Fisheries and Food, English Nature and National Rivers Authority (1992) *Environmental Procedures for Inland Flood Defence Works. A guide for Managers and Decision Makers in the National Rivers Authority, Internal Drainage Boards and Local Authorities.* MAFF, London.

Part 1
RIVER PROCESSES AND BIOLOGY

1.1 Introduction

Chapters 1.2 and 1.3 examine the hydrological link between rivers and their floodplains and the influence of fluvial processes on shaping river habitats. The potential impact of river engineering works on river hydrology and geomorphology is introduced.

Chapters 1.4 to 1.9 identify the habitat requirements of plants, mammals, birds, fishes, amphibians and reptiles and invertebrates. This is accompanied by an overview of the potential impact of engineering activities on the different groups.

1.2 The Hydrological and Ecological Link between Rivers and Floodplains

1.2.1   Introduction

1.2.2   Ecological importance of habitat diversity in rivers and floodplains

1.2.3   The hydrological impact of river regulation on river and floodplain habitats

1.2.4   Connectivity and river restoration/rehabilitation

1.2.1 Introduction

Rivers and their floodplains can encompass a great variety of habitats for wildlife. Relatively unmanaged rivers have a diverse physical structure with pools, riffles, secondary channels, backwaters, fringing marshes and floodplain woodland. Engineering works on rivers with the aim of reducing flooding or improving land drainage can have serious adverse impacts which can degrade both the ecological value of the main channel and that of adjacent floodplain habitats. Historical demands to protect people and property from flooding, and improve agricultural land have resulted in a legacy of insensitive land drainage and flood defence in the UK (Holmes, 1993). Such works tend to hydrologically isolate many of our rivers from their floodplains as a result of the decreased incidence and duration of flooding. This has resulted in habitat loss for wildlife and reduced the ability of the floodplain to carry out many of its natural functions, eg flood control, and nutrient and sediment storage. An inevitable consequence of this is that rivers have tended to be regarded as a downstream continuum comprising only the main channel and perhaps a narrow bankside border (or corridor). As a result, the wildlife value of the river floodplain and its associated habitats has largely been overlooked. However, a more integrated approach to rivers and their floodplains is now developing (NRA, 1993). Amoros *et al.* (1987) and Welcomme (1992) view rivers in this wider perspective, highlighting the inter-relationships and influence of surface water and groundwater on river and floodplain ecology.

The hydrological and ecological associations between rivers and their floodplains are central to our understanding of how rivers function. This chapter highlights the importance of river and floodplain habitat diversity for wildlife. It also explores the impact of a range of river management practices on the hydrological link between rivers and their floodplains.

1.2.2 Ecological importance of habitat diversity in rivers and floodplains

Large lateral variations in habitat are found in natural river systems; ranging from threadlike, braided gravel-bed highland channels (Plate 1) to broad periodically inundated river floodplains with extensive backwater systems (Plate 2). In-channel riffles are spawning areas for fish species, including dace and trout (Plate 3 and Section 1.7.2). Gravel bars may support a wide range of invertebrates such as beetles adapted to cope with both winter flooding and low summer flows (Plate 4 and Section 1.9.2). Eroding bankside cliffs provide nesting locations for a range of birds,

**Plate 1 (right)
Gravel–bed
upland channel**

**Plate 2 (far right)
Typical lowland
river with
bankside
floodplain
woodland**

Table 1: River and floodplain habitat continuum (adapted from Roux, 1982)

HABITAT	
aquatic	In-channel features: Pools Riffles Gravel bars Islands Banksides
↕ Lateral continuum	Continuously flowing side arm
	Backwater connected to main river at downstream end only (eg side arms)
	Backwaters without permanent connection to river. Strongly influenced by floods (eg abandoned channels)
	Backwaters without permanent connection to river. Rarely influenced by floods
	Areas of floodplain grassland/marsh subject to periodic inundation. Characterised by seasonal high water tables)
	Fen/swamp
	Marsh
terrestrial	Riparian/floodplain woodland

Plate 3 Pool–riffle channel; the Ober water in the New Forest

Nigel Holmes

Plate 4 Lateral bar and riffle on the Crooked Oak stream, Devon

Nigel Holmes

Plate 5 Eroding cliff on R Dane

Nigel Holmes

including sand martins and kingfishers (Plate 5 and Section 1.6.2). Table 1 summarises characteristic habitats of rivers and their floodplains.

Detailed examination of river and floodplain habitat (particularly in lowland rivers) in its unconfined natural state reveals it is characterised by a continuum of habitats from the flowing main channel to aquatic, semi-aquatic and terrestrial environments (Figure 1 and Plates 6–10).

Channel margins, backwaters and lowland wet grassland with high water tables are particularly valuable habitats for wetland plants (Chapter 1.4). Lowland wet grassland is species rich, with approximately 500 of the 1,500 British

vascular plants being found in this habitat. However, many of these habitats have been adversely affected by past river engineering works. Whether for land drainage or flood defence, these generally result in a reduction in the incidence and duration of flooding of river floodplains. Large and Petts (1992) examined the vegetation of the R Trent floodplain which has been extensively regulated since the 18th Century. They found extensive degradation in vegetation diversity compared with that associated with other such lowland rivers.

Backwaters are important for fish, birds, mammals, invertebrates and amphibians as well as plants. For example, backwaters act as refuge areas during periods of pollution and flood conditions (Holcik and Bastl,

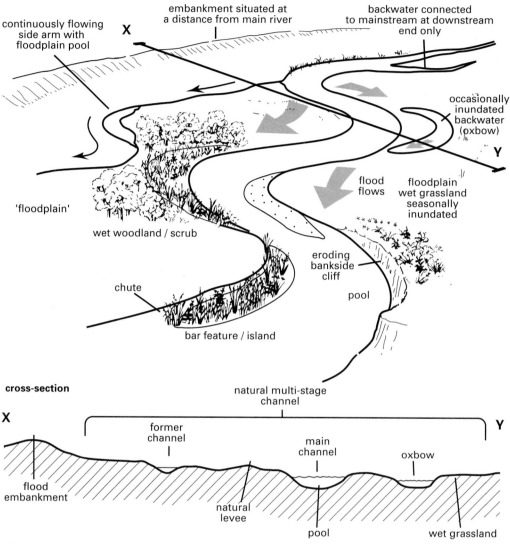

continuously flowing side arm with floodplain pool

embankment situated at a distance from main river

backwater connected to mainstream at downstream end only

X

Y

occasionally inundated backwater (oxbow)

flood flows

floodplain wet grassland seasonally inundated

'floodplain'

wet woodland / scrub

eroding bankside cliff

pool

chute

bar feature / island

cross-section

natural multi-stage channel

X

Y

former channel

main channel

oxbow

flood embankment

natural levee

pool

wet grassland

Figure 1
The lateral continuum of river and floodplain habitats

Plate 6 (below)
Continuously flowing side arm on R Soar

Plate 7 (below right)
Backwater connected to river at downstream end only

1976; Halyk and Balon, 1983). Backwaters are particularly important as refuges for young fish from the current of the main flow. Newly hatched dace can only swim at about 1.7 cm s⁻¹. Examination of the R Frome, Dorset, showed only 2–3% of the river had flow velocities of less than 2 cm s⁻¹ clearly illustrating the importance of such refuges (Mann and Mills, 1986). However, channelisation or flow regulation resulting in the reduction or even the loss of hydrological connectivity between the river and floodplain causes backwaters to be lost and significant declines in fish biomass (Valdez and Wick, 1983).

Paul José/Vernon Poulter

Paul José/Vernon Poulter

Nigel Holmes

Nigel Holmes

Plate 8 (far left) Backwater without permanent connection to the river, strongly influenced by floods

Plate 9 (left) Backwater on R Carron without permanent connection to river, rarely influenced by floods

Wet grassland and wet woodland within floodplains provide a range of feeding and breeding areas for a number of birds (Plates 11 & 12). Plants found in backwaters and on wet grassland provide both seeds and habitat for invertebrates, which are food for a variety of waterfowl. A number of the UK's most threatened bird species, including breeding and wintering waders and waterfowl, are associated with floodplain wet grassland (Section 1.6.2) (José and Self, 1993). Floodplain grassland provides a continuous habitat range from drier to wetter areas, which is used by breeding waders, eg lapwing, redshank and snipe. Wintering waterfowl exploit a range of water depths; with surface feeders such as teal feed on seeds and fruits in shallow water (*c* 20 cm), whereas diving ducks feed in water down to 2.5 m (Section 1.6.2).

Amphibians thrive in floodplain pools that occasionally dry out during the summer. Drying out eliminates predatory fish, which would otherwise have fed on the amphibians' young (Chapter 1.8).

Paul José/Vernon Poulter

Plate 10 (below left) Marshy area/floodplain pool on R Dove

RSPB

Plates 11 (centre right) Lowland wet grassland provides important habitat for breeding and wintering waders and wildfowl.

Plate 12 (below right) Wet woodlands have abundant invertebrate fauna providing important feeding sites for many birds.

Nigel Holmes

1.2.3 The hydrological impact of river regulation on river and floodplain habitats

The impact of channelisation and flow regulation on river and floodplain habitats in the UK has been immense. Most major lowland rivers in England (eg R Trent, The Great Ouse and R Thames) have been heavily impounded for navigation. The most serious impact of river engineering works, in order to meet the needs of flood protection, and land drainage, has been to isolate floodplains from water quality and flow variations in the main channel. The significance of channelisation on backwater environments can be illustrated by the percentage of channelised main river in the Trent basin (43%), (Brookes, 1985). Consequently, the remaining few backwaters within the Trent catchment are the last vestiges of former floodplain environments.

Rivers are dynamic systems, continually modifying their form. However, their ability to rejuvenate and create new habitat has been reduced or arrested by channelisation, (eg resectioning and the construction of embankments). Such activities have resulted in changes in the frequency and magnitude of flooding, altering seasonal patterns of flows and hydrograph form (Walker *et al.*, 1992). In addition, flow regulation has altered natural patterns of sediment transport and nutrient exchange in river systems. Reduction in the link between the river and its floodplain affects the relationship between surface water and groundwater in the alluvial aquifer (Bravard *et al.*, 1992).

The hydrograph is a measure of the magnitude and duration of high and low flows. Hydrograph form is strongly influenced by differences in rainfall and catchment geology. Hydrographs of rivers in 'hard' igneous or metamorphic rock upland areas (eg R Lune) (Figure 2(i))

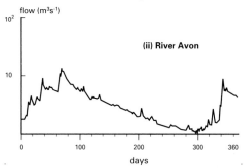

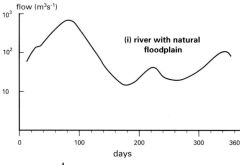

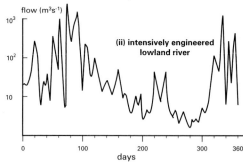

Figure 2
Characteristic annual hydrograph of (i) an 'upland' river with a 'hard' rock catchment. (ii) a lowland river with a 'soft' rock catchment.
Source: Lewin (1981)

Figure 3
Hypothetical annual hydrograph of (i) a river with a 'natural' floodplain (ii) an intensively engineered river with limited hydrological connectivity with its floodplain.

display more 'peaked' form than those in soft sedimentary rock lowland areas (eg R Avon, Hampshire); (Figure 2(ii)). However, channelisation of lowland rivers has significantly affected their hydrograph form. Figure 3 compares a hypothetical annual hydrograph of a river having a natural floodplain with that of an intensively engineered river having limited interaction with its floodplain. The natural system (Figure 3(i)) is characterised by a smooth (gradually rising and falling) hydrograph. Such unperturbed systems have slow drainage rates and maintain water in the floodplain for a greater part of the year. In contrast the channelised river (Figure 3ii) shows a more 'flashy' regime with faster rates of rise and fall.

At the river catchment scale, arterial channel works lead to larger flow peaks downstream, due to higher channel velocities and a reduction in overbank flooding and floodplain storage. This has direct implications for both in-channel and floodplain ecology. In-channel wildlife is adversely affected by not only the loss of habitat as a result of channelisation but also the change in hydraulic conditions, which make the remaining habitat less suitable. Bankside, backwater and floodplain grassland habitats can be affected by lowered water tables which may occur as a result of the construction of embankments, dredging or deepening works (Table 2; Chapter 1.3, Table 1). The breeding success of wading birds has, for example, been

Table 2: **The potential impact of different regulatory strategies on river/floodplain hydrology and water quality. Modified from José (1988)**

REGULATORY ACTIVITY	HYDROLOGICAL IMPACT ON FLOODPLAIN HABITAT	WATER-QUALITY IMPACT ON FLOODPLAIN HABITAT
(A) Channelisation		
1 Construction of embankments	Potential total loss of hydrological connectivity with mainstream except in extreme flood events above design criteria of embankment. - Loss of continuously flowing side channels/ cut-offs/side arms in permanent/occasional contact with mainstream - Replacement of above backwaters by temporary pond/oxbow type habitat.	Reduced renewal of nutrients from mainstream. Greater groundwater influence on floodplain habitats.
2 Resectioning	Reduced hydrological connectivity between river and floodplain. - Lowering of floodplain water table where channel deepening occurs — drying out of marshes/floodplain grassland. - Degree of loss of backwater habitat/ lowering of water table dependent on magnitude of dredging.	As above.
(B) Flow Regulation (By Dams)		
1 Compensatory low flows	- Marked reduction in mainflow influence on backwaters (ie loss of flushing ability). - Inundation depth and frequency greatly reduced	Water quality modified by upstream impoundment. Potential increase in nutrient concentrations due to reduced dilution. Consequent problems of eutrophication in backwaters connected to mainstream as a result of increased retention times.

adversely affected at many sites in the past, eg Pulborough Brooks on the Arun Valley, where dry conditions as a result of lowered water tables prevented the birds from probing the soil for food.

The nature (duration and amplitude) of the 'flood hydrograph pulse' is a fundamental control of the ecological productivity of a river and floodplain system (Junk *et al.*, 1989). A slow to moderate rate of increase on the rising limb of the hydrograph is associated with slowly changing water levels and release of nutrients from the surface. The result is increased plant and animal growth and reproduction. Studies

of floodplain fisheries (Welcomme, 1985) illustrate this point, with strong year-classes of fish tending to occur when flood levels change gradually. The fish respond to increased production of vegetation, associated food and habitat, as the water advances over the floodplain.

In addition to the effect of channelisation and flow regulation on river floodplain environments, eutrophication can have detrimental effects on floodplain habitat which still retains some degree of hydrological connectivity with the main stream (Table 2).

1.2.4 Connectivity and river restoration/rehabilitation

Sensitive river engineering offers major opportunities for developing good habitats in degraded stretches of rivers. However, although maintenance work can significantly enhance the conservation value of rivers, reinstatement of a more natural hydrological regime may be needed to rehabilitate and ultimately restore our rivers. An important principle is that the river and floodplain should be managed together (Newson, 1992). However, options for rehabilitation and restoration are influenced by the need to protect people and property from flooding. River reaches in low grade agricultural areas potentially provide greater opportunities than in built-up areas.

Consideration of the nature of flow regulation affecting a river (Table 2; part b) plays a role in determining the potential opportunities for habitat enhancement and rehabilitation which may be undertaken during engineering works. In nutrient enriched rivers proposals to rejuvenate or re-create backwaters to be in continuous contact with the mainflow must also consider water quality. Flow regulation may influence the length of time water is retained in the backwater (residence time) and may influence whether algal blooms build up and affect plant growth.

Additionally, stable water levels maintained by weirs and dams may in the long term (ie tens of years) result in reduced wildlife potential (Bayley 1991). Plants living in floodplains are adapted to fluctuating water levels and benefit from fresh sediment and nutrient inputs, which occur when a river is connected to its floodplain.

The creation, development and functioning of floodplains depend on fluctuating hydrological conditions. This fundamental principle should be remembered by both conservationists and engineers if habitats are to be safeguarded or re-created in a sustainable manner.

Key References

Amoros, C, Roux, A L, Reygrobellet, J L, Bravard, J P and Pautou, G (1987) *A method for applied ecological studies of fluvial hydrosystems*. Regulated Rivers 1:17-36.

Bayley, P B (1991) *The flood pulse advantage and the restoration of river floodplain systems*. Regulated Rivers 6(2): 75-86.

Gordon, N D, McMahon, T A and Finlayson, B L (1992) *Stream hydrology, an Introduction for ecologists*. John Wiley and Sons, Chichester.

Welcomme, R L (1992) *River Conservation Future Prospects. In River Conservation and Management*. P J Boon, P Calow, and G E Petts (eds.) pp 453-462. John Wiley and Sons, Chichester.

1.3 River Morphology and Fluvial Processes

1.3.1   Introduction

1.3.2   The influence of fluvial processes on shaping river habitat

1.3.3   The impact of engineering practices on fluvial processes and river morphology

1.3.4   River restoration/rehabilitation and recovery

1.3.1 Introduction

The range and type of natural habitats found in rivers are determined largely by fluvial processes. As water works its way downstream, energy is expended on the transportation and rearrangement of materials in the river channel and floodplain (Gordon *et al.*, 1992). Meanders can migrate, banks may erode, new channels form and old ones cut-off, creating backwaters. An understanding of fluvial geomorphology (the study of water-shaped landforms) is essential if such habitats are to be safeguarded or re-created. In the unmodified river it is the

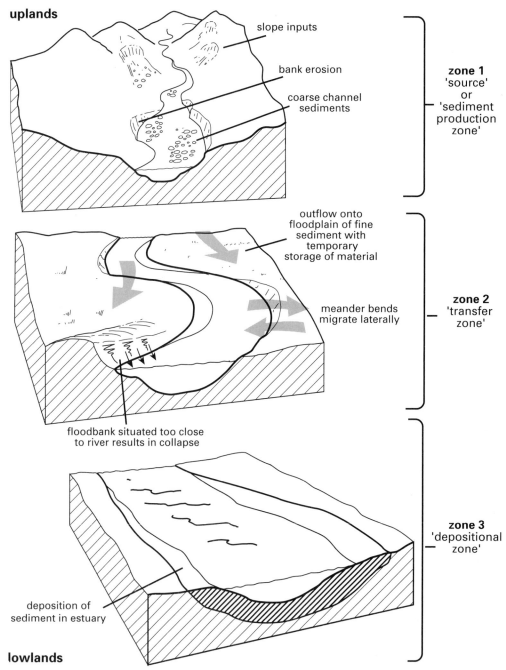

Figure 1
Variation in channel morphology and processes through a drainage basin (based on the concept of Schumm (1977)).

range of natural habitat features which represents its maximum wildlife potential and it is these which may be degraded or altered by management. General texts containing chapters which provide an introduction to fluvial geomorphology include: Gregory and Walling (1973), Petts and Foster (1985), and Richards (1982 and 1987).

For many aquatic plants the channel bed is used for rooting; animals may use this for

depositing and incubating eggs, or as a refuge during floods and drought (Minshall, 1984; Statzner *et al.*, 1988). Many organisms live temporarily in the water-filled voids between bed material, whereas others carry out their whole life-cycle deep within stony streambeds (Hynes, 1970).

1.3.2 The influence of fluvial processes on shaping river habitat

Several natural factors govern the physical processes in rivers and hence their morphology (Church, 1992). These include the volume and timing of water supplied from upstream, the amount and type of sediment as well as the nature of the material through which the river flows. Clearly, each of these may be beneficially or detrimentally influenced through human management of the river system as a resource, eg for navigation, or to mitigate hazards, eg flooding.

Channel size and form is determined in part by flood peak flows, which affect erosion and channel-shaping sediment transport. Observation and research has indicated that bankfull floods recurring once in about 1.5–2.5 years are the major channel forming flows (Richards 1982). However, large rivers flowing in fine, more easily mobilised sediment may be shaped by more frequently recurring flows. At the other extreme, the morphology of cobble gravel-bed streams is subject to major modification only during rarer floods.

Our understanding of the role of fluvial processes in shaping rivers can be enhanced by assigning them to one of three zones (Schumm, 1977). Figure 1 shows a hypothetical river which has been divided into Schumm's zones. The first, the upper

Plate 1 (far left) Bankside erosion on the R Oona, N Ireland, characteristic of Schumm's production zone

Plate 2 (below) Slopes impinging almost directly onto the banks of the upland R Greta

Malcolm Newson

Malcolm Newson

Plate 3 (left) The wide floodplain of the R Avon, the reach characteristic of Schumm's transfer zone

Plate 4 (right) The lowland R Soar redistributing fine sediment under flood conditions

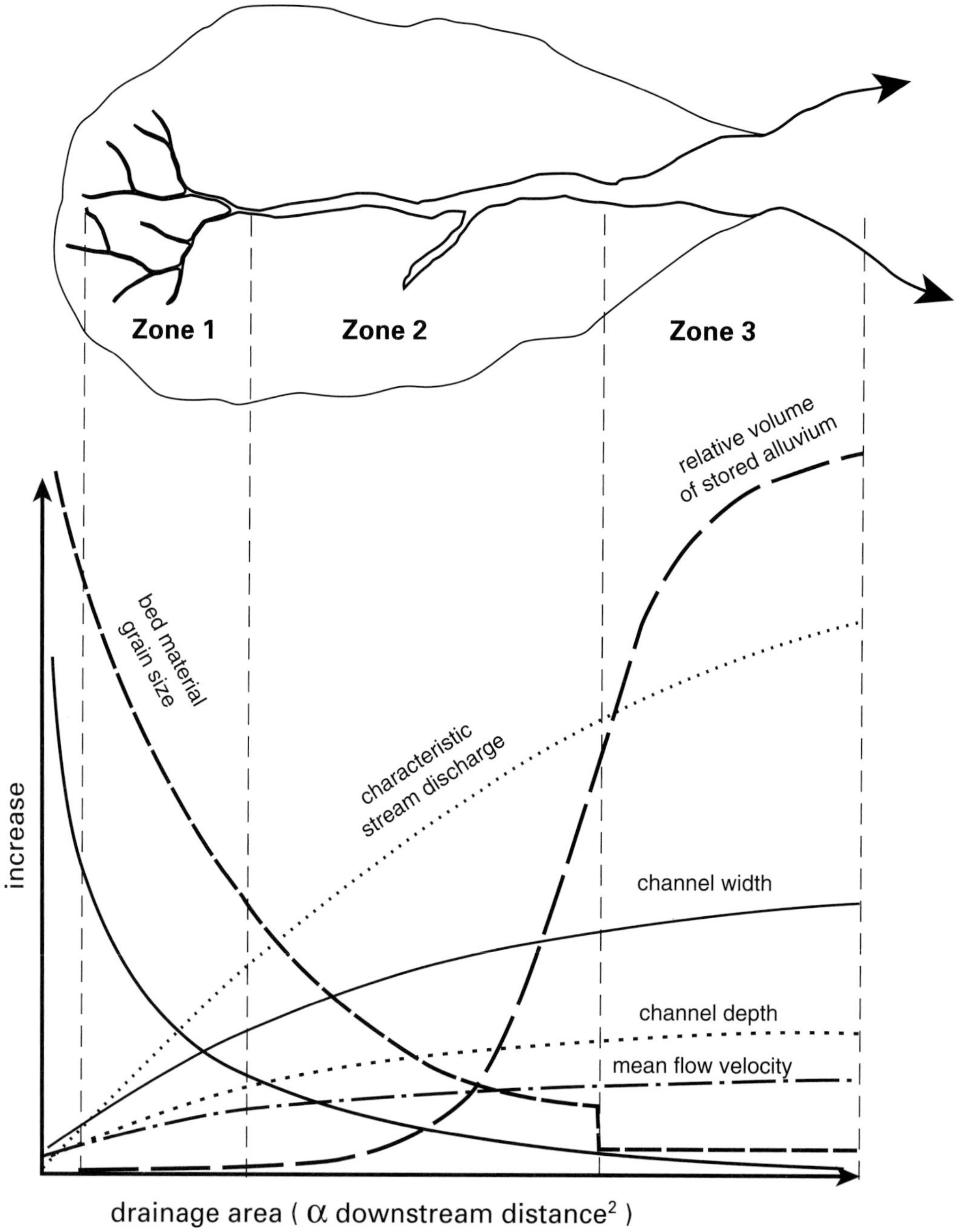

Zone 1   Zone 2   Zone 3

relative volume of stored alluvium

bed material grain size

characteristic stream discharge

channel width

channel depth

mean flow velocity

increase

drainage area (α downstream distance²)

**Figure 2
Changes in channel properties through Schumm's zones.
Source: Calow and Petts (1993)**

'source' area, is the main sediment production zone. This zone is characterised by valley slopes impinging almost directly on to the channel (Plates 1 and 2).

Second, the 'transfer' zone, comprises mainly the lowland reaches of the river where the channel is often bordered by a wide floodplain (Plates 3 and 4). In this zone the river redistributes sediment derived from upstream and bank and bed erosion. Sediment varies from cobble and gravel-sized material in the upper reaches to silt, clay and alluvium in the lower reaches.

The third zone in the estuarine reaches is the river's main 'depositional' zone.

Figure 2 shows a schematic representation of the variation in channel properties in the different zones.

The range of substrates found within the 'production' and 'transfer' zones together with the hydrological regime, determine the habitat characteristics of the river. UK rivers can tentatively be divided into three sedimentological categories in habitat terms; first, upland boulder bed and bedrock streams; second, coarse gravel-bed rivers with pools, riffles and point bars characteristic of the piedmont zone; finally, lowland rivers ranging from fine gravel-bed to rivers with silt/clay bed and bank material.

River channels in their natural state vary widely in form (Figure 3). Channels vary from straight to meandering (sinuous) and braided (multi-channel). Although channel form is influenced by a range of factors, eg nature of bank/bed substrate, it is largely determined by stream power. Stream power can be considered as an index of the erosive capacity of a river. Stream power increases with discharge. However, even though discharge increases in the downstream direction, stream power per unit area typically decreases because the gradient decreases. Braided channels, with coarse bank/bed material, are characterised by higher stream power. Meandering channels with lower gradients and more cohesive bank/bed materials

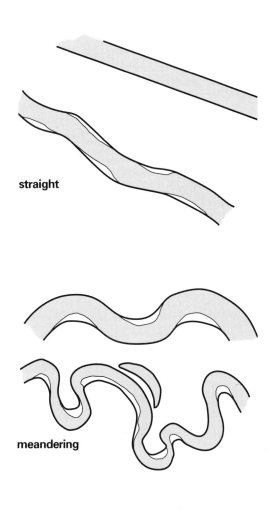

straight

meandering

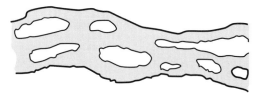

braided

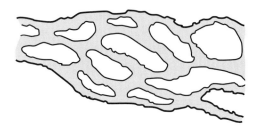

**Figure 3
Variations in river channel form.
Source: Gordon *et al.* (1992)**

typically have lower stream power.

Straight rivers are rare in nature. This is in part linked to the fact that velocity at a river cross-section is unevenly distributed

Figure 4
(i) Convergent and divergent surface flow in pools and riffles
(ii) Surface-flow vectors in a meander bend showing convergent flow in the pool at the bend and divergent flow in the riffle. (iii)(a) Where banks are cohesive secondary flows create midstream pools and riffles (b) Where banks are more erodible, lateral erosion and deposition produce a more sinuous form.
Source: Richards (1982)

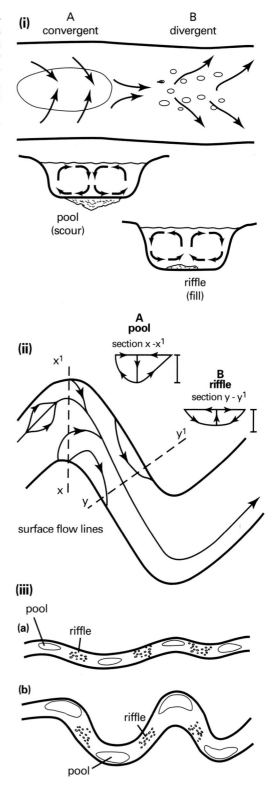

and as a result lateral or secondary flows develop (Figure 4(i) and (ii)). As a consequence, convergent and divergent patterns of downstream flow result in the development of a longitudinal sequence of pools and riffles. In streams where banks are cohesive, secondary flows create midstream pools and riffles (Figure 4(iii)). Where banks are more erodible, pools and riffles still occur but lateral erosion and deposition produce a more sinuous form. In terms of physical habitat the pool—riffle structure provides a great diversity of bed forms, substrate materials and local velocity variations.

It is important to bear in mind that rivers and floodplains are dynamic systems. They are continuously adjusting to changes in discharge and sediment load. Such changes affect the channels, altering courses, creating new ones, and cutting off old channels as they migrate laterally. The continual changes in river form are critical to wildlife.

Environmental problems have in the past resulted from the failure to recognise the dynamic nature of fluvial processes and their interaction with biological systems. This has been in part a consequence of reliance on an empirical 'regime' based approach to river engineering. In the regime approach a single discharge figure (the dominant discharge or the bankfull flow) was taken as representative of the flow range experienced and was thought to create the same channel morphology as a varying discharge. However, it is an oversimplification to assume a single flow can determine river channel form. It is therefore inappropriate to rigidly apply engineering formulae to design a scheme for a river, which, by its nature, is unstable. An understanding of fluvial

geomorphology and its application to river dynamics assists in identifying the source of a problem, possibly farther upstream or downstream and facilitates a solution which works in harmony with natural processes.

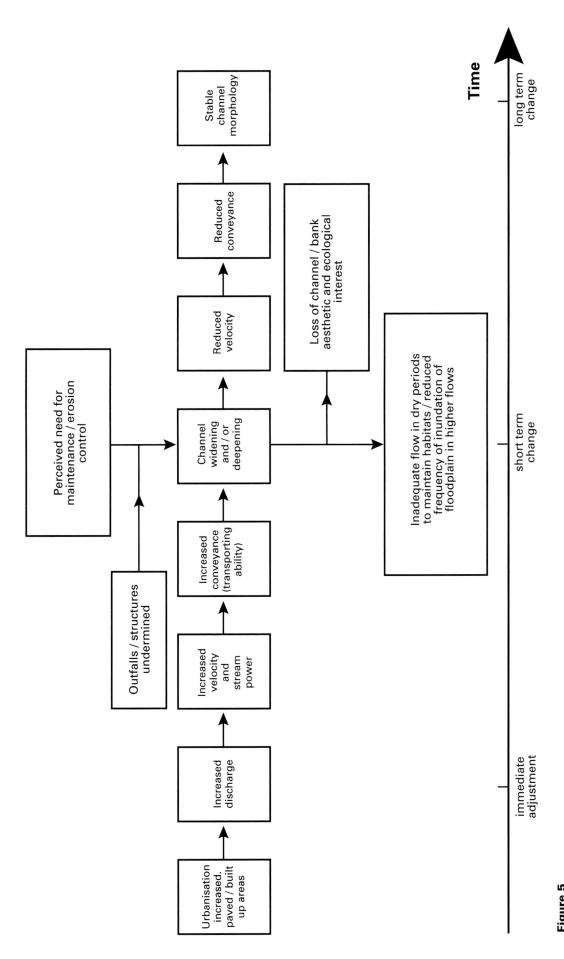

Figure 5
The impact of engineering practices on river morphology and fluvial processes.

Changes in fluvial processes affecting river channel form occur in response to alterations of flows and changes in sediment load. Lane (1955) showed these can be broadly anticipated by considering the balance between sediment load (Q_s), size of sediment (D_{50}), stream flow (Q) and stream slope (S):

$$Q_s \times D_{50} = Q \times S$$

In addition to providing a general indication of the way a stream will respond to natural change this relationship can assist in the determination of the impact of engineering practices on rivers (Figure 5). Unfortunately however, pressure for development, lack of space in many urban environments, and the need for flood protection may prevent rivers from recovering from changes naturally. All too often it is the immediate results of change due to urbanisation which have to be addressed.

1.3.3 The impact of engineering practices on fluvial processes and river morphology

River channels have been modified in the UK for many purposes including: flood alleviation, agricultural drainage, reducing bank erosion and maintaining navigation. These objectives have been achieved by a variety of engineering methods, including widening, deepening, straightening and embanking. Table 1 illustrates the potential ecological and geomorphological impact of river deepening (Plate 5). The impact of channel straightening on fluvial processes is shown in Figure 6.

Straightening increases slope by providing a shorter channel path. Consideration of Lane's (1955) relationship indicates that increase of slope enables the upstream end of a straightened reach to transport more sediment than is supplied from above the section. This results in erosion of the bed, which progresses upstream as a nickpoint in order to supply more sediment (Parker and Andres, 1976) (Plate 6).

Table 1: Potential, ecological and geomorphological impacts of river deepening

ENGINEERING OBJECTIVE	IMPACT
Reduce period of flooding on adjacent land and provide better freeboard to enable drainage	(a) Degraded channel morphology with loss of pool/riffle habitats. Channel destabilised upstream and downstream. (b) Decreased potential for backwater creation/rejuvenation (c) Bankside plants lost because of steep and rapid transition from permanently wet channel to dry banks. (d) Water table lowered in floodplain habitats adjacent to river leading to loss/reduction of wetland species.

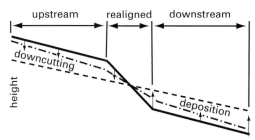

Figure 6
The impact of channel straightening on fluvial processes.
Source: Parker and Andres (1976)

**Plate 5
Slumping of a
riverbank as a
result of river
deepening
operations**

RSPB

Table 2: Geomorphological solutions to adverse impacts on a river channel due to changes within the catchment. Source: NRA Thames Region.

ACTIVITY WITHIN CATCHMENT	IMPACT ON CHANNEL	TRADITIONAL ENGINEERING RESPONSE	GEOMORPHOLOGICAL RESPONSE
Urbanisation	Lowered base flows and increased flood flows from decreased infiltration and lowered groundwater levels. Increased sediment load initially. Increased run-off from paved areas - increased discharge - widening through erosion (especially in non-cohesive glacial sands and gravels). Overwide channel encourages deposition of urban silts.	Enlarge channel. Line channel with concrete or similar armour layer. Sheet piling or concrete on both banks.	Source control of run-off using permeable pavements, storage ponds etc. Establish a two or multi stage channel to accommodate increased discharges while maintaining a low flow width. Sequence of pools and riffles placed in channel to enhance habitat. Wetland flora can be planted on higher berm. Erosion control using geotextiles (if necessary).
Realignment/ Diversion to accommodate development	Loss of pool/riffle sequence. An increase in slope – higher velocity – erosion of bed and banks – instability – wider, more uniform channel. Decrease in ecosystem habitat.	Straighten channel – shortest point A–B uniform, trapezoidal morphology.	Realignment should copy original plan geometry. Minimise slope increase and reinstate bends. Pools and riffles reinstated at regular intervals. Reinstate substrate.
Bank Protection	Loss of natural bank profiles. Loss of marginal habitats.	Toe boards, sheet piling, sandbags.	Planting of reeds, geotextile stretch fencing, gabions or rip-rap, willow spiling. These should be placed on the outside of a bend where flowlines converge.

Research indicates that where stream power exceeds a value of 35 Wm^{-2} channels will adjust to change (ie erosive power is enough to modify the bed if it is not rigid).

Figure 7 shows the impact of stream widening, raising floodbanks and straightening meanders on stream power, together with the resultant effect on sediment supply and erosion.

Nigel Holmes

Increased understanding of fluvial processes has enabled alternative engineering techniques, which work with nature, to be utilised, eg:

- establishment of low-flow channel in flood relief channels;

- reinstatement of pools and riffles where realignment using trapezoidal channels had been undertaken;

- use of natural bank protection, eg reeds and geotextiles, instead of sheet piling.

Table 2 illustrates a number of geomorphological solutions to adverse impacts on a river channel due to changes within a catchment.

**Plate 6
Degradation of a
stream bed
progressing
upstream as a
'nickpoint' in
order to increase
sediment supply**

Sediment transport capacity is broadly related to stream power. This index of a river's erosive power can easily be calculated:

$$\text{Stream power} = (w \times Q \times S)/b$$
(units = water per square metre)

w = specific weight of water (density x gravity)
Q = bankfull discharge
S = water slope
b = channel width at bed level

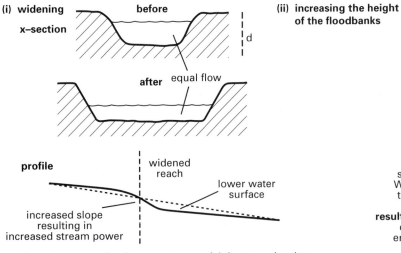

(i) widening x–section

before

after   equal flow

d

profile

widened reach

lower water surface

increased slope resulting in increased stream power

result: upstream erosion (transport > supply) because the slope of water is increased into the widened engineered section
Deposition in widened section because supply > transport

(ii) increasing the height of the floodbanks

before

d

after

d

under natural conditions, floods transfer stream energy and sediment to floodplain
With the embankments there is no transfer to floodplain so energy is high in channel.

result: bed and bank erosion as transport > supply
downstream sediment supply increased;
erosion spreads upstream as bed degrades.

(iii) altering slope by straightening meanders

result: channel bed and banks erode due to increase in stream power, and sediment supplied downstream increases

same fall of height in ³/4 of distance

**Figure 7
The impact of stream widening, raising floodbanks and straightening meanders on stream power.**

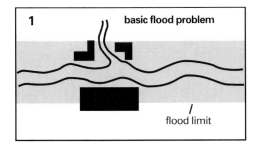

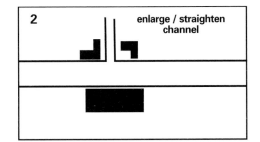

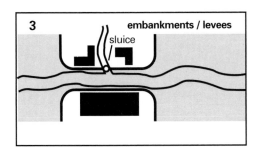

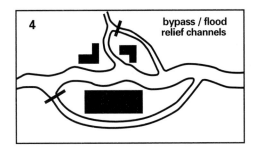

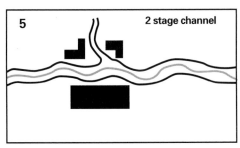

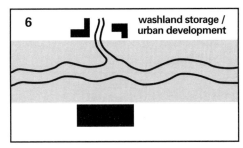

Figure 8
The range of flood alleviation options in an urban area and their potential impact in geomorphological and ecological terms. Adapted from Nixon (1966).

Additionally, where flood alleviation work has to be undertaken, it should be seen as an opportunity to protect and enhance the morphology of the channel. Figure 8 illustrates a range of flood alleviation options in an urban area and their potential impact in geomorphological and ecological terms. Where a channel has to be enlarged, options 5 and 6 are more desirable than option 2 in wildlife terms, as a result of reduced impact on the channel and floodplain.

Consideration of stream power is central not only to the evaluation of the impact of river engineering works but also to the evaluation of the success of river restoration, rehabilitation and recovery.

1.3.4 River restoration, rehabilitation and recovery

Most, if not all, UK rivers have been damaged in the course of engineering 'improvement' works; many rivers now infrequently flood their floodplains due to the construction of embankments and over-deepening. However, recognition of the role of fluvial processes in creating sustainable river habitats and the importance of the link between the river and floodplain is growing. In addition, the importance of the natural functions of floodplains, eg flood and sediment storage, are being recognised. Consequently, opportunities for river restoration and

Table 3: Impact of channel modification on low and high energy streams and potential for subsequent recovery. Adapted from Brookes (1992)

CHANNEL MODIFICATIONS	HIGH ENERGY STREAM/RIVER (STREAM POWER > 35 Wm^{-2})	LOW ENERGY STREAM/RIVER (STREAM POWER < 35 Wm^{-2})
Channel widening/ deepening	*Geomorphological Impact* Deepened reach may function as trap for sediment moving from upstream. Slumping of banks where sediment supply limited in over-deep reach. *Recovery* Ability to recover dependent upon availability of sediment source.	*Geomorphological Impact* ↓velocity ↑siltation Channel unstable in high flows. *Recovery* Little/no natural recovery, if no sediment supply. Artificial channel narrowing may be required to restore channel morphology. Install deflectors to enhance development of berms
Channel straightening	*Geomorphological Impact* ↑slope, ↑sediment transport from upstream. Break of slope (nickpoint) migrates upstream causing bed erosion and bank collapse. *Recovery* Channel remains unstable. In erodible material channel may attempt to regain sinuous form.	*Geomorphological Impact* ↑slope, ↑sediment transport Bank/bed erosion. *Recovery* Limited: dependent upon stream power and nature of channel material (ie erodible). Need to re-instate meanders/install deflectors alternately side to side to create sinuous channel.

rehabilitation must not be overlooked both in terms of engineering and wildlife benefits. They not only offer the opportunity to reverse past damage but may also reduce costly levels of maintenance.

Stream rehabilitation can take two approaches. The first is passive, in which disturbance is reduced and the stream is left to readjust naturally. Specific rehabilitation measures are applied in the second approach. Brookes (1992) shows that the morphology of some artificially widened or deepened channels have been observed to adjust or 'recover' without intervention. Although an enlarged river may be in equilibrium with its engineered design flow (usually a large flood), it may be out of equilibrium with lower flows. Widening reduces stream power and sediment is deposited and stabilised by vegetation as the channel tries to re-create a more natural low-flow width.

Brookes (1992) highlights the influence of stream power in determining the potential for recovery subsequent to overdeepening or widening and straightening of channels. Table 3 indicates the capacity for recovery in low and high energy streams. In addition, it points to whether or not intervention may be the most appropriate option. The lack of natural readjustment at low stream power sites means that physical rehabilitation of morphological features may have to be undertaken.

An understanding of fluvial geomorphology assists comprehension of the factors affecting the stability of the channel and allows engineers to work with nature rather than against it.

Key References

Brookes, A (1988) *Channelized rivers: perspectives for environmental management.* 326 pp, John Wiley and Sons, Chichester.

Brookes, A (1992) *Recovery and restoration of some engineered British River Channels. In River Conservation and Management.* P J Boon, P Calow, and G E Petts (eds.) pp 337–352. John Wiley and Son, Chichester.

Newson, M (1993) *Hydrology and the River Environment.* Oxford University Press.

Richards, K S (1982) *Rivers; Form and Process in Alluvial Channels.* Methuen and Co Ltd.

1.4 Plants

1.4.1 Introduction

1.4.2 The importance of plants and their habitat requirements
— The importance of plants to river systems
— Plants of different river habitats

1.4.3 River classification based on plants (a tool for the assessment of conservation value and restoration/rehabilitation potential of rivers)

1.4.4 The impact of river engineering works on plants

1.4.1 Introduction

Most plants of the British Isles can be found in the valleys of streams and rivers but only a few grow in the submerged parts of the channel. Algae, lichens, liverworts, mosses, ferns, herbs, grasses, sedges and trees are all represented in a wide variety of forms and combinations. Because of the vast range found, this chapter considers only those aquatic and wetland plants which are found in the channel and on the wet banksides. Consequently, only brief mention will be made of the rich and varied communities which occur on banks, and in the water bodies and wet grasslands that occur on the floodplain (Rodwell, 1992). Details of vegetation characteristics of other aquatic and wetland habitats can be found in Wheeler (1980a, b and c), and for standing waters in Palmer (1989).

The numbers and types of plant found in any river primarily depend on natural factors, such as geology, altitude, water chemistry, velocity, size of river and gradient. Geographical location also plays an important role. The prime external factors are the degree and type of management work that has previously taken place, and changes in water quality. Only 'aquatic' plants are found in the centre of most channels; with very specialist 'riverine' species in places where the velocity is rapid and the substrate coarse. Where velocity decreases and the bed is dominated by silts and clays, 'river' species decline and are often replaced by plants equally at home in lakes or ponds. Haslam (1978) illustrates preferred habitats for many of the aquatic plants of rivers. At the bank/water interface some of the most varied communities are present. If the bank has a shallow slope, wetland plants, some of which may be rare or declining, may be present. If the river has been deepened and the bank steeply re-sectioned, a limited plant assemblage only is present, mostly species that are *not* characteristic of rivers.

Rivers are not only important for the plants within the channel (Plate 1), but also for the influence they exert on plant communities in the floodplains (Plates 2 and 3). Unconstrained rivers spill on to their floodplains and inundate habitats on a regular basis; where land is low and close to the river, they also ensure water tables are high at all times. Past river improvements for agricultural drainage and urban flood alleviation have led to a massive destruction of neutral and wet grasslands, marshes, fens, mires and carrs, and the plants that they support (Williams and Hall, 1987; Thornton and Kite, 1990; Buisson and Williams, 1991). Watercourses in the Broadlands, the Gwent Levels and the North Kent Marshes are now the last large refuges for wetland plants which were previously commonplace. In nature

**Plate 1
In-channel
'aquatic'
vegetation on the
R Stour**

Nigel Holmes

**Plate 2 (left)
Botanically
diverse
floodplain
meadow, subject
to periodic
inundation**

**Plate 3 (right)
The marsh
marigold, a
species
characteristic of
marshy areas in
floodplains**

Nigel Holmes

Nigel Holmes

conservation terms, high priority must be given, to protecting wetland habitats and their plant communities, whether they

occur in river floodplains or at the water/bank interface.

1.4.2 The importance of plants and their habitat requirements

The importance of plants to river systems

Apart from having a conservation interest in their own right, plants in rivers fulfil many vital functions. Submerged species provide shelter and a source of food for many aquatic invertebrates, small fish and some birds. Such plants are also the 'substrates' on which coarse fish such as pike and bream lay their eggs. In rivers where physical habitats are uniform, the plant communities give habitat diversity. Lilies and other plants with floating leaves provide shade in hot weather, whereas reeds form a vital link between water and air for invertebrates, such as dragonflies, which have aquatic larval stages. Several research papers (eg Marshall and Westlake, 1978; Wright *et al.*, 1991) give accounts of how much richer, both in species and numbers, animal communities of rivers are when plant communities are varied too.

Bank plants are important for the shelter they provide for a range of invertebrates and for small mammals such as the water shrew. They are the favoured food of the water vole and their fruits and seeds are a much needed protein-rich food for many birds. Additionally, they provide pollen and nectar sources for insects. Marginal and bank plants also enhance riverbank stability and protect against flood and boat-wash erosion.

Public appreciation of rivers is greatly enhanced if attractive flowers such as flowering rush, water-lilies, crowfoot and arrowhead are seen emerging from the water, and the banks are lined by purple loosestrife, flag iris, meadowsweet and water-mint.

Plants of different river habitats

River and wetland plants have a range of habitats in which they will grow and thrive. For some the range is very wide; others are very specific in their requirements. For instance, most of the pondweeds (*Potamogeton*), must be submerged at all times and fringed water-lily (Plate 4) grows only where flow velocity is minimal and substrates soft. These represent typical plants of slow-flowing rivers, backwaters and floodplain

**Plate 4 (top)
The fringed
water-lily**

**Plate 5 (bottom)
River water-crowfoot**

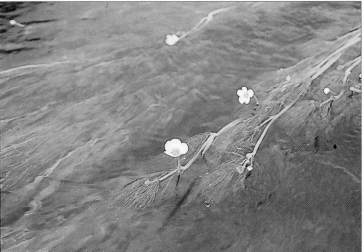

Nigel Holmes

Table 1: Aquatic River Plants

PLATE NO. IN KEBLE-MARTIN	SPECIES	ALTITUDE	SUBSTRATE — Clay Silt Peat Sand Gravel-Pebble Cobble-Boulder	FLOW — Nil-Slow Moderate Fast-Rapid	DEPTH — >1 m 0.5-1 m 0.1-0.5 m 0.1-dry	WIDTH — >20 m 10-20 m 5-10 m <5 m	CHEM. — Base poor Base neutral Base rich	WATER QUAL. — Clean Moderate Polluted	SHADE TOLERANCE	DISTURBANCE TOLERANCE	LIFE CYCLE

a   Free-floating, unrooted plants

34	Hornworts	L	○● ○○	●	●○●	○○○●	○●	○●○	●	●	A/P
88	[Duckweeds]	L	○○●●	●●	○●●●	●○●○	●●○	○○		●	A
59	*Fringed water-lily	L	●●	●	●●○	○○○○	●	○○		○	P
66	Bladderworts	Thr	●○●●	●	○○○	●○○○	○○○	●	●	●	A/P
79	Frogbit	L	○○●●	●	●○	○○○●	●	○●		○	A/P

b   Submerged, narrow-leaved plants
(some are part-emergent, some others have floating leaves)

34	Mare's-tail	L	○○●○●	○●●	○●●●	○●●○	○●	●○●		○	P
87	Bulbous rush	U/T	● ●○●●	○○●	●○●●	●●●○	●○	●●○	●	●	P
71	Shoreweed	U	● ○●●	●●○	●○○○	○○○●	●○●	●●○	●	○	P
34	*Water milfoils	Thr	○●●●○●	●○○	○○●	○○○●	○●●	○○●	○	○	P
39	*River water dropwort	L	●○ ○○	○●●	●○●	○○○●	●●	○○		○	P
90	Small pond-weed	L	○○●○○	●○	●○○	○○○○	○○○	○○○	●	○	A/P
90	[Fennel pondweed]	Thr	○○●○○●	○●○	○●○	○○○○	○ ●	●○●	○	●	P
90	Flat-stalked pondweed	L	○●	●	○●○	○○○○	○○	○○○	○	○	P
2	Cmn. water-crowfoot	Thr	●●●●●○	○○○	●○●○	●○○○	○○●	●○●		●	A/P
2	Fan-leaved water-crowfoot	L	●●	●●	○●●	○○○●	●	○○●	●	○	P

Key to Plant Habitat tables

The Keble Martin plate number refers to Keble Martin (1969), a useful illustrated guide to British plants, most of them in colour.

●-preferred conditions, most frequently found/high tolerance.
○-very commonly found/fair-good tolerance
o-occasionally found/moderately tolerant
⊘-when several species have been amalgamated, some prefer this condition and others shun it.
●-rarely found

blank   -absent/intolerant
NP   -no preference

L   -lowland only
U   -upland only   } altitude of site
T   -transitional only
Thr -throughout

A   -annual/biennial   } life-cycle
P   -perennial

*   -uncommon plant, recorded in fewer than 100 national kilometre grid squares, out of *c.* 2,600

34   -the plant may grow both in the channel and on the bank

[....] -very common, likely to recolonise unaided, not suitable for replanting.

Table 1 (cont)

2	River water-crowfoot	T/L	○● ○●○	○●○	○●●●	●○○●	●●○	●●			P
-	Pond water-crowfoot	T/L	○●●○●●	○●○	●○●○	●○●○	●○●	●○○		○	A/P
2	Thread-leaved water-crowfoot	T/L	○● ○○	○○●	○○○●	○○○○	○●	●○	○	●	A/P
79	Arrowhead	L	●● ●	●○	●○●	○○○○	●○●	○○○		●	A/P
91	Floating club-rush	U	○●○○○●	●●●	●●●	●○○○	●●	●		○	P
88	Unbranched bur-reed	L	○○●●●	○○●	●○○●	○○○○	●○○	○○		●	P
90	Horned pondweed	L	●●● ●○	●○	●○●	○○○○	○●○	○○●		●	P

c   Submerged, broad-leaved plants

38	Narrow-leaved water parsnip	L	○○●○●●	●○●	●○●○	●○○●	●○	●●	○	○	P
34	Starwort species	Thr	○○●●○○	○●●	●●●●	○○○○	⊘●⊘	●○●	○	○	A/P
89	Opposite-leaved pondweed	U	○● ○○	●○	○●○	○●●○	○●	○○			P
90	Curled pondweed	T/L	○○●○○●	○○○	●○●	○○○○	●●○	○○○	○	●	P
89	Shining pondweed	L	○○ ●●	●	○●●	○○○	○●	○○		●	P
89	Perfoliate pondweed	T/L	○○ ○○●	●○	○○○	○○○	○○	●○		○	P
79	[Canadian pondweed]	T/L	○○ ○○	○○●	○○○	○○○○	○○	○○○		●	A/P

d   Rooted, floated-leaved plants

5	[Yellow water-lily]	L	●○	●○	○○○	○○○○	●○	○○○	○	●	P
5	White water-lily	Thr	●○ ○	●	○○○	○○○○	○○○	●	○		P
89	Bog pondweed	U/T	○○● ○	○○○	●●○	●○○●	●○	●		○	P
89	Broad-leaved pondweed	Thr	○○○○○○○	○○○	●○ ○	○○○○	○○	○○●	●	●	P

Table 2: Marginal plants

PLATE NO. IN KEBLE-MARTIN	SPECIES	ALTITUDE	SUBSTRATE (Clay, Silt, Peat, Sand, Gravel-Pebble, Cobble-Boulder)						FLOW (Nil-Slow, Moderate, Fast-Rapid)			DEPTH (>1 m, 0.5-1 m, 0.1-0.5 m, 0.1-dry)				WIDTH (>20 m, 10-20 m, 5-10 m, <5 m)				CHEM. (Base poor, Base neutral, Base rich)			WATER (Clean, Moderate, Polluted)			SHADE TOLERANCE	DISTURBANCE TOLERANCE	LIFE CYCLE

a Emergent narrow-leaved plants ('reeds')

Plate	Species	Alt.	Substrate	Flow	Depth	Width	Chem.	Water	Shade	Dist.	Life
79	Water plantain	L	● ○	● ○	● ● ○ ●	● ● ○ ○	● ○ ●	○ ○		●	P
79	Flowering-rush	L	● ○ ● ○ ●	● ○ ●	● ○ ● ○	○ ● ● ● ●	● ●	○ ○		○	P
91	Spike rushes	Thr	○ ○ ○ ● ○ ○	○ ○ ○	● ○ ●	○ ○ ○ ○	○ ● ○				P
-	Water horse-tail	Thr	○ ○ ○ ● ●	● ●	● ● ● ○	○ ○ ○ ○	○ ○ ○	● ○	○	○	P
95	Common reed	L	○ ○ ○ ●	●	○ ○ ○ ●	○ ○ ○ ○	○		○		P

b Emergent broad-leaved plants
(note that all of these plants behave differently when growing on banks)

Plate	Species	Alt.	Substrate	Flow	Depth	Width	Chem.	Water	Shade	Dist.	Life
37	[Fool's water-cress]	L	● ○ ● ●	● ○	● ● ○ ●	● ○ ○ ○	● ○	○ ○	○	○	A/P
7	Water-cress	L	○ ○ ● ●	● ○	○ ●	● ○ ○ ●	○ ●	○ ○	○		P
74	Water dock	L	● ○ ● ● ●	●	○ ●	○ ○ ○ ●	● ●	○ ○			P
84	Blue water-speedwell	L	○ ● ● ●	● ○	● ○ ○	● ○ ● ○	○ ●	○ ○ ○	○	●	A/P

c Encroaching plants

Plate	Species	Alt.	Substrate	Flow	Depth	Width	Chem.	Water	Shade	Dist.	Life
93	*Water sedge	U	○ ○ ○ ● ●	● ○ ●	● ●	NP	○ ○ ●	● ○		●	P
94	Lesser pond-sedge	L	● ○ ● ● ○ ●	● ○ ●	○ ●	NP	○ ○	○ ○ ○	●	●	P
94	Greater pond-sedge	L	○ ○ ○ ● ●	● ●	○ ●	NP	○ ○	○ ○ ○	○	●	P
94	Bottle sedge	U/T	○ ○ ○ ○ ○	● ○ ●	○ ●	○ ○ ○ ○	● ○	○ ○ ○		●	P
94	Bladder sedge	U/T	○ ○ ● ● ●	○ ●	○ ●	○ ○ ○ ○	○ ○ ○	○ ○	●	○	P
97	Whorl grass	L	○ ● ● ○ ●	● ●	○ ●	○ ○ ○ ○	○ ●	○ ○ ○	○	○	P
97	[Reed sweet-grass]	L	○ ● ● ●	● ○	● ● ● ●	○ ○ ○ ○	○ ●	○ ○ ○	○	●	P
89	Bogbean	Thr	○ ○ ○ ● ●	●	● ○ ● ○	○ ○ ○ ○	○ ○ ○	● ●		○	P
93	Amphibious bistort	L	○ ○ ● ○	○ ○	●	NP	○ ○	○ ○ ○	○		P
7	Great yellow-cress	L	○ ●	● ●	○ ●	● ○ ○ ○	● ●	○ ○ ○		●	P
64	Pink water-speedwell	T/L	○ ○ ● ● ●	● ○	● ○ ○	● ○ ○ ○	● ○ ○	● ○ ●		○	P

Table 3: Bank plants

PLATE NO. IN KEBLE-MARTIN	SPECIES	ALTITUDE	SUBSTRATE (Clay, Silt, Peat, Sand, Gravel-Pebble, Bedrock)	FLOW (Nil-Slow, Moderate, Fast-Rapid)	BANK SLOPE (>60°, 30-60°, >30°)	HGHT. (>1 m, 0.5-1 m, <0.5 m)	CHEM. (Base poor, Base neutral, Base rich)	WHERE PLANT (Just submerged, At water level, Just above, >30cm above)	SHADE TOLERANCE, STABILIZING ABILITY, SCOUR RESISTANCE	LIFE CYCLE

a   Narrow-leaved, upright bank plants

Plate	Species	Altitude								Life cycle
79	Water plantain	L								P
93	Slender tufted-sedge	L								P
94	Lesser pond-sedge									
93	*Water sedge	U/T								P
93	Tufted-sedge	L								P
93	Common sedge	U/T								P
92	False fox-sedge	L								P
92	Great tussock-sedge	L								P
94	Pendulous sedge	L								P
91	Common spike-rush	Thr								P
83	Yellow Iris	T/L								P
87	Sharp-flowered rush	U								P
87	Jointed rush	U/T								P
87	Bulrush	U/T								P
86	Soft rush	U/T								P
86	Hard rush	T/L								P
95	Reed canary-grass	T/L								P
95	Common reed	L								P
88	Branched bur-reed	T/L								P
88	Narrow-leaved reedmace	L								P
88	Reedmace	L								P

b   Narrow-leaved, straggling bank plants

Plate	Species	Altitude								Life cycle
95	[Creeping bent]	T/L								P
95	*Orange foxtail	L								A
95	Marsh foxtail	T/L								A/P
97	Small sweet-grass	L								P
97	Floating sweet-grass	U/T								P
97	[Reed sweet-grass]	L								P
97	Plicate sweet-grass	T/L								P

37

Table 3 (cont)

c Broad-leaved, upright bank plants

No.	Species									
37	Fool's water-cress	T/L	● ● ● ● ●	○ ○ ●	● ○ ●	● ○ ○	○ ○	●	○ ● ●	P
38	Lesser water parsnip	L	○ ○ ● ● ●	○ ○ ○	● ●	● ○ ○	● ●	● ●	○ ● ●	P
67	Water-mint	T/L	○ ○ ● ○ ○ ●	○ ○ ○	● ○ ●	○ ○	○ ○	●	● ● ●	P
63	Water figwort	T/L	○ ○ ● ○	● ○	○ ○ ○	● ●	● ○ ○	○ ○	● ○	P
4	Marsh marigold	U/T	○ ● ○ ●	○ ○ ●	○ ●	○ ●	● ● ○	● ●	●	P
26	Meadow sweet	Thr	○ ● ○ ○ ● ●	○ ○ ○	○ ○ ●	● ● ●	○ ○	●	● ● ●	P
34	Purple loosestrife	L	○ ○ ○ ○	● ○	○ ○ ○	○ ○	○ ●	○ ● ○	○ ○	P
67	Gipsywort	L	○ ● ● ● ●	● ○	○ ○	○ ○	○ ○	○ ●	○ ○ ○	P
39	[Hemlock water drop-wort]	Thr	○ ○ ○ ○ ○	● ○ ●	● ○ ○	○ ● ○	● ○		○ ● ●	P
69	Marsh woundwort	T/L	○ ○ ● ○ ●	○ ○ ●	○ ○ ●	○ ○	○ ○	●	○ ● ●	P
46	Butterbur	T/L	○ ○ ○	○ ● ○	○ ○ ●	○ ○ ●	● ○	○ ●	● ● ●	P
46	Colt's-foot	Thr	○ ○ ● ○	● ○ ●	● ● ●	●	○ ○	●	○ ● ●	P
45	Bur marigold	L	● ○	●	●	● ●	● ○	●		A
60	Common comfrey	L	● ○ ● ○	● ○	○ ○ ●	○ ● ○	○ ○	● ●	○ ● ●	P
44	Hemp agrimony	T/L	○ ○ ● ○ ● ○	● ○	● ○ ○	○ ○ ●	○ ○	● ● P	● ● ●	P
35	Great willow-herb	T/L	● ● ● ○ ○	○ ○ ●	● ○ ●	○ ○	● ○	● ●	● ●	P
–	Royal fern	T/L	○ ○ ●	● ● ●	○ ○	●	○ ○ ●	● ●	● ● ○	P

d Broad-leaved, straggling bank plants

No.	Species									
7	Large bitter-cress	T/L	○ ● ○ ●	○ ○ ●	○ ○ ○	● ●	● ○	● ●	● ○ ○	P
42	Common marsh-bedstraw	T/L	○ ○ ○ ○ ●	● ○ ●	○ ○ ○	●	○ ○	●	○ ○	P
29	Water avens	Thr	○ ● ● ● ●	○	● ● ○	○ ● ○	● ○ ●	● ○	● ● ○	P
60	Water forget-me-not	T/L	○ ○ ○ ○ ○ ○	○ ○ ○	○ ○ ○	○ ●	○ ● ○	●	○ ● ●	P
15	Water chickweed	L	○ ○ ● ○	● ○	○ ○ ○	○ ○	○ ●	●	●	P
73	Amphibious bistort	L	○ ○ ● ○	● ○	○ ○ ○	○ ○	○ ○	●	○ ○	P
3	Lesser spearwort	Thr	○ ● ○ ● ○	● ● ○	● ○ ○	●	○ ● ○		○ ○ ●	P
3	Greater spearwort	T/L	○ ○ ●	● ○	● ●	○	○ ○	●	● ○ ○	P
3	Celery-leaved buttercup	L	○ ● ●	● ●	●	○ ●	○ ●	●	○ ○ ○	A
2	Ivy-leaved crowfoot	U	○ ○ ○ ●	● ●	●	● ●	○ ○	○		A/P
2	Round-leaved crowfoot	U	○ ○ ○ ○	● ●	●	●	○ ○			A
7	Great yellow-cress	L	● ● ●	● ●	● ●	● ● ●	○ ○	● ● ○	○ ○	P
7	Water-cress	T/L	○ ● ● ○ ●	○ ○ ●	● ●	● ○	● ●	● ●	○ ○	P
7	Marsh yellow-cress	T/L	○ ○ ● ●	○ ○ ●	● ● ●	●	○ ○	●		A
7	Creeping yellow-cress	T	● ○ ● ○	● ○ ●	● ● ●	●	● ○	●	○ ● ●	P
61	[Bittersweet]	T/L	○ ○ ● ○ ○	● ●	○ ○ ○	● ○	○ ○	○ ○ ○	● ○ ○	P
64	Brooklime	Thr	● ○ ○ ○ ○	● ○ ●	● ○ ●	●	● ● ●	● ○	○ ○ ○	P

Table 3 (cont)

e   Bankside trees and shrubs

77	Alder	T/L	○ ●○●●	○●○	●○●	●	●○○	●●	●●	P
42	Ash	T	○ ●○●●	○○●	●○●	●	○●	●	●●	P
77	Common oak	T/L	● ○	○●	●○●	●	○○	●	●●	P
77	White willow	Thr	○○○○ ●●	●○○	●○●	●	●○○	○○○●	●●	P
77	Common osier	T/L	●●○●○●	●○○	●○●	●	●○○	○○○○	●●	P
77	Goat willow (sallow)	Thr	●●○●○●	●○○	○○●	●	○○●	○○○○	●●	P
20	Alder buck-thorn	L	○●●●	○○	○○	●	●○	○○	●●	P
78	Native poplars	T/L	●●○●		○○○	●	○○	○●	●●	P

pools. In contrast, there are those which are confined to the main channel and rarely grow anywhere other than amongst boulders, pebbles and gravels, where fast-flowing water constantly tugs at them, eg many mosses and river water-crowfoot (Plate 5).

Tables 1-3 list a number of species that typify various riverine habitats: in-stream (Table 1) (Plates 6, 7 and 8); marginal (Table 2) (Plates 9, 10 and 11); and bank (Table 3) (Plates 12 and 13). The lists indicate what species are likely to be found throughout a range of riverine habitats.

Each table indicates the preference, and tolerance, of species to such variables as altitude, substrate types, river width, water depth, current velocity, soil and water chemistry, bank slope and degree of shade. The final column of each shows whether

Nigel Holmes

Nigel Holmes

Nigel Holmes

Nigel Holmes

Nigel Holmes

Nigel Holmes

Plates 6, 7 & 8 In-stream aquatic plants

Plate 6 (top left) The white water-lily

Plate 7 (middle left) Arrowhead

Plate 8 (bottom left) The moss *Rynchostegium riparioides* characteristic of 'runs' in intermediate/lowl and channels

Plates 9–11 Marginal plants

Plate 9 (top right) Amphibious bistort

Plate 10 (middle right) Branched bur-reed

Plate 11 (bottom right) Water-cress (all three above species may also be found in bankside habitats)

**Plates 12 & 13
Bankside plants**

**Plate 12 (left)
Hemp agrimony**

**Plate 13 (right)
Purple-
loosestrife**

the plants are long-lived (perennials) or live for just one (annual) or two (biennial) years. For edge and bank species a guide 'Where to Plant' is given to aid choice of species for planting in enhancement works (Chapter 3.6).

Tables 1–3 should thus be used to determine:

- what may be found in a reach – because of regional differences, geographical isolation, and the effects of past management, only field survey can show what actually *is* there;

- which plants might disappear as a result of river works – deepening, widening, regrading banks, increasing velocity, change in sediments, and increase in shade may change conditions so significantly that the plant community is replaced by a different one (with repercussions on the animal community);

- which plants are suitable for replanting – so that the plant community habitat structure can recover as quickly as possible from disturbance;

- the most appropriate plants to use in river restoration and rehabilitation projects to ensure the community will

not only establish quickly, but also be 'right' for the conditions.

For management purposes, understanding which plants should be expected in different in-stream habitats in different parts of the country is vital. For convenience, riverine habitats can be divided into three:

- Riffles – where shallow water flows rapidly over coarse gravels/stones/boulders;

- Runs – where deep water flows swiftly over firm substrates;

- Slacks/pools/backwaters – where water has minimal velocity often over clays or fine silts.

Table 4 lists typical plants associated with such in-stream habitats. To complement this, Table 5 shows plants of the riverbank associated with different habitats in different parts of the country. It is clear from these that mosses and liverworts dominate upland and rocky rivers, which rarely need or receive maintenance. In contrast, lowland rivers, which are often managed, are dominated by flowering plants.

Table 4: Typical plants associated with in-stream habitats in upland, intermediate and lowland channels

HABITAT	UPLANDS	INTERMEDIATE SECTIONS	LOWLANDS
Riffles	Alternate-flowered water-milfoil Bulbous rush Shore-weed *Hygrohypnum ochraceum* (moss) *Fontinalis antipyretica* (moss) *Solenostoma triste* (liverwort) *Chiloscyphus polyanthos* (liverwort)	Hemlock water-dropwort Brook water-crowfoot Stream water-crowfoot Canadian pond weed Intermediate water-starwort Blanketweed algae *Rhynchostegium riparioides*	Brook water-crowfoot Spiked water-milfoil Lesser water-parsnip Arrowhead Horned pondweed *Fontinalis antipyretica* *Rhynchostegium riparioides*
Runs	*Marsupella emarginata* (liverwort) *Nardia compressa* (liverwort) *Scapania undulata* *Hygrohypnum ochraceum* (moss) *Fontinalis squamosa* *Hyocomium armoricum* (moss) *Racomitrium aciculare*	Alternate-flowered water-milfoil River water-crowfoot Curled pondweed *Fontinalis squamosa* (moss) *Fontinalis antipyretica* *Rhynchostegium riparioides*	Spiked water-milfoil River water-crowfoot Common club-rush Fennel pondweed Unbranched bur-reed *Fontinalis antipyretica* *Rhynchostegium riparioides*
Slacks	Intermediate water-starwort Common water-starwort Floating sweet-grass Bog pondweed Floating club-rush Least bur-read *Sphagnum* moss	Perfoliate pondweed Broad-leaved pondweed Canadian pondweed Water-cress Branched bur-reed Curled pondweed Common duckweed	Yellow water-lily Flowering rush Shining pondweed Nuttall's pondweed Branched bur-reed Blunt-fruited water-starwort Fat duckweed

Table 5: Typical plants of river banks/margins in upland, intermediate and lowland channels

HABITAT	UPLANDS	INTERMEDIATE	LOWLANDS
Wet ledges within channel	Shoreweed Jointed rush Marsh spearwort Blinks Monkeyflower Ivy-leaved water-crowfoot	Indian balsam Brooklime Water forget-me-not Pink water-speedwell Creeping yellow-cress Water plantain	Marsh foxtail Common bulrush Blue water-speedwell Celery-leaved buttercup Great yellow-cress Great waterdock
Shallow waterlogged margins	Marsh violet Marsh stitchwort Bulbous rush Greater bird's-foot-trefoil Round-leaved water-crowfoot Marsh ragwort	Fool's water-cress Amphibious bistort Marsh yellow-cress Bittersweet Marsh woundwort Marsh marigold	Pink water-speedwell Fool's water-cress Water-cress Yellow flag Plicate sweet-grass Marsh horsetail
Reed/sedge/rush edge	Soft rush Sharp-flowered rush Bottle sedge Common sedge Floating sweet-grass	Reed canary-grass Hard rush Common spikerush Hairy sedge Slender tufted sedge	Common reed Greater pond-sedge Lesser pond-sedge Greater tussock sedge Reed sweet grass
Steeper banks	*Pellia epiphylla* (liverwort) *Polytrichum commune* (moss) Purple moor-grass Mat-grass Tormentil Meadowsweet	Water figwort Water-mint Comfrey Butterbur Angelica	Great willow-herb Purple loose-strife Teasel Hemp agrimony Water chickweed Gypsywort

1.4.3 River classifications based on plants

(a tool for assessment of the conservation value and restoration/ rehabilitation potential of rivers)

The network of British rivers traverses land ranging from the high peaks of Scotland to the rich flat farmlands of East Anglia. Different rivers support different plant communities, and assemblages of plants invariably change from source to mouth. Many attempts have been made to classify zones of, and whole, rivers (Hawkes, 1975). The first major study of this type using plants was Butcher (1933). He suggested that rivers which flowed over similar rock types, which rose at a certain height and had common water velocities and water chemistry characteristics, also had plant communities with much in common. His findings are still supported today but have been advanced considerably in the past two decades in Great Britain and Europe (Haslam, 1987).

In the last 10 years, a new classification has evolved for conservation assessment. Details are given in DoE (1987), Holmes (1983a, 1989) and Holmes and Rowell (1993).
The classification system that developed has given a clear picture of what types of river system can be expected in any region of the country based upon geology, altitude and physical characteristics. This information enables the extent of any river type in all regions to be assessed and provides a system to compare similar rivers more objectively. Thus, no river in Scotland or Wales will have 'chalk river' communities, and no 'highland' or low-nutrient rivers will be found in East Anglia.

The classification derived has a number of levels. At the simplest, the sites with broadly similar plant communities are placed in one of four Groups A–D (Figure 1). Refinement of the classification involved further sub-divisions of the four main Groups into smaller sub-groups (Figure 2).

Group A communities are associated with

rivers with low altitudinal sources, low gradient, with fine and/or rich substrates.

Group B communities have intermediate characteristics but have a very close affinity with areas of sandstone and hard limestone.

Group C river communities normally occur on neutral shales and metamorphic rocks where velocity and shade are much greater than in the Groups A and B.

Group D communities occur in rivers that have very nutrient-poor soils and water chemistry, steep gradients and boulder-strewn substrates.

Each of the 'Groups' and 'Sub-groups' have characteristic plants. Examples which illustrate close affinities with individual 'Groups' are shown in Table 6; those with even closer association with one or more sub-groups are shown in Table 7. Both show that there are also a number of generalists which span the ranges within both 'Groups' and 'Types'.

Reference to Figure 2 confirms that altitude, geographical location and geology hold the key to plant communities in rivers. Because of this, no river conforms to the classic popular vision that they have a source in windswept mountains followed by a rapid descent through rolling uplands to sluggish meanders in the flat lowlands. In reality, rivers that start in mountains with a 'Group D Community' rarely have lowland reaches with plant communities in 'Group A', which dominate all sites in lowland England (even in their uppermost reaches).

This classification system is not only useful for assessing the conservation value of rivers but also provides a tool to assist in determining appropriate goals for the restoration or rehabilitation of degraded rivers using the techniques described in Part 3.

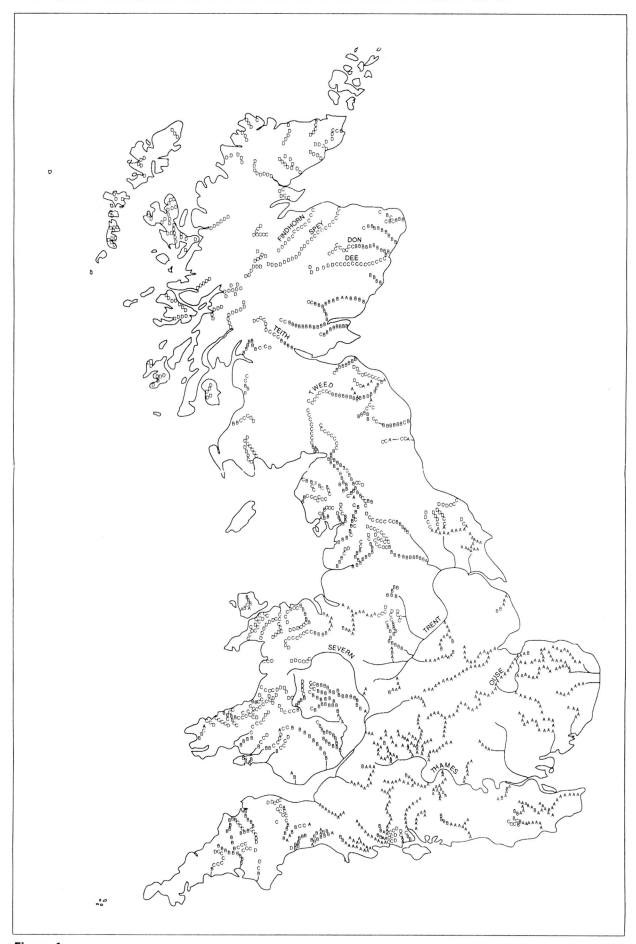

Figure 1
Distribution of Group A, B, C and D plant communities in British rivers (after Holmes and Rowell, 1993).

Table 6: Examples of species from the four main groups

GROUPS SPECIES	A	B	C	D
Nuphar lutea	■	□	□	□
Oenanthe fluviatilis	■	□	□	□
Ceratophyllum demersum	■	□	□	□
Potamogeton lucens	■	□	□	□
Sagittaria sagittifolia	■	□	□	□
Rorippa amphibia	■	□	□	□
Berula erecta	■	□	□	□
Callitriche obtusangula	■	□	□	□
Rumex hydrolapathum	■	□	□	□
Veronica anagallis-aquatica	■	□	□	□
Scirpus lacustris	■	□	□	□
Carex riparia	■	□	□	□
Carex acutiformis	■	□	□	□
Glyceria maxima	■	■	□	□
Zannichellia palustris	■	■	□	□
Apium nodiflorum	■	■	□	□
Epilobium hirsutum	■	■	□	□
Polygonum amphibium	■	■	□	□
Ranunculus calcareus	■	■	□	□
Elodea canadensis	■	■	□	□
Potamogeton crispus	■	■	□	□
Potamogeton perfoliatus	■	■	□	□
Myriophyllum spicatum	■	■	□	□
Freshwater sponge	□	■	□	□
Lysimachia vulgaris	□	■	□	□
Scirpus sylvaticus	□	■	□	□
Cladophora glomerata - alga	■	■	■	□
Sparganium erectum	■	■	■	□
Eupatorium cannibinum	■	■	■	□
Alisma plantago-aquatica	■	■	■	□
Solanum dulcamara	■	■	■	□
Cinclidotus fontinaloides - moss	□	■	■	□
Hildenbrandia rivularis - alga	□	■	■	□
Ranunculus penicillatus	□	■	■	□
Callitriche hamulata	□	■	■	■
Myriophyllum alterniflorum	□	■	■	■
Eleocharis palustris	□	■	■	■
Equisetum fliviatile	□	■	■	■
Fontinalis squamosa - moss	□	□	■	■
Hygrophynum luridum - moss	□	□	■	■
Pellia epiphylla - liverwort	□	□	■	■
Scapania undulata - liverwort	□	□	■	■
Solenostoma triste - liverwort	□	□	■	■
Brachythecium rivulare - moss	□	□	■	■
Racomitrium aciculare - moss	□	□	■	■
Achillea ptarmica	□	□	■	■
Ranunculus flammula	□	□	■	■
Montia fontana	□	□	■	■
Carex nigra	□	□	■	■
Carex rostrata	□	□	■	■
Littorella uniflora	□	□	■	■
Nardia compressa - liverwort	□	□	□	■
Marsupella emarginata - liverwort	□	□	□	■
Sphagna - moss	□	□	□	■
Dicranella palustris - moss	□	□	□	■
Schistidium agassizii - moss	□	□	□	■
Viola palustris	□	□	□	■
Juncus bulbosus	□	□	□	■
Potamogeton polygonifolius	□	□	□	■
Filamentous algae - alga	■	■	■	■
Fontinalis antipyretica - moss	■	■	■	■
Rhynchostegium riparioides - moss	■	■	■	■
Angelica sylvestris	■	■	■	■
Filipendula ulmaria	■	■	■	■
Mentha aquatica	■	■	■	■
Myosotis scorpioides	■	■	■	■
Salis species	■	■	■	■

■ Common component
□ Absent or rare

Source: *British Wildlife*

Table 7: Characteristic species of eight community types

Symbols indicate occurence of each species
- □ Absent
- ❖ 1-24%
- ◆ 25-49%
- ● 50-74%
- ■ 75-100%

Source: *British Wildlife*

	SPECIES	A2iv Clay Rivers	A3i Chalk Rivers	B2i Large Old Red Sandstone Rivers	B4ii Hereford Sandstone Rivers	C1i Upland Rivers	C3v New Forest Rivers	D1i Mountain Rivers	D3ii Moorland Rivers
		COMMUNITY TYPE							
Butomus umbellatus	Flowering-rush	●	□	□	□	□	□	□	□
Sagittaria sagittifolia	Arrowhead	■	□	□	□	□	□	□	□
Nuphar lutea	Yellow water-lily	■	□	□	□	□	□	□	□
Rorippa amphibia	Great yellow-cress	●	□	□	❖	□	□	□	□
Potamogeton pectinatus	Fennel pondweed	●	□	◆	◆	□	□	□	□
Rumex hydrolapathum	Great water-dock	❖	■	□	□	□	□	□	□
Berula erecta	Lesser water-parsnip	□	■	□	□	□	□	□	□
Phragmites australis	Reed	□	■	□	□	□	□	□	□
Zannichellia palustris	Horned pondweed	□	■	□	◆	□	□	□	□
Veronica anagallis aquatica	Blue water-speedwell	❖	■	□	□	□	□	□	□
Ranunculus calcareus	Brook water-crowfoot	❖	■	■	◆	□	□	□	□
Callitriche obtusangula	Blunt-fruited WS	□	■	□	□	□	●	□	□
Carex paniculata	Great tussock-sedge	□	■	□	□	□	□	□	□
Fontinalis antipyretica	Willow moss	◆	■	■	■	■	●	■	◆
Rhynchostegium riparioides	moss	❖	●	■	■	■	●	■	❖
Potamogeton crispus	Curled pondweed	◆	◆	■	□	□	□	□	□
Eleocharis palustris	Common spike-rush	□	□	■	■	□	□	□	□
Ranunculus fluitans	River water-crowfoot	□	□	■	■	□	□	□	□
Elodea canadensis	Canadian pondweed	●	■	■	●	◆	□	□	□
Hildenbrandia rivularis	red alga	□	□	■	◆	●	□	□	□
Thamnobryum alopecurum	moss	□	□	●	❖	■	□	□	□
Cinclidotus fontinaloides	moss	□	□	■	●	●	□	□	□
Oenanthe crocata	Hemlock water-dropwort	❖	●	◆	◆	■	◆	□	□
Hygrohypnum ochraceum	moss	□	□	□	□	■	□	■	●
Chiloscyphus polyanthos	liverwort	□	□	□	□	■	◆	●	□
Fontinalis squamosa	moss	□	□	□	□	■	□	◆	◆
Callitriche hamulata	Intermediate water-starwort	□	□	□	□	□	■	●	◆
Juncus bulbosus	Bulbous rush	□	□	□	□	□	■	■	■
Ranunculus omiophyllus	Round-leaved crowfoot	□	□	□	□	□	●	□	◆
Potamogeton polygonifolius	Bog pondweed	□	□	□	□	□	●	❖	●
Marsupella emarginata	liverwort	□	□	□	□	□	□	❖	■
Nardia compressa	liverwort	□	□	□	□	□	□	❖	●
Sphagnum species	mosses	□	□	□	□	□	❖	□	■
Montia fontana	Blinks	□	□	□	□	□	◆	●	□
Calliergon cuspidatum	moss	□	□	□	□	□	□	■	□
Dichodontium pellucidum	moss	□	□	□	□	□	□	■	□
Philonotis fontana	moss	□	□	□	□	□	□	■	❖
Bryum alpinum	moss	□	□	□	□	□	□	■	❖

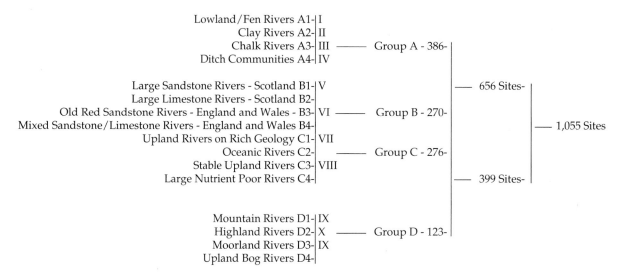

Figure 2 The macrophyte classification of British rivers derived from 1,055 survey sites showing Groups A-D, 16 sub-groups (Holmes, 1983, 1989) together with the sub-groups included in the ten SSSI river 'types' (NCC, 1989).

1.4.4 Impact of river engineering

The extinction of flowering river plants is unlikely because the whereabouts of rare species is usually known. It is important to note that there are two flowering river plants that are nationally rare and vulnerable (sharp-leaved and loddon pondweeds); both are on the Red Data list of flowering plants. There are no fewer than 26 species of fen, bog, marsh and open water plants vulnerable to extinction (Newbold, 1981). In addition, there are many vulnerable and declining lower plants (especially mosses, liverworts and lichens) associated with shaded rivers in the west of the country. In the western parts of Britain rivers are of major European significance for liverworts and mosses, which demand a damp atmosphere (Hodgetts, 1993).

The major impact of engineering works on riverine plant communities is that alterations in habitat may result in community changes. Where habitat is lost and greater uniformity created by engineering works, the diversity of plant species suffers. However, this is in contrast to ancient meadows that are ploughed, woodlands that are felled or fens that are drained, where wildlife interest may be totally destroyed.

Key References

DoE (1987) *Methods for the Use of Aquatic Macrophytes for Assessing Water Quality 1985—86*. Methods for the Examination of Waters and Associated Materials. HMSO, London.

Haslam, S M (1987) *River Plants of Western Europe*. Cambridge University Press.

Holmes, N T H (1983a) *Classification of British Rivers According to their Flora*. Focus on Nature Conservation No. 3. NCC. Peterborough.

1.5 Mammals

1.5.1   Introduction

1.5.2   The species and their habitat requirements
   — Otter
   — Water shrew
   — Water vole
   — Mink
   — Bats

1.5.3   Habitat management for otters
   — Management objectives and considerations
   — Protection and management of existing habitat
   — Rehabilitation and enhancement of habitat

1.5.1 Introduction

There are three native mammal species that are particularly associated with rivers in the UK: the otter, water shrew and water vole (Corbet and Harris, 1991). Particular consideration should be given to their requirements when planning works on rivers and associated land. In addition, the mink, an introduced species, is closely associated with rivers and streams, and another introduced species, the coypu, has recently been eradicated from rivers in East Anglia. A number of bat species regularly feed over rivers and several other mammals, both large and small, use rivers for foraging and drinking. Table 1 lists the mammals most closely associated with rivers and gives details of their distribution and requirements.

Otters and bats, and their places of shelter, are protected under the Wildlife and Countryside Act 1981.

Table 1: Requirements and distribution of mammals particularly associated with UK rivers

COMMON NAME	HABITAT	UK DISTRIBUTION	FOOD SOURCES	COMMENTS
Otter	Rivers/wetlands and coastal areas (eg N & W Scotland). Needs cover of marginal vegetation, trees and reedbeds. Secure breeding sites essential.	Only abundant in NW Highlands & islands of Scotland. Now largely absent from Central & S England.	Predominantly fish, particularly eels. Frogs and occasionally young birds and mammals.	*Protected Species.* Largely nocturnal.
Mink (non-native)	Rivers and wetlands, with cover of marginal vegetation and/or trees.	Became established in late 1950s, now widespread and still expanding.	Fish, birds and their eggs, small mammals and large invertebrates.	Now thought not to compete with otter. Mainly nocturnal.
Water shrew	Clear, unpolluted streams and wetlands, with plant cover.	Throughout. Scarce N Scotland	Predominantly insects also small fish, snails and frogs.	Small burrows in banks. Active day and night.
Water vole	Lowland rivers, canals, ponds and drainage ditches, particularly with good marginal vegetation.	Throughout, but declining rapidly	Water plants – very selective feeder.	Small burrows in banks. Semi-colonial. Day-active.
Natterer's bat	Woodland adjacent to rivers.	Throughout, no longer common.	Moths, dusk-flying insects.	*Protected species.* Nocturnal. Summer roosts in buildings. Winters in caves.
Daubenton's bat	Over open water.	Throughout, no longer common.	Insects at/above water surface.	*Protected species.* Nocturnal, roosts in hollow trees and under bridges.
Whiskered bat	Open areas and woodland, especially with rivers and ponds.	Throughout, no longer common.	Small insects and spiders.	*Protected species.* Nocturnal. Summer roosts often in buildings, winter in caves, cellars and trees.
Noctule	Over rivers and lakes.	Throughout, no longer common.	Large insects such as cockchafers.	*Protected species.* Nocturnal but first to emerge at dusk. Roosts in trees.
Pipistrelle	Over or near water and grassland.	Throughout, common but declining.	Small insects, especially midges.	*Protected species.* Roosts in a variety of confined spaces, in winter in buildings

1.5.2 The species and their habitat requirements

Otter

Formerly common throughout Britain, the otter (Plate 1) has experienced a substantial decline from the late 1950s onwards. The decline has been linked primarily to the effects of pollution particularly , organochlorine pesticides, and extensive habitat loss . Activities such as wetland drainage, insensitive dredging practices, and increased grazing on riverbanks have resulted in the destruction of holt sites and removal of bankside cover. However, this trend is now being reversed by implementation of river management practices to maintain or improve bankside habitat.

Surveys in the mid-1980s (Andrews and Crawford, 1986; Green and Green 1987; Strachan *et al.*, 1990) indicated that, although the numbers of otters had increased in much of Wales, the south-west and northern England, there appeared to be little change elsewhere in England and Wales. Otters are still absent or rare in much of central, southern and eastern England. A survey of otters in Ireland in 1980/81 found 92% of sites occupied by otters, probably due to the relatively low levels of pollution and human disturbance. Similarly, in Scotland, particularly in the Highlands and Islands, good populations were found. Figure 1 shows a broad assessment of the distribution of otters in Great Britain in 1993 (NRA, 1993b). Pollution (possibly as a result of polychlorinated biphenyls (PCBs)),

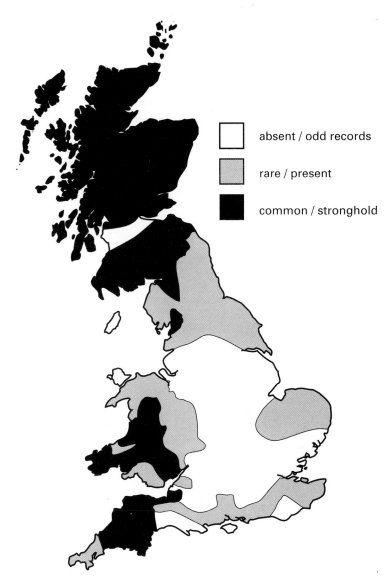

☐ absent / odd records

▨ rare / present

■ common / stronghold

Figure 1
A broad assessment of the distribution of otters in Great Britain (1993). Source: NRA (1993b)

Plate 1
Otter

RSPB

Plate 2 Otter holt

Nigel Holmes

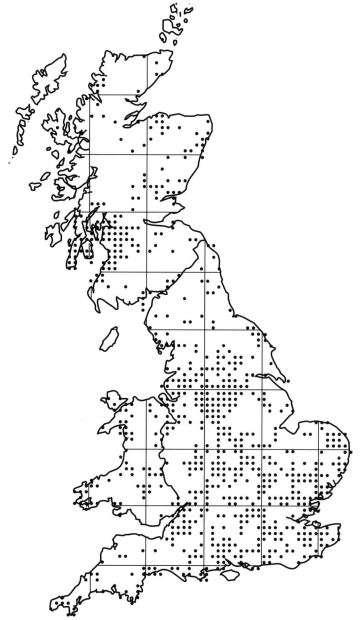

Figure 2
Shrew distribution in Great Britain. Source: Arnold (1993)

disturbance (particularly from increased recreational activity), road deaths, drowning in fyke nets, and lack of habitat may be preventing population recovery in places. When only small numbers of animals are present in an area, opportunities for pairing, even when habitats are suitable, are limited. Consequently affected populations may take a considerable time to recover.

Male and female otters both hold home ranges, the size varying with the quality of the habitat, availability of food and dominance of the individual otter. Dog otter home ranges rarely overlap but may overlap with those of bitches. Sizes vary from approximately 4-40 km of river per otter.

Otters are largely nocturnal and require dense cover for feeding, resting and breeding. Favoured areas of cover include low, dense vegetation, such as hawthorn, blackthorn, willow, bramble and gorse. Cavities among bankside tree roots, especially oak, ash and sycamore are often used as holt sites and are of immense importance (Plate 2). The fibrous roots of willow and alder are often unsuitable, though otters may lie up in the crowns of pollarded willows. Rock cavities, peat burrows and old culverts may also be used (Smith and Drury, 1990). Reed and sedge beds are important as they are often undisturbed and contain ditches and dykes with abundant food, eg eels.

The most secure holts are chosen for giving birth and rearing cubs. Of the few known breeding sites, most have been in dense, impenetrable scrub in undisturbed areas with secure space available for cubs to play. Different holts are used as the cubs

Heather Angel

Plate 3 Water shrew

mature. Otters can breed at any time of year, but more births occur in spring (Mason and Macdonald, 1986; The Wildlife Trusts, 1991).

Diet varies according to habitat range and prey availability, but fish comprise 95% of the diet; species such as roach and eels are preferred. Voles, waterfowl, molluscs and amphibians may be also taken.

Water shrew

This is the only aquatic species of the three British shrews (Plate 3). It is widespread, but is absent from Ireland and some of north Scotland (Figure 2). A good swimmer, the water shrew is closely associated with clear, fast-flowing unpolluted rivers and streams, but also occurs around ponds and ditches. It may also occasionally occur in small numbers some distance from water. Cover at the water's edge is essential to give protection from predators. Population densities in water-cress beds, a favoured habitat, vary from 3-6 per hectare (Churchfield, 1988). Water shrews use extensive tunnel systems in riverbanks with entrances both above and below water. Their young are reared in nests of moss and other dry material, usually in the burrow.

Shrews are more active at night, travelling up to 60 m along watercourses. They have a voracious appetite (Churchfield, 1984, 1985) and can dive to depths of 75 cm or

more to catch their prey. Water shrews consume the equivalent of their body weight in food in a day. Invertebrates such as freshwater hoglice and shrimps and caddisfly larvae are taken in the water; on land earthworms, beetles and spiders form the main prey. Water shrews also occasionally take fish and frogs.

Water vole

Water voles (Plate 4) are largely associated with slow-flowing rivers (Woodall, 1977). They are widespread in the lowlands of Britain but are absent from north and

Plate 4 Water vole

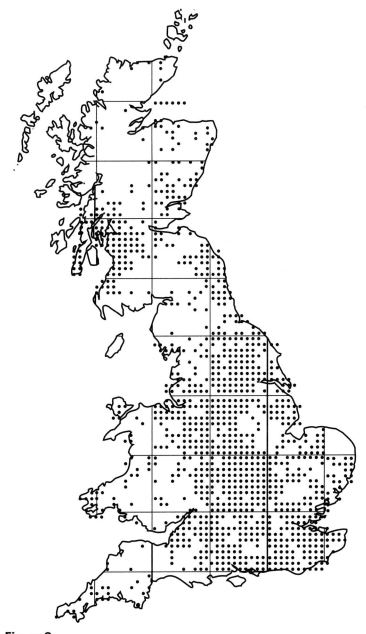

Figure 3
Water vole distribution in Great Britain. Source: Arnold (1993)

north-west Scotland, many islands and Ireland (Figure 3). Water vole populations have decreased in many parts of Britain in recent years, possibly as a result of pollution, habitat loss and predation by mink. They are also less common in areas populated by brown rats.

Male water voles have a home range of approximately 130 m of river whilst females occupy about 80 m^2, depending on habitat quality (Stoddart, 1970). In summer, breeding females occupy exclusive linear home ranges along riverbanks. Within the home range is at least one main burrow with entrances above and below the water. The nest is normally underground in a complex burrow, but when the water table is high, voles may nest in tussocks of vegetation. Coarse vegetation is used to line the nest.

Water voles are active both day and night, usually for periods of 2-4 hours. They create runways in dense vegetation within 1 m of the water's edge. In summer they actively range along riverbanks, but most of the winter is spent within the burrow although they do not hibernate. Water voles are vegetarians and need a supply of plant food all year round (Pelikan, 1974). They can eat up to the equivalent of 80% of their body weight in a day, taking green shoots in preference to seeds, fruits and roots. In winter they have to rely more on below-ground rhizomes. Preferred species include river margin reeds, rushes, bur-reed, reedmace and reed sweet-grass (Holisova, 1965). Except for willow, woody vegetation is not eaten.

Water voles have been shown to prefer banks greater than 1 m high, with slopes of less than 35°, and vegetated to the water's edge. It appears that vegetation is a more important factor than soil type, but loamy and sandy banks are preferred for burrowing. Water voles also appear to be more abundant on streams with muddy bottoms. Deep streams, 1-3 m wide, with slow flowing water are also preferred as the animals swim and dive well.

Mink

Mink have become naturalised along many rivers of the British Isles since they first escaped from fur farms in the 1950s. Mink are good swimmers and are sometimes confused with otters. However, adult mink (male 60 cm, female 50 cm) are half the length of otters and only a tenth of the weight (Plate 5). The most frequent fur colour of mink is dark (almost black), brown except for white patches on the chin and chest, but many variations occur.

Mink favour eutrophic streams, rivers and lakes with dense bank cover. Dens are commonly beneath, or in, waterside trees, within rabbit burrows or among rocks close to water. The mink is an opportunistic predator taking a wide variety of mammals (particularly rabbits), birds (notably moorhens and ducks), fish (eels are favoured), and invertebrates (including crayfish). Though minks' diet overlaps with that of the otter there is no

Plate 5
Mink

RSPB

evidence of competition and it is now felt highly improbable that they have any adverse effects on otter numbers (Birks, 1990). Owners and keepers of fish-farms, game and poultry regard the mink as a pest but its effect on waterfowl and other wildlife is controversial. Though mink are easily trapped, they are so well established that they are very difficult to eradicate.

Bats

Of the 15 species of bat found in Britain, five are particularly associated with watercourses (Table 1). These are Daubenton's bat, whiskered bat, Natterer's bat, noctule and pipistrelle (Stebbings and Jefferies, 1982; Sargent, 1991). Bat populations generally are declining and the retention of mature trees with cracks or holes will help to provide roost sites, particularly in the summer.

Daubenton's bats are found in all but the extreme north of Scotland, usually in small roosts close to water, in treeholes, bridges, buildings and caves. They hunt low over slow flowing open water, foraging in long straight beats and sheltered by overhanging trees (Nyholm, 1965). Watercourses greater than 9 m wide, where there are large mayfly and caddisfly populations are preferred. Daubenton's

bats need a minimum foraging area of 0.5 ha.

Whiskered bats roost in trees and buildings and tend to select rivers less than 10 m wide for feeding, where bankside vegetation is 1-5 m high. Small arthropods are taken from the foliage.

Natterer's bats generally prefer buildings as a roost site, so need to travel to rivers to feed. They feed primarily by taking insects from bankside vegetation, flies, beetles, spiders and caterpillars being the principal prey.

Noctule bats roost in trees, often in woodpeckers' old holes, and are usually the first species to emerge at dusk. They fly fast and high, direct to their preferred feeding areas, such as over rivers and lakes. Prey is caught and eaten in flight.

Pipistrelles use a variety of habitats for foraging, including farmland and woodland as well as rivers and ponds (Swift and Racey, 1983; Swift *et al.*, 1985). They feed on dense swarms of insects and therefore prefer wide rivers with wide open spaces. They fly considerable distances (up to 5 km) between roosts and foraging areas.

1.5.3 Habitat management for otters

Otters have been a particular focus of conservation activity in recent years. Consequently the following section highlights important factors of habitat management for these mammals. Habitat improvements undertaken for otters will also inevitably benefit other wildlife, whether or not otters recolonise.

When developing a management strategy to benefit otters, it is essential to consider the whole catchment because they inhabit long stretches of river. The management of tributaries and adjacent catchments should also be considered because otters travel

considerable distances to seek out suitable home ranges not occupied by other otters.

Whole river catchment management plans for otters are being developed and implemented in partnership with landowners, river managers and users. Typically, these partnerships may include Wildlife Trusts, the NRA, the statutory nature conservation agencies, the CLA, individuals and angling organisations. These plans are designed to integrate with catchment plans being prepared by the NRA. Although otter plans are developed primarily with the species in mind, the whole river environment is intended to benefit from measures taken.

Before undertaking conservation work, it is best to contact the appropriate water management organisation, eg NRA, for advice as some management activities may require consent from them or from other statutory bodies.

Management objectives and considerations

Habitat management for otters should primarily aim to conserve existing otter populations and enable expansion to neighbouring rivers. The most important factors determining whether otters will spread are the presence of a successfully reproducing population nearby, good water quality, adequate food supply, and sufficient cover and shelter (for secure areas, vital for giving birth and rearing cubs) (NRA, 1993b).

These factors should not be considered in isolation. Although many rivers in Wales currently have adequate cover, many potential holt sites are under pressure from overgrazing and the potential for natural regeneration of cover is minimal. In a few decades the number of resting sites could be significantly reduced unless management is undertaken now to redress this. Appropriate measures include planting trees and erecting fencing to reduce riverbank grazing pressure, thereby encouraging natural tree and scrub regeneration. A single young oak or ash sapling may seem insignificant, but retaining it might result in an important holt site for otter use being available in 100 years time.

Management action for otters needs to be directed in two ways:

- protection and management of existing habitat;
- rehabilitation/enhancement of habitat.

Protection and management of existing habitat

The maintenance of good habitat depends upon the production and management of terrestrial vegetation to ensure that suitable breeding sites and cover remain. In addition, the otters' food supply may be affected by channel works, which alter the habitat available for fish. The practices (described in Part 3) of leaving aquatic plants and marginal vegetation as refuges for fish, maintaining pools and riffles, only partially dredging a channel, and retaining meanders, are all important for otters.

Riverside scrub, reedbeds, dense herbaceous vegetation and woodland should all be maintained to provide good cover. Fencing off trees and scrub from livestock not only protects existing cover but also encourages future regeneration. Retention of tall vegetation or leaving cutting until late in the year is also valuable. Trees and scrub should be coppiced or pollarded rather than being removed; if removal cannot be avoided, the root system should be left as a potential holt site (several landowners on the R Eden in Cumbria have adopted a policy to preserve tree roots). As trees favoured as holt sites often lean out over the channel appropriate positioning of current deflectors may reduce erosion and maintain the holt feature. Often it may be desirable to top trees to increase their stability. This is particularly important in the case of ash, oak and sycamore, where root systems are often favoured holt sites. Licences, issued by EN, CCW or SNH, are required for maintenance of trees which are used as resting places.

Adoption of a low-maintenance policy minimises disturbance to otters in river corridors and retains wetlands in the floodplain. Best practices include working from one bank and limiting access in sensitive areas. Where vegetation management (both aquatic and terrestrial) is essential for flood defence purposes it should be carried out on suitable rotations to encourage the permanent development of scrub and dense vegetation (Chapter 3.7). For example, rotational cutting, particularly on the smaller becks in areas of importance for otters, is being employed by the NRA. Dense vegetation may also be encouraged by using natural bank protection to encourage establishment of scrub behind it.

Rehabilitation and enhancement of habitat

Provision of cover is particularly important in river systems where little currently exists. This is especially true where disturbance is a significant factor. Cover may be improved in a variety of ways.

- *Planting trees and scrub.* Bramble, hawthorn, blackthorn and sycamore provide dense cover for lying up or even breeding. A mixture of local species to provide quick cover and long-term holt sites is best (NRA, 1993b and Chapter 3.7). Planting field corners minimises land-take and the costs of protecting from grazing. Planting adjacent to the riverbank to provide cover is also important.

- *Wetland creation.* This includes the creation of sedge or reedbeds and water level management to encourage wetland vegetation regeneration. Replanting of aquatic vegetation may also be necessary to assist the process (Chapter 3.5). Ideal sites are those which will flood regularly and have lost their previous ecological interest due to intensification of land use.

Careful de-silting of old ponds and backwaters or creation of new ones can provide alternative feeding areas (Section 3.3.3). Ideally, they should be located as close to the river as possible, with adequate cover provided to allow travel to and from the river. Backwaters in continuous connection with the main channel are particularly desirable. Liaison with NRA or the appropriate water management agency should be undertaken to determine whether any proposed works are likely to require land drainage consent.

- *Logpile and artificial holts.* These may be essential if otters are to make immediate use of rivers with impoverished cover. They should be constructed as a short-term measure in conjunction with the creation of new habitats which will provide the long-term cover. Holts should be sited as close as possible to the water where the otter can have easy access and be free from disturbance. They should be above frequently occurring flood levels to prevent the holt and its occupants being washed away. Plate 6 shows the entrances/exits to an artificial holt on the R Dee. Methods of construction of log pile holts are

**Plate 6
Artificial otter
holt on the R Dee**

Steve Garner

**Plate 7
A pipe and
chamber holt
under
construction
(R Avon)**

David M Green

**Plate 8
The completed
artificial holt
which showed
signs of otter
usage within six
months of
completion**

David M Green

considered in Chapter 3.7. Figure 4
shows a theoretical example of an
artificial pipe and chamber hold. These
can be used in exceptional
circumstances, when there is little
natural cover and no local material for
log piles (which should be used in
preference). Plates 7 and 8 show the

design of an artificial holt constructed by
the Worcestershire Nature Conservation
Trust in the R Avon catchment. The
favoured location for this type of holt is
along the lower 200–400 m of
tributaries, which provide good habitat
but lack natural holt sites. This
arrangement provides easy 'otter' access

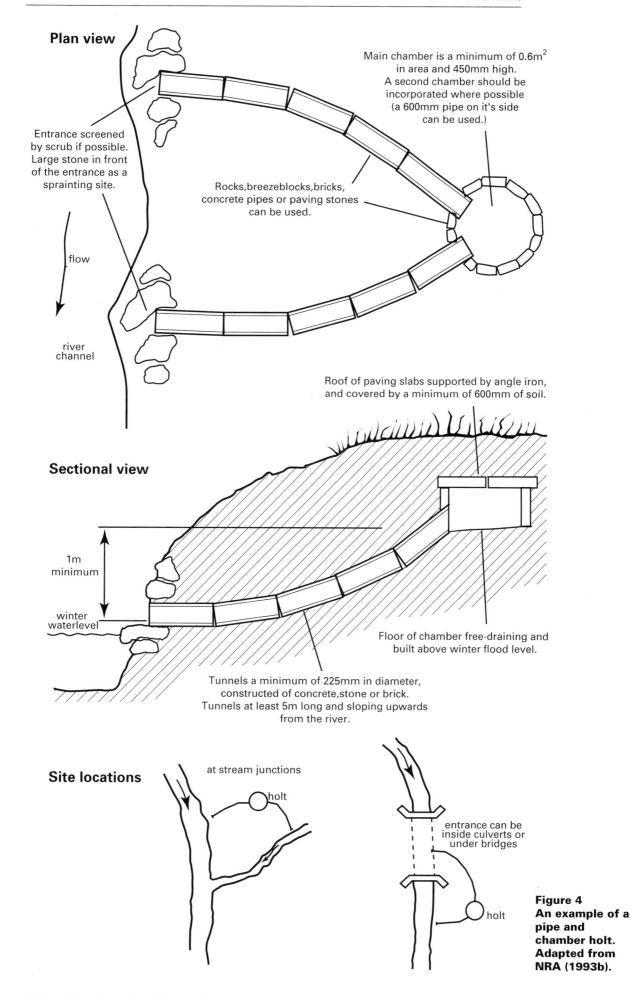

Plan view

Entrance screened by scrub if possible. Large stone in front of the entrance as a sprainting site.

flow

river channel

Rocks, breezeblocks, bricks, concrete pipes or paving stones can be used.

Main chamber is a minimum of 0.6m² in area and 450mm high. A second chamber should be incorporated where possible (a 600mm pipe on it's side can be used.)

Roof of paving slabs supported by angle iron, and covered by a minimum of 600mm of soil.

Sectional view

1m minimum

winter waterlevel

Floor of chamber free-draining and built above winter flood level.

Tunnels a minimum of 225mm in diameter, constructed of concrete, stone or brick. Tunnels at least 5m long and sloping upwards from the river.

Site locations

at stream junctions

holt

entrance can be inside culverts or under bridges

holt

Figure 4 An example of a pipe and chamber holt. Adapted from NRA (1993b).

to the more abundant food supply to be found in the larger river. Advice should be sought from the appropriate water management organisation if planning to install a pipe and chamber holt.

Heightened awareness is leading to increasing interest in mammals, especially otters. Organisations and landowners have been working together to secure the future of otters, which is of overall wildlife benefit. Whilst rehabilitation focuses on the physical habitats, it must also address the problems of water quality, including pollution from pesticides, which have been linked to past loss of otter populations.

Key References

Andrews, E, Howell, P and Johnson, K (1993) *Otter Survey of Wales 1991*. The Vincent Wildlife Trust, London.

Chanin, P R F (1993) *Otters*. Whittet Books.

Churchfield, S (1981) *The Natural History of Shrews*. A and C Black..

Corbet, G B and Harris, S (1991) *The Handbook of British Mammals*. Blackwell Scientific Publications, London. 2nd edition.

National Rivers Authority (1993). *Otters and River Habitat Management. Conservation Technical Handbook, Number 3*. National Rivers Authority, Bristol.

The Wildlife Trusts (1991) *Focus on otters – a guide to their natural history and conservation*. The Wildlife Trusts, Lincoln.

Strachan, R and Jefferies, D J (1993) *The water vole* Arvicola Terrestris *in Britain 1989-1990: its distribution and changing status*. The Vincent Wildlife Trust, London.

1.6 Birds

1.6.1   Introduction

1.6.2   Habitat requirements of river birds
      1.6.2.1 Upland rivers
      1.6.2.2 Lowland rivers
            – River channels and banks
            – Floodplain grassland
            –Floodplain trees and woodland

1.6.3   Implications for river management

1.6.1 Introduction

More than 20 bird species are regularly found breeding or feeding along rivers in either the lowlands or the uplands of the British Isles. Only the dipper is confined largely to the uplands. Several other species are found principally on rivers at least in the nesting season – they include goosander, common sandpiper, kingfisher, sand martin and grey wagtail. Many riverine birds are more abundant on lakes, reservoirs, gravel pits and even ponds; this almost certainly reflects past and present management of the respective habitats. The loss of backwaters and islands, the removal of bankside vegetation, and the lower frequency and magnitude of winter flooding greatly reduce the suitability of rivers as bird habitats especially in the lowlands. Two species that breed in wet grassland, redshank and snipe, have undergone such declines that they are now included as candidate species in the *Red Data Book of British Birds* (Batten *et al.*, 1990). However, birds can rapidly recolonise previously degraded habitat once conditions become favourable and there are many ways in which sensitive engineering practice and rehabilitation measures can help.

Good information on the current and past distribution of birds in Britain and Ireland can be found in the *New Atlas of Breeding Birds in Britain and Ireland* (Gibbons *et al.*, 1993).

Most river birds are widespread across the British Isles in suitable habitat. Their distribution is strongly influenced by river type, especially the distinction between 'upland' rivers with stony or rocky beds and 'lowland' rivers on clays and silts with luxuriant plant growth (Plate 1). However, some species range across all types of rivers.

**Plate 1
A typical slow-flowing lowland river with ample plant growth for nesting and feeding**

Paul Jose/Vernon Poulter

1.6.2 Habitat requirements of river birds

Most river birds feed on invertebrates such as molluscs, worms, spiders and insects. Even those species such as mallard which are mainly plant-feeders have young that feed on invertebrates. In general, food begins to become more plentiful in spring when plants begin to grow and invertebrates hatch from overwintered eggs or emerge from pupae. Invertebrates are the main food resource during this period and are particularly important for the rapid growth of young birds.

There is another flush of food in the form of seeds from summer into autumn. At the end of the growing season, food becomes scarcer as the numbers of adult invertebrates decline and plant stocks are depleted. Additionally, much food material may be swept away by high flows, which also alter the amount of accessible feeding habitat. Where the river is retained within its channel, all shallows may be flooded out so that only birds which dive and can cope with the flow rate can reach their feeding areas. Only if the river overtops into the floodplain are feeding conditions improved as previously inaccessible seeds and invertebrates are floated out of vegetation into shallow,

Table 1: Characteristics of major bird species breeding in close association with upland rivers

SPECIES	STATUS	HABITAT CHARACTERISTICS	MAIN FOOD	NEST SITE
Red-breasted merganser	Widespread north and west Scotland also Northern Ireland and spreading in North England and Wales. Absent during winter months when predominantly marine.	Well-oxygenated unpolluted upland rivers, with boulders, riffles and sand banks. Banks with dense vegetation such as heather, scrub and often woodland.	Predominantly fish with some invertebrates.	Nests on ground among tree and scrub roots, in hollows in banks and cliffs or concealed in thick vegetation.
Goosander	In breeding season restricted to Scotland and North England but spreading in Wales. In winter widespread throughout Britain. Absent from Ireland.	Clear, unpolluted, upland rivers particularly where close to mature trees during breeding season, more open waters during winter months.	Primarily fish <10 cm and occasionally invertebrates.	Prefers to nest in tree holes over or close to water.
Common sandpiper	Widespread in upland areas north of a line from Humber to Severn estuaries. Summer visitor only.	Water courses with shingle margins, banks and islands; rough vegetation on or near to river.	Invertebrates particularly insects taken from bars, margins or grassland at waterside.	Nests in rough cover on the riverbank, islands or some distance away, usually well above normal flood levels.
Dipper	Widespread in north and west, absent from England east of line Humber – Isle of Wight. Present throughout the year.	Fast-flowing streams and rivers with rocks, boulders, shingle, water-falls and rock outcrops with shallow water.	Invertebrates largely taken from the stream bed. Fish	Nests in holes in rock outcrops, earth-bank overhangs and tree roots; regular use of man-made structures such as bridges and weirs.
Grey wagtail	Widespread though absent in much of central and eastern England. Present throughout the year.	Turbulent streams with gravel bars; weirs, mill races. Favours wooded reaches.	Insectivorous, taking food from ground and just above ground and water surface.	Nests in cavities among rocks, tree roots; also on man-made structures.

relatively slow-moving water. Such food resources are much more abundant in unimproved pasture, marsh, scrub and wet woodland than in improved pastures.

Birds deal with the seasonal variations in food availability in one of three ways: by changing their diet; changing their feeding method; or by moving away.

The availability of nest sites is important. Except for mute swans, which can defend their nests from most predators, most birds place their nests where they are concealed or, failing that, inaccessible. Dense, tall, herbaceous vegetation is favoured by many species because it gives cover against bird predators such as crows and magpies; as well as rats, foxes, stoats, weasel and mink. For birds that nest early this means that the cover must have stood over the winter and not have been cleared by management or broken down by livestock. Other birds, such as moorhens, may use limbs of trees that are trailing in the water. A few species, eg great crested grebe and coot, construct floating nests in emergent vegetation. Some bird species, eg common sandpiper and mute swan, prefer to nest on islands, which offer some protection from ground

breeding oystercatchers, which nest on shingle bars or margins and feed in the surrounding pastures. Ringed plovers and little ringed plovers can also occur on similar nest sites but are much less common. Two duck species are widely but sparsely distributed on upland rivers during the breeding season, particularly on wooded reaches (Table 1). The goosander is almost entirely confined to Britain while the red-breasted merganser also occurs in much of Ireland. Sand martins are widespread on many upland as well as lowland rivers; they require regularly eroding banks which offer sheer earth faces in which to tunnel. Kingfishers are also present on upland rivers but are absent from most of Scotland. Table 1 summarises the status, habitat, food and nesting requirements of five bird species characteristic of upland rivers.

Plate 2
An eroded bankside cliff, an ideal nesting place for sand martins and kingfishers

predators, from trampling by stock and from human disturbance.

Some species, eg sand martin and kingfisher, nest in holes excavated in eroding banksides where they are out of reach of ground predators. The availability of such features along a stretch of river influences the bird species able to live there (Plate 2).

1.6.2.1 Upland rivers

Plate 3 (left)
Dipper; upland rivers

Plate 4 (right)
Grey wagtail; upland rivers

The most widespread and characteristic birds of upland rivers are common sandpiper, dipper and grey wagtail (Table 1, Plates 3 and 4), the last two species are also found on well-oxygenated streams in lowland Ireland and Britain. Many northern British rivers also support

1.6.2.2 Lowland rivers

The lowland rivers tend to support more species of breeding and wintering birds than those of the uplands. They generally offer a much larger range of food and habitat than upland watercourses due to the wider range of vegetation types and associated aquatic invertebrates (Table 2).

River channels and banks

Lowland rivers are now often heavily modified and all but the immediate banks are usually subject to cultivation or

Table 2: Characteristics of major bird species breeding in close association with lowland rivers

SPECIES	STATUS	HABITAT CHARACTERISTICS	FOOD	NEST SITE
Great crested grebe	Widespread, mainly in lowland areas. Present throughout the year.	Open lake-like sections of 1 ha 0.5-5 m deep, per pair during breeding season. Well-developed fringing emergent vegetation especially reeds.	Fish; aquatic invertebrates	Nests of vegetation within emergent vegetation or trailing branches.
Little grebe	Widespread and sometimes numerous especially in south. Present throughout the year on lowland rivers.	Shallow waters often <1 m deep and < than 1 ha extent. Luxuriant aquatic, emergent and marginal vegetation, overhanging branches, bushes and scrub.	Insects; molluscs; tadpoles; small fish	Floating nest platforms attached to emergent vegetation trailing branches.
Mallard	Very common and widespread on both lowland and upland rivers.	Waters with emergent vegetation, bankside scrub; rank vegetation and submerged aquatics. Very adaptable.	Omnivorous and opportunistic, small young dependent on invertebrates	Generally on ground in thick cover but also in holes in trees. Where habitat on riverbanks is not ideal will freely nest at distance from water in ditches, in hedges or scrub. Young then brought to water.
Tufted duck	Widespread, rather scarce but sometimes at high density. Present throughout the year.	Open lake-like sections with good marginal emergent vegetation. Depths in excess of 5 m but usually less than 1 m during breeding season.	Omnivorous: fish, aquatic invertebrates; green plant material. Mainly taken from riverbed.	Nests in tussocks or dense vegetation over or close to water. Apparent territories on rivers may involve birds actually nesting on nearby lakes, pools or gravel pits.
Mute swan	Widespread in lowland areas; numerous in south. Present throughout the year.	Wide or open sluggish channels with islands, backwaters, spits or stands of emergent vegetation, eg reeds and abundant submerged aquatics in depths less than 1 m.	Mainly aquatic vegetation; also emergent plants and seeds. Also graze on land, particularly early in season.	Nests on bank, islands or within emergent vegetation in shallow water.
Moorhen	Very common and widespread. Present throughout the year.	Prefers waters sheltered by woodland or tall emergent plants but utilises open bankside habitats for feeding.	Omnivorous; may feed within river but also often in adjacent damp pasture.	Nests in emergent vegetation, trailing branches or in bushes. May nest well away from river if suitable habitat is lacking.
Coot	Common, widespread in south, more scarce in north. Present throughout the year.	Moderately wide but slow-flowing, open channels, with shallows and marginal emergent vegetation such as reeds and bulrushes. Overhanging and trailing scrub or branches important for early nests. Adjacent wet pasture may be important for feeding early in season.	Omnivorous; plants, frequently obtained by diving down to 2 m.	Nests over water anchored to rushes, reeds or trailing branches.

Table 2 (cont)

SPECIES	STATUS	HABITAT CHARACTERISTICS	FOOD	NEST SITE
Kingfisher	Widespread and quite common except in Scotland where scarce and absent in the Highlands. Present throughout the year.	Still or gently flowing rivers and streams with shallow areas of clear water, low overhanging branches or other perches essential.	Mainly small fish but also tadpoles and aquatic invertebrates	Nests in tunnels excavated in steep or vertical bank normally over water. Most nests 90-180 cm above water.
Sand martin	Widespread; summer visitor Mar–Sept.	Vertical earth and sand banks soft enough for burrowing. Open areas without woodland. Mainly along rivers in the north but artificial sites such as gravel workings in the south.	Aerial insects often taken over open water.	Nests in burrows excavated in soft or sandy cliffs generally over water. Nest site an average 1.8 m above water. Opportunistic and may nest in pipes in walls.
Reed warbler	Widespread but local in south; absent north England, Scotland, Ireland and much of Wales. Summer visitor Apr–Sept.	Almost entirely restricted to areas with reedbeds or fringes, uses other bankside vegetation when feeding.	Predominantly insectivorous	Large numbers usually confined to extensive reedbeds but scattered pairs in reed fringes elsewhere. Nests typically attached to reed stems, well above ground or water level.
Sedge warbler	Widespread and numerous throughout lowland Britain. Summer visitor Apr–Sept.	Low dense vegetation generally along water's edge, utilises reeds, willow carr, scrub and bushes.	Insectivorous	Nests low down in dense bankside vegetation, occasionally over water.
Reed bunting	Widespread and common. Present throughout the year.	Marshy areas, reedbeds, fringing emergent vegetation, hedgerows and ditches, rank vegetation.	Mainly seeds but insects during breeding season.	Nests in thick vegetation close to the ground. Formerly restricted to marsh or riverine areas – but now occasionally in rough ground in agricultural areas.

livestock grazing. The range of vegetation cover and hence suitability for birds has consequently been reduced. The commonest breeding species, mallard and moorhen (Table 2), are often able to survive on highly managed rivers, although their breeding success can be poor. Other typical species, such as little grebe, mute swan and coot (Table 2), are more dependent on the presence of in-channel vegetation and are often restricted to undisturbed backwaters. Other characteristic birds depend on the banks of lowland rivers; kingfishers and sand martins require nest holes excavated in steep exposed banks, and sedge warblers and reed buntings need bankside patches of tall herbaceous vegetation or scrub (Table 2, Plates 5, 6 and 7).

The seeds of submerged and emergent plants are a valuable food, which is quickly dispersed by currents but may be trapped by stands of emergents or locally concentrated by eddies, in bays and backwaters. Mallards, water rails, moorhens and coots take many seeds in late summer and autumn. Almost all river birds also take invertebrates, including insects, crustaceans, molluscs and worms but the extent to which they do so depends upon season and stage in the insect's lifecycle. Several species that are omnivorous, like mallard and moorhen, or plant-feeders like coot and mute swan, require insects on which to rear their young and the large losses amongst newly hatched ducklings and sometimes, cygnets,

RSPB

**Plate 5 (top)
Kingfisher;
upland and
lowland rivers**

**Plate 6 (below
left)
Sand martin and
nest hole**

**Plate 7 (below
right)
Sedge warblers
require tall
vegetation**

RSPB

RSPB

may be due to the inadequacy of this food supply on insensitively managed watercourses.

Fish are the main sources of food for several breeding bird species. On larger lowland rivers, great crested grebes feed primarily on fish (Plate 8) whereas little grebes probably take more invertebrates than small fish. Kingfishers are almost exclusively fish feeders and may be present on the smallest waters. To rear a brood successfully, kingfishers need to catch about 100 small (about 50 mm) fish a day for up to four weeks. Though they can plunge from hovering flight, kingfishers fish with least energy expenditure by using perches over water.

Herons normally nest colonially in trees away from water. However, they are

regular visitors to rivers in both lowlands and uplands where there are suitable shallows in which the birds can wade. They can also fish the surface layers of deep water provided the bank is accessible. neither too steep nor covered in tall, impeding vegetation, or with a continuous tree canopy. Herons are also predators of amphibians, small mammals and other birds.

Floodplain grassland

Most lowland river valleys formerly contained meadows with a high water table and were subject to regular winter flooding. They were cut for hay in late spring/early summer and then grazed in autumn. The vegetation comprised a wide variety of grasses, sedges, rushes and

Table 3: Characteristics of major bird species breeding in close association with river floodplains

SPECIES	STATUS	HABITAT CHARACTERISTICS	FOOD	NEST SITE
Lapwing	Widespread but now scarce in lowland England and Wales. Present throughout the year.	A mosaic of arable and pasture with ploughed or open ground for nesting and grassland, preferably damp or with standing water for rearing chicks.	Ground-living invertebrates	Nest placed on the ground in open areas with short or sparse vegetation <5 cm tall
Redshank	Widespread but now very scarce in lowland England. Present throughout the year.	Damp meadows, marshland and estuarine marshes often with some standing water.	Invertebrates obtained by pecking and probing	Nest usually placed in tussock of grass or sedge in open habitat.
Snipe	Widespread but now scarce on lowland farmland, present throughout the year.	Wet meadows, rough grazing and upland bog with tussocky vegetation, needs wet or damp ground to probe for invertebrates.	Invertebrates obtained by probing	Nests on the ground in tussocky grass, rushes or sedges. Usually concealed.
Yellow wagtail	Widespread throughout England and Wales but declining, rare in Scotland, absent from Ireland.	Lowland flood meadows and damp grazing especially where vegetation low and near to shallow surface water.	Insects and other small invertebrates	Nest placed on the ground, in tuft of vegetation usually within rank grass.

herbs, producing abundant seeds which were floated out by winter floods. This attracted large numbers of wildfowl, such as teal, as well as grazing species like wigeon and geese. In addition wildfowl and waders fed on soil invertebrates. The effect of livestock grazing on this diverse vegetation was to produce an uneven sward offering good feeding conditions to breeding waders, most commonly lapwing, snipe, redshank plus curlew in the uplands, and yellow wagtail (Table 3). The breeding waders, redshank, snipe and lapwing, all require access to soil invertebrates which are only available in moist soils or along ditch margins. Lapwings are able to survive in drier habitats but breed in much higher numbers in wet or damp habitats. All three species also require large open areas with open views unimpeded by hedgerows or other structures. Being used for hay, floodplain meadows are free from livestock in late spring and early summer so nests and chicks are not at risk from trampling. The habitat is also a rich hunting area for barn owls.

Floodplain trees and woodland

To birds, different kinds of trees have different values. For instance, in winter alder produces abundant small seeds, which are an important food resource for two small finches that breed mainly in conifer forests - redpoll and siskin. In

**Plate 8
Great crested grebe; primarily a fish eater**

RSPB

England and Wales, alder, willows and birches are the main nesting trees for the willow tit. Unlike other tits, this species excavates its own nest hole and requires rotting, soft-textured tree trunks, branches and stumps.

Willows, birches and oaks have a very abundant invertebrate fauna and are therefore particularly important feeding sites for many birds, including woodpeckers, warblers, flycatchers and tits.

Species which come into leaf or flower early in the spring have high value because they provide new feeding opportunities after the shortages of winter. Willows are an early source of pollen for insects emerging from hibernation and so attract many insectivorous birds at this time. In the uplands, pied flycatchers returning from Africa may feed first in the riverside alders while waiting for conditions to improve in the oakwoods higher on the hill where they will breed.

Where both banks are tree-lined, relatively calm air conditions prevail. In Northern Ireland, where woodland is scarce, spotted flycatchers make much use of this habitat, catching aquatic insects flying above the river surface.

1.6.3 Implications for river management

The preceding sections have described how birds use river channel and floodplain features in a number of ways. However, their presence or absence along a river can, to an extent, be dictated by the river management that is undertaken. For a series of detailed management recommendations for breeding birds, see Table 4.

Before management work is started, the bird species that occur on the river should be identified (Chapter 2.6). Tables 1, 2 and 3 list the species most likely to occur on upland and lowland rivers and on lowland floodplains along with the features of particular importance. It should be noted, however, that some reaches in the upland fringes often contain features of both upland and lowland rivers and may be particularly rich in birds.

In general terms, the more time that has elapsed since management work was last carried out, the more likelihood that the river will hold a good variety of birdlife. One of the aims of river management should be to retain as much diversity as possible. However where habitat reinstatement is the object, rather than management, emphasis should be placed on establishing features or habitats of particular value to species that are scarce or declining within the region (Table 4). With careful consideration it may prove possible to attract species back to a river from which they have been absent for a number of years.

Key References

Batten, L, Bibby, C J, Clement, P, Elliott, G D and Porter, R F (1990) *Red Data Birds in Britain.* T and A D Poyser, London.

Gibbons, D W, Reid, J B and Chapman, R A (1993) *The New Atlas of Breeding Birds in Britain and Ireland.* T and A D Poyser, London.

Table 4: Management recommendations for breeding birds

FEATURE OR VEGETATION TYPE	SPECIES LIKELY TO BENEFIT	MANAGEMENT RECOMMENDATION	BENEFIT
Vegetated islands	Common sandpiper, mallard, tufted duck, mute swan	Size of islands not important but need to be protected against erosion, height should be just above predicted flow during March–May. A cover of dense herbaceous vegetation should be maintained.	Provides protection from ground predators for ground-nesting birds, can provide additional shallow water edges for feeding birds and can help to create areas of slack water.
Shoals and bars	Common sandpiper, oystercatcher, ringed plover, little ringed plover, grey wagtail, pied wagtail	Maintain or create small areas from 0.1 ha for nesting birds but always close to more extensive areas of 0.5 ha or more for feeding, areas should be maintained several centimetres above predicted maximum April–June flows and kept vegetation-free.	Provides open, vegetation free, nesting and feeding areas for oystercatcher, ringed and little ringed plovers and feeding areas for other species.
Pools and riffles	Red-breasted merganser, dipper, grey wagtail	In upland areas pool–riffle systems with rocks and boulders and shallow areas should be retained, at least some within wooded areas.	Provides suitable feeding conditions for dipper and grey wagtail. Dippers in particular require exposed rocks and boulders in riffles from which to dive for invertebrates.
Shallows	Mallard, grey heron	Should be located where sediments, seeds and organic material will accumulate to slow colonisation by emergent vegetation. Large areas may be required.	Shallows provide areas where dabbling duck can sift organic matter from the riverbed and where wading birds can locate invertebrates and fish.
Bays and backwaters	Great crested grebe, little grebe, mallard, tufted duck, mute swan, moorhen, coot, kingfisher	Slack water, bays and backwaters should be retained where possible and managed to ensure mixed conditions of open water over 1.5 m deep and shallows up to 0.3 m deep as well as areas with emergent and bankside vegetation.	Provides calm areas where food productivity is high, with abundant cover for feeding birds including vulnerable young.
Submerged aquatic plants	Mute swan, coot, little grebe, tufted duck, grey heron	Existing beds of submerged aquatic plants should be retained and conditions created suitable for their growth in sheltered bays and backwaters.	Provides direct food for mute swan and coot and habitat for invertebrates and fish taken by other species.
Emergent plants	Little grebe, great-crested grebe, coot, moorhen, reed warbler, sedge warbler, water rail	Existing stands of emergent vegetation should be retained wherever possible, larger blocks are more valuable. New stands can be established by transferring dredged material to areas of shallow water. Existing stands should not be broken up where this will open the reach to human disturbance.	Important as feeding areas for many birds, and nesting sites for grebes, coot and moorhen. Reeds in particular are the main nesting habitat for reed warblers and can provide roost sites for many species.

Table 4 (cont)

FEATURE OR VEGETATION TYPE	SPECIES LIKELY TO BENEFIT	MANAGEMENT RECOMMENDATION	BENEFIT
Unvegetated margins	Wading birds, dabbling ducks, moorhen and wagtails	Restricted lengths of unvegetated margins can be maintained or created by allowing limited livestock access. Care should be taken to protect important existing emergent and bankside vegetation.	Open areas of poached ground can provide good feeding conditions for snipe, redshank and other birds providing that trampling is not excessive.
Herbaceous vegetation	Red-breasted merganser, mallard, tufted duck, common sandpiper, sedge warbler, reed warbler and reed bunting	Extensive irregular bands of tall herbaceous bankside vegetation should be allowed to develop by excluding livestock. The value to birds can be increased by allowing adjacent to areas of emergent vegetation. Where necessary cutting should not take place until after August, vegetation should be allowed to stand over winter to provide nest sites the following spring.	Important as nesting cover for wildfowl, sedge warbler and reed bunting and provides feeding opportunities for a range of other insectivorous and seed-eating birds, if not too tall, can also provide hunting areas for barn owl and kestrel.
Bankside scrub	Red-breasted merganser, mallard, tufted duck, sedge warbler and other species not restricted to rivers and wetlands	Should be managed in association with other bankside vegetation, if possible should be cut on a 10-year rotation to maintain thick cover down to ground level and various stages of growth.	Can provide nest sites for mallard tufted duck, sedge warbler and a range of other species.
Bankside trees	Goosander, moorhen, coot, kingfisher	Planting of native species particularly those associated with rivers or wetlands such as willows or alder should be encouraged in small areas along the bankside. Where present, older trees, should be retained. Branches overhanging the water should also be retained where possible.	Native trees contribute seed fruit and invertebrates of value to birds, older trees with cavities are used for nesting by barn owls and goosander, overhanging branches are used as perches by kingfishers and trailing branches as nest anchorages by moorhens and coots.
Earth cliffs	Kingfisher, sand martin	Natural erosion should be permitted wherever possible otherwise new sheer faces at least 2 m high can be cut over water and recut at intervals.	Earth cliffs provide opportunities for burrow-nesting birds such as kingfisher and sand martin to excavate nest holes.
Winter flood meadows (floodplain wet grassland)	Snipe, lapwing, redshank, golden plover, mallard, teal, wigeon	Wherever possible areas of grassland should be established within the floodplain and allowed to flood at times of high flow. The maintenance of high water tables throughout the year should be considered.	Winter floods help to float out abundant seeds for wintering wildfowl and improve feeding conditions for snipe, golden plover and lapwing. High water tables will enhance breeding conditions for snipe, lapwing and redshank.

1.7 Fishes

1.7.1 Introduction

1.7.2 Classification and habitat requirements
    – Taxonomic and ecological groupings
    – Habitat requirements

1.7.3 Impacts of river management and opportunities for enhancement and
    rehabilitation
    1.7.3.1 Impacts
    1.7.3.2 Opportunities
        – Management practices
        – In-channel enhancements
        – Backwater and bay creation and rehabilitation
    1.7.3.3 Post-project appraisal

1.7.1 Introduction

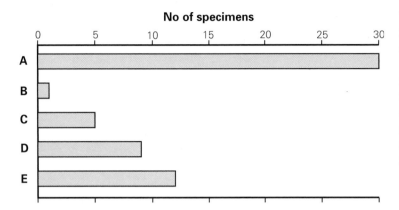

Figure 1
An analysis of current status of British freshwater fishes (including introduced species) (Wheeler 1992a).
A All species that spawn in fresh water and the eel - omits fishes which inhabit estuaries (total 30).
B The only species which is extinct in Britain (the burbot) (1)
C Species whose range and abundance have been severely reduced (5)
D Species whose range and abundance have increased (9)
E Introduced species which have established breeding populations (12)
A full listing of the above categories is included at the end of the chapter

The British Isles have a relatively limited native freshwater fish fauna when compared with the rest of Europe (Figure 1, column A). Even within Britain there is a marked reduction in species from south to north. For example a river on the north coast of Scotland may have fewer than 10 species, but an equivalent river on the south coast of England may have around 20 species.

1.7.2 Classification and habitat requirements

Table 1: Classification by family of the more common British freshwater fishes

FAMILY	SPECIES
Salmonidae	Atlantic salmon, brown trout, rainbow trout
Thymallidae	Grayling
Esocidae	Pike
Cyprinidae	Common carp, crucian carp, barbel, gudgeon, tench, bream, silver bream, bleak, minnow, rudd, roach, chub, dace, goldfish
Cobitidae	Spined loach, stone loach
Anguillidae	European eel
Gasterostidae	Three-spined stickleback, nine-spined stickleback
Percidae	Perch, ruffe
Cottidae	Bullhead

Note: for details of more threatened species, eg and arctic charr, refer to Maitland and Campbell, 1992.

Taxonomic and ecological groupings

Freshwater fishes of the British Isles can be classified into a number of taxonomic families. These include the salmonids, eg salmon, the cyprinids, eg roach and the percids, eg perch. (Table 1 lists many of the species and their family names).

Fishes have also traditionally been used to classify rivers according to their pattern of 'longitudinal zonation' (Table 2, Figure 2) in river systems (Huet, 1949). The upper reaches, characterised by more turbulent water, are inhabited by fishes with high swimming speeds, such as trout or salmon. The lower reaches are characterised by slower swimming fishes such as tench and bream. However, as a result of numerous factors, including variations in geology, the influence of river engineering works and artificial introductions, zonation can only be a generalisation.

Table 2: Longitudinal zonation of fish in river systems. Adapted from Huet (1949)

RIVER SYSTEM	ZONE	CHARACTERISTICS	SPECIES
Upstream ↕ Downstream	Trout Zone (fast flowing brooks and streams)	Very steep gradient, very fast flow rates, highly oxygenated, cool, silt free, oligotrophic	Trout, salmon, parr, bullhead, stone loach
	Grayling Zone (medium fast streams and river reaches)(1)	Steep gradient, fast flow, well oxygenated, clean gravel	As above plus:grayling, to barbel, chub, dace
	Barbel Zone (medium flowing river reaches)(2)	Gentle gradient, moderate flow, good oxygen content, mixed substrate (silt & gravel)	All above plus roach, rudd, perch, pike, eel
	Bream Zone (slow flowing/ sluggish river reaches)	Very gentle gradient, slow flow good oxygen content, variable temperature, silty substrate, turbid, eutrophic	Roach, rudd, perch, pike eel, tench, bream, carp

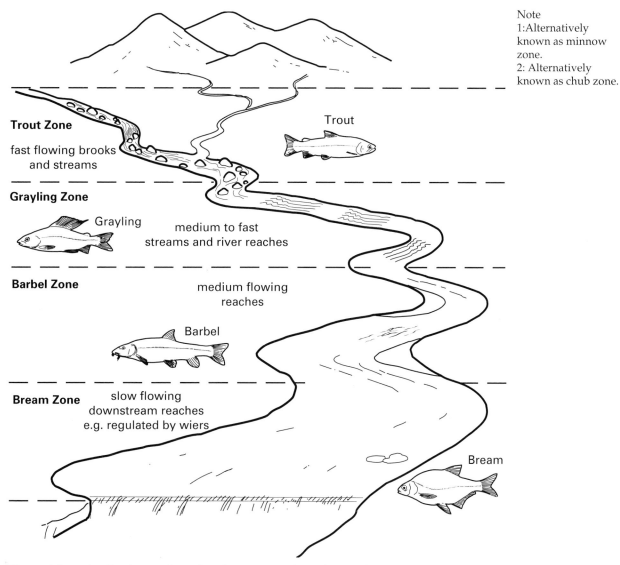

Note
1:Alternatively known as minnow zone.
2: Alternatively known as chub zone.

Trout Zone

fast flowing brooks and streams

Trout

Grayling Zone

Grayling

medium to fast streams and river reaches

Barbel Zone

medium flowing reaches

Barbel

Bream Zone

slow flowing downstream reaches e.g. regulated by wiers

Bream

Figure 2 Longitudinal zonation of a river system based upon fish zones.

**Figure 3
The range of
habitats
potentially
available within
the lateral
continuum of a
lowland river
floodplain.**

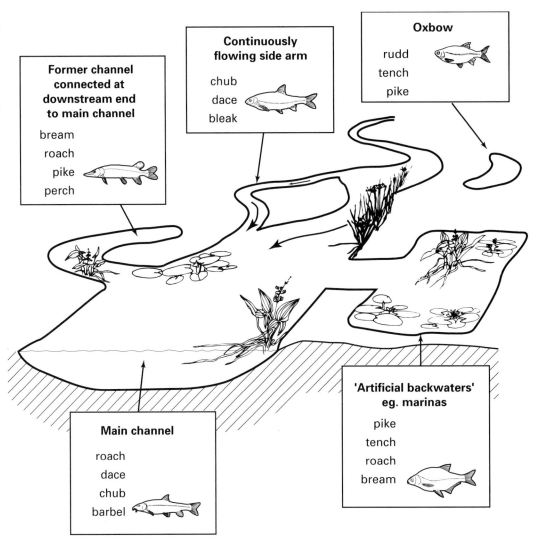

Oxbow

rudd
tench
pike

**Continuously
flowing side arm**

chub
dace
bleak

**Former channel
connected at
downstream end
to main channel**

bream
roach
pike
perch

Main channel

roach
dace
chub
barbel

**'Artificial backwaters'
eg. marinas**

pike
tench
roach
bream

**Plate 1
Shallow gravel
riffle with
bankside and in-
channel
vegetation,
providing good
habitat for
species such as
minnow and dace
fry.**

Mark Pilcher

In addition to longitudinal changes in
species, lateral variations in river habitat,
eg cut-offs and secondary channels,
influence fish distribution, particularly in
reaches with more extensive floodplains
(Figure 3). Small, faster flowing channels in
lowland reaches are favourable to species
such as minnow or dace (Plate 1). In slow-
flowing reaches and backwaters
permanently connected to the main river,
characteristic species include bream (Plate
4) and roach. Where flow rate is moderate
and the channel deeper, species such as
barbel and chub are present.

In backwaters, such as oxbows no longer in
contact with the main flow except in

extreme flood, characteristic species include tench (Plate 6), rudd and pike (Plate 5). Again, as with the 'longitudinal' zonation of fish fauna, 'lateral' zonation should be viewed only as a generalisation.

Habitat requirements

The habitat requirements of fish vary between species, with age and other factors, including the presence of predators. Table 3 summarises the general habitat requirements of a number of common freshwater fishes.

Species characteristic of upland channels, eg salmon and trout, require clean, silt-free gravel-bed rivers in which to breed. Typically spawning between November and early January, they bury their eggs in gravel redds of pea to walnut-sized pebbles. These are sometimes raised above the mean riverbed level to ensure that the

eggs receive a constant flow of oxygen-rich water. The young also require a gravel-bed with well-oxygenated, silt-free water.

Coarse fish, including chub (Plate 3), roach, bream (Plate 4) and carp, vary in their habitat preferences (Copp, 1991). Species

Plate 2 Backwater on R Colne connected at one end to mainstream, providing good habitat for roach, fry and adults.

Table 3: The generalised habitat requirements of several of the more common British freshwater fish

SPECIES	RIVER TYPE (in preferred order)	WATER VELOCITY	HABITAT	SEASON	SPAWNING SUBSTRATE
Salmon	1,2,3*,4*	I-II	i,ii	Wi	Gr
Trout	2,1,3*,4*	I-II	i,ii	Wi	Gr
Pike	3,4,	III-IV	iv,v	Sp	Pl
Eel	3,4,	III-IV	iii,v	-	-
Carp	3,4	IV	iv,v,iii	Su	Pl
Tench	4,3	IV	iv,v,iii	Su	Pl
Barbel	2,3	II-III	ii	Su	Gr
Gudgeon	3,4,2	II-III	ii,iii	Su	Pl/Gr
Roach	3,4,2	III-IV	iv,v	Sp	Pl
Rudd	4,3	IV	iv,v	Sp	Pl
Chub	3,2,4	III-IV,II	i,iv	Sp.Su	Pl/Gr
Dace	2,3,	II,III	i,ii	Sp	Gr
Bream	4,3	IV,III	iii,iv,v	Sp/Su	Pl
Perch	3,4	III-IV	iv,v	Sp	Pl
Zander	4	IV	i	Sp	Pl

Key: River type: 1 Upland; 2 Piedmont; 3 Upper reaches of lowland rivers; 4 Lower reaches of lowland rivers.
   *shows use of region during migration.
Water velocity of preferred habitat: I Fast; II Moderate; III Slow; IV Very slow.
Habitat: i Open Water; ii On gravel; iii On silt; iv Among plants; v In backwaters.
Spawning season: Wi Winter (Nov–Feb); Sp Spring (Mar–May); Su Summer (Jun–Aug).
Spawning substrate: Gr Gravel; Pl Plants.

Mick Rouse

Mick Rouse

Plate 3 (left) Chub

Plate 4 (right) Bream

such as barbel and dace tend to spawn in gravelly areas (ie the tail-end of riffles) in the mainstream or in continuously flowing backwaters. In contrast, species such as tench and carp spawn in densely vegetated backwaters out of the main current. Species such as roach will spawn in the margins of the main channel on plants away from the influence of the main current. Comparison of the habitat requirements of fishes at different stages of their life history (Table 4) illustrates the importance of lateral habitat diversity in river systems. For example, the habitat requirements of dace vary with age. Fry can tolerate only slow-flowing water, tending to occupy vegetated channel margins and side-channels. Adult dace prefer deeper, gravel-bed areas with faster flows.

Many freshwater fishes are unselective, opportunist feeders. Salmon, trout and to some extent grayling, feed on aquatic invertebrates, particularly crustaceans and insects on or near the stream bed. An important component of their diet is terrestrial insects which have fallen (or been blown) from trees, bankside plants, or simply out of the air. Windblown invertebrates are also important for fishes, such as dace and chub in lowland streams. This demonstrates the importance of bankside trees, bushes and scrub as valuable sources of these food organisms. Most cyprinids eat insect larvae, crustaceans and plant material. Dace, barbel and bleak generally prefer animal to plant material. The pike (Plate 5) and, where present the introduced zander, prey on other fishes (although both eat invertebrates when young). They have different feeding strategies; the pike lurks in plant beds before making a charge at prey sighted close by, whereas the zander lives in mid-water, feeding at twilight.

Table 4: The physical habitat requirements of dace at different life history stages

LIFE-STAGE	VELOCITY (cm/s)	DEPTH (cm)	SUBSTRATE
Fry	5–25	10–30	Instream plants
Juveniles	15–35	30–70	Mud/silt/sand
Adults	20–70	50–100	Silt/sand/gravel
Spawning	55–100	20–80	Silt/sand

Bullock *et al.*, 1990

Plate 5
Pike

Mke Suckling

1.7.3 Impacts of river management and opportunities for enhancement and rehabilitation

1.7.3.1 Impacts

Most British rivers have been heavily modified. The impacts of such works have been the deepening, straightening and embanking of natural channels. Many rivers now have increased hydraulic efficiency, but uniform structure, depth and velocity, and lack the varied physical features necessary for fish to thrive. Brookes (1988) provides a useful summary of the impact of channelisation on fish.

Generally, freshwater fishes are adaptable survivors under a variety of conditions. A reduction in diversity of species and numbers occurs when habitats are affected by insensitive engineering or a decline in water quality. Particularly sensitive species are salmon and trout. The most damaging

period is shortly after the spawning season, when the eggs, larvae and fry are in spawning areas. Disturbance of breeding adults may prevent spawning and loss of or a reduction in the number of fry for that particular year. River micro-habitats, such as weed beds, backwaters, small tributaries and even ditches, which fry use as nursery grounds, are easily damaged during even routine maintenance.

Channelisation can prevent periodic flow fluctuations from 'flushing out' accumulated silt and mud. Thus, as a result of the reduction of hydrological connectivity (Chapter 1.2) between the river and its floodplain, backwaters silt up. This often leads to the development of anoxic conditions unfavourable even for tolerant species such as tench and eels.

1.7.3.2 Opportunities

Habitat enhancement and rehabilitation cannot be considered in isolation from water quality, which must also be taken into account when improving fishery potential.

Fishes are used, as an indicator of conservation and river-quality status and as a resource for recreational and commercial fishing. For this reason a large part of fishery improvement has been concerned with stocking artificially reared fish to achieve better catches. However, for most fisheries, stocking alone has only short-term benefits; to achieve long-term improvements, the habitat requirements of the fish must be taken into account.

Before embarking upon any fisheries enhancement or rehabilitation scheme it is essential clearly to define the objectives and the species or group of species which it is meant to benefit. It is pointless to produce slow, weedy stretches of river ideal for roach and bream, if the objective is to improve habitat for game fishes. In planning enhancement/rehabilitation and management work, it is essential to determine that any proposed physical modifications are appropriate for a particular stretch of river. Where necessary land drainage consent should be obtained from NRA etc, before undertaking such work. Fisheries improvements should target species or communities and fisheries uses that are compatible with overall conservation needs and activities. Considered planning and consultation from the very outset of any work, and with all interested parties, will ensure that this is the case.

It is important to discriminate between factors that enhance fish populations and factors that enhance angling, though they are not necessarily mutually exclusive. Trees, for example, not only add significantly to the ecological and landscape value, but they can also contribute to the food supply for fish, by means of invertebrates, which colonise roots, and drop into the water from the branches and leaves. However, trees may block good casting points or prevent access

to anglers altogether. Therefore, tree planting needs to be carried out with care: tree species selected by ecologists, but then positioned after consideration by fishermen, ecologists and engineers.

The principles behind detailed planning assume an understanding of the ecological requirements of the target species and this will create perceptions of the work needed. The design of rehabilitation and enhancement schemes must aim to allow the creation and maintenance of conditions which would enhance the growth and reproduction of target species of fish and their food supply.

There is an increasing number of successful rehabilitation projects, which have been carried out in conjunction with engineers, thereby ensuring that they meet ecological and engineering criteria. The following section summarises options that may be considered. The techniques utilised are addressed in detail in Part 3 of the handbook.

Clearly any proposals to rehabilitate and enhance habitats damaged as a result of previous engineering operations, eg pool–riffle reinstatement, must take into account geomorphological processes (Chapters 1.3, 3.2 and 3.3) and work with them to produce 'self-sustaining' habitats (Hey, 1990).

Management practices

Management practices such as weed cutting to increase flow capacity can adversely affect fish if they coincide with spawning or the hatching of fish fry. If carried out sympathetically, eg after the spawning season and by partial cutting, both flood defence and fisheries objectives may be met. Excessive cutting of overhanging bankside vegetation may remove the only cover for fish in a stretch of river and may also reduce the invertebrate input to the river. Where permissible, fallen trees and branches should be left in the river where they will create flow diversity and refuge areas for species such as chub and barbel (Plate 7). Many species of fish are intolerant of, or avoid, full sun, so where trees are growing by a river they should be retained wherever possible to create shade. Tree planting can provide protection against channel erosion (Chapter 3.7) as well as valuable habitat and should be encouraged where appropriate.

In-channel enhancements

Various in-channel features have been specifically designed to create particular effects of scour and flow variability. Weirs maintain water depth and have been used in many instances to ameliorate the effects of low flows or overwidened channels. Groynes and deflectors are usually designed to cause a break in the uniformity of the channel and thus to vary flow. Siting of such structures must be carried out with care to avoid erosion of the opposite bank of the channel. They are made from a range of materials such as rock or wooden stakes and can create localised habitat diversity. Other features constructed specifically for fishery improvement include artificial overhangs, which create cover for fish. Artificial reefs may be especially useful where there are very few invertebrates as a result of previous engineering works; a number of materials, including brushwood and even unwanted Christmas trees, have been used. Care must be taken when using this technique to ensure that the reefs do not pose an unacceptable obstacle to navigation or floodwaters or are easily washed out to create a blockage downstream.

Such structures immediately create habitats sought by fish but which are often removed by engineering works. They produce variations in flow and substrates, and provide shelter for fish from strong flows and predators.

Backwater and bay creation and rehabilitation

Former meanders and secondary channels cut off from the main flow as a result of channelisation can be reconnected to the main channel to create valuable refuges for fish during periods of high flow and pollution incidents. Consideration should be given to producing a range of habitats from secondary channels in continuous contact with the mainstream to floodplain

Mick Rouse

pools, relatively uninfluenced by the main flow (Table 2: Chapter 1.2). Such pool-like backwaters provide breeding habitat for species such as pike, rudd and tench (Plate 6), whereas continuously flowing side arms will form suitable habitat for dace, chub and barbel (Plate 7).

**Plate 6
Tench**

Creation of bankside bays can provide slower-flowing refuges for fry particularly in the absence of suitable backwaters. In addition to creating areas of refuge for fish, bays and backwaters are also valuable conservation resources. They add significantly to the range of habitats in the river and will increase the diversity and abundance of plants and animals that the river can support. The presence of additional plants and animals may also significantly enhance the spawning and rearing potential of fishes, such as roach and bream, which require slower waters

**Plate 7
Barbel**

Mick Rouse

with abundant weeds. A wide range of fisheries rehabilitation techniques and examples are covered by Cowx (1994).

1.7.3.3 Post-project appraisal

Clearly post-project appraisal should be an integral part of flood defence and fishery enhancement schemes. For example, there is little point in constructing deflectors to vary flow in a straightened channel, if the subsequent erosion produced on the far bank is unacceptable to either landowner or flood defence engineer. There is, therefore, a great need for these management techniques to be monitored as part of the overall programme of river improvement.

Key References

Alabaster, J S (1985) (ed.) *Habitat modification and freshwater fish.* 278pp. Butterworths.

Cowx, I G (1994) (ed.) *The rehabilitation of freshwater fisheries.* Fishing New Books, Blackwell Scientific Publishing, Oxford.

Maitland, P S and Campbell, R N (1992) Freshwater *Fishes of the British Isles.* 368pp. Harper Collins Publishers, London.

Mills, D (1990) (ed.) *Strategies for the rehabilitation of salmon rivers.* 210pp. Atlantic Salmon Trust, The Institute of Fisheries Management and the Linnean Society of London.

O'Grady, K T, Butterworth, A J B, Spillet, P B and Domaniewski, J C J (eds.) *Proceedings of the 21st anniversary conference of the Institute of Fisheries Management, held at Royal Holloway College, Egham.* Institute of Fisheries Management, Nottingham.

Philips, R and Rix, M (1985) *Freshwater Fish of Britain, Ireland and Europe.* 144pp. Pan Books Limited, London.

Templeton, R G (1984) *Freshwater Fisheries Management* p.83-96. Fishing News Books.

Wheeler A (1992a) A list of the common and scientific names of fishes of the British Isles. Academic Press, London. p 37

The status of British freshwater fishes

A Native Freshwater Fishes

Eel[1]
Allis shad[2]
Twaite shad[2]
Barbel
Gudgeon
Tench
Crucian carp
Silver bream
Bream
Bleak
Minnow
Rudd
Roach
Chub
Dace
Stone loach
Spined loach
Pike
Vendace
Schelly
Pollan[3]
Salmon
Trout
Charr
Grayling
Three-spined stickleback
Ten-spined stickleback
Bullhead
Perch
Ruffe

B Extinct Species

Burbot

C Threatened Species

Allis shad
Twaite shad
Vendace
Schelly
Charr

D Significant extensions to range in last two centuries

Barbel
Tench
Crucian carp
Bream
Rudd
Roach
Chub
Pike
Perch

E Established introduced species (at least one self-sustaining population)

Rainbow trout
Brook charr
Bitterling
Carp
Goldfish
Orfe
Wels
Black bullhead
Zander
Rock bass
Large-mouth bass
Pumpkinseed

[1] Breeds in the sea
[2] Mostly estuarine
[3] Inland only
  Lampreys not included as Agmatha not fishes
  Excludes burbot

Source: Wheeler (1992b)

1.8 Amphibians and Reptiles

1.8.1   Introduction

1.8.2   Classification and habitat requirements
    — Amphibians
    — Reptiles

1.8.3   Management and enhancement

1.8.1 Introduction

Many amphibians and reptiles are not commonly thought of as riverine. However they may be indirectly dependent on the river as their habitat is part of the floodplain system. These species may be threatened not only by direct loss of backwater habitat, as a result of changes in land management and insensitive spoil disposal (Section 3.1), but also by management practices, eg dredging, which may result in a fall in water-table levels in floodplain grassland adjacent to the channel. (Chapter 3.2–3.4).

1.8.2 Classification and habitat requirements

There are six species of amphibians and six species of reptiles native to Britain (Table 1). Of these, natterjack toads, smooth snakes and sand lizards are unlikely to occur in river or floodplain habitats.

Adult amphibians and reptiles feed on a range of invertebrates, foraging for food primarily on land. The adults and tadpoles of amphibians provide food for a range of birds, fish and mammals.

Amphibians

Amphibians tend to breed in still or slow-flowing water bodies. They spend much of their lives foraging for food in bankside margins, wet floodplain grassland and areas of scrub or woodland.

Suitable breeding habitats for amphibians include backwaters (including oxbows) and temporary floodplain pools. However, they may use vegetated margins of slow-flowing watercourses. Frogs lay clumps of spawn in water about 10 cm deep (Plate 1), whereas toads use water about 30 cm deep (Plate 2). Newts lay eggs singly, wrapped in submerged leaves, in deep or shallow water. Temporary pools are particularly favourable breeding areas because drying out eliminates fish and predatory

Plate 1 (left) Common frog: Several mating pairs and spawn in a shallow pond.

Plate 2 (right) Spawn of common toad laid in strings among water plants.

F Greenaway/Bruce Coleman

Jane Burton/Bruce Coleman

Table 1: Habitat requirements of amphibians and reptiles associated with rivers

	DISTRIBUTION	HABITAT REQUIREMENTS
AMPHIBIANS Smooth newt	Widespread, Britain and Ireland	Prefers still, hard water. Likely to be found wherever warty newts occur, though much more abundant. Will rapidly colonise sites, including urban sites.
Great crested or warty newt	Rare in Britain, absent in Ireland	The most aquatic species, breeds in still or slow-flowing water above pH 5.5. A hard water species, rare in the north and west. Not very good at colonising new sites.
Palmate newt	Widespread in Britain, absent in Ireland. Found in the west and north of Britain, but rare in central England and East Anglia	Rarest and smallest, found in still soft water but sometimes breeds in flowing water.
Common frog	Widespread in Britain, not native in Ireland, declining	Typically breeds in warm, shallow (*c* 10 cm) edges. Spawn can be anchored to submerged vegetation and can survive substantial increases in water velocity or depth.
Common toad	Widespread in Britain, absent in Ireland	Perhaps most likely amphibian to be found in rivers. Wind strings of spawn around plants in water about 30 cm deep.
REPTILES Common or viviparous lizard	Widespread in Britain and Ireland	Often in moist well-vegetated habitats. Swims well.
Slow worm	Widespread in Britain, absent in Ireland	A legless lizard. Secretive; most often found by turning over stones in damp areas.
Grass snake	Widespread in England only. Absent in Ireland	Most aquatic of reptiles, often swims. Hunts tadpoles and other amphibians in water. Egg-laying.
Adder	Widespread in Britain, absent from Ireland	Quite often found on banksides.

invertebrates which feed on tadpoles. The still conditions in backwaters and floodplain pools allow the build-up of algae, which provide food for the tadpoles.

Outside the breeding season amphibians require different terrestrial habitats. Toads are adapted to withstand a dry environment, whereas frogs and newts are restricted to more moist surroundings, such as shallow, vegetated channel margins and wet grassland. Limited areas of tree and scrub provide shelter, foraging and hibernation sites. However, areas with too much cover, which results in excessive shade and cool conditions, are avoided.

Reptiles

Reptiles are less aquatic than amphibians and do not breed in water. However, four of the six species are often found in damp habitats associated with rivers, including vegetated bankside margins. They generally prefer habitats with deep vegetation in which to forage and shelter, with open, unshaded areas nearby in which to bask. Reptiles tend to be most conspicuous from mid-March to May,

**Plate 3
Grass snake in a
typical riverside
habitat.**

George McCarthy/Bruce Coleman

when basking following hibernation. Reptiles hibernate underground in holes on slopes facing the sun. All species in Britain are declining, mainly because of loss of suitable habitat. Grass snakes are the most aquatic and may enter the water to catch prey (Plate 3). They are dependent on warm egg-laying sites and in natural river systems they lay their eggs in decomposing vegetation left after floods. Compost- or dung-heaps can be used as an alternative.

1.8.3 Management and enhancement

Amphibians and reptiles rarely use main channel habitats, therefore river works within the channel itself may have little direct effect on them. However, deepening of channels may have serious consequences if lower water tables result in the drying out of adjacent damp areas and pools. In areas where frogs are suspected to be hibernating, dredging operations should be avoided if possible during the hibernation period (this may be taken mid-October to the end of February, although this varies between regions). Close mowing of banks is inappropriate for all species, resulting in a reduction in cover and associated invertebrate food, and the potential for increased predation. Lack of cover may also restrict movement of both groups between feeding and breeding sites. Improved land drainage resulting in the reduction in water-table levels can have a detrimental effect on amphibians, which in turn causes declines in grass snakes as amphibians are a major component of their diet. Depositing dredged spoil in small hollows can destroy breeding and feeding habitat.

By-products of management, including logs and other woody debris, can be used to provide refuges for amphibians.

Key References
Arnold, E N and Burton, J A (1978) *A field guide to the reptiles and amphibians of Britain and Europe.* Collins, London.
Corbett, K (1989) *Conservation of European reptiles and amphibians.* Christopher Helm, London.
Frazer, D (1983) *Reptiles and amphibians in Britain.* Collins New Naturalist Series, London.

1.9 Invertebrates

1.9.1 Introduction

Invertebrate assemblages are associated with particular types of river. However, local variations in current speed and substrate often determine their precise distribution. The maintenance of natural habitat diversity within river reaches is therefore essential to support a rich and varied invertebrate fauna.

Of the estimated 30,000 British species of terrestrial and freshwater invertebrates, over 1,000 exploit the water-edge habitat and more than 3,500 species spend all or part of their life cycles in fresh water. Table 1 lists the main groups and classes of invertebrates commonly found in fresh water in Britain. In general, upland streams have fewer species and lower faunal abundance than do weedy/gravelly stretches in the middle or lower reaches of rivers (Armitage and Petts, 1992).

Invertebrates perform a range of functions in the aquatic environment:

- They influence nutrient recycling by transforming and transporting nutrients from one part of the ecosystem to another (Kitchell *et al.*, 1979). Feeding activities change the size, shape and form of dead organic matter and other living plant and animal material. Burrowing animals redistribute nutrients from the sediment and in some cases release toxins into the water column. In contrast, filtering organisms remove particles from the water.

Thus, nutrient recycling is important for the general health of the river.

- River invertebrates are a direct major source of food for both fish (Crisp *et al.*, 1978; Mann, 1974 and 1982, Mann *et al.*, 1989) and insectivorous birds such as dipper and grey wagtail (Ormerod and Tyler, 1987).

- Invertebrates are sensitive to changes in habitat, and pollution. Invertebrate communities thus provide a means of assessing sites for river water quality.

Table 1: The numbers of species in major groups of macroinvertebrates in fresh water

GROUP	NO OF SPECIES
True flies	1,385
Water beetles	342
Water mites	323
Caddisflies	198
Worms	126
Molluscs	91
Water bugs	62
Mayflies	48
Dragonflies	45
Crustaceans	40
Wasps	39
Stoneflies	34
Leeches	16
Flatworms	12
Alderflies	7
Moths	5

1.9.2 The distribution and habitat requirements of invertebrates

Many species have very specific environmental requirements. Rivers offer a wide range of conditions and micro-habitats from source to mouth and this range is reflected in the diversity of invertebrate life (Figure 1). Different conditions are preferred by different invertebrates, which have adapted to

exploit a range of habitats successfully. The adaptations that they exhibit fall into eight categories shown in Table 2 (Merritt and Cummins, 1984). Not all invertebrates fall conveniently into one category; they may behave in several 'modes' during different stages of their life cycles to make use of available habitats. Many insects, eg

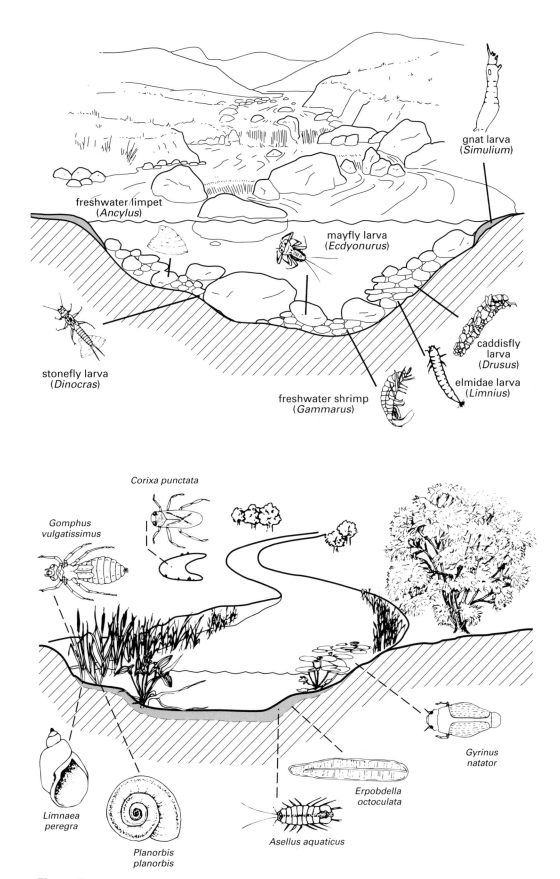

Figure 1
Invertebrates of micro-habitats: (i) upland rivers; Adapted from Hynes (1970) (ii) lowland rivers

Table 2: The most common invertebrate life-forms or adaptations to living in water

1. *Skaters* (eg pond-skaters) living on the water surface and scavenging on organisms trapped in the surface film.

2. *Plankton* (eg phantom midge larvae, mosquito larvae) living in open slack water.

3. *Divers* (eg water boatmen, diving beetles) in slowly flowing waters and pools, obtain oxygen from the surface and diving and swimming when alarmed.

4. *Swimmers* (eg some mayflies) which usually cling to rocks or vegetation but which are adapted for short bursts of 'fishlike' swimming.

5. *Clingers* (eg some mayflies, blackflies, leeches, limpets) have behavioural and morphological adaptations for attachment in fast flows which include flattening or silk pads, claws, suckers or sucker-like feet.

6. *Sprawlers* (eg many damsel, dragonfly larvae and some mayflies) inhabit the surface of macrophytes or maintain a position on top of fine sediments.

7. *Climbers* (eg dragonflies) inhabit macrophyte vegetation, tree roots and overhanging submerged branches and move vertically up and down these surfaces.

8. *Burrowers* (eg worms, molluscs, some mayflies, chironomid midges) are found in fine sediment but may also occur tunnelling in plant tissue or wood.

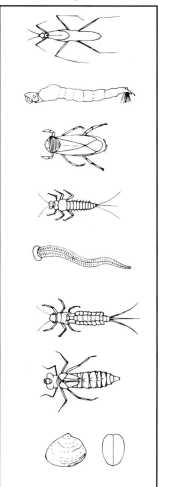

dragonflies and mayflies, have larval aquatic stages before maturing into adults with aerial lifestyles.

1.9.2.1 Use of micro-habitats

Longitudinal zonation is a feature of invertebrate communities along most rivers. In the relatively short rivers of the British Isles there is often much overlap between the range of species, therefore 'zones' based on invertebrate communities are rarely clear-cut. A more useful approach is to consider the range of micro-habitats colonised according to preferred feeding habitats and mode of existence. These can be divided into two main categories: vegetation- and sediment-based habitats together with a number of special habitats which merit separate consideration, eg springs/seepages and winterbournes (intermittent streams).

Figure 2 illustrates the importance of micro-habitats, or substrates, for invertebrates based on a set of 26 lowland rivers (Wright *et al.*,1991). Emergent vegetation tends to support the widest variety of families but there is a wide range of values for the richest and poorest sites. Clay and sand substrates generally have fewer families.

Vegetation-based habitats

River plants provide a range of contrasting habitats for many species within which to exploit a variety of food resources, including decaying plant matter.

Emergent vegetation provides sites for insects such as dragonflies and damselflies to hatch. Still water areas associated with marginal vegetation offer pond-like conditions and living space for water beetles and water boatmen. The plant stems themselves support a variety of water snails and caddisfly larvae. Large populations of water fleas and copepods (Crustaceans) may develop in these areas. Such habitats are more prevalent at the margins of rivers, in sheltered backwaters (Plate 1), slacks and ponded sections more than 1 m deep, above weirs.

Mid-stream vegetation may range from the water-lilies and long-stalked pondweeds of slow-flowing deep waters, to water-crowfoot in shallower fast-flowing sections. Dense vegetation in deep water (>1 m) may impede flow, resulting in the development of pond-like animal communities in slow-flowing or still conditions.

Shallow, fast-flowing water crowfoot sites support species adapted to rapid flows. These include mayflies (Baetidae and Ephemerellidae), caddisflies (Brachycentridae and Leptoceridae), blackflies (Simuliidae) and molluscs. These are most common on the surface of plants where velocities are greatest. During the growing season, silt and detritus are often trapped by plants and still-water species such as worms and non-biting midges can then inhabit these reaches.

Dense growths of filamentous algae are a common habitat for invertebrates. Most often these algal growths are associated with some form of organic pollution and/or physical damage. However, the large surface area is ideal for many invertebrates. Numbers of individuals are frequently very high but species variety may be poor. In upland regions, moss provides a habitat for large numbers of invertebrates. Tree roots are important in rivers where plants are scarce.

Sediment-based habitats

These habitats include not only in-channel features such as pools and riffles but also periodically inundated banksides, gravel bars and islands.

The range of mayflies illustrates well how different species are adapted to exploit sediment-based habitats in rivers. The genus *Rhithrogena* consists of flattened

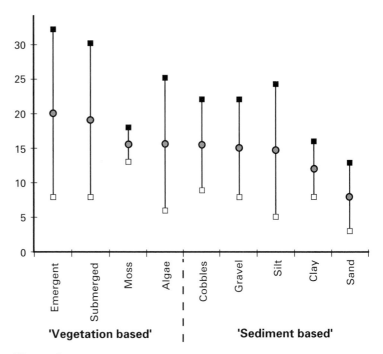

Figure 2
Numbers of invertebrate families occupying different micro-habitats.

animals enabling them to live on the surface of stones, whereas *Ecdyonurus* have strong limbs which allow them to cling to the undersides of rocks, and in the family *Baetidae* nymphs are streamlined to avoid being washed away.

Bed material such as large rocks with many spaces between stones of different sizes support different communities than do beds with more compact gravels or sand. In fast-flowing waters invertebrates must cling to stones or search out crevices where turbulence is reduced, to avoid being

Plate 1
Vegetation-based habitat in a sheltered backwater.

washed out of the system. Other ways of surviving are the use of silk as an anchor (blackfly larvae), a broad foot (river limpet) and strong posterior 'claws' for attaching to vegetation (caddis larvae such as *Rhyacophila*).

Gaps between rocks are important for the survival of many river invertebrates. They are favoured habitats of invertebrate larvae, such as net-spinning caddis larvae which construct silk nets in which they lie waiting to trap food particles. Long and flattened stonefly nymphs, eg *Leuctra* and *Chloroperla*, are able to avoid high flows by burrowing into smaller spaces under large rocks. Some animals, eg freshwater shrimp, are flattened laterally enabling them to fit easily into small cracks and spaces in the substrate. The invertebrate community within rock spaces is very varied and rich, ranging from flatworms and worms to juveniles of many species of aquatic insects, crustaceans and molluscs. Total numbers are greatest where gaps are largest (Williams and Hynes, 1974).

Plate 2 Apparently lifeless gravel bars provide habitat for many specialised semi-aquatic and terrestrial 'Red Data Book' or nationally scarce invertebrate species.

Clean gravels and coarse sandy gravels support a wide range of invertebrates but rarely contain species with elaborate adaptations to overcome fast flow. The porosity of the gravels is important; if they become clogged with silt, impoverishment of the community occurs. The mayfly *Ephemera danica* is a common inhabitant of sandy gravels in which it burrows and filters out small organic particles.

Silty sand and silt riverbeds generally support fewer invertebrate species but the numbers of individual animals may be very great. For example, in a slow-flowing millstream in Dorset a square metre of mud was found to harbour about 30,000 individual animals, 85% of which were chironomid midge larvae, worms and molluscs (Crisp and Gledhill, 1970).

In slack water, accumulations of organic detritus from leaves, and habitat created by twigs provide suitable sites for a number of caddis larvae, freshwater shrimps, pond skaters and many molluscs.

Apparently lifeless gravel bars (Plate 2) and shoals provide habitat for many specialised semi-aquatic and terrestrial 'Red Data Book' or nationally scarce invertebrates. These are adapted to cope with winter flooding and reduced flows during the summer period. Two of the commonest strategies to cope with these conditions are burrowing and running. Shingle beetles (particularly staphylinids) move vertically between the gravel in search of food and in response to changing water levels. Other ground beetles and spiders hunt on the shingle surface moving farther up gravel bars as water levels rise.

Although there is a degree of overlap, there are substantial differences between the invertebrate faunas of coarse gravel and fine sand shoals. Particle size is a critical determining factor. Sand banks are ideal for burrowing and, in addition to many specialist beetles, they support a range of *Diptera*, such as craneflies, whose larvae live in soft, moist sediments. Other *Diptera* families that are well represented on sandy riverbanks include the *Dolichopodidae*, *Empididae* and *Therevidae*. A few species of spider-hunting wasps are also characteristic of sandy shingle banks.

Table 3 summarises the characteristics of shingle habitats and gravel bars, which are likely to be of particular importance for invertebrates.

There are still many good examples of shingle banks and gravel bars in rivers in Scotland, northern England and Wales, but

Nigel Holmes

Table 3: Characteristics of shingle areas/gravel bars of benefit to invertebrates

Size	Larger areas more likely to contain a greater range of niches.
Matrix	Areas with large range in particle size from sand to large pebbles will support greatest diversity of invertebrates.
Gradient/slope	Variation in surface height of feature essential to allow invertebrates to move upwards or downwards as river levels rise and fall.
Adjacent habitat	Areas of riparian wet woodland and floodplain grassland provide additional habitat during flood events.
Trampling	Trampling of shingle matrix by cattle can have a damaging impact.

many other sites have been lost through a combination of past river engineering schemes, gravel extraction, loss of adjacent semi-natural habitats and livestock access. Although shingle banks can look natural after artificial disturbances, the fauna is usually significantly impaired (Plachter 1986), so it is important to protect those that remain if the range of invertebrates is to be conserved.

Special habitats

Springs and seepages and winterbournes provide unusual habitats for invertebrates and merit separate consideration.

Springs and seepages. These habitats are frequently found in bankside margins and at the headwaters of some rivers. They offer relatively constant conditions in comparison with the fluctuations of temperature and flow observed in running water. Species such as the flatworm *Crenobia alpina* are restricted to cool spring streams and larvae, eg *Elaeophila* and *Pedicia*, are found in cool, shady places at the edges of streams. Thin sheets of water flowing over rock faces also provide a specialist habitat for midge larvae and the unusual caddisfly, *Tinodes maclachlani*. There may be some movement of species between the stream proper and some of these edge habitats which can be essential for the completion of their development. For example, small beetles of the family Hydraenidae are often found as adults in stony rivers and streams but their larval stages are spent at the edge as air-breathers. In contrast, larvae of riffle beetles (Elmidae) live in water and then leave to pupate within 10–15 cm of the

water's edge. The importance of varied edge habitats for invertebrates, therefore, cannot be too highly stressed.

Winterbournes. Invertebrates of winterbournes are often very specialised because they have to survive regular periods of no flow each year. Hynes (1972) concluded that burrowing into the substrate, production of drought resistant eggs, sealing over shell openings and larval cases (eg molluscs and caddisflies) and reinvasion from elsewhere were common strategies for survival. Some invertebrates are actually triggered by lack of flow to complete their life cycles. If flows fail for many years due to combined effects of drought and groundwater abstraction, specialist species which cannot fly to recolonise, eg flatworms, may be lost altogether.

1.9.2.2 Food and feeding

Stream invertebrates can also be categorised, on the basis of their adaptations for acquiring food, into 'functional trophic groups' (Cummins, 1973; Merritt *et al.*, 1984). These include shredders, grazers, predators and collectors (Figures 3 and 4). Despite some overlap between categories, and the difficulty of placing some taxa in a single category, this is a useful way of looking at the composition of faunal communities in relation to organic resources available to the stream animals. Figure 3 shows a typical shift in relative abundance of the different invertebrate functional groups from upstream to downstream in a river system. Abundance of many families changes dramatically on passing

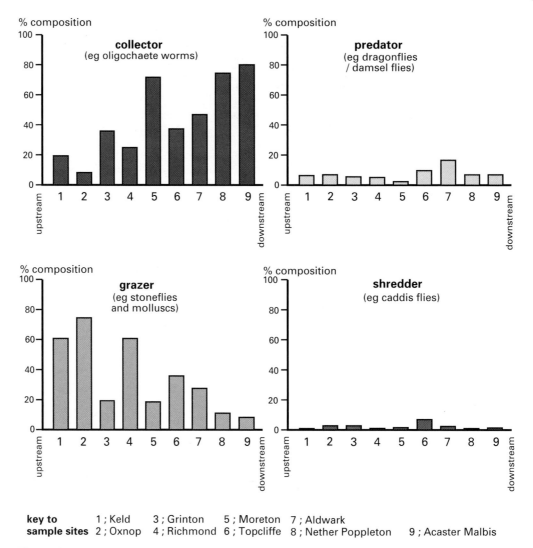

key to
sample sites

1 ; Keld	3 ; Grinton	5 ; Moreton	7 ; Aldwark		
2 ; Oxnop	4 ; Richmond	6 ; Topcliffe	8 ; Nether Poppleton	9 ; Acaster Malbis	

Figure 3
Typical shift in relative abundance of the different invertebrate functional groups from upstream to downstream in the R Swale/Ouse, Yorkshire.

downstream as a result of food availability. The Swale/Ouse system in Yorkshire is unusual in Britain because it has a mountainous source and a long lowland section. Figure 4 shows changes in the proportion of different feeders down such a river with grazers declining as collectors increase on passing downstream. Figure 3 also names some of the characteristic invertebrates within the categories 'Shredder', 'Collector', 'Grazer' and 'Predator'.

1.9.3 Impact of river management on invertebrates

River management such as dredging may affect both the physical structure of the channel and banks and the hydrology of adjacent bankside and floodplain habitats. These aspects and their implications for riverine invertebrates are introduced in the following section.

River management practices affecting invertebrate communities are listed in

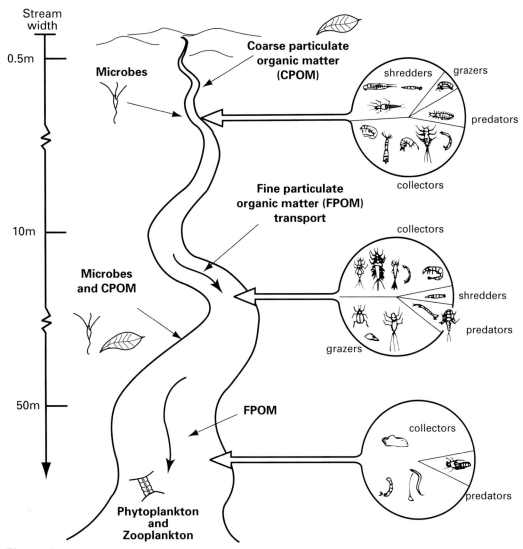

Figure 4
Generalised changes in the proportion of different categories of invertebrates in an hypothetical river with increasing distance downstream. Adapted from Calow and Petts (1992)

Table 4. The table shows management activities which are potentially harmful, but sympathetic approaches can mitigate or even enhance habitat against any detrimental effects.

Little research has been undertaken into management and reinstatement of watercourses specifically for invertebrates so broader ecological aims often prevail. These are usually to improve or maintain diversity and quality of habitats in combination with protecting water quality. This is generally a piecemeal approach. However, the catchment as a whole should be considered. Invertebrates recolonise

from four directions: downstream by drift; upstream by migration; vertically upwards from within the substrate; and downwards from aerial sources, eg through egg-laying. Williams and Hynes (1976) showed that for a denuded section of stream in Canada, drift contributed over 40% of the new colonisers, aerial sources were next in importance and upstream migration and movement from within the substrate each made smaller, but nevertheless significant, contributions.

An essential prerequisite of river management for invertebrates is knowing what is initially present. This information

**Table 4: The effects of river management on aquatic and water's edge invertebrates.
(A cross indicates possible impacts on invertebrates due to the action specified)**

POTENTIAL IMPACTS	ACTIVITY		
	AQUATIC WEED CUTTING	CHANNEL WORKS	BANK WORKS
1. Loss/removal of part of the invertebrate population from the water or riverbank.	X	X	X
2. Disturbance, leading to increased drift of aquatic invertebrates and dispersal of populations.	X	X	X
3. Reduction in cover provided by aquatic and bankside plants, leading to increased predation, also drift of aquatic invertebrates and dispersal of populations.	X	X	X
4. Loss of emergence sites (eg reed stems) for insects.	X	X	X
5. Removal of food plants, leading to the elimination of specialist plant-feeding invertebrates.	X	X	X
6. Instability of riverbed and consequent loss of firm attachment sites for aquatic invertebrates.	X	X	(X)
7. Reduction in habitat diversity (eg loss of riffles, meanders, trampled margins, beds of aquatic plants) causing impoverishment of invertebrate communities.	X	X	X
8. Increased suspended solids loading and siltation, which may clog gills, smother eggs and young stages, or decrease the oxygen concentration of the water.	X	X	X
9. Localised reduction in flow, leading to lower oxygen concentration		X	(X)
10. Reduction in shade because of the removal of trees etc, leading to increased insolation, higher water temperatures and increased submerged plant growth.		X	X
11. Reduction in food supply for aquatic and water's edge invertebrates because of the removal of bankside vegetation.		X	X
12. Nutrient enrichment, siltation and pollution with pesticides following drainage of surrounding land and intensification of agriculture.		X	X
13. Loss of wet peripheral habitats because of lowering of water table and reduction of flooding, leading to elimination of whole invertebrate communities.		X	X

can be acquired from:

- distribution atlases
- results of biological water quality monitoring
- specific surveys
- the Invertebrate Site Register (ISR)

Atlas information may be out of date and may only reflect the distribution of interested naturalists; generally invertebrate samples are only identified to family level and are not related to habitats. However, it is important to take account of what information is available. As a general rule it is preferable to retain scarce species than it is to try to reintroduce them if they are lost. Habitat protection or enhancement is likely to be more successful than introducing a species, which would depend on the precise habitat being available.

1.9.3.1 Impact of in-channel works

River management has the potential to alter the complex in-channel habitat structure. Typically this may involve removal of silt deposits, vegetation or organic debris or the reshaping of the bed by redistributing existing substrate material. Such operations will inevitably affect the invertebrate community. Physical uniformity of the channel will result in a less diverse fauna although numbers and biomass of successful species may increase. A significant loss of invertebrate variety and abundance has been shown to result from channelisation and dredging, which removes the pool–riffle–run structure of the river. Engineering techniques which cause minimal disturbance to the channel are likely to maintain diverse invertebrate communities.

The sensitive management techniques advocated in Part 3 all help to maintain and enhance riverine invertebrate communities. Retention of features and habitats of note, together with those which are commonplace, ensures the maximum range of micro-environments is available to invertebrates at all times.

Retention of good habitat features is preferable to re-creation. However, if they cannot be retained, it may be possible either partially or fully to re-create certain habitats. The introduction of various sizes of stone substrate to create riffles or gravel beds is just one example of enhancing in-stream habitat variety; shallowing steep trapezoidal banks to create wet margins helps edge communities. All such attempts at re-creating diverse habitats are, however, unlikely to match exactly those of a pristine river: the favoured conservation option is to 'retain the best'.

Preventing removal of invertebrates

Dredging, desilting and shoaling operations (Chapter 3.2) can remove considerable numbers of invertebrates from a watercourse. Where species of conservation value are known to occur, modifications to operations may be desirable. Alternatively, a system for returning individual animals to the river during the operation should be considered.

Some invertebrates, such as the freshwater shrimp, are able to migrate back to the river from the spoil dumped along a bank if the spoil is placed close to the edge. This may not be possible for more sedentary species such as mussels. However, placing spoil on or very close to the bank edge may be detrimental to plant communities.

Where important species are present especially when in large numbers, it may be practical to 'rinse' dredgings before placing them on the bank. For example, during dredging beds of reed sweet-grass from the R Beane in Hertfordshire the number of crayfish being removed was reduced by 40% using this technique. Advantages for individual species have to be balanced against possible increases in turbidity and sedimentation downstream.

Impact of changes in flow regime and water levels

Altered flow regimes will affect invertebrate species and their habitats. Modification of flow conditions may change the pattern and rate of sedimentation and affect the nature of the bed material. Increased flows may cause the development of a coarser substrate, as fine sediments are removed, making it more difficult for plants and invertebrates typical of slow flows and silt beds to recolonise after the engineering works.

The effects of altering flow regimes can be mitigated on a local scale by incorporating physical structures in the channel. Large rocks, logs, groynes and mid-channel deflectors create localised areas of flow variations (Section 3.4.4). Small weirs, or riffle areas, can be constructed to create the desired flow conditions for some distance upstream, in addition to being valuable habitat features in their own right. (Sections 3.2.6 and 3.4.5; and Case Studies 3.2e, 3.2f and 3.4i). Prior to undertaking work in such instances land drainage consent should be obtained from the appropriate body (eg NRA).

Channel modifications often cause changes in water level. Reductions in normal water level can have serious effects on invertebrate communities not only within the channel but also along the river margins. In the short term, invertebrates may be stranded and subject to drying or freezing. Although more mobile species, such as water beetles, may be able to migrate with the falling water, or leave the site altogether if they are able to fly, less mobile species, such as molluscs, may be significantly affected.

Water-level changes may also cause successional changes in the vegetation, with loss of aquatic and wetland species and replacement by common terrestrial ones. Such changes will affect the invertebrate community.

Suspended sediment transport

River engineering operations release sediments into suspension, raising turbidity, and at least short-term deposition of sediment downstream. This may cause direct damage to insects, through deoxygenation, smothering, and clogging of gills or it may cause indirect damage through changes to substrate composition and alteration of habitat. In some circumstances toxic material may be released from disturbed sediments.

Construction of a silt trap between a dredging site and a sensitive location downstream may be required. Where there is a risk of toxic materials being released, take advice from relevant pollution prevention authorities.

1.9.3.2 Impact of bank engineering and construction works on bankside habitats

Invertebrates likely to be affected by bank engineering and construction works are:

- those which demand relatively still water conditions and cannot survive in the main flow, eg water beetles and bugs;

- those which depend upon emergent vegetation for completion of their life cycle, eg damselflies;

- those which feed on particular emergent species or use such vegetation for shelter, eg gastropod molluscs.

Careful design can ensure that appropriate habitats are retained along at least one bank and that there are suitable areas, eg low-level berms, off-channel bays and backwaters, where vegetation can be retained or replanted (Chapter 3.3). It should be remembered that the classic trapezoidal channel makes no allowance for development of a marginal fringe.

Where adjacent land use does not permit the creation of a low-level berm or where geomorphological considerations require it, it may be necessary to provide erosion protection to the toe of the bank. A natural fringe of emergent vegetation could have fulfilled this function but sympathetic artificial toe-protection provides a very good range of habitats for invertebrates includes hazel faggots, willow spiling, reed, sedge and mixed herbage (see Case Studies 3.5e and 3.5g). Again, land drainage consent should be obtained when undertaking such work, thereby ensuring conservation needs are integrated with flood defence requirements.

River management works frequently require machine access along riverbanks or their use for disposal of spoil. Both activities can destroy riverside vegetation, which often supports a wide range of invertebrates. Such invertebrate communities are of interest in themselves and are also of particular value for insectivorous insects (dragonflies), birds (warblers) and mammals (bats). In addition, insects that fall into the water from bankside vegetation often form a significant component of the diet of fish, such as trout.

The structure of riverbank vegetation is an important influence on the suitability of a site for dragonflies. Tall vegetation will provide shelter from strong winds but must include open areas, particularly over the channel, where dragonflies can hunt.

Bankside vegetation may also directly influence aquatic invertebrate communities. A significant part of the diet of some species, such as the water hoglouse, may consist of organic leafy material that has fallen into the river. Such materials may also be of importance for some species of case-building caddis fly.

Management of existing bank vegetation, together with the selection of species for replanting, and their density and siting, can be important for retaining invertebrates (Chapter 3.6). As bare earth is a preferred habitat of some rare species, eg ground beetles, care should be taken also to include unvegetated areas and retain earth or sand cliffs and slumps.

1.9.3.3 Impact on floodplain wetlands

The invertebrate communities in floodplains are generally significantly different from those in the main watercourse because of the range of habitat types, such as fen, marsh, backwaters and ditches. As a wetland area dries out, invertebrate communities change and because many of the species present in such areas are rare or endangered, this has major conservation significance. Additionally, as the water table in adjacent wetlands falls, invertebrates may move downwards in the soil, becoming unavailable to birds such as waders.

Key References

Armitage, P D (1984) Environmental changes induced by stream regulation and their effect on lotic macroinvertebrate communities. In A Lillehammer and S J Saltreit (eds.) *Regulated Rivers*. Oslo University Press, Norway. pp 139–165.

Boon, P J (1988) The impact of river regulation on invertebrate communities in the UK. *Regulated Rivers: Research and Management* 2: 389–409.

Gore, J A (1985) *The restoration of rivers and streams*. 280 pp. Butterworths, Boston.

Hynes, H B N (1972) *The ecology of running waters*. University Press, Liverpool.

Wright, J F, Blackburn, J H, Westlake, D F, Furse, M T and Armitage, P D (1991) Anticipating the consequences of river management for the conservation of macroinvertebrates. In *River conservation and management*. P J Boon, P Calow and G E Petts (eds). John Wiley and Sons, Chichester.

Part 2
SURVEY METHODS

2.1 Introduction to Survey Methods

Part 2 of the handbook provides an overview of ecological and geomorphological survey methods. It shows how the wildlife value of a river is determined and how to understand the physical processes operating at a location. Knowledge of both factors is essential in determining the most appropriate river management options, to satisfy the needs of both flood defence and conservation, as well as other river users. The subject areas include:

2.2   River Morphology Survey
2.3   River Corridor Survey
2.4   Plant Surveys
2.5   Otter Surveys
2.6   Bird Surveys
2.7   Fish Stock Assessment and Surveys
2.8   Amphibians and Reptile Surveys
2.9   Invertebrate Survey

Chapters 2.2–2.9 follow a similar format, each divided into two main components. The first, larger, component addresses how, why, when, what and where to survey; the second addresses the use and interpretation of data. However, because of the diverse subject areas examined, this should only be considered as a broad indication of structure. The section should be regarded only as an introduction to survey methods and used as a source of more detailed information.

Health and safety factors are of paramount importance when undertaking fieldwork on rivers. For this reason a section examining these issues is included as Appendix I.

2.2 River Morphology Survey

2.2.1 Introduction

Geomorphological assessments aim to establish the character of a river in terms of stability, morphology, sedimentary and hydraulic characteristics, vegetation and engineering features. Fieldwork is the basis for such assessments supplemented by map data and aerial photographs. It provides the background for designing the scheme and establishes the relationship between different hydraulic processes, which control erosion, deposition and channel form. Geomorphological assessment is therefore a key component when determining sustainable options for maintenance, enhancement, rehabilitation and restoration work (Brookes, 1992; RIZA, 1992).

Why undertake a geomorphological survey?

Geomorphological survey is carried out to define the existing morphological, sedimentary and hydraulic conditions. The objectives of such a survey for river management purposes may include one, or a combination of, the following:

- to assess the stability of an existing river channel in terms of erosion or deposition;
- to determine how a river channel has been affected by past engineering works;
- to recommend suitable criteria for restoration, rehabilitation or enhancement;
- to enable scheme designs to work with, not against, natural river processes.

2.2.2 Objectives, recommendations and types of survey

There are at least three levels at which information can be collected:

- a rapid catchment survey of long lengths of watercourse to assess the relative naturalness of channels for planning purposes;
- a project-specific survey to characterise the river morphology at a site (eg for the purpose of environmental assessment);
- a topographic survey to record more precisely morphological variables for subsequent analysis and calculation (eg for input to a shear-stress or stream power equation).

The methods presented here are those which have been developed through experience in practical river management to facilitate rapid collection of data. Details of the method for rapid assessment of a complete catchment are described in Brookes and Long (in prep).

Similar methods for the appraisal of capital and maintenance works are documented in Brookes (1991). Project specific and topographic surveys are outlined below.

2.2.2.1 Project-specific morphological survey

The procedure for river channel morphology assessment was developed in 1989 by A Brookes (NRA Thames Region) specifically for channelised rivers in the UK. Its use is particularly suitable when assessing rehabilitation options.

The procedure should be repeated for each homogeneous reach, ie a length of channel within which processes or previous channel management are relatively uniform. These reaches may vary in length from a few metres to several hundred metres.

Survey sheets

The use of river channel morphology survey assessment sheets (Table 1) is outlined below:

- Sheet A enables the scope and location of the survey to be recorded. Historical sources such as maps, aerial photographs, and maintenance histories provide an insight into the types of change that have already occurred or are anticipated at a

Table 1: Example of River Channel Morphology Assessment

SHEET A : SCOPE OF SURVEY

Description of problem (if any):

Channel widened and regraded as part of a flood alleviation scheme.
Suffering from siltation and inadequate depth at low flow.

Purpose of river morphology assessment:

To assess the existing situation and make recommendations for mitigation/enhancement.

Details of survey:

DATE: *4/90*   SURVEYOR: *AB*   CATCHMENT: *Stort*

RIVER: *Stort*   STUDY REACH: *RS54*

PHOTOGRAPH Nos: *21; 22*

General comments:
(including general description of river channel type, likely changes determined from historical sources such as documents, maps and aerial photographs; geological description taken from maps).

Lowland channel in park close to urban area. Most recent records show channel to have been enlarged as part of a flood alleviation scheme; old maps show channel may have been locally straightened at some time in the past.

Channel cut into alluvium, overlying glacial head deposits.

---

particular site (Kondolf and Sales, 1985; Nielsen, 1992). It is important to take photographs of representative sections of the reach being surveyed.

• Sheet B allows general site details to be recorded, principally about the river valley, adjacent and upstream land uses, and the nature of the channel pattern.

• Sheet C enables a description of channel characteristics to be recorded based on field observation and measurement. This is best undertaken at low flow, when substrate and bar features are obvious. For some rivers with firm beds this also allows the survey to be undertaken by walking the channel. Checklists are provided which should be ticked: in some instances more than one tick may be necessary and some indication is then given of the most abundant features represented.

Measurements should be taken at a representative section in the reach, eg a riffle or the interchange area between a riffle and a pool. Choosing a representative section means that consistency can be achieved between record sheets for adjacent reaches. When considering enhancement and rehabilitation, the low-flow water width is an important variable to record. In channels artificially over-widened to carry floods, this dimension may be too large, leading to siltation and an inadequate depth of flow to support appropriate in-stream life.

• Sheet D concerns management interpretation, including observations on recovery and possible recommendations for enhancement. To gain a 'feel' for what a now degraded river channel should look like, it is necessary to walk and record unaffected reaches either upstream or

SHEET B : GENERAL DESCRIPTION

VALLEY DESCRIPTION:

Terrain:		Valley floor:	
Mountains	___	Flat	X
Uplands	___	Floodplain	X
Hills	___	Low-slope	X
Plains	X	Terraces	___
Lowlands	___		

LAND USE OF VALLEY FLOOR:

Left bank		Right bank
___	cultivated	___
___	pasture	___
___	urbanised	X
___	partly built up	___
X	riparian buffer strip*	___

PLANFORM DESCRIPTION:

Pattern Type:		Activity:	
straight	X	inherently stable	X
sinuous	___	confined	___
irregular meanders	___	active migration	___
regular meanders	___		
tortuous meanders	___		

Guidance on definition of fluvial-geomorphological terms can be found in Petts (1983).
*Strip which protects the river from enhanced sediment load and gives bank stability.

downstream or within an adjacent catchment of similar character. In particular, the low-flow width dimensions of a natural reach or comparable channel can be compared with those of an artificially widened channel so that recommendations can be made for channel narrowing that is in keeping with the 'natural' state.

A representative cross-section and a plan of the reach could also be drawn to give an indication of the location and nature of specific channel characteristics (Figure 1).

These can also be described in terms of habitat features for in-stream ecology, eg riffles used by spawning fish and berms supporting marginal vegetation.

When filled-in by an experienced geomorphologist, an individual record sheet and sketch should take no more than 15 minutes to complete, once the reach has been walked. For a uniform drainage channel in lowland England, it is possible to walk and observe about 10–20 km per day per surveyor. This is possible because few record sheets need to be completed;

SHEET C : CHANNEL CHARACTERISTICS

CHANNEL DESCRIPTION:-

Dimensions (metres):   Channel shape: Pool riffle sequence:

Bankfull width _14.0_ Natural
                        Asymmetrical/
                        Symmetrical   ____   Highly developed   ____

Bankfull depth _2.5_   Incised   ____   Moderately developed ____

Low-flow water depth _1.0_ Artificial earth _X_   Poor development   _X_

Low-flow water width
(existing)   _11.0_ Artificial controls ____   Uniform bed   _X_

                        Mannings roughness, n; _0.030_

Slope: high ____   moderate ____   low _X_

Slope (calculated):   _0.0018_

BANK CHARACTERISTICS:

Bank materials: Bank stability: Bank profile:

Left bank Right bank   Left bank   Right bank   Left bank   Right bank

____ Clay ____   _X_ Cohesive _X_   ____ Asymmetrical ____

____ Silt ____   ____ Non-cohesive ____   _X_ Symmetrical _X_

_X_ Silt/clay _X_   ____ Eroding ____   ____ Cliff ____

____ Sand ____   ____ Slumping ____   ____ Berm ____

____ Sand/silt ____   ____ Tree-lined ____   _X_ Artificial _X_

____ Gravel ____   _X_ Vegetation ____

____ Sand/gravel ____   ____ Bedrock _X_

____ Cobbles ____   _X_ Artificial ____

____ Boulders ____   ____ Protection _X_

____ Artificial ____   ____

SUBSTRATE CHARACTER

Bed sediment type: Bed stability: Bar forms:

Clay ____   Naturally mobile ____   Pools/riffles ____

                   Bedrock ____   Alternate bars ____

Silt _X_   Segregated ____   Mid-channel bars ____

Sand ____   Armoured ____   Point bars ____

Gravel ____   Deposition evident _X_   Tributary Junction bars ____

Cobbles ____   Structures ____   Vegetation Stabilising bars _X_

Boulders ____   Instream vegetation _X_

Bedrock ____

Artificial _X_

SHEET D : MANAGEMENT INTERPRETATION

Dominant characteristics of upstream catchment:		Previous works in reach:	
Natural	____	None	____
Cultivated	X	Agricultural drainage	____
Pasture	____	Flood alleviation	X
Urbanised	X	Realignment	X
Road development	____	Maintenance dredge	X
Reservoir	____	Bank protection	____

Evidence of recovery from impact:		Enhancement recommendations:	
None	____	Recreate planform	____
Re-meandering	____	Channel narrowing	____
Width narrowing through deposition	X *(some)*	Substrate placement	____
Pool-riffle	____	Pools/riffles	____
Alternate bars	____	Check weirs	____
Point bars	____	Natural bank protection	____

Sensitivity to channel maintenance:-	
High	____
Moderate	X
Low	____

Additional interpretation:
Channel will recover further in the absence of further intervention. Silt moving from upstream will tend to deposit on the inside of the bend as a point bar, leading to channel narrowing. This will be a slow process (20 yrs+).

Note: The above procedure was devised by A Brookes of Thames NRA.

however, for meandering semi-natural channels with great variability in structure, record sheets have to be more numerous to reflect such variations and a far shorter length of river (5–10 km in a day) may be covered. Interpretation of Sheet D should be undertaken by a trained fluvial geomorphologist.

2.2.2.2 Procedure for detailed topographic survey

River channels vary greatly in cross-sectional shape but are mostly bounded on one or both sides by a fairly well-defined bank separating the channel from floodplain or valley side. The bankfull dimensions of a channel, together with a depth–velocity relationship (such as the Manning equation) determine the discharge it can convey. Channel dimensions are not arbitrary but are adjusted by erosion and deposition so that the channel can contain all but the highest flows it experiences. A typical river overtops its banks, at most, only once or twice per year.

The procedure involves surveying the channel cross-section and existing channel slope and estimating 'roughness' for input to a flow equation.

Cross-section measurement

- For stream channels less than 4–5 m wide a tape measure should be stretched horizontally across the channel from bank to bank and held by two pegs or pins. Vertical depth measurements are then made from this datum point to the channel perimeter or floodplain surface. Petts (1983) recommends that at least 20 measurements of depths are taken at each section (Figure 2(i)).

- For stream channels with a width greater than 4–5 m more sophisticated techniques are required because tape sag and wind effects reduce accuracy. A standard quickset level and graduated staff should be used (Pugh, 1975) (Figure 2(ii)).

The surveyed natural cross-section can then be plotted and bankfull level can be delimited by reference to the break of slope separating the channel from the floodplain. Width, average depth, cross-sectional area and form ratio can be determined from the

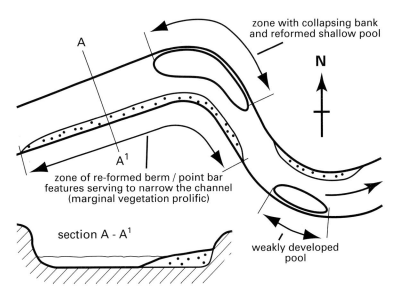

Figure 1
Example sketches of a reach affected by maintenance works involving over-widening

plotted section. Hydraulic radius (R) is a description of the cross-sectional shape of a channel (the ratio of cross-sectional area to wetted perimeter). As 'R' decreases the length of the water-boundary contact increases, and the efficiency of a river to convey water decreases.

Slope measurement

Measurements of gradient are dependent on scale because the slope obtained over a very short reach corresponds to bed-forms and not to the general bed elevation trend. An approximate channel slope may be obtained from 1:10,000 or 1:25,000 maps by measuring the plotted length of a river's plan-form between two contours. However, field survey is recommended to take account of variations resulting from pools and riffles. Slope may be obtained by measuring over three riffle crests, the middle riffle being used as the site for a surveyed cross-section.

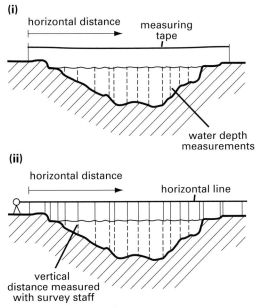

Figure 2
Surveying stream cross-sections: (i) with a measuring tape and rule using the water surface as a horizontal line; (ii) with a level and staff.
Source: Gordon *et al* (1992)

Roughness calculation

Manning's 'n' is a measure of roughness (the greater the roughness the greater the impedance of flow) and can be calculated for each stream by reference to tables in Chow (1959) or photographs in Barnes (1967). The value of 'n' depends on channel bed and bank materials, sinuosity, cross-sectional shape and the size and extent of aquatic and bankside plant growths.

2.2.3 Utilisation of measurements

The variables collected by field measurement can be put into a number of equations, each of which assist in scheme design, impact assessment, and give guidance for functional restoration. Calculations of velocity and stream power are essential.

Velocity

Velocity calculations utilise geomorphological field measurements of slope, hydraulic radius and Manning's 'n'. Roughness data can be derived using the Manning equation (glossary).

Stream Power

Stream power may be defined as the rate of energy expenditure per unit length of channel (the rate of doing work) and is highly dependent on gradient. Hence geomorphological survey data on bed slope are used alongside discharge information in equations incorporating gravity and unit weight of water. The equation to derive stream power is shown in chapter 1.3. The equation derives 'gross' stream power; to determine the availability of energy per unit width, or 'specific' stream power measured variables of channel width, mean velocity and mean bed shear stress are used.

The importance of stream power to modern river management in relation to the geomorphological characteristics of a river is outlined in Chapter 1.3. For instance, thresholds have been identified between erosion and deposition.

2.2.4 Summary

The survey methods described have been developed specifically for rivers in England and Wales and may need to be refined or extended for other environments. More detailed analysis of channels may be required for specific purposes, including an accurate evaluation of the stability of bed and bank sediments, eg measurement of cohesiveness and sediment size-distribution. Standard methods are available for measuring the shear strengths of bed and bank materials (eg Gardiner and Dackombe, 1983).

Geomorphological processes should be considered as an integral component when determining solutions to river management problems (Iversen *et al.*, 1993; Kondolf and Micheli, 1993; Perrow and Wightman, 1993). By taking a catchment-wide geomorphological perspective and determining the cause of a problem, sustainable solutions to river management problems can be developed. For projects, whether capital, maintenance, enhancement or rehabilitation, geomorphological survey and evaluation enable the range of potential options to be determined together with requirements for long-term monitoring.

Key References
Brookes, A (1991) Geomorphology. In *River Projects and Conservation: A Manual for Holistic Appraisal.* J L Gardiner (ed.) pp 57–66. John Wiley, Chichester.

Gardiner, V and Dackombe, R (1983) *Geomorphological field manual.* Allen and Unwin, London.

Petts, G E (1983) *Rivers.* Butterworths Publications, London.

Pugh, J C (1975) *Surveying for field scientists.* Methuen, London.

RIZA (1992) *Contributions to the European Workshop: Ecological Rehabilitation of Floodplains.* Arnhem. Report No. II–6, CHR.

2.3 River Corridor Survey

2.3.1   Introduction

2.3.2   How and why river corridor surveys are undertaken
      — Why undertake river corridor surveys?
      — The basic river corridor survey methodology

2.3.3   Use of river corridor survey data and future application and
      development of the methodology
      — Audits and post-project appraisal
      — Strategic surveys and national overview of enhancement potential
      — Developments in river habitat evaluations

2.3.1 Introduction

The River Corridor Survey (RCS) was developed in the early 1980s. This coincided with changes in legislation (Wildlife and Countryside Act 1981) and its effect on the manner in which river management works are planned, designed and carried out. Since that time, use of RCS has become accepted as an essential prerequisite of the planning process for any major works affecting rivers (Ash and Woodcock, 1988; Holmes, 1986; Rheinalt, 1990). This chapter briefly considers RCS in the context of river management, not in its broadest application to resource evaluations of rivers, floodplains and catchments.

2.3.2 How and why river corridor surveys are undertaken

Why undertake river corridor surveys?

Rivers, and the corridors of land through which they flow, are one of Britain's major wildlife resources. Without RCS it is impossible to determine existing conservation interest or evaluate potential threats. The first stage in ecological data gathering begins with an RCS. Some of the uses of the output are listed in Table 1.

Table 1: Key applications of River Corridor Survey output

- Evaluating and setting priorities in conservation efforts;
- determining how proposed engineering works will be undertaken sensitively;
- auditing management and scheme works to highlight impacts/enhancements and improve approaches for the future;
- influencing floodplain developments;
- preparation of sensitive long-term prescriptions for managed rivers.

The basic river corridor survey methodology

The survey methodology is outlined in the technical handbook River Corridor Surveys: Methods and Procedures (NRA, 1992). The RCS methodology is a habitat-based approach to surveying, essentially recording details of vegetation and physical structure rather than comprehensive species accounts. It involves mapping or sketching defined stretches of river of approximately 500 m in length and including a minimum corridor of 50 m on either side of the river.

A standard river corridor survey should include four zones (Figure 1):

- aquatic zone
- marginal zone
- bank zone
- adjacent land zone (floodplain).

Where important wetlands are present in the wider corridor, these are noted and included in the survey. A survey report comprises an annotated map/sketch, supporting text and photographic record.

Figure 2 is an example of a map produced during a RCS and Figure 3 shows the symbols and abbreviations used in mapping. Table 2 lists the background information which should be included with RCS maps.

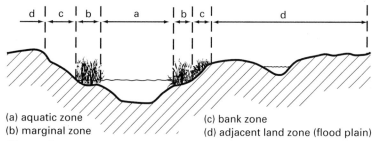

(a) aquatic zone
(b) marginal zone
(c) bank zone
(d) adjacent land zone (flood plain)

Figure 1
Diagrammatic cross-section of river corridor survey zones.
Source: NRA (1992)

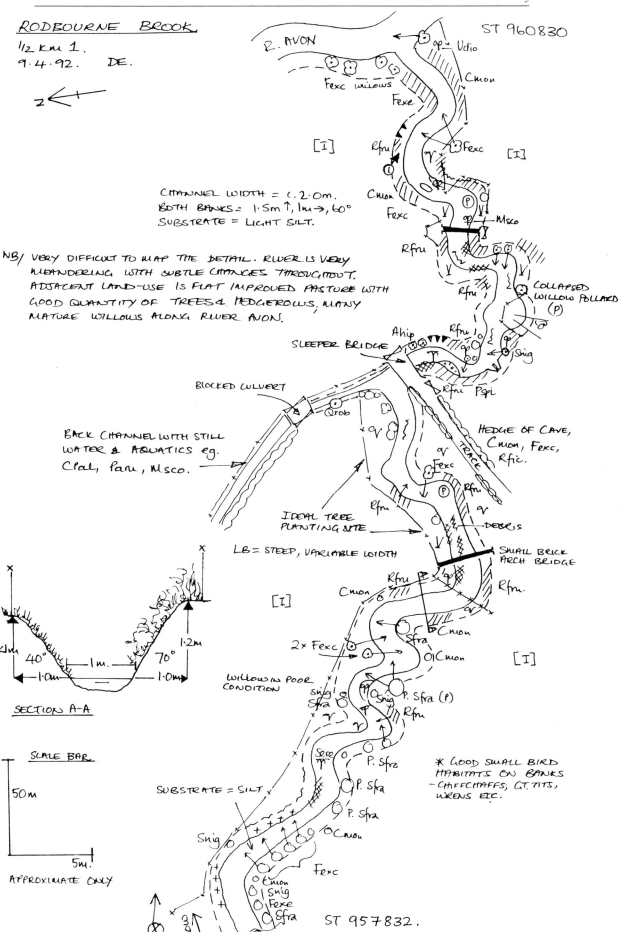

Figure 2
Minimum acceptable standard for a river corridor survey map in a final RCS report
Source: NRA, 1992.

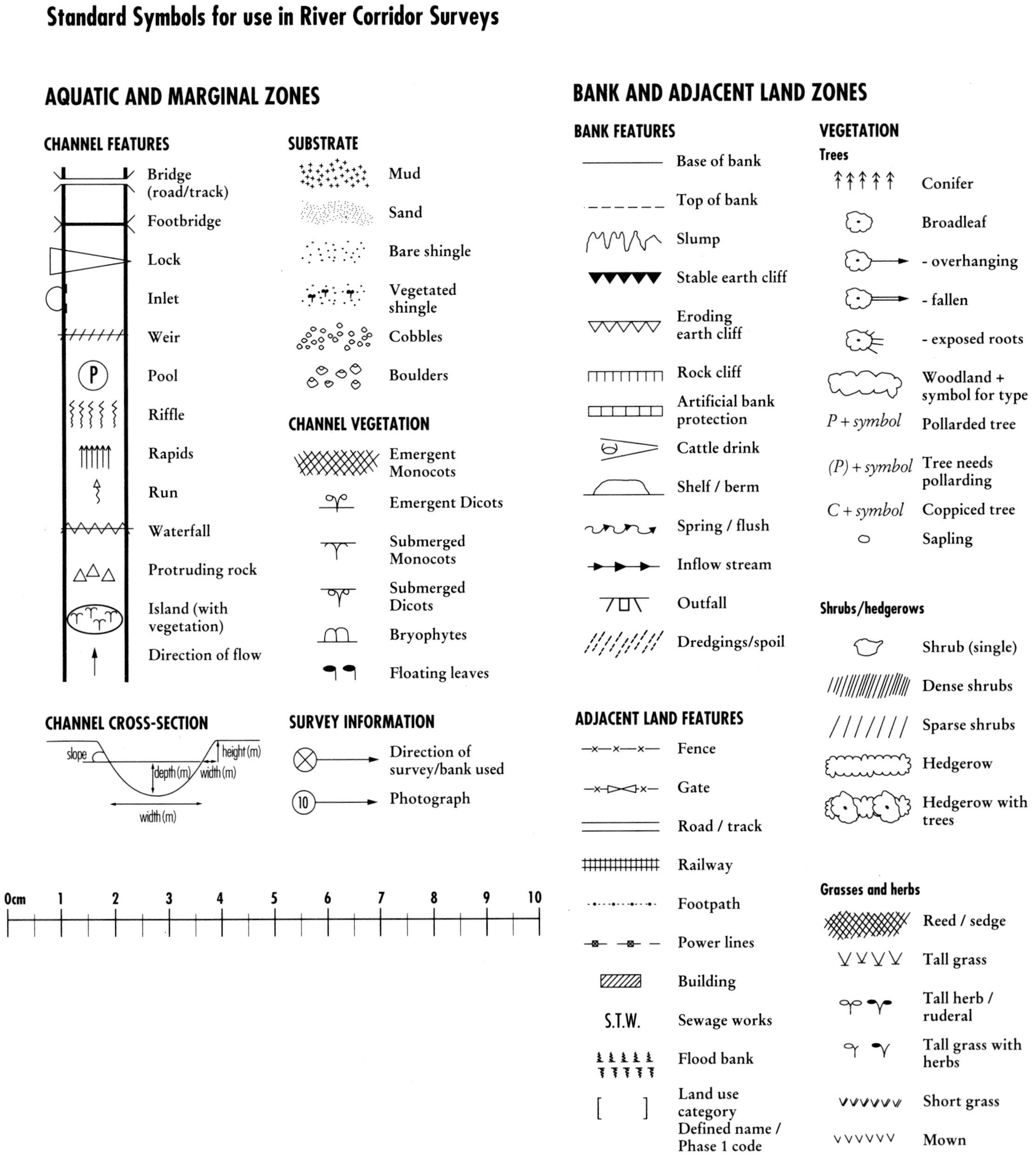

Standard Symbols for use in River Corridor Surveys

AQUATIC AND MARGINAL ZONES

CHANNEL FEATURES

Bridge (road/track)
Footbridge
Lock
Inlet
Weir
Pool
Riffle
Rapids
Run
Waterfall
Protruding rock
Island (with vegetation)
Direction of flow

CHANNEL CROSS-SECTION

slope
height (m)
depth (m)
width (m)
width (m)

SUBSTRATE

Mud
Sand
Bare shingle
Vegetated shingle
Cobbles
Boulders

CHANNEL VEGETATION

Emergent Monocots
Emergent Dicots
Submerged Monocots
Submerged Dicots
Bryophytes
Floating leaves

SURVEY INFORMATION

Direction of survey/bank used
Photograph

0cm 1 2 3 4 5 6 7 8 9 10

BANK AND ADJACENT LAND ZONES

BANK FEATURES

Base of bank
Top of bank
Slump
Stable earth cliff
Eroding earth cliff
Rock cliff
Artificial bank protection
Cattle drink
Shelf / berm
Spring / flush
Inflow stream
Outfall
Dredgings/spoil

ADJACENT LAND FEATURES

Fence
Gate
Road / track
Railway
Footpath
Power lines
Building
S.T.W. — Sewage works
Flood bank
Land use category Defined name / Phase 1 code

VEGETATION

Trees

Conifer
Broadleaf
- overhanging
- fallen
- exposed roots
Woodland + symbol for type
P + symbol — Pollarded tree
(P) + symbol — Tree needs pollarding
C + symbol — Coppiced tree
Sapling

Shrubs/hedgerows

Shrub (single)
Dense shrubs
Sparse shrubs
Hedgerow
Hedgerow with trees

Grasses and herbs

Reed / sedge
Tall grass
Tall herb / ruderal
Tall grass with herbs
Short grass
Mown

Figure 3
Standard symbols for use in river corridor surveys
Source: NRA, 1992.

Maps are prepared in black and white to facilitate photocopying. Critical areas, ie those easily damaged and not easily re-creatable, are highlighted on the maps using an asterisk (*). For management purposes maps are annotated to show where features of interest must be retained and where habitat enhancements are possible (Figure 4).

In addition to plan-form sketches, cross-sections showing the character of the river between bank tops (or through floodbanks and into the adjacent riparian zone where appropriate) are also shown. These are required to indicate channel width, margin and bank character, and height of banks and adjacent land in relation to river water and riverbed levels. One representative sketch for each 500 m stretch is required for

Table 2: Background information included on all RCS maps

- The name of river and reach reference number;
- surveyor's name or initial;
- date of survey;
- north orientation point;
- grid reference of the upstream and downstream limits of the stretch;

uniform rivers but more profiles are shown where there is greater variety of physical features.

The best time for survey is between late April/early May and early October when vegetation should be readily identifiable. However, variation in the beginning and end of the season must be taken into consideration.

2.3.3 Use of river corridor survey data and the future application and development of the methodology

Surveys, employing the RCS methodology, are now carried out by all regions of the NRA for major planned flood defence works. They are also undertaken for catchment inventories for river and floodplain features, conservation assessment and give baseline data for impact assessment for developments, water resource schemes, etc.

Development of the RCS methodology and its application has moved in tandem with its increasing use by the water industry. Principal areas of development and application are highlighted below.

Audits and post-project appraisal

Audit surveys were first undertaken in the Anglian Water Region in 1987. The prime purpose was to ascertain how effectively the implementation of the RCS methodology integrated wildlife and engineering requirements. In simple terms the reaches of rivers were re-surveyed following the completion of maintenance

dredging works.
Amongst other things, audits address three key areas:
- the degree to which high interest features have been retained;
- the general environmental sensitivity of the finished works;
- the extent to which there has been an uptake of the enhancement recommendations.

By 1988 Wessex Water (Exton and Crompton, 1990) had embarked upon audits and more regions of the NRA have done so since (Holmes, 1991). Exton and Crompton (1990) concluded that the introduction of audit surveys have been invaluable as a basis for reviewing the impact of individual river management practices. They have also helped to recognise which operatives are practising good conservation measures and this encourages others to follow their example. In particular, audit surveys constructively bring together the knowledge and skills of all those concerned with maintenance

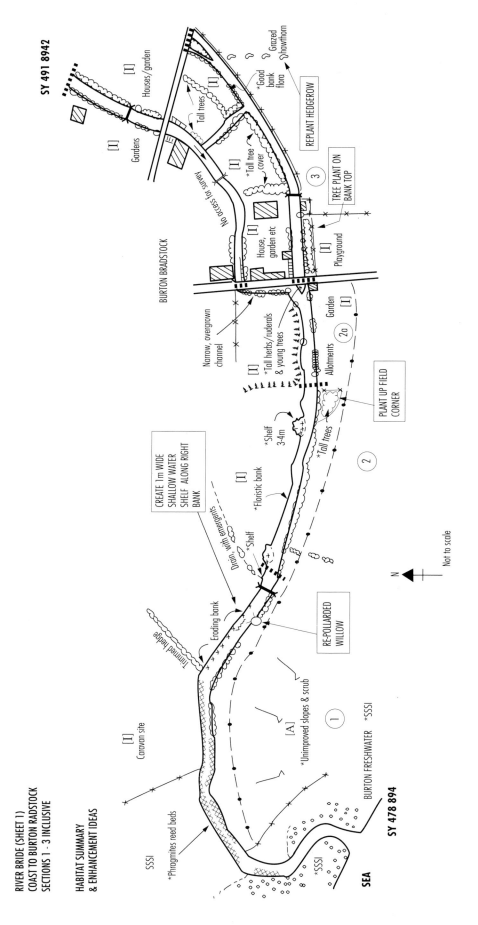

Figure 4
Summary map showing main habitat features and enhancement suggestions included in a final RCS report. Source: NRA, 1992.

operations; this includes the conservation staff, decision makers and operatives.

Currently the basic RCS methodology maps only habitats and key plants or islands of vegetation within 500-m lengths; inevitably, the depiction of features on to maps has been regarded as crude. As such, basic RCS is not very suitable for objective and detailed post-project appraisal of either potentially damaging river works or enhancements. However, the method was not devised to serve such a detailed purpose but was intended to be the 'backbone module' to which more detailed information could be added as necessary.

Strategic surveys and national overview of enhancement potential

The success of river corridor surveys has masked some of their disadvantages. The technique was introduced as a response to proposed works, driven by decisions and demands of the flood defence programme rather than any environmental rationale. This means that they are short-lived and piecemeal.

Strategic surveys adopt the same basic RCS methodology but generally cover whole rivers (or systems). They differ from reactive surveys in being promoted because of a desire to influence management strategies, not in response to proposed works. The rationale behind strategic surveys is to enable an integrated approach to habitat conservation within the overall needs of river management. This allows important river lengths requiring particular sensitivity, and others which could be the subject of a programme for restoration, to be highlighted.

The main problems associated with widespread implementation of strategic surveys are time penalties, cost and potential redundancy of data before they are properly utilised. For these reasons, most strategic surveys are undertaken on rivers where one or more of the following is proposed:

- preparation of catchment management plans;
- flood defence requirement involving strategic action to address causes of the problem, not local action to ameliorate symptoms;
- river restoration and enhancement efforts;
- investigation into catchment effects of water resource developments.

A review of mapping systems ranging from RCS to satellite imagery, was undertaken by the Institute of Freshwater Ecology (Dawson *et al.*, 1992). It concluded that development of a strategic overview of conservation value and enhancement potential is feasible using a combination of remote sensing and existing map data.

Developments in river habitat evaluations

The NRA is currently developing a simple form of river habitat evaluation based on physical structure. The method includes separate assessments of in-channel, marginal, bank, riparian buffer strip and floodplain character along representative reaches of river. The objective is to 'type' rivers and their 'physical architecture' to provide a rapid appraisal of extant features requiring protection and also identifying the potential for restoration. Outputs from this procedure will include an inventory of river features and also an evaluation of habitat, which will complement that already existing for water quality. Both can be used for catchment planning and national reporting purposes. The method will also allow the NRA to determine the relationship between physical habitats, floristic structure and management so that future river works can be instrumental in sustaining and furthering conservation.

Key References

Nature Conservancy Council (1984a) *River Corridor Survey: Draft Methodology.* NCC, Peterborough.

National Rivers Authority (1992b) *River Corridor Surveys; Methods & Procedures* Conservation Technical Handbook No. 1, National Rivers Authority, Bristol.

2.4 Plant Surveys

2.4.1   Introduction

2.4.2   What are macrophytes and why survey them?
  — What are macrophytes?
  — Why should macrophyte surveys be undertaken?

2.4.3   Survey methodologies
  2.4.3.1   Background to methods currently employed for macrophyte surveys in Great Britain
  2.4.3.2   Methodologies
    — Mapping macrophytes
    — Surveys of long reaches
    — Surveys of short reaches

2.4.4   Practical considerations

2.4.5   Recording results

2.4.1 Introduction

It was not until the first half of this century that Butcher (1933) undertook surveys of many rivers in England, culminating in a classification based on plants. In the last 25 years much more attention has been paid to surveying the vegetation in rivers. This is because there is now a far greater awareness of the value of plants to the general well-being of rivers and the habitats which they create for river animals. Many detailed surveys have been undertaken on selected rivers in most areas of the country although national plant surveys have been confined to those undertaken by Haslam (1978, 1981, 1982), Holmes (1983, 1989); and Holmes and

Rowell (1993). The NRA also holds an increasing amount of information on river plants.

There are a number of other survey methodologies which could, and should, be used for other aquatic and wetland habitats. It is important to use established methodologies for individual habitat types, rather than to try to adapt others or pursue personal preferences. Both such approaches may lead to the data collected being incompatible with any other and render it potentially useless. This chapter considers survey methodologies solely for rivers.

2.4.2 What are macrophytes and why survey them?

What are macrophytes?

The majority of plant surveys on rivers involve larger plants called macrophytes. The term 'macrophytes' describes plants which are:
- large enough to be easily seen;
- readily identifiable in the field without microscopes;
- found submerged, emergent, floating or at the water's edge.

Large algae, lichens, bryophytes (liverworts and mosses), ferns, horsetails, and all higher plants which are aquatic or associated with the water's edge are included.

Limited expertise in identifying mosses and liverworts means more attention is paid to higher plants. However, in rivers with rocks and shade, bryophytes are the key components of the river and bank flora.

Why should macrophyte surveys be undertaken?

Macrophytes have several advantages as diagnostic tools. They are large, there are

relatively few species and most are rooted, thereby ensuring that unexpected absence is immediately noted. Being rooted and therefore unable to move away, they also have to endure pollution incidents. However, there are disadvantages in that most (bryophytes excepted) die back in the winter, thus preventing their use for environmental monitoring all year round. Plant surveys therefore complement invertebrate surveys (Chapter 2.9).

There are many reasons why plant surveys of rivers are desirable. Three of the most important are:

- Assessment of conservation value of the river. It is important to find out what plants occur in different parts of a river system. Data collected using a standard method can be used to classify a river into a 'Type' and identify which rivers are 'the best of their Type' (Chapter 1.4). Data from each site can contribute to the development of knowledge on the extent of various river community types nationally and regionally so that conservation strategies can be set. All surveys can, and should, help data gathering on rare and declining species so that reasons for their demise can be postulated and attempts made to reverse the trends.

• Scheme impact/enhancement potential assessment. These surveys usually involve identifying the presence or absence of vulnerable species so that scheme design can be modified to protect them. It also enables the creation of habitats so that plant assemblages can be protected or enhanced. Monitoring surveys are also important to show if a

predicted end-state is achieved, or to identify problems so that remedial measures can be introduced.

• Pollution or damage detection. Plants have often been neglected as water quality monitors (being regarded merely as weeds which may hinder flow). However, several systems can be employed, the data often enabling damage caused by physical impacts on habitats to be determined, and/or deteriorations in water quality and quantity to be identified.

2.4.3 Survey methodologies

2.4.3.1 Background to methods currently employed for macrophyte surveys in Great Britain.

Four methods have been used to classify British rivers:

• Butcher (1933) made subjective observations of key species within sites with undefined limits.

• Haslam (1978) studied many rivers from bridges.

• Goriup (1978) surveyed and classified rivers in southern England based on 30 m representative lengths of river.

• Holmes (1983a+b) surveyed more than 200 rivers for the NCC and developed a standard method with a standard checklist. The unit lengths were 1 km, divided into two 500 m representative sections.

The work of Goriup (1978) and Holmes (1983) indicated that survey length is critical when assessing the floral communities of a river. The smallest survey unit that has been used systematically to classify river sites is 30 m (Goriup, 1978).

The national surveys of rivers undertaken by Holmes for the NCC between 1978 and

1982 attempted to develop plant survey methodologies as well as provide a classification of rivers in Britain. The validity of surveying two 500 m stretches every 7–10 km was checked by recording 100 m and 500 m lengths within the whole 1 km site (Table 1).

2.4.3.2 Methodologies

It has been acknowledged by the DoE (1987) that plants can be used in a variety of ways for assessing water quality in both rivers and lakes. This reference is also the

Table 1: Occurrence of macrophyte numbers in various survey lengths.

500 m lengths contain approx 37% more spp than 100 m*

1 km lengths contain approx 56% more spp than 100 m*

1 km lengths contain *only* 13.5% more spp than 500 m*

2 km lengths contain *only* 2.5% more spp than 1.5 km[+]

97% of river species and 94% of bank species which occur in more than 2% of 500-m reaches surveyed in whole rivers are found in 1 km sites located approx 7 km apart.[+]

1 km sites surveyed every 7 km enables the majority of species to be recorded in 14% of the time it would take to survey a whole river.[+]

* Results based on over 50 1 km sites surveyed on more than 10 river systems in England and Wales in 1978.
+ Results based on analysis of data gathered for a source to mouth

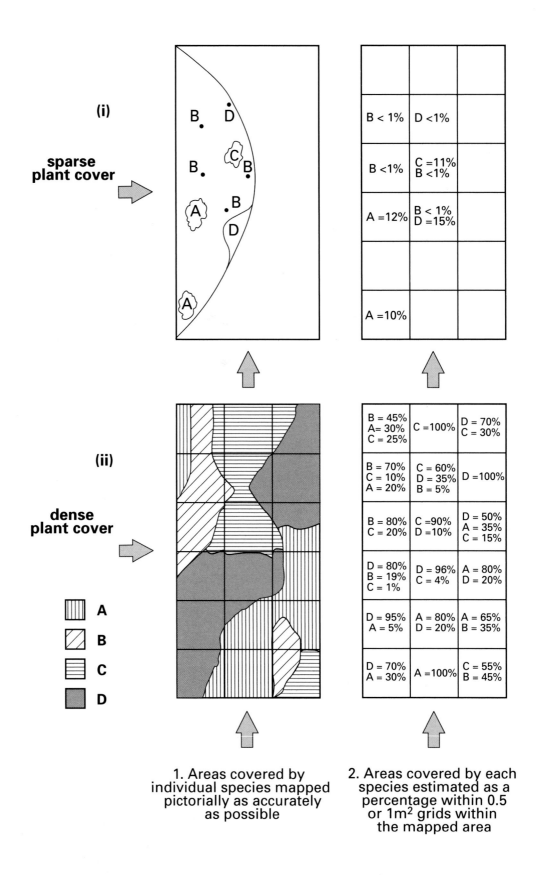

Figure 1
Two mapping techniques; each method being illustrated by examples with:
(i) sparse cover; (ii) dense cover.

best source of information on plant surveys other than mapping. For mapping, the best reference is Wright *et al.* (1981). It is most important that the appropriate methods are used to meet the predetermined objectives of the survey.

Mapping macrophytes

The value of mapping vegetation is that it primarily provides quantifiable information enabling future monitoring of individual species. Thus responses to natural processes, imposed external changes and management strategies can be measured. Mapping is time consuming, but provides reproducible results which justify the effort. The method is most applicable to shallow, wadable water and for short lengths of river or individual habitat features.

The method of mapping may vary according to the density of vegetation. Figure 1 illustrates two methods. One shows mapping of individual species and the other percentage cover of species within grid squares. The former is easy in rivers where cover and species richness is very limited but is impossible where cover is dense and varied. Transect mapping is useful for general monitoring but individual habitat maps, eg for riffles, are particularly useful for determining changes in relation to abstraction, flow regulation, flow augmentation or flood events.

Against the general advice that only wadable rivers should be surveyed,

transects of l m width across deep and wide rivers may be mapped if that is the only habitat available. Scuba-diving may be needed to collect accurate data.

Surveys of long reaches

Surveys of 500 m lengths along representative river reaches are well suited to providing broad yet detailed descriptions of macrophyte communities. This length is regarded as the minimum required to gather sufficient data to enable a site to be assessed adequately for species richness. One kilometre is considered 'ideal' for classifying a length of river into a national type (Chapter 1.4).

Surveys of short reaches

River lengths used above are not suitable for some purposes, eg point monitoring at sites to assess the impact of discharges. In this instance shorter survey lengths of 10–100 m are recommended. Although use of a shorter length means a significant proportion of species may not be represented, this is balanced against the ability to survey a greater number of closely spaced sites in a given time. Such surveys can be effectively combined with invertebrate and fish sampling.

DoE (1987) provides details on the options and merits of using different survey lengths for survey purposes.

2.4.4 Practical considerations

Prior to embarking upon surveys it is important to consider what equipment is needed to undertake the job properly. The DoE (1987) provides simple yet comprehensive recommendations. In addition to guidance on equipment, the same document draws attention to safety considerations and gives practical help on visual assessments of percentage cover. Information on plant identification guides is given at the end of this chapter. Table 2 provides practical advice for plant surveyors.

Table 2 : Key advice for surveyors:

- Do not attempt to rush your survey – someone else will use your data to undervalue the river.
- Only record macrophytes systematically when conditions are good. This means never survey in spate, when the water is turbid, or outside the main growing season of May–October.
- Always use a checklist so that future surveyors know what you were, and were not, recording.
- Ask for help on plant identification when you have problems.
- Don't try to undertake habitat, bird or other surveys whilst doing your macrophyte surveys – full attention to individual tasks is required. If necessary, complete one before embarking on the next.

2.4.5 Recording results

When undertaking surveys, it is essential that a checklist is used for standard recording (several available in DoE, 1987). For instance, the use of the appropriate checklist is absolutely essential if a site is to be classified an NCC SSSI Type.

Whatever surveys are being conducted, a checklist should be compiled to aid future assessment. It is recommended that the species listed by Palmer and Newbold (1983) as being of special importance in different regions of the country are included.

All macrophyte surveys should be supported by clear information on site location, date of survey, surveyor and physical characteristics of the surveyed unit. Simple maps are recommended as support documentation. They should show habitat features and give details of river width, depth and substrate. Where accompanied by faunal surveys, the location of the survey sites should also be shown.

Note: For surveys of canals, ditches, ponds, lakes and wetlands different methods should be employed; contact JNCC, EN, CCW or SNH for guidance.

Plant identification guides:
Books specific to aquatic plants:

Haslam, S M, Sinker, C A and Wolseley, P (1975) *British Water Plants*. Field Studies Council 4: 243–351.

Spencer-Jones, D and Wade, M (1986) *Aquatic Plants. A Guide to Recognition*. ICI, Surrey.

General texts:

Garrard, I and Streeter, D (1983) *The Wild Flowers of the British Isles*. MacMillan, London.

Keble-Martin, W (1976)*The Concise British Flora in Colour*. Ebury Press and Michael Joseph.

Taxonomic works with keys:

Clapham, A R, Tutin, T G and Warburg, E F (1981) *Excursion Flora of the British Isles*. 3rd Edition. Cambridge University Press.

Clapham A R,Tutin, T G and Moore, D M (1989) *Flora of the British Isles*. Cambridge University Press. 3rd Edition; paperback.

Rose, F (1981) *The Wild Flower Key*. Warne, London.

Stace, C E (1992) *A New Flora of the British Isles*. Cambridge University Press.

Key References

DoE (1987) *Methods for the Use of Aquatic Macrophytes for Assessing Water Quality 1985– 86. Methods for the Examination of Waters and Associated Materials*. HMSO, London.

Haslam, S M (1978) *River Plants; the Macrophytic Vegetation of Watercourses*. Cambridge University Press.

Holmes, N T H (1989) *British Rivers, A Working Classification*. British Wildlife. BW Publishing, Rotherwick, Hants.

Palmer, M and Newbold, C (1983) *Wetland and Riparian Plants in Great Britain. An assessment of their Status and Distribution in Relation to Water Authority, River Purification Board and Scottish Islands Areas*. Focus on Nature Conservation No 1. NCC, Peterborough.

Wright, J F, Hiley, P D, Ham, S F and Berrie, A D (1981) Comparison of three mapping procedures developed for river macrophytes. *Freshwater Biology* 11: 369–379.

2.5 Otter Surveys

2.5.1   Introduction

2.5.2   Survey methodologies
   – Full survey
   – Short survey (bridge search survey)

2.5.3   Signs to look for when surveying for otters

2.5.1 Introduction

Otters are among Britain's rarest mammals. They and their shelter sites are protected by the Wildlife and Countryside Act 1981. Where river management is planned in areas believed to hold otters, surveys should be undertaken to establish whether or not they are present.

As otters are largely nocturnal and rarely seen, populations cannot be counted by simple observation. The main indicators of their presence are their spraints (droppings) and tracks (Figure 1). Repeated visits to a reach of river are necessary to determine whether otters are temporary visitors or resident. Unless cubs are observed, it is very difficult to know whether breeding is taking place.

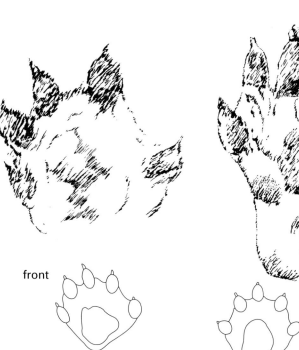

front

Hind

Mink

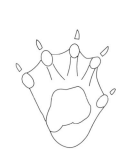

Otter spraint

(i) black and tar like

(ii) when fresh have a distinctive musky odour

(iii) fish bones visible

Mink scat

(i) twisted appearance

(ii) distinctive unpleasant smell

Figure 1
Indicators of otter presence;
(i) otter and mink footprints,
(ii) otter spraints and mink scats (not to scale).
Source: NRA (1993b)

2.5.2 Survey methodologies

Surveys combine a search for signs that indicate the presence of otters together with a general description of the river corridor and factors affecting their distribution. For this purpose river corridor surveys (Chapter 2.3) provide valuable background information. Table 1 and Figure 2 show a simplified version of the national otter survey form which outlines the key parameters to be recorded in basic otter surveys. These include information on recent weather conditions, water levels and potential holt sites, eg tree root cavities or impenetrable vegetation, as well as any signs of otter and mink. If spraints are found, the age (fresh, recent, old) should be noted.

It is also important to record where signs of otters have not been found, although it should be remembered that a lack of signs does not always mean that otters are absent.

Table 1: Basic otter survey recording/monitoring form

RIVER: *Eden*		DATE: *31.7.92*	MAP: *OS 85*
SITE: *Grinsdale to Boomby Gill*			
MAP REF: *369-578 to 371-571*			
WEATHER: *Warm and breezy*		RECENT WEATHER: *Warm/dry*	
WATER LEVEL: *Summer low flow*		LAND TENURE:	
OTTER RECORDS		SPRAINTS: FRESH *2* RECENT *2* OLD *3*	
		TRACKS: *Yes (at 2 sites)*	
COMMENTS: *(see attached map)*			
MINK RECORDS:		SCATS: *none*	TRACKS: *yes*
COMMENTS: *none*			
HABITAT DESCRIPTION: *Steep wooded bank, with vegetation comprising Himalayan balsam, nettles and hogweed. Trees included alder, ash, hawthorn and willow. Well developed root systems along bankside at 371-572 adjacent to small bar in channel.*			
HABITAT EVALUATION: *Reasonable but prone to disturbance (see below)*			
HUMAN IMPACT: *Area used for walking dogs and fishing*			
OTHER NOTABLE SPECIES: *Goosanders present*			
RECOMMENDATIONS			
1. *Potential to plant alder, willow and hawthorn to provide cover at 369-577.*			
2. *Sign post bank top footpath to reduce bankside disturbance.*			
3. *Install logpile holt at 370-574.*			
			SURVEYOR:

Sketch of site on reverse

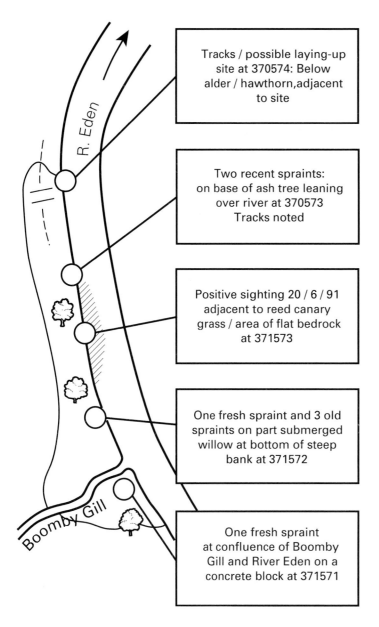

Tracks / possible laying-up site at 370574: Below alder / hawthorn, adjacent to site

Two recent sprains: on base of ash tree leaning over river at 370573 Tracks noted

Positive sighting 20 / 6 / 91 adjacent to reed canary grass / area of flat bedrock at 371573

One fresh sprint and 3 old sprains on part submerged willow at bottom of steep bank at 371572

One fresh sprint at confluence of Boomby Gill and River Eden on a concrete block at 371571

**Figure 2
Otter survey map**

Two main options are recommended for otter survey: both using a similar methodology. These are outlined below:

Full survey

Whole stretches of river are examined for signs of otters. The riverbank and any notable features, either at the toe of the bank or within 10 m of the bank top should be searched. This can be done mainly by walking the bank. However, wading may be necessary to examine features such as root cavities and overhanging vegetation. Either bank can be used and may be

changed according to ease of access or number of prominent features.

This method is most applicable:
- where a river corridor survey has not been carried out;
- where a detailed catchment plan specifically for otters is being developed (plans are being drawn up for key rivers by County Wildlife Trusts, the National Rivers Authority and river owners to protect existing otter populations and encourage recolonisation through improvements in habitat and water quality);
- when an environmental impact assessment is undertaken in areas holding or potentially holding otter populations that may be affected by the proposed development;
- as a means of pre- and post-project appraisal to assess the success of rehabilitation schemes.

Short survey (bridge search survey)

Sites are selected usually 5–8 km apart where bridges cross rivers or where a road runs close by. Access is usually easier at these points and bridges are often good places to look for sprains. A stretch 300 m upstream and the same downstream should be searched, looking for signs as outlined in the survey methodology above.

A degree of flexibility in using this approach is sensible unless it is for the National Survey. For example, if a prominent feature such as a weir is located 500 m away from the bridge, it is worth including in the search. Tributary junctions often provide suitable habitat and are worth investigating.

The main disadvantage of this methodology is that it is less effective at low otter densities than the full search.

This type of survey may be most appropriate when:
- a river corridor survey has been carried out and further information is required;
- time constraints exist – a working day is required to cover 3–6 km for a full survey.

2.5.3 Signs to look for when surveying for otters

Sightings of otters are unlikely without a good deal of luck or patience! Many reported sightings of otters are found to be mink. Consequently, the principal signs used in surveying for otters are their spraints and tracks. However, it is not always easy to differentiate between otter and mink spraints and tracks in the field.

Figures 1(i) and 1(ii) indicates the difference between otter spraints and tracks and those of mink.

Spraints are the main sign used in surveying for otters. Spraints are generally left in prominent places such as boulders and bankside ledges where the 'calling

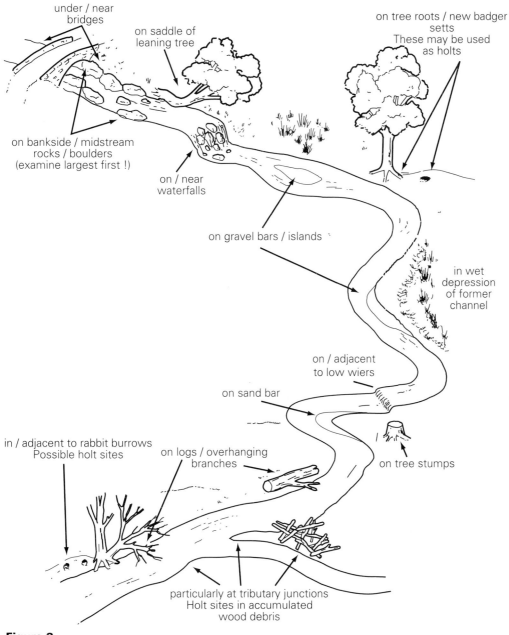

Figure 3
Spraint location guide (after Lenton)

Table 2: Comparative guide to the recognition of otters and mink. Source: NRA (1993)

	OTTER		MINK	
		Size:		
		Average total body length:		
female	104 cms		female	51 cms
male	119 cms		male	60 cms
		Average weight:		
female	7.4 kg		female	0.63 kg
male	10.3 kg		male	1.14 kg

Colour:
Uniform chocolate brown with paler chin and throat patch.

Variable in colour from very dark brown to silver. White patches on chin and/or throat.

Fur:
Two layers, water resistant long guard hairs, dense soft underfur. Coat looks spiky when wet and dries quickly.

Less water resistant. Glossy winter coat which flattens to body when wet.

Shape:
Flattened square-shaped head. Eyes, ears and nose on same plane. Broad muzzle. Torpedo-shaped body. Short legs. Broad based, flattened tail tapering to the tip, approx half total body length.

Similar body shape. More pointed nose. Tail thin, cylindrical, approx one-third total body length.

Feet:
Average width across 5 toes:

female	55 - 60 mm		female	25 mm
male	65 - 70 mm		male	30 mm
cub	45 - 50 mm		kit	up to 25 mm

card' will be most noticed by other otters passing through. Figure 3 illustrates the most common places to search for spraints. Heavy rain and spates wash spraints away and thus may give a false indication that otters are absent.

Spraints are used to mark the otter's home range. The degree of sprainting behaviour varies with the season and with the sex of the animal. Females tend to spraint less and may spraint in the water when they have cubs to avoid drawing attention to themselves. Otters also tend to spraint less when they are fewer in number.

Tracks may be found in mud, sand or snow. Otter prints characteristically show four, but occasionally five toes and are 45–70 mm wide. Mink prints rarely show the fifth toe and are up to 30 mm wide. Dog and fox prints never show five toes and are more symmetrical (Table 2).

Other signs include otter 'runs' (or 'slides') to and from the river. Short cuts across land, especially where rivers meander, can be taken and 'slides' are prevalent here.

2.6 Bird Surveys

2.6.1   Introduction

2.6.2   Survey methodologies
   – Territory mapping
   – Surveys to determine relative value of reaches of habitats for birds
   – Habitat mapping
   – Long-term monitoring

2.6.1 Introduction

Birds are an easily visible indicator of ecological change: they enable us to monitor the effects of our actions on the environment and to assess whether conservation measures are working or whether more are required. It is important that standardised, repeatable techniques are used when surveying birds (Bibby, *et al.*, 1992).

The standard way of counting breeding birds on rivers is by making repeated visits to a site, ideally 10, and to map out territories. A method which involves less intensive effort is to make just two or three visits to map and count the number of contacts with birds. This approach is adequate for comparison between areas in the survey year but not between years. Bird survey information should be integrated with information on habitat.

2.6.2 Survey methodologies

Territory mapping

A mapping survey will give the most accurate count of birds in the census area. Such an approach is to be recommended if the counts are intended to be part of a continuing process of monitoring the consequences of management or other changes over a number of years. The use of 10 visits reduces the effects of bias due to changes in observer, in skill or weather. It also has a further advantage that data of similar quality can be gathered from many rivers for comparison.

During the breeding season, many species are territorial. Especially among songbirds, territories are often marked by conspicuous song, display and periodic disputes with neighbours. In such cases, mapped sightings and soundings of birds, referred to as registrations, should fall into clusters coinciding with territories. Mapping relies on locating these signs on a series of visits and using them to estimate locations and numbers of clusters or territories (Figure 1). Detailed instructions have been produced by the BTO and should be consulted by anyone contemplating a study (Taylor, 1982).

Study areas need to be adequately mapped at a scale of about 1:2,500. In open areas, it is helpful to mark selected trees or other features to enable accurate plotting of birds. The length of route depends on access.

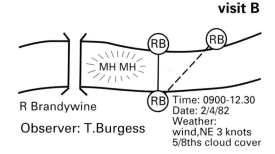

visit B

R Brandywine

Observer: T.Burgess

Time: 0900-12.30
Date: 2/4/82
Weather:
wind,NE 3 knots
5/8ths cloud cover

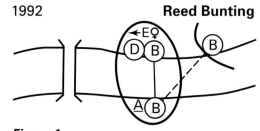

1992 **Reed Bunting**

Figure 1
1. A Reed Bunting was recorded singing on a tree near an old bridge (the scene of a fight between two Moorhens) on the second visit of the season (visit B). The bird was then seen to fly to another tree across the channel and resume singing. A second Reed Bunting was then heard singing against the first.
2. The information relating to the fighting Moorhens and singing Reed Buntings is entered on the *visit map*, using the appropriate species codes and activity symbols.
3. At the end of the season, Reed Bunting registrations from all visits are transfered to a Reed Bunting *species map*. Song registrations from visit B now appear as *B* on the species map.
Source: BTO Waterbird Survey Instructions (1982)

The International Bird Census Committee has adopted 10 visits as a standard. In southern England, visits should take place between mid-March and mid-June, but later farther north. Ideally visits should be spread uniformly at weekly intervals. Their total number and the length of season should give all species enough registrations to clarify clusters. The important visits for most resident species fall in the first half of the survey, whereas later-arriving migrants will not normally be recorded until the latter half.

Early morning is the best time to carry out the visits, although it is best to avoid the first hour at dawn. At this time, bird activity peaks vary markedly. There is a period of more uniform activity lasting from about an hour after dawn to nearly midday. On hot days, these periods may be briefer. Since time of day and differences of effort can cause bias, it is important to record date and start and finish times as part of the documentation of a visit. The starting points should be alternated between visits.

Table 1: Selected BTO mapping codes for a number of bird species associated with rivers, lowland wet grassland and wetlands. Source: BTO WBS Instructions (1992)

CODE	SPECIES		
LG	Little grebe	LP	Little ringed plover
GG	Great crested grebe	RP	Ringed plover
CA	Cormorant	L	Lapwing
H	Grey heron	DN	Dunlin
MS	Mute swan	RU	Ruff
GJ	Greylag goose	SN	Snipe
CG	Canada goose	BW	Black-tailed godwit
EG	Egyptian goose	CU	Curlew
SU	Shelduck	RK	Redshank
MN	Mandarin	GK	Greenshank
WN	Wigeon	CS	Common sandpiper
GA	Gadwall	BH	Black-headed gull
T	Teal	CM	Common gull
MA	Mallard	CN	Common tern
GY	Garganey	KF	Kingfisher
SV	Shoveler	SM	Sand martin
PO	Pochard	YW	Yellow wagtail
TU	Tufted duck	GL	Grey Wagtail
RM	Red-breasted	PW	Pied wagtail
	merganser	DI	Dipper
GD	Goosander	CW	Cetti's warbler
OP	Osprey	GH	Grasshopper warbler
WA	Water rail	SW	Sedge warbler
MH	Moorhen	MW	Marsh warbler
CO	Coot	RW	Reed Warbler
OC	Oystercatcher	WH	Whitethroat
		RB	Reed bunting

Table 2: Standard mapping census symbols. Source: BTO WBS Instructions (1982)

RB, 3RB Juv, **RBm, RBf** **RBm/f, RB2m**	Reed Bunting sight records with age, sex or number of birds, if appropriate (use *m/f* for male and female together).	It is useful if the visit maps carry an indication of which registrations, in close proximity to one another, are definitely of different birds, or belong either definitely (or even doubtfully) to the same bird. The following conventions should be used:	
DI fam	Juvenile Dippers with both parents in attendance.		
DI	A contact with a Dipper giving an alarm call or any other vocalisation (other than song) thought to have territorial significance.	(RB)- - -(RB)	Different Reed Buntings in song at the same time.
(DI)	A Dipper in song.	RBm- - -RBm	Different male Reed Buntings in view at the same time.
—DI DI—	An aggressive encounter between two Dippers.	(RB)——(RB)	Singing bird seen to take up a new position.
***DI**	An occupied nest of Dippers. Unoccupied nests can be recorded in this way if a suitable note is appended to the registration.	(RB)-?-(RB)	Thought to be the same bird in a changed position but not certain.
***MH on**	Moorhen nest with an adult sitting.	If there is no line joining the registrations it will be assumed that they were probably different birds.	
MH mat	Moorhen with nest material in beak.	Additional activities of territorial significance, such as display or mating, should be noted using an appropriate clear abbreviation.	
DI food	Dipper with food in beak.		

The identity and activity of all birds should be mapped using standard codes for species and for activities (Tables 1 and 2). Care should be taken to record as much detail as possible, such as the sex and age of the bird (were two different birds close together the adults of a pair or were they both males and thus presumably near a territory boundary?).

Most useful is the location of individuals of the same species that can be seen or heard simultaneously. A key feature of analysis assumes that territory boundaries fall between such records. One way some birds respond is to chase rivals to their territory boundaries. Species such as dippers will often fly readily within their territory but be reluctant to go beyond it. Occasionally, the neighbours might be seen or heard responding in confirmation that a boundary has been reached.

The time taken to undertake a visit will vary according to the variability of habitat and density of birds as well as the competence of the observer. For a surveyor capable of identifying birds and their song with confidence, approximately 2 km/h can be covered (with a similar time to analyse the results). Some 10 km can therefore be walked in a morning.

Field maps should be generated for each visit, containing all records of all species. For analysis, registrations are copied from all the field maps to a single species map where the species code is replaced by a visit code. Interpretation of maps is not a simple process as there may be more than one 'correct' way to interpret a particular map. Guidelines are provided by the BTO (Taylor, 1982).

The analysis should produce non-overlapping rings round clusters of registrations that refer to one pair of breeding birds. These clusters are called territories and results are presented in terms of number of territories. In perfect circumstances, a species map would show a group of distinct clusters, each of which would contain records of one or two birds on most or at least several visits. There would also be several records of the males singing against their neighbours.

To register a 'cluster', there must be at least two registrations if there were eight or fewer effective visits for the species and at least three registrations for nine or more effective visits. For migrants the number of effective visits is the number from the first visit on which the species was detected. If 10 visits at weekly intervals started in late March, many migrants will not be seen at all in the first 2–5 visits. In this case they will all have eight or fewer effective visits, so they only need two registrations per cluster.

Individual records in a cluster must be at least 10 days apart to avoid counting a temporary migrant present for only a few days. A single record of a nest with eggs or young can be counted as a cluster even in the unlikely event of the adults not having been seen at a level to qualify. Broods of flying juveniles or newly hatched young of species such as mallard or lapwing should not be counted in the same way as a nest because they might have moved from a territory already recorded.

The mapping method only works well for species that show clear clusters. For species that defend small areas near a nest site but range widely, group clusters are drawn. Such species include mallard or reed warbler. The clusters must include a potential nest site. If adjacent group clusters contain similar maximum numbers of birds on different visits they should be amalgamated.

Surveys to determine relative value of reaches of habitats for birds

Surveys based on fewer visits are adequate for descriptive purposes such as deciding which sections of a catchment are most important for birds or which habitats hold particular species. They provide a general description of what species occur in different areas where but they cannot be relied on to provide results comparable to a full mapping survey. Results from fewer visits are also more prone to observer bias.

Surveys based on fewer visits are conducted in the same way as those for mapping census. The results are summarised as numbers of registrations by species. These results have no absolute meaning but may be compared between areas. However, anomalous results can occur as a result of a limited number of visits being undertaken in different time periods (eg different seasons). Care should be taken to spread the timing of visits across plots and to avoid days when weather conditions are not good. If more than one observer is used, they should be equally competent and ideally swapped between visits to particular stretches.

Habitat mapping

Even when bird census work is undertaken, the mapping of habitat features, an integral part of river corridor survey, is important. Although the bird survey will show where, for example, kingfishers or common sandpipers actually bred in the study year, it will not detect potentially valuable features.

Long-term monitoring

Long-term monitoring of birds may be used to ensure that environmental conditions are not deteriorating. In many habitats, birds are easily monitored indicators of environmental change. However, in river corridors, this is less clearly the case. For example, most birds are sensitive to the effects of engineering works and also to disturbance or predators such as mink, so it may be difficult to identify the reasons for observed change.

Long-term monitoring is expensive and should be designed with great care. Priority when monitoring or surveying should be given to species of high conservation value or species which give quick, sensitive, cost-effective indications of habitat change.

Key References

Bibby, C J, Burgess, N D and Hill, D A (1992) *Bird Census Techniques*. British Trust for Ornithology and The Royal Society for the Protection of Birds. Academic Press. London.

Taylor, K (1982) *Waterways Bird Survey Instructions*. British Trust for Ornithology, Tring.

2.7 Fish Stock Assessment and Surveys

2.7.1 Introduction

2.7.2 Why fisheries surveys are undertaken, what they show and who carries them out

2.7.3 Survey/stock assessment methods
    2.7.3.1 Active survey methods
        — Electric fishing
        — Netting
        — Echo-sounding or hydro-acoustics
    2.7.3.2 Passive catch-related methods
        — Angling catches
        — Catch statistics
    2.7.3.3 Census methods
        — Redd counts
        — Fish counters
        — Fish traps

2.7.4 Survey requirements
    — Absolute estimates versus relative estimates
    — Selection of sampling area and sites
    — Measurement of actual density/abundance and identification of environmental impacts on fish populations
    — Choosing the best method

2.7.5 Reporting of fisheries survey and associated data

2.7.1 Introduction

Stock assessment and fisheries surveys are important because they provide information for fisheries management and conservation decisions. Stock assessment is the most practicable way of describing the fisheries resource of a river. It addresses the question of how many and what kind of fish *are* present and raises the question of how many and what kind *should be* present. Stock assessment usually requires data from active surveys, eg electric fishing (Section 2.7.3.1). Assessment of the status of fish stocks can also be made using data from a variety of passive sources, such as fish traps or catch statistics from anglers and commercial fishermen (Section 2.7.3.2). Active surveys, using nets or electric fishing, are aimed at a site, tributary or sub-catchment of particular interest. A wide range of fish sampling methods are available (von Brandt, 1984) because of the range of species, habitats and questions posed. It is essential that the appropriate

method of survey or assessment is used. Many of the survey methods are sophisticated and highly technical. Some require significant manpower, equipment and safety resources and are costly. Others are simple and cheap because not all questions require complex or costly answers.

The information obtained from fishery surveys assists with:

- assessment of environmental impacts on fish populations (eg low flows, pollution and engineering works);
- evaluation of need for habitat/water quality and quantity improvements;
- conservation of fish species, especially rare ones;
- assessment of long-term population changes;
- evaluation of the need for restocking.

2.7.2 Why fisheries surveys are undertaken, what they show and who carries them out

Fish are a good indicator of general river quality. Overall, they are more sensitive to many chemicals than invertebrates because they have a higher metabolic rate and require more oxygen. They cannot endure large reductions in oxygen for long periods and their absence is often a sign of organic or other forms of pollution that deoxygenate water. Many invertebrates survive such pollution but fish are either killed or avoid the pollution by swimming away. Fish also have specific physical habitat requirements: bankside features, eg chub require overhanging trees for cover; backwaters, which act as refuge areas during floods and provide breeding habitats for many coarse fish; in-stream features such as riffles and gravel bars which provide spawning redds for salmonids. Consequently, absence or low

numbers of fish may be the result of poor or degraded habitat. Appropriately varied and abundant fish populations are a good guide to angling and recreational potential, as well as indicating the conservation status of a river.

Fish stock assessment and surveys involve fish capture, identification, counting and collection of biological data such as size and scale samples. Comparison of population statistics with previous years or other similar sites allows conclusions to be drawn about the composition and abundance of fish, ie are they what was expected? Aspects of natural water quality, eg nutrients, greatly influence growth and biomass and, therefore, should also be taken into account when sampling.

Fisheries are subject to property rights and consequently it is necessary to inform fishery owners of proposed survey work and seek their agreement. They will in most cases be interested in the outcome of the survey and be a valuable source of information about the river and its fishes. If the survey requires fish to be caught, even temporarily, by methods other than licensed angling or licensed netting, the consent of the appropriate authority will be required. Methods such as netting and electric fishing are illegal unless specifically consented. Reference should be made to the NRA in England and Wales, to SOAFD in Scotland and DANI in Northern Ireland.

When commissioning fisheries survey work the competence of the staff concerned should be established because of the need for safe working practices. Any team should contain experienced, trained members who comply with relevant codes of practice. It is difficult to get good results during periods of high flow. It can also be unsafe to sample at these times. Therefore, most surveys are undertaken during the period of lower flows between March and September. In nutrient-rich waters, where extensive growth of marginal and in-stream weeds occurs, it may be necessary to carry out surveys before the end of May, to avoid problems caused by excessive weed growth.

Regular strategic monitoring programmes are undertaken in England and Wales by the NRA. These generate survey information on a three-or-five-year basis, for coarse fish, and annually for many juvenile migratory salmonid populations. This frequency of sampling is necessary to detect weak year classes and to identify any potential decline in population numbers. Observed changes are evaluated and management action taken if necessary. Fishery survey work is also undertaken by SOAFD, District Fishery Boards and other fisheries organisations in Scotland, by DANI in N Ireland, and by fishery owners or angling clubs.

2.7.3 Survey/stock assessment methods

2.7.3.1 Active survey method

Electric fishing

This is the most effective way of estimating the density and survival of juvenile salmonids in small streams using handheld equipment and wading (Kennedy and Strange, 1981 and Anon, 1988). It is also used from boats in wider and deeper rivers (Cowx, Wheatley and Hickley, 1988) but is generally less effective in large, deep, slow-flowing rivers and where the electrical conductivity of the river is high. A portable generator passes a current through the water between two electrodes. This stuns the fish temporarily. They are collected by handnet, (Plate 1) counted, examined (Plate 2) and released at the end of the operation. The development of the technique and its effects upon fish are well

**Plate 1
Electro-fishing of a small stream**

Mark Pilcher

Mark Pilcher

**Plate 2
Measurement of
fish length
during a fisheries
survey**

covered in Cowx (1990). Electric fishing may be used in combination with other methods, such as netting, to raise the capture efficiency of net trawls. Training is essential for all practitioners and the electric fishing equipment must meet safety requirements, and be routinely and professionally checked (Hickley and Milwood, 1990; NRA, 1991).

Netting

Nets are commonly used for surveys in larger, slow-flowing rivers. The mesh size is chosen according to the size of fish to be captured and the required efficiency of capture. They are used in large rivers which are not easily sampled by other methods. Nets, such as seine nets or their derivatives are most commonly used in survey work. They may be flat sheets of net or may have a bag sewn into their centres. The net is rigged with a series of floats on the top and weights on the bottom to keep it taut and prevent fish swimming under or over it. It is then pulled around the fish by boat to encircle them from the shore. Both ends of the net are then beached, the net pulled to the bank and the fish removed. They can be used on their own but also within stop nets blocking off a section of river, for good quantitative estimates. A good account of this method for population estimates is given by Coles, Wortley and Noble (1985). Many different techniques of setting and drawing in nets are used to achieve high efficiency under a range of different conditions (Matthews, 1971; Bubb, 1980; Penczak and O'Hara, 1983).

In large, uniform rivers and channels where access is difficult for normal netting, or a higher than usual sampling frequency is required, trawls may be towed behind boats to obtain fish survey data (Adams, 1988).

Echo-sounding or hydro-acoustics

After many years of use in marine fisheries, echo-sounding is being applied with increasing success in rivers (Kubecka, *et al.,* 1992). The equipment is expensive, but where it is possible to use this method it can quickly and cost-effectively generate fish biomass estimates over large areas of a river. However, 'background noise' from turbulent water can prevent the use of hydro-acoustics in some habitats.

2.7.3.2 Passive catch-related methods

Angling catches

Angling records, particularly catches during matches provide valuable information about fish populations. These usually relate to coarse fish and are expressed as catch per unit effort (CPUE). Fishing effort is measured as the number of days or weeks fished by anglers, the number of fishing permits sold or the number of fishing match participants. CPUE data provide a useful measure of stock abundance where it would be difficult or expensive to sample using more conventional methods, eg large lowland rivers. Use of these data assumes that they are representative of the sites in question and their use has been discussed by Cowx (1991). Representativeness has been shown for coarse fish by Axford (1979), Cooper and Wheatley (1981) and Cowx and Broughton (1986). However, catch rates of coarse fish from different parts of the same river vary greatly (Cowx, 1991) and this may be caused by factors such as disease, age group variations and population movements (Axford 1991).

Catch statistics

Catch returns are required, by law, for salmon and sea trout from anglers and commercial fishermen, by the NRA in England and Wales and from fisheries owners in Scotland by SOAFD. The NRA also requires eel catch returns in some areas. Catch statistics are generated from these catch returns and provide a general indication of overall long-term trends.

2.7.3.3 Census methods

Redd counts

Salmon and sea trout deposit their eggs in the riverbed gravels when spawning. The disturbed areas 'cut' by the fish are known as redds and their number and location indicate the distribution and abundance of spawning migratory salmonids. However, it is often very difficult to count redds where spawning takes place in the main river channel. The accuracy of the counts is also dependent upon the skill of the observer and the water conditions, such as depth and clarity.

Fish counters

Electronic fish counters have been installed in some rivers to count automatically the numbers of salmon and sea trout migrating upstream and downstream in a river system. In most cases this involves building a weir to channel fish through the counter. Because these large in-river structures are expensive to build it is usual to have just one counter in a river system. The scientific background to fish counters is given by Bussell (1978).

Fish traps

Fish traps are used to provide information on fish movement and abundance (Shearer, 1988), although many traps are only operated for short periods of the year. In some cases traps are used to obtain counts and details of salmon and sea trout smolts moving downstream.

2.7.4 Survey requirements

Irrespective of the sampling method chosen, the objectives of a survey determines the sampling design/strategy adopted. Sampling should be undertaken in a manner that meets the requirements of the desired objectives in terms of accuracy and precision (Table 1). This section examines how to meet such requirements.

An introduction and further details on sampling design and strategies are provided in Bayley (1990) and Hillborn and Walker (1992).

Absolute estimates versus relative estimates

The objectives of the study and the nature of the estimates required – either 'absolute' variables such as total population size or 'relative' measures such as changes with time – (Table 1) determine both the level of precision and accuracy required. Costs increase with an increased level of precision, therefore it is essential to avoid a higher level of precision than is needed. Bohlin *et al.* (1989) and Bohlin (1991) examine these aspects further.

Selection of sampling area and sites

This may be undertaken in three stages:

*Stage 1 select the target area.*The 'target area' is the length of river to which the stock assessment applies. Selecting the target area requires some knowledge of the fish distribution and the probability of their efficient capture.

Stage 2 select sites within the target area. Ideally, the sites within the target area should be selected at random. However, practical considerations, such as habitat variability and access difficulties, will influence site choice. The number of sites needed for a study will depend upon several factors; in particular the variation between sites and the overall variability in fish numbers. The higher the required precision and the larger the target area, the greater the number of sample sites needed. However, if the objective is to estimate a change in population size, rather than the absolute population size at two different

Table 1: Survey objectives and the required level of accuracy and precision

OBJECTIVE	NATURE OF ESTIMATE	ACCURACY [1]	PRECISION [2]
1 To obtain information on species distribution	relative	low	none
2 To estimate relative abundance	relative	low	low/med
3 To estimate annual or triennial trends in abundance	absolute or relative	low	low/med
4 To calculate actual density or abundance	absolute	high	med/high
5 To identify and evaluate environmental and man-made effects	absolute	high	med/high

Note: [1] Accuracy refers to how close an estimate is to the truth and is a function of the selectivity and efficiency of the equipment used
[2] Precision refers to how consistent the estimate of population size is, depending mainly upon the number of sites sampled

points in time, this will reduce the number of sites needed. Bohlin *et al.* (1989) have developed a formula to enable the estimation of the required number of sampling sites needed.

Stage 3 sample fish from within each site.
Table 2 illustrates how the way in which fish are sampled determines the necessary level of accuracy of the sampling. Greater efficiency of sampling may result from the use of many small sites as opposed to a few large sites, but this relates to the fishes' distribution. Cowx (1991) provides further

Table 2: The way in which fish are sampled within a site determines the necessary level of accuracy of the sampling

ACCURACY	PROCEDURE
Low ↑↓ High	Fish until something is caught
	Fish until a particular species is caught
	Fish for a set period of time or over a specific area without stopnets (ie catch per unit effort)
	Complete one fishing exercise within stopnets (ie a minimum estimate)
	Perform 2 or 3 successive fishing exercises within stopnets removing the fish each time (precise estimate)

information on the effectiveness of sampling strategies.

Measurement of actual density and abundance and identification of environmental impacts on fish populations

In order to provide actual density and abundance measures or identify environmental impacts on fish populations (Table 1, rows 4 and 5) additional sampling techniques such as 'mark and recapture' are needed to produce the high quality of data required. This and other additional techniques are examined in Zippin (1958), Seber and Le Cren (1967), Carle and Strub (1978) and Cowx (1991).

Choosing the best method

There is no one method of sampling fish populations that can be applied to all sites and all habitats. An important part of survey design is to ensure that the proposed sampling methods are practical, safe, efficient, appropriate and cost-effective. Although electric fishing is the best way of sampling many sites, it is less effective than, for example, netting in larger deep rivers.

2.7.5 Reporting of fisheries survey and associated data

The biomass (the aggregated weight per unit area) or the density (number per unit area) and age structure of a fish population (determined from rings on fish scales) can reveal relevant information about the present and past nature of a site. Fish are long-lived, and healthy populations should have a pyramid of numbers with more younger individuals than older ones. The absence or low numbers of particular age groups may be a result of previous pollution or other damage, whereas large numbers of a single year class may well reflect a particularly successful year for spawning, survival and growth. A distorted pyramid of numbers, with more older or larger fish than would normally be expected is often evidence of substantial stocking to improve angling.

In addition to biological data, some assessment of physical habitat should be made. Habitat features will often explain some of the attributes of fish populations, especially presence or abundance of some species. Factors such as altitude, width, mean channel depth, depth variation, amount of cover, gradient, flow, conductivity and riverbed substrate are all important. A fuller account of habitat features and their importance is given by Milne *et al.* (1985). Data from river corridor and habitat surveys, as well as those relating to the biology and chemistry of the water, are useful background information when formulating plans for fisheries surveys. Furthermore, such information will enable a better interpretation of survey results to be made.

Before undertaking a survey, it is worthwhile researching any previous fish surveys, no matter how old or poorly executed, as these may help with the process of survey design. It is unlikely that these will relate specifically to the target site or be up to date enough to obviate the need for a survey, but they may provide useful background information, enable identification of change and also highlight the practical difficulties of sampling some of the chosen sites.

At the end of the sampling period it is of the utmost importance that the data are properly analysed and a report produced. If this is not done very few benefits will result from the work and there will be no record for comparison with subsequent surveys. The report should be of a length consistent with both the size and complexity of the survey and with getting the information across clearly and simply. Data should be summarised into tables and graphs and the raw data listed in an appendix or on a computer floppy disk. A clear account should be given of the procedures undertaken in the field as well as the conclusions drawn. The report should set out the survey objectives at the beginning and end with a concise statement of the conclusions.

Key References

Anon (1988) *Methods for sampling fish populations in shallow rivers and streams.* DoE Standing Committee of Analyses. HMSO

Bayley, P B (1990) Sampling strategies for fish populations. In: *Fisheries in the year 2000* pp253–259 Proceedings of the 21st anniversary conference of the Institute of Fisheries Management, held at Royal Holloway College, Egham. O'Grady, K T, Butterworth, A J B, Spillett P B and Domaniewski, J C J (eds.) Institute of Fisheries Management, Nottingham.

von Brandt, A (1984) *Fish catching methods of the world.* Third edition. Fishing News Books. 418 pp.

Hillborn, R and Walker, C J (1992) *Quantitative fish stock assessment: choices, dynamics and uncertainty.* Chapman and Hall, New York and London. 570 pp.

2.8 Amphibian and Reptile Surveys

2.8.1   Introduction

2.8.2   Amphibians
    — Survey methodologies
    — Common frog
    — Common toad
    — Smooth and palmate newts
    — Great crested newt

2.8.3   Reptiles
    — Survey methodology

2.8.1 Introduction

Amphibian and reptile surveys may be carried out for various reasons, for example to locate breeding sites, identify species present or assess population trends.

Although most British amphibians are easy to identify, newts, particularly females, may be difficult to differentiate. Reptiles may also be difficult to identify as often the observer has no more than a brief glimpse. Good field guides are essential for accurate identification (Arnold and Burton, 1978). Figures 1 and 2 provide an introduction to identifying reptiles and amphibians.

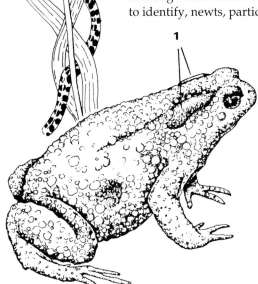

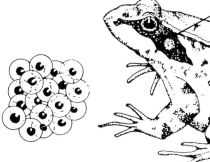

Frog and spawn
Dark 'mask' marking behind eyes (1)
Generally smooth moist skin
Pronounced 'hump'(2)
Moves on land by hopping

Common toad and spawn
No mask
Prominent glands on head (1)
Rarely hops – usually walks

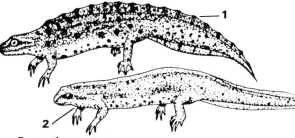

Smooth newt
Usually <10 cm
Male has undulating crest to the tip of tail – female lacks crest (1)
Female differs from palmate newt – white throat with dark spots (2)

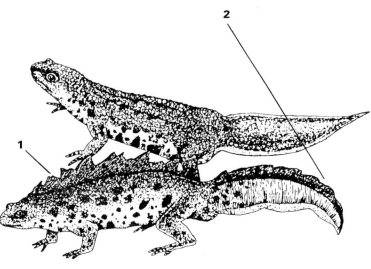

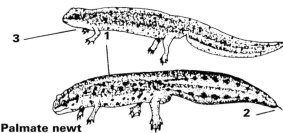

Palmate newt
Usually <9 cm
Male has low smooth–edged crest (1)
Distinctive tail tip – ends abruptly, with thin filament (2)
Female told from smooth newt – pinkish throat, never spotted (3)

Great crested newt
Up to 16 cm
Rough, granular skin
Male has serrated crest (1), terminating at base of tail (2)

Figure 1 Identification of amphibians in breeding condition

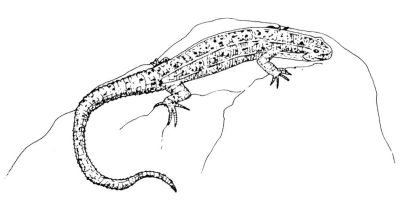

Common lizard
Length to 13 cm including tail.
Distinguished from newts by dry, scaly skin.

Slow-worm
Legless lizard, not a snake. Length up to 45 cm, but often shed tails, like other lizards, and may just have a stump.
Very smooth and glossy, grey or brown
Tiny scales, scarcely visible
Closable eyelids (1)

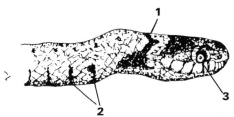

Adder
Short, thick snake less than 65 cm long
Distinct zigzag on back (1) (normally dark brown pattern on straw-coloured background in female, black on dirty white in male, but variable, reddish or even black)
Red eye, cat-like pupil, no eyelids (2)
Moves away at a steady pace

Grass snake
Long and thin, female about 100 cm, male 70 cm. Olive green.
Distinct black and yellow collar (1)
Vertical black bar markings (2)
Yellow eye with round pupil, no eyelids (3)
Tends to dash away very fast

Figure 2
Identification of reptiles
Adapted from: Inns (1992)

2.8.2 Amphibians

Surveys should be undertaken in the breeding season when amphibians are easily observed (Figure 3). To locate potential amphibian sites it is best to walk the area marking them on a suitable map (eg Ordnance Survey 1:25,000) before the breeding season. The timing of breeding is directly related to weather, particularly temperature, being delayed by freezing temperatures and advanced by mild, wet weather.

To assess the population sizes the following methods should be used and the results compared with the population scores in Table 1. In each case, repeat counts might be helpful.

Survey methodologies

Common frog

Timing: February to early April, a few days after spawn is laid.

The frogs in a single riverine or floodplain water body will usually spawn almost simultaneously and the adults may be in the water only for a week or so. Regular

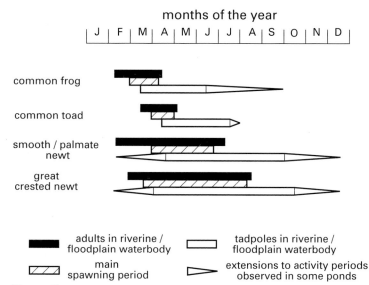

months of the year

| J | F | M | A | M | J | J | A | S | O | N | D |

common frog

common toad

smooth / palmate newt

great crested newt

▬▬▬ adults in riverine / floodplain waterbody

▭ tadpoles in riverine / floodplain waterbody

▨▨ main spawning period

▷ extensions to activity periods observed in some ponds

Figure 3
Periods when different amphibians are likely to be found in riverine and floodplain water bodies.
Adapted from: Griffiths (1987)

Method: Estimate the number of spawn clumps dvisible in the backwater or habitat being examined. Most clumps will be deposited close to one another, forming a mat. Small temporary floodplain pools should not be overlooked when surveying.

Common toad

Timing: March to April when toads are spawning. Like frogs, they may be in the water only for a week or so and are easily missed.

Method: Spawn is difficult to count as it is laid in strings, often wrapped around submerged vegetation. Additionally, females may lay their spawn close together so it is generally best to count adults. Visit the riverine or floodplain water body on a mild, wet night with a powerful torch. Count the number of heads above the surface and any toads at the sides, using a hand-held counter if available. Only 75% of the males are likely to be present at any one time, and only about 50% of them will be visible. Females will usually amount to around 20–30% of the male numbers.

inspection is therefore advisable as spawning time is easy to miss. The survey should be repeated at least once more, about a week later, in case further spawning has occurred (mark location of spawn clumps on a map to prevent them being counted twice).

Table 1:   A simple way to test the extent of a riverine/floodplain waterbody's amphibian population

SPECIES	METHOD	LOW POPULATION Score 1	GOOD POPULATION Score 2	EXCEPTIONAL POPULATION Score 3
Gt crested newt	Seen or netted in day Counted at night	<5 <10	5–50 10–100	>50 >100
Smooth newt	Netted in day Counted at night	<10	10–100	>100
Palmate newt	Netted in day Counted at night	<10	10–100	>100
Common toad	Number of adults counted	<100	100–1,000	>1,000
Common frog	Spawn clumps counted	<50	50–500	>500

Using methods described in the text to survey for the widespread native species, add up the score.   Add 1 bonus point if the pond has four species, and 2 bonus points if there are all five species.   Add another two points if natterjack toads are present.   This method should only be used for natural populations (ie *you shouldn't use data for species that are known to be non-native, eg marsh frog*).   Where several ponds lie close together use the highest counts for each species to produce a score for the site.   This is based on a method devised by the former Nature Conservancy Council (now English Nature).

Smooth and palmate newts

Timing: March to May when both species will be in the water.

Method: Use a net during the day or count early in the night using a torch. Netting is best carried out with a strong net (mesh 2.5 mm in diameter) at the edges of the riverine or floodplain waterbody where there are stands of emergent vegetation or beds of aquatic weeds. Count the numbers caught in 15 minutes on each stretch of 50 m or less (30 minutes for 50–100 m, etc).

Great crested newt

Timing: March to May when in the water.

These newts are best surveyed by torchlight at night or egg counts by day (although this only confirms presence). A licence is required to handle this species, therefore specialist advice should be sought from the statutory conservation agencies, who issue these licences.

2.8.3 Reptiles

There is no accepted 'standard' methodology for surveying reptile populations, as there is for amphibians. Estimating population size is difficult and survey is usually directed towards determining presence or absence. However, counts can be used to give an indication of the relative importance of a site and to monitor how populations change between years. Reptiles are cold-blooded and therefore must gain warmth from their surroundings to maintain their body temperature. To do this reptiles bask in sunny spots in order to absorb warmth. Look in likely basking areas; gaps between tussocky vegetation, at the edge of bushes or, for lizards, on logs. Reptiles can also get too hot and may be difficult to observe when the weather gets too warm. This sort of searching is unlikely to reveal even one-third of the animals on a site, even in good weather conditions and with experienced observers.

Survey methodology
Small sheets of tin laid on the ground where they can be warmed by the sun will attract reptiles, especially snakes and slow worms, which bask under them. Once the animals are warm enough they will move away, and they are unlikely to be under the sheets in hot sun. The best times to check the sheets will be when the temperature beneath them is in the high 20s to low 30s degrees Centigrade. Suitable times are late morning or early evening in May; particularly in sunny, hazy, warm conditions which follow a period of wet, cooler weather.

The above technique is unlikely to permit quantitative assessment of populations but, if repeated yearly, will allow any trends in populations to be identified.

Key References
Arnold, E N and Burton, J A (1978) *A Field Guide to the Reptiles and Amphibians of Britain and Europe.* Collins, London.

2.9 Invertebrate Survey

2.9.1   Introduction
    — Why use invertebrates?

2.9.2   Objectives, recommendations and procedures for invertebrate
    surveying
    — How often to sample and in how much detail

2.9.3   Sampling techniques

2.9.4   Use of invertebrate data in score systems

2.9.5   Summary

2.9.1 Introduction

Invertebrate surveys are carried out for four main reasons: basic scientific research, conservation assessment, impact assessment and biological monitoring. The methodologies employed change to reflect objectives and cost constraints.

Invertebrate surveys are used to measure the possible impacts of, for example, bridge construction or pipeline crossings on the river fauna. To be most useful at least three surveys should be undertaken; before, during and after the construction. Sometimes, in the case of a pollution incident, it may only be possible to assess the impact after the event by reference to unaffected stretches upstream of a similar physical nature.

Biological river monitoring is carried out throughout the UK on a regular basis. Such surveys provide a general indication of the state of the rivers.

Why use invertebrates?

Invertebrate communities are particularly sensitive to changes in habitat and the presence of organic pollution. Invertebrates differ in their tolerance to organic pollution (Figure 1). Polluted sites generally contain fewer species, restricted to more tolerant groups. Invertebrate communities need time to establish a population so their existence implies that previous conditions have been suitable. Thus they act as continuous monitors of the physical and chemical conditions in a river, indicating both recent and past variations in habitat and water quality. The advantages of using invertebrates for pollution monitoring, many of which are also applicable to assessing the impact of channel works, are shown in Table 1 (Hellawell, 1977).

unpolluted   **polluted**

increasingly tolerant

Stonefly nymphs   Mayfly nymphs   Caddis larvae   *Gammarus pulex*   *Asellus aquaticus*   Chironomid larvae   Worms

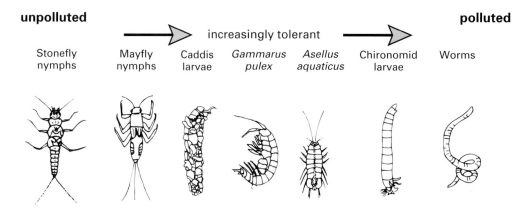

Figure 1
Differences in pollution tolerance of different invertebrate groups.

Table 1: Advantages of invertebrates in pollution monitoring

- Wide diversity and abundance in almost all freshwater habitats.

- Relatively sedentary means that the occurrence of most taxa can be related to the conditions at the place of capture.

- Life cycle of the many species is longer than six months and provides an overview of prevailing, not just immediate, conditions; they therefore reflect a wide range of environmental stresses.

- Qualitative sampling to family level is relatively simple and inexpensive, provides good information on water quality status but has major limitations for conservation assessment.

2.9.2 Objectives, recommendations and procedures for invertebrate surveying

Objectives differ from survey to survey, but the basic requirement for raw data for analysis is the same. Information is needed on the types and numbers of invertebrates in particular areas of the river. These data may subsequently be used to:

- describe the environmental quality of the site;
- determining environmental impacts, eg pollution/abstraction;
- identify habitat preferences of fauna;
- provide information for a database which will be useful to water managers in the future when assessing wildlife resources, potential impacts and enhancement opportunities.

It is important to have the aims of a project clearly defined, together with an appreciation of the need for and ultimate use of the data. The following questions should be addressed before starting any invertebrate survey programme:

- *Can the invertebrate survey be integrated with other survey work?* It is prudent to attempt to integrate invertebrate survey with the activities of other survey teams, eg water quality, so that unnecessary duplication of effort is avoided. Integration also permits more comprehensive reporting with a wider perspective.

- *Is the survey a 'one-off' or will it be the start of a sampling programme lasting many years? What are the financial constraints?* Long-term sampling programmes can be expensive, especially if invertebrate survey to species level is required. Family-level identification is a cheaper alternative, which will still provide a means of monitoring. The value of long-term data sets cannot be overemphasised because only they can indicate the process of change and natural variation which is essential to the understanding of the river ecosystem.

- *How will the results be expressed and to whom will they be directed?* When analysing the results of the survey it should be clear to whom, and where, the report or recommendations are to be directed. Long lists of scientific names are unhelpful to engineers and planners without biological background. Brief presentations with summary statistics, eg species richness in relation to habitat types, identification of rare species or unusual communities, and clear, succinct recommendations are preferred by 'river managers' to detailed and extensive texts. The complete data set for a survey must, of course, be retained for future reference.

- *Is invertebrate survey information available from any other sources?* Surveys are carried out for a number of purposes by a wide range of bodies. This means that in addition to the databases held by IFE, government ministries and departments, statutory conservation agencies, the NRA, SRPBs and DoE NI, many other organisations will hold data on streams and rivers. Examples are universities, natural history societies (both local and national), environmental organisations (eg Greenpeace), county councils, museums and water companies. Often fairly comprehensive databases are collected by suppliers of power, and international construction and engineering firms.

The objective of the invertebrate survey will determine whether *qualitative* or *quantitative* sampling is undertaken. Qualitative sampling is where only a species list is produced, whereas quantitative sampling is where the numbers of individuals of different species are counted. These can be expressed as numbers per unit area of riverbed surface.

Qualitative samples can provide, relatively cheaply, sufficient data for biological assessment, especially for pollution monitoring. However, more subtle impacts arising from reduced flows or shading often require quantitative data to identify the degree of the impact and determine whether species are being lost.

Assessments of site quality primarily using qualitative data can be determined using the River Invertebrate Prediction and Classification System (RIVPACS). This technique uses the environmental attributes of a site to predict the macroinvertebrate community to be expected in the absence of environmental stress, eg pollution. This 'target' community can then be compared with the observed fauna to establish impacts on the site (Wright *et al.*, 1991). In the survey area all micro-habitats are sampled in proportion to their occurrence and bulked together to form a sample.

More specialised studies on species–habitat relationships, in contrast, require the separation of all microhabitats within a river reach, preferably using quantitative sampling (Smith *et al.* 1991). Wright *et al.* (1991)), in another habitat-based study, have concentrated their effort on associating invertebrate communities with particular aquatic plants (macrophytes) with a view to providing guidelines for the management of aquatic vegetation in rivers.

How often to sample and in how much detail?

With greater frequency of sampling, more information becomes available about subtle changes in relation to habitat requirements, seasonal differences and annual population fluctuations. Replication of samples to provide a measure of the variability of the results is desirable for accurate analyses but it is frequently the first casualty of cost-cutting. In one-off surveys replication may

be important but regular surveys of sites may offset the need.

Some invertebrates are seasonally abundant, eg mayflies, and it is essential for comprehensive surveys that sampling is carried out sufficiently often throughout the season to ensure capture of these transient species. Another point in connection with seasonality is the natural variation in numbers of taxa in the absence of any man-induced stress detectable by survey. For example, in a set of samples

(i)

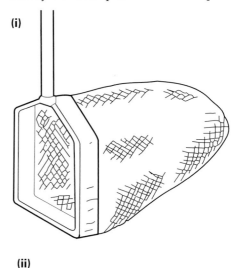

(ii)

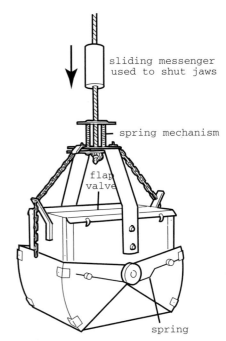

Figure 2
Invertebrate sampling equipment:
(i) hand net; (ii) Eckman grab.
Source: Hellawell (1989)

Table 2: Taxonomic classification of the club-tailed dragonfly

Order	Odonata (all British Dragonflies)
Sub-order	Anisoptera (comprises five British families)
Family	Gomphidae (comprises two British species)
Species	*Gomphus vulgatissimus* (Club-tailed dragonfly)

taken monthly over a year in the R Otter, Devon, at a site unaffected by pollution, the mean number of families of invertebrates taken in each month was 33, but actual numbers ranged from 29–40. It is important, therefore, to take account of this inherent variability before drawing too many conclusions.

The taxonomic level of identification to which samples are taken is another important consideration. Invertebrates can be categorised and hence identified to different levels. Table 2 illustrates this with reference to the club-tailed dragonfly. Identification to species level is time-consuming, expensive, and involves a high level of expertise. The information content of the sample is however considerably increased. Species data are essential to determine the distribution of 'rarities' but costs may be reduced by concentrating on particular 'indicator' species known to be sensitive to change. For many purposes, including flood defence works, identification to family level or to a subset of families may provide sufficient information initially to assess environmental quality.

Another common tendency is for survey work to be restricted to the supposed main area of impact. However, there are many cases where the effects of stress can be detected for long distances downstream. Construction of reservoirs is known to affect the whole length of a river (Petts, 1980), and pollution effects will extend far beyond the point of entry of the effluent (Guiver, 1976; Hynes, 1960). These are factors which must be taken into account when planning surveys. Sampling programmes should include all areas likely to be affected by proposed changes; for example surveys undertaken in relation to flood defence works should be taken at, above and below the proposed working area.

There is also the longer term to consider. Most impact-related surveys are carried out within a calendar year but it may be important to continue into succeeding years to follow the process of recovery or change. Better management decisions in the future would be facilitated by such a strategy. For example, in the R Stour (Kent), only 25 families were recorded in 1987 following dredging and clearance of marginal vegetation: this was below the RIVPACS predictions for a river of that type. However, later surveys between 1988 and 1990 showed recovery (30 and 29 in 1988 and 1989) and then a further reduction to 27 families in 1990. Without these follow-up surveys an erroneous conclusion of serious impact would have been drawn.

2.9.3 Sampling techniques

The range of techniques for invertebrate sampling is wide and a full description of them is beyond the scope of this section. Detailed accounts of the options available for biological surveillance and sampling methods are given in Hellawell (1978 and 1986). A summary is presented in Table 3. Different sampling techniques may be selected if specific invertebrates are of interest. Any of the methods may be used to assess impacts of flood defence works but it is important to use a standard method. Because invertebrates are caught more easily by one method or another, it is always vital to standardise methodologies for any monitoring.

The most commonly used method of obtaining qualitative information in rivers of wadeable depth is the kick sweep sample (Armitage *et al.*, 1974; Furse *et al.*, 1981) (Figure 2(i)). This involves disturbing the substrate and, where there is sufficient current, allowing this to carry organisms downstream into a net held at right angles to the flow. Where current velocities are low, the net is swept back and forth over the disturbed substrate. If the kicking effort is kept constant it is possible to obtain comparable samples with an estimate of the relative abundance. Armitage *et al.* (1974) have shown that, when sampling effort is concentrated in one spot it is

Table 3: Recommended methods for sampling in shallow water (quantitative methods are also applicable for qualitative surveys)

FLOW	SUBSTRATE TYPE	QUALITATIVE SURVEYS	QUANTITATIVE SURVEYS
Swift	Boulders, large stones	Lifting stones upstream of hand net	Box or Surber sampler - where this can be located correctly
Moderate	Gravel	Artificial substrates Kicking and hand net	Box or Surber sampler Air-lift if depth adequate
Slow	Gravel – sand	Shovel samplers, Grabs Dredges	Cylinder samplers Grabs, dredges Air-lift if depth adequate
Very slow or static	Sand or mud	Shovel samplers, Grabs Dredges	Core samplers Air-lift if depth adequate

possible to provide approximate quantitative values per unit area. Kick sweep sampling was the chosen method of sampling used in the 1990 National River Quality Surveys.

In deep water use of dredges may be more appropriate. These methods will provide information on taxa present and also give an indication of their relative numbers; if more accurate data are required, quantitative samplers must be used. The type chosen will depend on the substrate, ranging from dredges and grabs (Figure 2(ii)) for use in coarse deposits to corers for sampling fine gravels, sandy and silty mud. In rapidly running water, box samplers, which isolate an area of stream bottom, can be used effectively.

2.9.4 Use of invertebrate data in score systems

The ease of sampling and their response to pollution makes invertebrates natural indicators of water quality and this has led to the development of numerous indices. The most recent, nationally-used index is the Biological Monitoring Working Party (BMWP) score system (National Water Council, 1981). All score and index systems are based on the varying degrees of tolerance shown by species and/or families to pollution (usually organic). Thus sensitive taxa are given high scores and tolerant taxa low scores (see Table 4). The sum of the scores of individual families recorded at a site constitutes the 'BMWP score'. Although the BMWP score does not have an upper defined limit, values over 200 are rare. Low scores being indicative of poorer water quality and high scores of good water quality. If the BMWP score is divided by the number of individual families recorded, the average pollution tolerance of the taxa (ASPT) is indicated.

Scores such as ASPT and BMWP provide a convenient way of summarising large quantities of data. However, all score systems possess two basic flaws:

Table 4: The amended DoE/NWC 'Biological Monitoring Working Party' score system

GROUP	FAMILIES	SCORE
Mayflies	Siphlonuridae, Heptageniidae, Leptophlebiidae, Ephemerellidae, Potamanthidae, Ephemeridae	10
Stoneflies	Taeniopterygidae, Leuctridae, Capniidae, Perlodidae, Perlidae, Chloroperlidae	10
River bug	Aphelocheiridae	10
Caddis	Phryganeidae, Molannidae, Beraeidae, Odontoceridae, Leptoceridae, Goeridae, Lepidostomatidae, Brachycentridae, Sericostomatidae	10
Crayfish	Astacidae	8
Dragonflies	Lestidae, Agriidae, Gomphidae, Cordulegasteridae, Aeshnidae, Corduliidae, Libellulidae	8
Mayflies	Caenidae	7
Stoneflies	Nemouridae	7
Caddis	Rhyacophilidae, Polycontropodidae, Limnephilidae	7
Snails	Neritidae, Viviparidae, Ancylidae	6
Caddis	Hydroptilidae	6
Mussels	Unionidae	6
Shrimps	Corophiidae, Gammaridae	6
Dragonflies	Platycnemididae, Coenagriidae	6
Bugs	Mesoveliidae, Hydrometridae, Gerridae, Nepidae, Naucoridae, Notonectidae, Pleidae, Corixidae	5
Beetles	Haliplidae, Hygrobiidae, Dytiscidae, Gyrinidae, Hydrophilidae, Clambidae, Helodidae, Dryopidae, Elmidae, Chrysomelidae, Curculionidae	5
Caddis	Hydropsychidae	5
Craneflies/ Blackflies	Tipulidae, Simuliidae	5
Flatworms	Planariidae, Dendrocoelidae	5
Mayflies	Baetidae	4
Alderflies	Sialidae	4
Leeches	Piscicolidae	4
Snails	Valvatidae, Hydrobiidae, Lymnaeidae, Physidae, Planorbidae	3
Cockles	Sphaeriidae	3
Leeches	Glossiphoniidae, Hirudidae, Erpobdellidae	3
Hog louse	Asellidae	3
Midges	Chironomidae	2
Worms	Oligochaeta (whole class)	1

- They set the same target for all sites despite the fact that different types of unpolluted stream, eg lowland clay v upland gravel-bed rivers, have different natural scores.

- The results are effort dependent (Armitage *et al.*, 1983) as increased sampling effort biases results due to the greater number of species and families caught and the higher index value

Table 5: Examples of environmental variables used in RIVPACS predictions

Water width (m)
Water depth (cm)
Altitude (m)
Distance from source (km)
Substratum composition
Discharge
Slope
Alkalinity(mgl^{-1}CaCo$_3$)

achieved.

BMWP scores have been used since 1980 in the national River Quality Survey, but only in the 1990 survey was it used alongside RIVPACS. Prior to RIVPACS, BNWP scores were rarely useful in assessing how far the faunal communities at a site deviated from the pristine state, because there was no ready standard for comparison. Through the RIVPACS methodology this is now available, because invertebrate data and environmental data are combined (Table 5). Several taxonomic options are available and predictions can be made for single seasons or combinations of seasons. These include:

- families (qualitative)
- BMWP families (qualitative)
- species (qualitative).

The options can be applied according to the quality of the field data. For example, if only a limited amount of taxonomic expertise is available, data can be collected at family level and family option of RIVPACS used for analysis. The 'predicted' family lists can then be compared with the observed lists. Similarly, a species option is provided where in-depth surveys are undertaken. The options provide a means of comparing like with like and increases the flexibility of the system.

Data from RIVPACS can be used to predict biotic indices for most stretches of river. For example, at a hypothetical site A, environmental variables fed into the system would provide a predicted BMWP score. This would be the expected value at this site if it were not 'stressed' and hence could be regarded as a river quality objective. Recent developments of the system allow 95% confidence limits to be associated with the predicted value, thus enabling a range of expected BMWP scores to be produced. If the observed score is divided by the predicted score, an Environmental Quality Index (EQI) is obtained. This ratio provides a measure of the status of the site. Values approaching 1.0 suggest that the invertebrate community is not under stress.

The range of options offered by RIVPACS for assessing the quality of a site are shown in Table 6.

RIVPACS has been used to investigate the effects of river regulation (Armitage *et al.* 1987), organic pollution (Armitage *et al.*, 1990) and heavy metal pollution and physical disturbance (Armitage *et al.* 1992). The system is currently being used by the NRA in national surveys. No correlations between RIVPACS results and those from

Table 6: The range of options offered by RIVPACS for assessing the quality of a running water site from its macroinvertebrate fauna

1. Comparison of predicted and observed taxa. Where species or families are unexpectedly present or absent, clues as to the cause of the environmental stress may be provided.

2. The predicted and observed biotic parameters, BMWP score, number of scoring taxa and ASPT can be compared with the predicted values that occur within an acceptable range for similar unpolluted sites.

3. The three parameters in (2) above can be used to provide an Environmental Quality Index (EQI).

4. The EQI values could be divided into a series of bands related to the chemical classification system. This may be useful for presenting nationwide statistics but the information loss associated with banding makes this unsuitable for specific river surveys.

2.9.5 Summary

databases for other faunal groups or
macrophytes are yet available.
As for all biological surveys, aims should
be clearly defined. For invertebrate surveys
cost implications are also very important.
Use of family-level data can be more than
adequate for routine monitoring but for
conservation assessment more expensive
species data are required.

Correct procedures will result in
invertebrate surveys that have a direct
application to the needs of river engineers,
resource managers and conservationists. In
addition, careful and detailed surveys will
contribute to the body of knowledge on
running waters and provide data that will
help in the maintenance of good
environmental quality in our rivers.

Key References

d'Aguilar, J, Dommanget, J-L, Prechac, R *A Field Guide to the Dragonflies of Britain, Europe and North Africa*. Collins, London.

Ball, I R and Reynoldson, T B (1981) *British Planarians. Synopses of the British Fauna* (New Series) No 19. Cambridge University Press.

Croft, P S (1986) A Key to the Major Groups of British Freshwater Invertebrates. *Field Studies* 6:531–579

Friday, L E (1988) A Key to the Adults of British Water Beetles *Field Studies* 7:1–151

Hellawell, J M (1978) *Biological surveillance of rivers–a biological monitoring handbook*. Water Research Centre, Medmenham. 332pp.

Hellawell, J M (1989) *Biological indicators of freshwater pollution and environmental management*. Elsevier Applied Science. London and New York. 546pp.

HMSO (1978) *Methods of Biological Sampling: Handnet Sampling of Aquatic Benthic Macroinvertebrates 1978*.

HMSO (1980) *Quantitative Samplers for Benthic Macroinvertebrates in Shallow Flowing Waters 1980*.

HMSO (1983) *Methods of Biological Sampling: Sampling of Benthic Macroinvertebrates in Deep Rivers 1983*.

Macan, T T (1959) *A Guide to Freshwater Invertebrate Animals*. Longman.

Miller, P L *Dragonflies*. Naturalists Handbooks 7, Cambridge University Press.

Identification Guides

Institute of Freshwater Ecology publication Number

13. *A Key to the British Fresh- and Brackish-water Gastropods*, by T T Macan, 4th ed., 1977.
16. *A Revised Key to the British Water Bugs (Hemiptera-Heteroptera)*, by T T Macan, 2nd ed., 1965. (Reprinted 1976).
17. *A Key to the Adults and Nymphs of the British Stoneflies (Plecoptera)*, by H B N Hynes, 3rd ed., 1977. (Reprinted 1984).
20. *A Key to the Nymphs of British Ephemeroptera*, by T T Macan, 3rd ed., 1979.
22. *A Guide for the identification of British aquatic Oligochaeta*, by R O Brinkhurst, (1963).
23. *A Key to the British Species of Freshwater Triclads (Turbellaria, Paludicola)*, by T B Reynoldson, (1978)
24. *A Key to the British Species of Simuliidae (Diptera) in the larval, pupal and adult stages*, by L Davies (1968)
31. *A Key to the Larvae, Pupae and Adults of the British Dixidae (Diptera)*, by R H L Disney, 1975.
35. *A Key to the Larvae and Adults of British Freshwater Megaloptera and Neuroptera*, by J M Elliott, 1977.
37. *A Key to the Adult Males of the British Chironomidae (Diptera)*, by L C V Pinder, 1978.
40. *A Key to the British Freshwater Leeches*, by J M Elliott and K H Mann, 1979.
43. *Caseless Caddis Larvae of the British Isles*, by J M Edington and A C Hildrew, 1981.
45. *A Key to the Larvae of the British Orthocladiinae (Chironomidae)*, by P S Cranston, 1982.
47. *A Key to the Adults of the British Ephemeroptera*, by J M Elliott and U H Humpesch, 1983.
48. *Keys to the Adults, Male Hypopygia, Fourth-instar Larvae and Pupae of the British Mosquitoes (Culicidae), with notes on their Ecology and Medical Importance*, by P S Cranston, C D Ramsdale, K R Snow and G B White, 1987.
49. *Larvae of the British Ephemeroptera: A Key with Ecological Notes*, by J M Elliott, U H Humpesch and T T Macan, 1988.
50. *Adults of the British Aquatic Hemiptera Heteroptera: A Key with Ecological Notes*, by A A Savage, 1989.
51. *A Key to the Case-bearing Caddis Larvae of Britain and Ireland*, by I D Wallace, B Wallace and G N Philipson, 1990.

Part 3
MANAGEMENT PRACTICES TO BENEFIT WILDLIFE

Introduction

This Part of the handbook considers a range of engineering and vegetation management techniques that when undertaken in an environmentally sensitive manner will benefit and enhance wildlife.

Clearly, for the precise design of schemes, engineering expertise and reference to technical river engineering manuals are of paramount importance.

Part 3 provides a framework within which engineering and management options can be considered. The key message is that only techniques hydraulically and ecologically suitable for the site in question should be used. The tables below provide direction to the range of techniques highlighted in the text.

Table 1: In-channel river management techniques

ENGINEERING		VEGETATION (AQUATIC)			
		Control		Establishment	
	Page		Page		Page
● partial dredging	175	● cutting	239	● planting	247
● deepening	176	● desilting/dredging	240	● screening	250
● narrowing	177	● aquatic herbicides	241	● rare species	250
● shoal/island creation	180	● nutrient stripping	245	● bank protection	251
● pool/riffle creation	181	● shading	245	● buffer strips	252
● deflectors	218	● straw bales (algae)	246		
● weirs and sluices	225				
● on-line flood storage	230				

Table 2: Bankside/floodplain river management techniques

ENGINEERING		VEGETATION			
		Control		Establishment	
	Page		Page		Page
● retain/create margins	186	● grazing	256	● seeding	261
● backwaters and bays	189	● mowing/cutting	257	● sowing	262
● multi-stage channels	195	● herbicides	259	● nurse species	262
● bend reprofiling	202	● selective thinning	274	● turf transplants	264
● embankments	208	● working around trees	274	● trees and shrubs	281
● realignment/by-pass	212	● branch removal	276	● 'soft' revetments	286
● 'hard' revetments	218	● coppicing	277		
● off-line flood storage	230	● pollarding	278		

The use of professional judgement is essential to ensure that the techniques implemented are appropriate to the site concerned in both hydraulic and ecological terms.

3.1 River Management Techniques to Benefit Wildlife

3.1.1   Introduction and general principles

—Concepts for the selection of river management options

—Disposal of the by-products of management

—Access, choice of machinery and working bank

3.1.1 Introduction and general principles

Management of rivers is undertaken for a wide variety of purposes. The principal reasons have been primarily to maintain or improve land drainage and flood defence as well as maintaining conditions suitable for navigation. In recent decades works for visual amenity, fishery enhancement, improved geomorphic stability and wildlife conservation have all featured more prominently, and have led to a more integrated and holistic approach to river management, which this handbook endorses.

This prescriptive part of the handbook is divided into six sections, each dealing with common management practices undertaken on rivers. The six sections are:

3.2 In-channel Works – dredging, reprofiling, introduction of material to improve substrate diversity and bed stability, etc

3.3 Riverbank Works – resectioning, reprofiling to create marginal habitats, backwaters, etc

3.4 Structural Works – construction of weirs, revetments, floodbanks, flood storage areas and by-pass channels, etc

3.5 Aquatic Vegetation Control and Establishment

3.6 Management and Establishment of Bank and Floodbank Vegetation

3.7 Tree and Scrub Management and Establishment

Table 1 lists the principal activities and the locations at which they are undertaken.

The aim of this section is to highlight what environmental features need to be considered in major engineering and maintenance work which meet the needs of flood defence and other river users. This is achieved through an integrated, approach involving engineers, hydrologists, geomorphologists, landscape architects and specialists with knowledge of recreation, fisheries and wildlife conservation. It is not the intention of this handbook to cover the expertise required to undertake the many engineering aspects of river management. Extensive information on this subject is available and reference to technical engineering manuals is included in the bibliography.

Whenever river management is planned, there are often a range of options available to achieve the same objectives. Each of the following chapters gives the primary reasons why river management utilises the described techniques. Guidance is given on management works that minimise adverse impacts, and therefore benefit wildlife. Some management is undertaken solely for good flood defence reasons and has no benefit to or may even be detrimental to wildlife. Such practices are dealt with in little detail because their use is to be discouraged. Where ecological impacts of such works can be minimised or mitigated against, guidance is given. Wildlife interests are the prime consideration, although in the vast majority of cases public enjoyment of rivers will also benefit from the adoption of the 'best ecological practice' approach recommended.

This Part of the book makes little reference to the effects that different management techniques have on individual species. The effects of management activities are primarily related to changes to in-stream, bank and flood-plain habitats. Part 1 relates fauna and flora to their required habitats and describes how these vary on different river types. Part 2 describes survey techniques, and how these may be used to help determine the most appropriate option.

Concepts for the selection of river management options

All but minor management activities affect natural river processes; therefore, a thorough understanding of how changes are induced is vital. All new works need to

Table 1: Schedule of key engineering operations

ENGINEERING OPERATION	BASIC PURPOSE OF OPERATION	LOCATION OF OPERATION/PROFILES
1 Desilting / dredging	Retain capacity lower water level / table	
2 Regrading / dredging	Increase capacity lower water level / table	
3 Resectioning	Increase capacity / stabilize erosion	
4 Embanking	Contain floods away from natural floodplain	
5 Realignment	Increase capacity. Avoid costs in road building developments. Increase land for agriculture	
6 By–pass	Increase capacity	
7 Deflectors	Control bed form	
8 Revetments	Control bank form	
9 Weirs	Control water level / dissipate energy and reduce headward recession	
10 Sluices	Control water level / flow	
11 Storage	Control water flow	
12 Weed cutting	Maintain capacity and control water level	
13 Bank cutting	Reduce flow resistance, maintain capacity and enable inspection	
14 Tree mangement	Control destruction to flow. Maintain stability of trees and banks	

work towards keeping, or returning a river to, a more 'natural' regime, thereby reducing the need for future engineering. Where works are essential they are often best achieved through mimicking natural systems. More importantly, treatment of causes, not the symptoms, is likely to be both cost effective and more environmentally acceptable. These

principles apply equally whether engineering works for flood defence are the driving force, or whether ecological rehabilitation is the aim.

Another important principle is always to attempt to keep natural features intact. Although there are good examples of habitat rehabilitation, it remains to be proven that artificially created habitats are as good as those which have been destroyed. This principle is embodied in the many guidance manuals (a selection is listed in the bibliography) which have been produced to promote sensitive management practices.

Habitat retention, rehabilitation or creation when undertaking river management all require an understanding of river processes (Chapter 1.3). Plants and animals depend upon the way fluvial processes shape habitats. Determining how these may change according to which management approach is adopted requires measurement of the physical parameters summarised in Table 2 and discussed in Chapter 2.2. This is a vital task because more problems have arisen, or opportunities for enhancement been lost, through inadequate understanding of the physical processes involved than for any other reason. Some concepts that support both objectives of engineering function and habitat protection and enhancement are listed in Table 3.

An ancient mill site on the R Great Ouse near Huntingdon (Case Study 3.4(h)) demonstrates the importance of clearly identifying management options and the environmental potential of a site, at an early stage of design. Here a multitude of channels and structures have resulted in good habitat diversity within the river and floodplain, although a simple option of a single armoured channel with a lock and sluice could have functioned equally well in engineering terms. However, this would not have provided the environmental value that the site represents today.

Ford Brook (Case Study 3.1(a)) is an example where a design has been acclaimed as an environmental enhancement but was undertaken at a reduced cost from the original potentially damaging, design of a trapezoidal, armoured channel.

Table 2: Physical parameters measured when planning engineering works

- The level and gradient of the river valley or floodplain.
- The level and gradient of the river channel or bed (normally flatter than the floodplain due to meandering).
- The alignment of the river within its floodplain and location of significant physical features (normally based upon OS Maps).
- The location and level of significant soil types occurring in the riverbank and bed, eg clay, gravel, sand.
- Soil types and groundwater levels in any diversion routes contemplated (obtained via boreholes, piezometers and shallow inspection pits).
- The cross-section of the river channel and floodplain at frequent intervals.
- The range of flows that prevail in the channel and corresponding water levels and velocities.

Table 3: Basic concepts for integrating engineering and wildlife needs

● Energy	The primary hydraulic forces that exists to varying degrees in all streams. Use these forces creatively; do not ignore them. They are very significant in Piedmont streams.
● Straight channels	Rarely exist in nature, often have high energy and may erode and meander. Geometric repetition is undesirable; lack of space may demand unnatural alignments and profiles but this leads to reduced habitat variety.
● Habitat	Use works as an opportunity to protect, rehabilitate and create wildlife habitat.
● Space	Maximum environmental gain usually demands maximum space. Do not stint on space, a natural river is "inefficient" in spatial terms when compared to a clean, trapezoidal channel; create room.
● Simulate	Look at the river, protect or simulate what is good in what you see and seek to modify degraded sections by copying good sections. Work with indigenous plants and materials.
● Horizons and scope	Consider extremes. What happens in drought and flood? Do not overlook conditions that will

Disposal of the by-products of management

Many river management activities produce material that has to be removed from site or be 'lost' within the area of the works. Dredging, resectioning, construction works, weed control, bank mowing and tree management may yield material that is potentially damaging to wildlife unless it is disposed of sensitively. However, there are many examples where by-products of management can be utilised for environmental gain, eg river dredgings to supply vegetation for planting schemes and brush used in spiling and faggotting. Safe disposal, or effective utilisation, of the by-products of river management works is an important environmental consideration.

All too commonly spoil is placed directly on the top of riverbanks which can result in rank vegetation displacing the natural communities of riverbanks. Another damaging practice for wildlife is filling up 'low spots' in adjacent fields, often these contain important plants and invertebrates and can be breeding or feeding areas for amphibians and many birds.

It is important, therefore, that any works that create spoil dispose of the material appropriately. Table 4 lists major points to be considered. Whatever method is selected, spoil should be kept well clear of the riverbank and margins, utilising the full reach of the excavator. Wherever sensitive or ancient habitats are present within this zone, no spoil should be spread over them because disturbance and enrichment is likely to destroy them. If in doubt, consult conservation staff for advice.

Access, choice of machinery and working bank

The choice of access routes and selection of excavators for river works can have a significant bearing on the environmental success of a scheme. Choice of access will depend upon the preferred bank for working. This is influenced by the amount of tree and other vegetation cover; where

Table 4: Considerations for spoil disposal

- Does the spoil contain plants which could be utilized for recolonisation on the affected river or elsewhere? (Chapter 3.5)
- Can it be used? (eg sand and gravel on access roads, or for flood embankments)
- Can it be used for developing in-stream habitat features; eg gravel for riffles, rock for weirs and silt for berms?
- Can it be ploughed into arable fields rather than spread on meadows or pasture?
- Would the overall scheme benefit by haulage off site?
- Has the pre-works planning process identified good areas for disposal and areas which must be avoided?
- Is reinstatement of topsoil over any spread spoil needed or can these areas be prepared and seeded with low maintenance herb-rich mixes? (Chapter 3.6)

spoil can be disposed of, and breeding areas for animals. Pre-work river corridor surveys assist in identifying the ecological sensitivity of banks and adjacent land with respect to spoil disposal and machine routing. For example, the use of established tracks, even if less convenient, is preferable to gaining access through valuable meadowland or woods.

Where access is a problem due to environmental sensitivity, choice of machinery becomes important. Depending on circumstances a smaller or larger machine may eliminate the problem and do the same job at no extra cost. The viability of using dredgers and other machinery on floating platforms should be examined in slow-flowing rivers. Some small machines will work well by tracking along the bed of shallow, firm-bedded rivers, with the practical working depth being about 300 mm. In-channel working can substantially reduce disturbance to riverside habitats, although spoil disposal requires more careful organisation. However, benefits to riverside habitats should be weighed against the potential impact upon the in-stream habitats, and the least damaging option taken.

Whatever the type of work, the approach of environmental assessment as outlined in the Environmental Procedures for Inland Flood Defence Works issued by MAFF (1993) should be adopted.

3.2 In-channel Engineering Works

3.2.1 Introduction

The presence of an excavator on a riverbank inevitably attracts the attention of anyone with an interest in rivers because it signifies that change is imminent. Some will see the excavator as a threat to their interests, whereas others will see it as a blessing, possibly long overdue. Whatever the viewpoint, the excavator is often the essential tool through which opportunities for environmental development can be realised. They are no longer the exclusive tools of drainage engineers but are employed to benefit environmental, angling and other recreational interests.

This chapter provides guidance on the integration of interests, by highlighting opportunities that can arise from in-channel works and suggesting techniques to achieve both ecological and engineering objectives. It concentrates on engineering activities that remove, redistribute or reinstate bed materials. For convenience, works that affect river margins are dealt with in Section 3.3.2.

Practices of in-channel excavation may be considered in three broad categories:

- Desilting/dredging. Work is restricted to the removal, or partial removal, of recently deposited sediments. Often referred to as *desilting* because silt is commonly the most troublesome sediment but also includes removal or redistribution of gravel.

- Regrading/dredging. The longitudinal profile, or gradient, of the riverbed is changed. Historically, this invariably meant deepening and widening to uniform dimensions but more recently the term *bed reprofiling* has been introduced, which implies the introduction of variations in water depth and velocity which benefit wildlife.

- Resectioning/reprofiling. This involves the excavation of material from either riverbank or bed (or in extreme cases both). It can be referred to as *bank reprofiling* when the objective is simply to change the shape of the bank rather than increase the size of the channel. Reprofiling can include narrowing as well as widening (Section 3.2.4).

A range of channel and bank excavation techniques are practised, some of which can assist with environmental rehabilitation whereas others are more likely to affect habitats adversely (Table 1). Whatever type of excavation is undertaken, certain general principles apply. The more important aspects pertaining to physical factors are listed in Table 2.

Suction dredging is an alternative to excavation from the bank. It will normally require a lagoon for dewatering of spoil but this can be located well away from the river in areas of low ecological value. For example, this was used on the R Blackwater in N Ireland, where burying large amounts of spoil on the banks within Caledon Estate was unacceptable.

Most maintenance dredging should be regarded as 'partial dredging' as it is now considered bad practice to dredge continuous lengths of river from bank to bank (Plate 1). Figure 1 (i, ii and iii) illustrates a range of options for the retention of plants during dredging works. Occasionally both the channel and banks require desilting. Even in such instances, selective retention of individual clumps or strips of plants can be achieved. This also applies to small watercourses (Plates 2 and 3).

**Plate 1
The unacceptable consequences of continuous dredging**

Nigel Holmes

Table 1: Schedule of channel excavation techniques

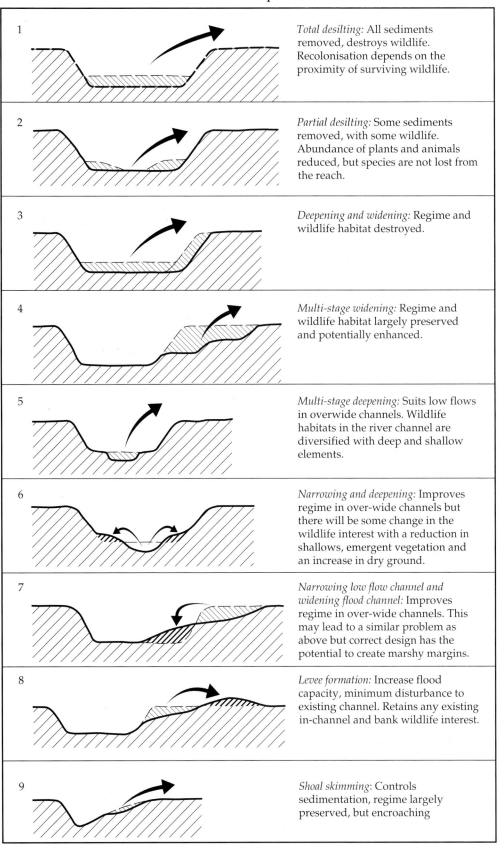

1	*Total desilting:* All sediments removed, destroys wildlife. Recolonisation depends on the proximity of surviving wildlife.
2	*Partial desilting:* Some sediments removed, with some wildlife. Abundance of plants and animals reduced, but species are not lost from the reach.
3	*Deepening and widening:* Regime and wildlife habitat destroyed.
4	*Multi-stage widening:* Regime and wildlife habitat largely preserved and potentially enhanced.
5	*Multi-stage deepening:* Suits low flows in overwide channels. Wildlife habitats in the river channel are diversified with deep and shallow elements.
6	*Narrowing and deepening:* Improves regime in over-wide channels but there will be some change in the wildlife interest with a reduction in shallows, emergent vegetation and an increase in dry ground.
7	*Narrowing low flow channel and widening flood channel:* Improves regime in over-wide channels. This may lead to a similar problem as above but correct design has the potential to create marshy margins.
8	*Levee formation:* Increase flood capacity, minimum disturbance to existing channel. Retains any existing in-channel and bank wildlife interest.
9	*Shoal skimming:* Controls sedimentation, regime largely preserved, but encroaching

Note: Combinations of the above operations may generally be found to comprise 'best practice' for application to any specific dredging scheme.
eg 9 +6 for Piedmontal ensures all dredgings re-distributed in river.

(i)

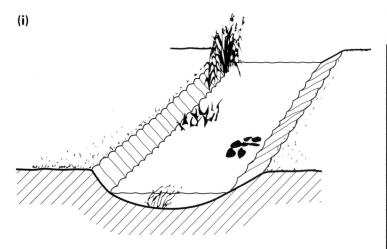

(ii)

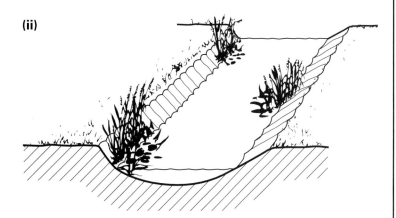

(iii)

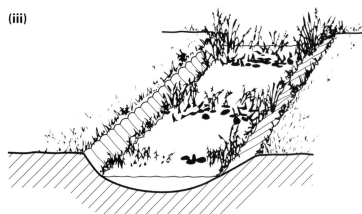

Figure 1
Retention of vegetation stands when undertaking major dredging works. (i) Individual species left where surveys indicate. (ii) Clumps or communities left either randomly or because of species assemblages. (iii) Random strip across channel and along margins; may produce series of small pools to increase interest. Source: Brandon (1989)

Table 2: General principles for dredging and resectioning works

- Obtain conservation advice relating to the site.
- Keep all excavation to a minimum unless system uniform and degraded.
- Leave banks untouched wherever possible, sparing bankside vegetation unless impoverished by previous works.
- Leave the channel as varied as possible.
- Comply with recommendations from Fishery/Biology/Habitat Surveys where possible.
- Work from one bank to minimise overall disturbance and retain areas to act as a basis for recolonisation.
- Careful spoil disposal avoiding transport over, and deposition on, sensitive areas.
- Design to include environmental enhancement features.
- Consider the whole riverine environment including adjacent land.
- Leave all mature trees and encourage self-set replacements.
- If tree management is required for access, pollard and coppice in keeping with the species and landscape.
- Preserve or reinstate natural channel forms like pools and riffles.
- Avoid dredging through gravel seams. This may drain nearby wetlands.
- Work from downstream up so that plants and animals have a chance to recolonise.
- Consider the effects both upstream and downstream of the works.
- Work at the appropriate time of the year.
- Consider the landscape.
- Use suitable machinery to minimise damage to the river corridor.
- Get necessary machinery to riverbank through land of low ecological interest.

recovery of habitat previously lost as a result of environmentally insensitive management practices.

The objective of removing, replacing or redistributing materials should be to create self-cleansing flow regimes which sustain or create habitats and minimise long-term commitments to sediment removal or vegetation control. A balanced hydraulic regime of sediment transport and deposition will provide suitable habitats for wildlife and reduce future maintenance requirements. Even if the need to desilt cannot be totally eliminated, eg in artificial drains, the frequency and extent can often be reduced.

River management involving in-channel works is not confined to removal or redistribution of sediments. Increasingly, rehabilitation work requires importing material into river channels to re-establish lost substrates and to encourage 'natural'

Judith Crompton

Judith Crompton

**Plate 2 (left)
Partial dredging
of one side of a
channel to
increase
conveyance, yet
retaining
vegetation.**

**Plate 3 (right)
The same
channel, one year
later, effectively
carrying flood
waters with
recolonisation of
the partially
dredged bank.**

3.2.2 Partial dredging

Partial dredging can take the form of selective removal of shoals, 'high spots' in the bed, and other obstructions. It can also include creating a deeper channel in one part of the bed. This technique is particularly desirable where elements of the in-channel vegetation are to be retained or marginal plants need to be left in situ. It is important that, as a consequence of lowering part of the bed, the water level is not lowered excessively to the detriment of the remaining marginal vegetation.

**Case Studies:
R Lyde (3.2(a)),
R Blackwater at
Eversley Cross
(3.2(b))**

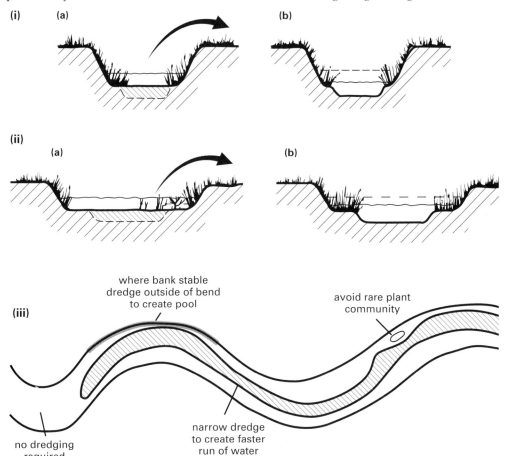

**Figure 2
Partial dredging. (i) Maintaining thin margins untouched in narrow watercourse.
(ii) Creation of wide margins on wider rivers. (iii) Plan-form illustrates the preferred
practice of varying widths dredged, in order to retain habitat and accommodate
natural river processes. Adapted from Brandon (1989)**

Table 3: Advantages and disadvantages of partial dredging

ADVANTAGES
- Minimum channel disturbance
- .Cheaper and quicker than 'full' dredging
- Less spoil to dispose of
- Can create greater self-cleansing velocities
- May locally lower water levels where these are required without taking river out of regime
- Naturally leads to habitat diversity while maintaining parts of existing environment intact

DISADVANTAGES
- Not necessarily suitable if overall flood capacity is important
- Perception that the job is not 'complete', so requires careful explanation and negotiating skills
- Needs detailed plans and supervision
- Records need to be kept for the next dredge so that the same features are retained and any changes noted and understood.

Figure 2 (i, ii and iii) illustrates the concept of partial dredging where reinstatement of previous capacity or increased capacity is required. However, partial dredging can take many forms, ranging from simple removal of a particular silt or gravel accumulation to a continuous mid-channel excavation along a long length of river. Retain as much undisturbed bed as possible where the channel has high wildlife interest. Scope for manipulation is

greater if rehabilitation of a degraded site is required.

In wide channels that suffer from excessive weed growth, excavation of a deep 'central' section leaving shallower edges may be helpful. In these cases, it is important that the centre of the channel is deep enough, with sufficient velocity, to prevent rapid recolonisation of weeds. The R Blackwater at Eversley Cross (Case Study 3.2(b)) illustrates the approach and Table 3 lists a number of advantages and disadvantages of the technique.

Experience has shown that a good plan has to be drawn up and followed carefully. It is necessary to explain clearly to all involved the objective so that the work is carried out sensitively.

Partial dredging can increase habitat diversity and reduce management of emergent reeds if undertaken in conjunction with river narrowing. This is particularly appropriate where rivers suffer from exacerbated low flows or have been over-widened in the past. The R Lyde (Case Study 3.2(a)) illustrates the technique and the benefits to wildlife and cost effective flood-defence management.

3.2.3 Deepening channels

Deepening whole stretches of river, with or without some widening, is very rarely undertaken except where flood relief schemes require a large increase in flow

Table 4: Important principles for deepening (or widening) channels

- Create a non-uniform and asymmetric channel designed on good geomorphological principles, or mirror an existing good section of channel found elsewhere on the river.
- Widen one bank only, alternating sides to accentuate sinuosity to maintain instream diversity.
- Vary bank slopes to give habitat diversity ranging from steep cliffs to long shallow slopes.
- Design for islands and shoals in what will be an 'oversized' channel.
- Design for tree growth at water's edge to avoid the need for subsequent removal of those that grow naturally.
- Always consider medium and low discharges so that design caters for stable average conditions as well as flood conveyance.

conveyance. From an ecological perspective this is undesirable unless it can be achieved while retaining habitats, and flora and fauna of interest within the existing channel. Even if safeguards can be built into the scheme, deepened channels may change the natural fluvial processes, increase siltation and destroy the hydrological connectivity of river and floodplain. Alternatives such as by-pass channels and multi-stage channels (a form of widening but leaving the bed width unchanged, Section 3.3.4) should be considered.

Where deepening and/or widening is essential, the principles in Table 4 should be pursued. Selection of engineering options should include consideration of whether deepening could be avoided and, if adjacent banks were of minimal wildlife interest, whether channel capacity could be increased be widening.

In rural areas there are often opportunities to adopt sensitive widening techniques using the principles in Table 4. Such an approach may greatly enhance an impoverished river but degrade a good one. In urban areas channel deepening may be the only option because of constraints of space, in which case, in-stream habitat enhancements are essential. These can take the form of habitat creation through importing substrates (R Ock, Case Study 3.2(e)), or constructing vegetated ledges which form edge habitat and create narrow, self-cleansing, low-flow channels (R Pinn, Case Study 3.5(j) and Ford Brook, Case Study 3.5(c)).

When creating ledges, the level of the soil surface to normal water level is crucial (Figure 3 (i) and (ii)). In the R Pinn scheme ledges were set 0.4 m above normal water level and these have tended to dry out and encourage undesirable, rank vegetation. By contrast the ledge on the Ford Brook scheme was set at a lower level and is regularly inundated.

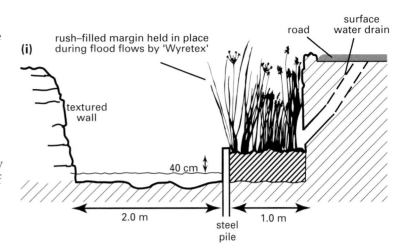

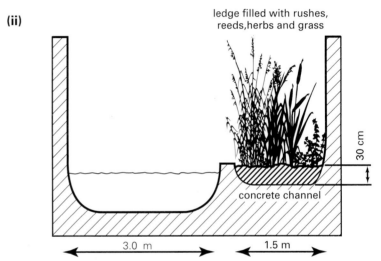

Figure 3
Edge enhancements in deepened/widened streams.
(i) R Pinn flood alleviation scheme. A wet ledge is created in a small, flashy urban watercourse. The ledge created on the inside of the sheet pile (used for bank strengthening purposes) appears to be situated 'too high' above the normal flow level, but it is kept wet by use of a surface water drain. The vegetation in the ledge not only provides bank habitat in an otherwise barren reach, but also functions as a silt trap and may potentially improve the quality of the surface water discharge. (See also Case Study 3.5 (j)).
(ii) Ford Brook flood alleviation scheme. Ledge creation within the constraints of an urban concrete channel. The ledge which forms the second stage of the flood channel is regularly innundated and remains wet (see also Case Study 3.5 (c)).

3.2.4   Narrowing channels

Many river channels in Britain are too wide to enable normal fluvial processes (which transport and deposit sediments) to maintain a variety of in-channel and edge habitat features. Extensive re-sectioning in the past and reduction in summer flows caused by excessive groundwater abstraction can produce anything between deep wide silt traps to very wide, shallow, reaches with a trickle of a flow.

Engineering works that narrow these channels are often aimed at restoring self-

cleansing flows, which reduce long-term maintenance needs. The NRA Southern Region booklet, *A Guide to Bank Restoration and River Narrowing,* provides guidance on these aspects particularly in relation to chalk streams. The aim is to increase velocities locally within the existing channel without significantly raising critical levels upstream. In some rivers (Plate 4) this readjustment occurs naturally and consideration should be given to allowing this to continue and then

Case Studies:
The Dyke
(3.2(c)), R Dun
(3.2(d))

Plate 4
Natural
readjustment
resulting in
narrowing on the
R Piddle.

retaining the new form. When artificially narrowing with chalk ballast, care should be taken not to destroy existing marginal habitat. Work should preferably be undertaken in reaches with low habitat

interest. In areas with good marginal habitat, narrowing can still be achieved by the creation of in-channel islands (Section 3.2.5).

Figure 4 shows channel narrowing techniques for sluggish, over-widened rivers. Further improvements can be made by reinstating former pool and riffle formations. The same principle of narrowing can be applied to chalk streams suffering low flow problems. The technique is well illustrated on the R Dun at Hungerford, Case Study 3.2(d). On the R Dyke (Case Study 3.2(c)) this method was further developed to provide artificial habitats suitable for crayfish (Plate 5).

Several reaches of the R Coln and R Windrush have been narrowed in recent years. On the R Coln (Plate 6) water crowfoot and coarse gravel substrates had declined dramatically over a 10-year period as reeds and silt had become dominant. Fisheries and macro-invertebrate surveys also indicated major declines. A reach was narrowed in 1991/92 using limestone blocks, back-filled with soil excavated locally. By 1993 wetland plants had become well established on the new berm and the concentrated flow was resulting in both

Nigel Holmes

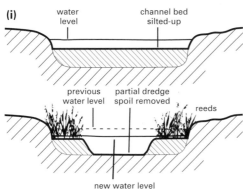

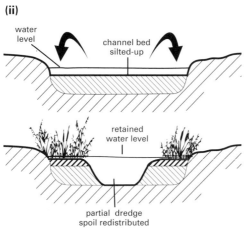

Figure 4
Channel narrowing for over-wide channels where retained water levels cause silt deposition. (i) Silt removed in central one-third to one-half of channel, enabling reeds to grow at edges and accrete silt. Central deep section has increased velocity and decreased deposition. R Stour, East Anglia 1986. (ii) Silt removal in central half of channel and deposited at edges to create low to medium flow channel, edge habitats, and increased velocities and decreased siltation. R Colne at Watford — 1990.

Plate 5
Results of channel narrowing on the R Dyke

Alistair Driver

Plate 6
River narrowing on the R Coln using limestone blocks. Excavation of the backfill used to narrow the channel resulted in the creation of a new pond, an additional wildlife resource.

sediment cleansing and the formation of pool–riffle sequences.

On the R Windrush at Worsham, channel narrowing was also undertaken in late 1991 (Plates 7, 8, 9 and 10). Coir fibre matting and larch poles were used to retain spoil introduced into the over-wide channel (Figure 5). Due to previous land drainage works and reduced flows resulting from abstractions the 8 m wide channel was reduced to 4.5 m. After two winters the channel has remained stable, with self-cleansing flows increasing velocity and substrate diversity in the narrowed

Plates 7-10
River narrowing on the R Windrush at Worsham.
Coir fibre matting and larch poles were used to retain the spoil.
Plate 7: (above) Installation of the larch poles and coir matting.
Plate 8: (below) Site immediately after backfilling (November 1991).
Plate 9 (left) Recovery from narrowing operations approximately 10 months later (September 1992).
Plate 10 (below left) Aerial view of narrowing operations.

**Figure 5
Use of matting
and other
materials to
retain spoil in
river narrowing
operations (see
Worsham
example in text)**

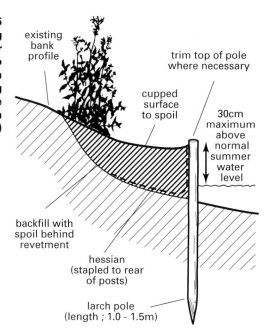

existing
bank
profile

trim top of pole
where necessary

cupped
surface
to spoil

30cm
maximum
above
normal
summer
water
level

backfill with
spoil behind
revetment

hessian
(stapled to rear
of posts)

larch pole
(length ; 1.0 - 1.5m)

channel, the infilled section being inundated during floods. After two years water crowfoot has returned, thereby achieving a key objective of re-creating conditions in which it could naturally recolonise.

Stabilisation of imported spoil is a crucial aspect of channel narrowing. In this respect using faggots (Chapter 3.7) is considered cheap and as effective as man-made materials in many locations. Faggots also have the benefit of providing habitat variability for invertebrates at the margin. If the woody material needed can be cut as part of a riverbank maintenance exercise a double benefit is gained.

3.2.5 Shoals and islands

Shoals may be defined as deposits in the channel bed which are above the mean grade line (mean channel gradient). Riffles and islands are good examples (Plates 11 and 12). Islands are important refuges for animals and plants. Potentially remote from human disturbance and grazing animals, they may support quite a different plant community when compared with the more accessible banks. The construction of flood by-pass channels in particular (Sections 3.4.3, Case Study 3.4(c), R Alne) and narrowing operations (Section 3.2.4) both provide the opportunity for island creation.

Unfortunately, they have frequently been removed in the past in the, sometimes mistaken, belief that they impede flow. Shoals are usually formed by the normal sediment transport processes of the river. To remove them may simply hasten their return. Consequently, before removing a shoal it is important to consider factors listed in Table 5.

**Plate 11 (above)
Unvegetated gravel bar on the R Axe**

**Plate 12 (below)
Vegetated island on the R Stour**

Nigel Holmes

Nigel Holmes

A common feature of shoals and islands is that they increase current velocities around them. This may induce bank scour. On wide, slow-moving channels, shoals can help create silt-free channels. This is illustrated by works on the R Lyde (Case Study 3.2(a)). An island was created on the R Ash at Spelthorne, W London in 1991 in a straightened urban section of river as part of narrowing operations to improve self-cleansing flows. In channels such as this creating shoals to produce faster flowing low-flow channels can result in a relatively stable regime. Shoals and islands can also

Table 5: Considerations necessary before removing shoals

- Understand the mechanism causing the formation.
- Check if it is really an impediment and whether it is stable.
- Assess how much, if any, needs to be removed.
- Consider deflectors to sustain a changed shoal section.
- Consider if a shoal should be reformed elsewhere or the material used for another feature.
- Examine ways of lowering all or part of the shoal to ensure that hydraulic requirements are met while retaining as much as possible of the habitat.

be created by installing hurdles or stone blocks as revetments to induce local scour and deposition (Section 3.4.4).

3.2.6 Pools, riffles and substrate conservation/reinstatement

Case Studies:
R Ock (3.2(e));
R Blackwater, Northern Ireland (3.2(f))

Pools and riffles are natural formations particularly noticeable in gravel-bed rivers. They are rarely consistent in form being reprofiled during flood events. A constant supply of material is needed to maintain them so removal of too much gravel during dredging will often result in erosion of the riverbanks or bed.

During light maintenance dredging it should be possible to leave riffles and pools largely untouched. Heavy dredging may result in their removal. Where this operation is unavoidable the loss of bed structure should be mitigated by appropriate bed reprofiling and/or localised narrowing of the bed width. Table 6 summarises guidelines on reinstating pools and riffles given by Brookes (1990). Figure 6 illustrates how a variety of dredging methods can be employed to create or save existing riffles and pools.

Channel narrowing (Section 3.2.4) and use of groynes/deflectors (Section 3.4.4) both offer ample opportunity for the reinstatement of pool—riffle sequences. Channel narrowing on the R Windrush and

Table 6: Guidelines for reinstating pools and riffles (from Brookes, 1990)

- Assess the channel and flow characteristics to determine if pools and riffles are appropriate features.
- Determine the size and spacing of the features, typically about six times the channel width for riffles.
- Identify and locate the size of the bed materials to be used in riffle formations; this should not be a problem where original materials are re-used.
- Riffles should be 300–500 mm above the natural gradient, pools should be a minimum of 300 mm deep.
- Individual pools and riffles should be between one and three channel widths long.
- Use should be made of the natural meandering of the channel so that pools are formed on the outside of bends with diagonal riffles at the exit.

Richard Vivash

**Plate 13
Redistribution of introduced material by floodwaters to form a new riffle section downstream of the 'created' riffle (Harper's Brook)**

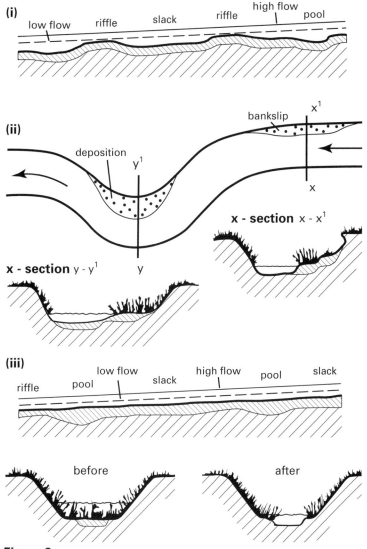

R Coln (Section 3.2.4) provide good examples. A natural channel bed may have become firmly imbricated, and have developed a consolidated surface or armoured layer, thereby ensuring a degree of stability which replaced gravels will not initially have. Consolidation and strengthening with large stones may be required to ensure adequate stability. Artificially reinstated riffles at Harpers Brook near Thrapston (Plate 13), Northants, rapidly underwent reconfiguration by flood waters, which re-sorted material to form a variety of gravel and sand riffles within the same reach.

Properly constructed in appropriate locations, new riffles and pools can add significantly to the ecological interest of a river without the need for extra or indeed any maintenance (Plate 14). With planning this is achieveable in a channel of good conveyance with a new bed-level enabling better discharge from land drains. Although 'extra engineering' is required both in the design and carrying out of the maintenance dredging, this effort is small compared with the environmental benefits. This was illustrated in the R Ock (Case Study 3.2(e)) where riffles were deliberately created in a deepened channel and suitable rock material placed on the newly exposed bed to provide the necessary substrate for plants, invertebrates and riffle-spawning fish.

In some chalk streams loss of fish spawning gravels as a result of siltation has caused increasing concern in recent years. Historically horse-drawn harrows were used to loosen silts, suggesting the problem is not new. In some streams the method is being reintroduced, harrowing taking place in key locations in late autumn to maximise the benefit of winter cleansing flows and have the beds prepared in time for spawning.

Figure 6
Creating or retaining riffles and pools
(i) Existing pool–riffle sequence maintained by dredging to the pool–riffle profile along length; where gravels are removed and clay exposed on riffles, gravels need to be returned to the bed eg R Ock.
(ii) Narrowed channel formed by slippage from bank to create deeper and faster water saved by asymmetric dredging of cross-section to increase capacity.
(iii) Even bed profile engineered to create pools, slacks and riffles; import of material may be needed to form riffle, (eg Scotsgrove Brook). Source: Brandon (1989)

Plate 14
Result of pool–riffle reinstatement operations on Scotsgrove Brook

Alistair Driver

3.3 Riverbank Engineering Works

3.3.1   Introduction

3.3.2   Retention and creation of margins

3.3.3   Backwaters and bays

3.3.4   Multi-stage channels

3.3.5   Bend reprofiling

3.3.1 Introduction

Riverbank engineering works described in this section concentrate on reprofiling using mechanical excavators. Revetments that require the use of imported rock or man-made materials are considered in Section 3.4.4 while bank protection measures that utilise only live trees and shrubs are described in Chapter 3.7.

The straightforward engineering solution to bank profiles, rule-straight batters, is not always a good solution both from an engineering consideration (they can develop slips), and from an environmental viewpoint (they lack diversity).

Wherever possible a preferred alternative is to create 'natural' banks incorporating undercutting, vertical, steep and shallow sloping areas. Where banks already have high wildlife interest, alternatives to reprofiling should always be considered. As a last resort only the bank with the lesser wildlife interest should be reprofiled. Ideally, the reprofiled bank should be re-created to resemble a natural bank. The bank can be made 'rough' by creating holes, ledges, crumbling slopes, shelves and shallow slopes. With the ever-increasing reach and performance of modern hydraulic excavators this operation is becoming more practicable on both banks while working from a single bank.

The profile of the bank below normal water level is as important as that above. Again straight forms are to be avoided and interesting features like shelves and shallow berms should be retained or created. Channel processes dictate that on the outside of bends, the banks will be steeper and deeper, whereas on the inside they will be shallow and gently sloping. However, on straight reaches features can be created, to form a wide range from shallow ledges to waterlogged shelves. Figure 1 (i–v) illustrates a variety of edge/bank reprofiling which have been undertaken to enhance wildlife features.

To create steeper features where soils are not highly cohesive, some extra support is needed until stabilising vegetation takes over. Examples of this type of protection are willow spiling, faggots, timber sheeting and rocks, (Chapter 3.7 and Hemphill and Bramley, 1989). Alternatively dredging can be planned so that natural features at the toe of a bank are left and the channel widened above them. In some situations banks have so little interest that it is advantageous to completely reprofile them right down to the water's edge. The R Bain Case Study (3.3(b)) is a good example which combined total reprofiling and planting on the ledges created.

For the full range of bank features to develop and be sustained, trees and shrubs such as alder, willow and ash are important (Plate 1). These allow vertical and undercut features to develop without loss of bank stability because the roots extend laterally. Banks which rely on support from trees should not be reprofiled but preserved wherever possible.

Riverside trees are retained and replanted to reduce bank erosion, but specialised methods of faggoting, spiling and incorporation of trees and shrubs with stone revetments are more commonly used (Chapter 3.7). Reeds and other vegetation are also used to protect banks from fluvial erosion and damage from boat wash; examples of this are given in Chapter 3.5. Margins, that is the damp areas between

**Plate 1
An 'ideal' set of bank features with a range of trees (alders and white willows) present.**

Nigel Holmes

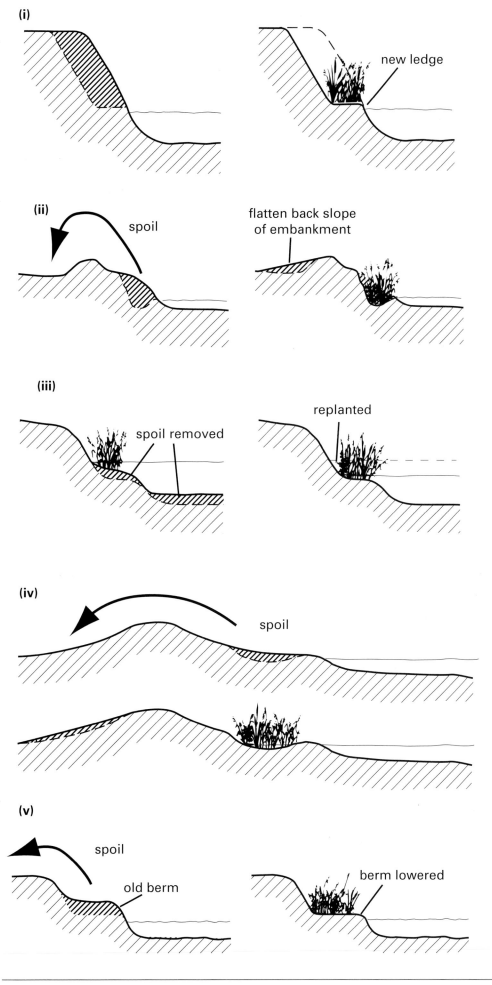

**Figure 1
Examples of bank
reprofiling to
benefit wildlife
(i) R Beult — Kent.**
Ledge formed *c*15
cm above low-
flow. Bank too
steep and high to
be trampled or
grazed. Ledge
always damp
below but firm
enough for
fishing. Rapid
colonisation of
wetland plants —
meadowsweet,
purple-loosestrife
(Case Study 3.3
(a)).
**(ii) R Bain —
Lincolnshire.**
Ledge formed at
low-flow level.
Bank grazed
periodically.
Emergents planted
into hollows from
old river channel.
Instant reed fringe
along river
forming habitat
for fish and
invertebrates with
reed sweet-grass,
rush, ragged-
robin, brooklime,
water-cress, etc
replacing nettles
(Case Study
3.3(b)).
(iii) R Eden — Kent.
Underwater toe of
bank re-created at
lower level to stop
drying-out as
centre of channel
lowered.
Trampling and
grazing regime
unaltered. Bur-
reed and
flowering-rush
maintained with
shallow water
retreat for fry and
invertebrates.
**(iv) R Avon —
Warwickshire.**
Lowering of linear
strip along berm
to enable wetland
habitat to develop
on the foreshore
of the floodbank.
(v) Padgate Brook,
machinery/access
berm lowered to
within 20 cm of
the low water
level.

Case Studies:
R Beult (3.3(a)),
R Bain (3.3(b))

3.3.2 Retention and creation of margins

normal water level and the dry part of the bank, are very important areas for wildlife because many specialised plants and associated animals occur only in this zone. It is frequently here that plants and animals which were once commonplace in the floodplain now find a suitable refuge. Figure 2 (i–iii) illustrates creation and

retention techniques for margin habitats.

As margins are so important, they should be retained if at all possible during dredging. Where disturbance cannot be avoided, mitigation should include the creation of new marginal habitat. If a channel is widened, opportunities to create valuable margins will be provided. If wide enough, margins potentially develop good plant communities. To ensure diversity of habitat, the margin should be varied in height and profile as well as width. In overwide channels the margins can be redesigned, as at the R Dun at Hungerford (Case Study 3.2(d)), to facilitate channel narrowing. Provided that locally derived dredgings are used, new margins may require no planting but may require temporary protection against scour until plant growth is well established. Marginal habitat enhancement also occurs when backwaters and bays are created (Section 3.3.3).

In general, it should be possible to retain or create margins on at least one bank of even the smallest watercourse. Both marginal and instream diversity can be created by reprofiling uniform existing banks. There is considerable scope for this type of work on trapezoidal channels. The reprofiling of one bank can provide greater capacity, which offsets reduced vegetation control to benefit wildlife further.

The R Beult in Kent is a good example of creating marginal wetland habitat just above water level and leaving natural establishment to determine the final form (Case Study 3.3(a)). On the R Eden in Kent margins were reprofiled to diversify underwater and edge habitats (Plates 2, 3 and 4). The additional land-take was accepted and encouraged by the landowners. On Padgate Brook (Plates 5, 6 and 7) in NRA Northwest Region edge profiling has incorporated the creation of a meander associated with ledges in a previously straight channel. Figure 3 shows widening of Spittle Brook at Woolston Park in the mid-1970s. The widening

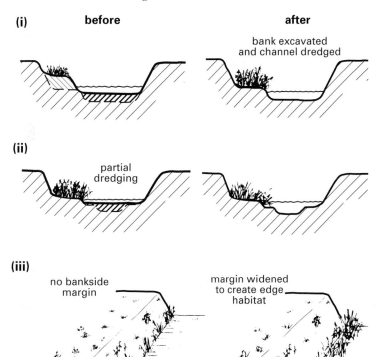

Figure 2
(i) Enhancing; (ii) retaining, and (iii) creating edge habitats.
Adapted from Brandon (1989)

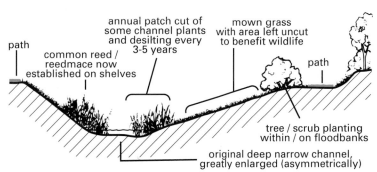

Figure 3
Creation of marginal habitats at Spittle Brook, Warrington.
Source: Lewis and Williams (1984)

Nigel Holmes

Nigel Holmes

Nigel Holmes

Plates 2—4
Reprofiling of channel margins on the R Eden, Kent

Plate 2 (top left): Before works undertaken

Plate 3 (left): Immediately after reprofiling

Plate 4 (above): Development of marginal habitat after reprofiling

incorporated ledge habitats within the design standard, making provision for reed growth on these margins. Reeds have established extremely well, with desilting of the channel needed every 3–5 years to retain capacity and keep the reeds in check. The urban watercourse now has a very diverse range of edge and aquatic plants whereas before the widening it had little wildlife interest. The same principle was copied on the Wyre near Catterall where low berms were created, which have been colonised by a range of marginal plants, but principally reed canary-grass. The berms have enhanced wetland habitat, remained within scheme design, and provided better access for maintenance excavators.

**Plates 5–7
Reprofiling of channel margins and
meander creation on Padgate Brook**

**Plate 5 (top): Trapezoidal channel;
before work was undertaken**

**Plate 6 (centre): Margin/meander
re-creation in process**

**Plate 7 (bottom): Site after work was
undertaken**

3.3.3 Backwaters and bays

(i)

1 deflection of current to opposite bank

2 flow sustains bay

3 shoal forms in eddy currents (can be built)

4 riffle forms as extension of shoal

5 mature tree forms a useful anchor point

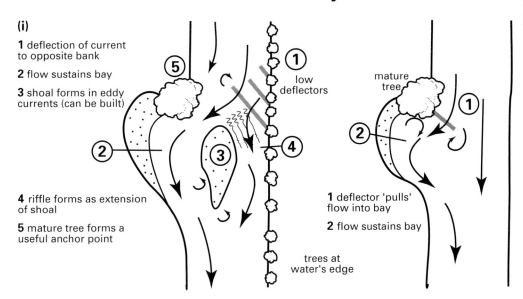

low deflectors

mature tree

1 deflector 'pulls' flow into bay

2 flow sustains bay

trees at water's edge

Backwaters and bays are immensely important features in rivers, providing a range of different habitats, from side channels, to temporary floodplain pools. Engineering works which deepen and straighten rivers usually result in the loss of these habitats so every opportunity should be taken to rehabilitate and re-create them. In particular widening schemes increasingly present the opportunity to rehabilitate and enhance backwaters and bays.

(ii)

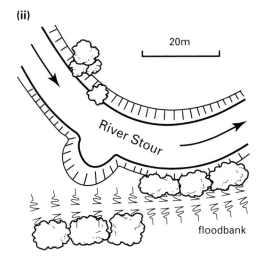

20m

River Stour

floodbank

Figure 4
Bay creation/rehabilitation (i) The excavation of artificial bays within riverbanks requires a design that utilises some of the energy of the river to sustain the basic form through scour. This reduces the tendency towards siltation but care must be taken to keep works small scale.
(ii) Bay creation – R Stour, Redhill, Bournemouth: The shallow bay with banks graded to 1:4 was excavated in the outer bank of a realigned bend during flood alleviation works by Wessex Water in the early 1970s. The bay is still in place in 1993 and is colonised by a range of emergent plants including bur-reed, wetland plants such as orange balsam and water pepper and aquatic species including hornwort and milfoil. Situated close to a housing estate, the bay is a popular fishing peg.
Source: Lewis and Williams (1984)

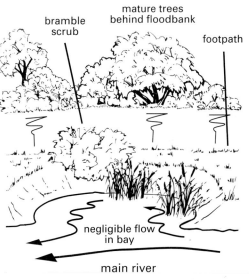

bramble scrub

mature trees behind floodbank

footpath

negligible flow in bay

main river

Judith Crompton

Judith Crompton

Plate 8
Bay creation on
the R Stour

The habitat value of backwaters and bays can be enhanced by appropriate management of animal access. Some poaching by cattle can increase the diversity of marginal habitats and provide feeding areas for waders. However, on many watercourses livestock cause serious damage to banks and margins, and fencing is required. It should, however, be remembered that fencing can impinge on the landscape as well as resulting in the loss of poached habitats of conservation importance. A hedge is a valuable alternative to fencing. Advice on the suitability of fencing should be sought from conservation staff.

Plate 9
The impact of
deepening and
straightening
operations on a
lowland river,
resulting in a
reach devoid of
backwaters and
bays

Provision of drinking bays for livestock can benefit wildlife too. Site selection should be made following river corridor survey so that no interesting bank or channel habitats will be destroyed.

Cattle-drinks provide incidental benefits as refuges for fish in times of flood and habitats for 'edge' plants and animals, purpose-built bays designed to benefit wildlife are often more beneficial. Figure 4 (i–ii) illustrates theoretical aspects of bay creation and work undertaken on the R Stour (Plate 8). Here greater attention to design and construction can provide shelter for fish and their fry, with underwater and edge profiles shaped to provide habitat enhancements for invertebrates and plants.

When re-creating or rehabilitating backwaters on a reach it should be remembered that on a natural, unconfined channel a selection of the range of backwater types found in Chapter 1.2, Table 1 could potentially be present. Work should therefore aim to re-create and rehabilitate the range or continuum of backwater types representative of the reach in its natural state. Use of historical map sources that indicate the location of former backwaters and old river courses is a good first step when deciding on suitable sites. Backwaters in continuous connection with the mainstream are of particular value, providing refuges to fish in both floods and periods of pollution as well as habitat for other wildlife and plants.

The R Cole is typical of many managed lowland rivers, where progressive loss of backwater habitat resulted in a floodplain and main channel of reduced ecological interest (Plate 9). Project Kingfisher, undertaken in the mid-1980s on the R Cole (Case Study 3.3(c)) and resulted in the creation of two backwaters, and is typical of the increasing number of schemes being undertaken. The success of this scheme was such that one backwater has since been enlarged and others created.

The following specific examples highlight both backwater retention and re-creation.

A proposal for straightening, deepening and embankment works on the R Witham in 1974, as part of an agricultural drainage scheme, could have resulted in the permanent 'cut-off' of a former meander loop at Westborough, Lincolnshire (Figure

Nigel Holmes

5 (i)). However, an objection from the local landowner resulted in the meander loop being retained. A low weir was installed together with a 45 cm diameter pipe (laid through the embankment at low summer water level) to maintain flows through the backwater.

In the late 1980s, Eske borrow pit (Figure 5 (ii) and Plate 10) situated in a meander loop of the R Hull was connected to the main river to create a 60–70 ha backwater area. The backwater functions as a flood by-pass channel (Section 3.4.3) in times of high flow, with lower flows accommodated in the natural channel. Armouring of the inlet and outlet prevents erosion and potential cut-off of the meander loop. The outlet is at a higher elevation than the inlet in order to maintain and enhance water-table levels in Pulfin Bog which was feared to be drying out. Plant, fish and invertebrate recolonisation at the site has been rapid and large numbers of wading birds and wildfowl currently use the site. This site is one of several wetland sites constructed and managed by the NRA in the R Hull valley.

Shallow borrow pits at Breaston Bridge, dug to provide material for the Pennington Brook flood alleviation scheme (NRA North West region), have been connected to the mainstream via a culvert and flap valve producing more than 2 ha of wetland habitat on which water levels can be managed. Creation of shallows, deeper water and islands has produced a range of habitats. Guidelines on the design of such features can be found in the RSPB handbook *Gravel Pit Restoration for Wildlife* (Andrews and Kinsman, 1990).

Other backwater creation schemes include those at Bidford Grange (Plate 11 and Figure 5 (iii)) and Clifton (Plate 12 and Figure 5 (iv)) on the R Avon, the R Ash (Plates 13 and 14) and the Great Ouse at Olney near Bedford (Plate 15).

At Bidford Grange a ditch entering the river close to a backwater was excavated to form a large pool. The Clifton backwater maximises the 'edge' area available, together with the creation of islands, and shallow and deeper water areas. The R Ash

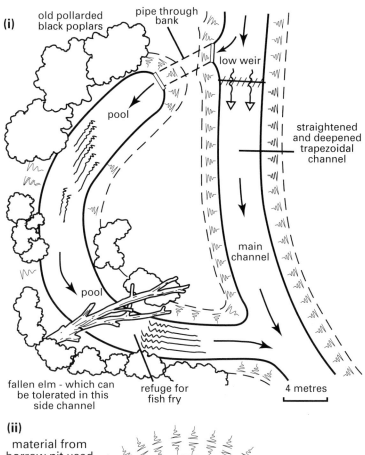

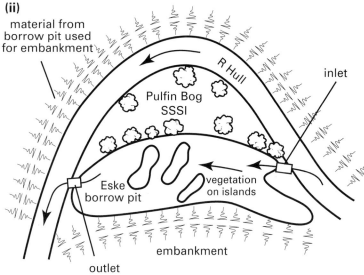

Figure 5
(i) Backwater retention at Westborough, R Witham, Lincolnshire. Source: Lewis and Williams (1984)
(ii) Backwater/bypass creation (Eske borrow pit), R Hull, (NRA Northumbria and Yorkshire region).

scheme illustrates that even in confined urban areas significant environmental enhancement may be possible. The Olney example illustrates reconnection of a backwater to the main channel, cut off by a former engineering scheme.

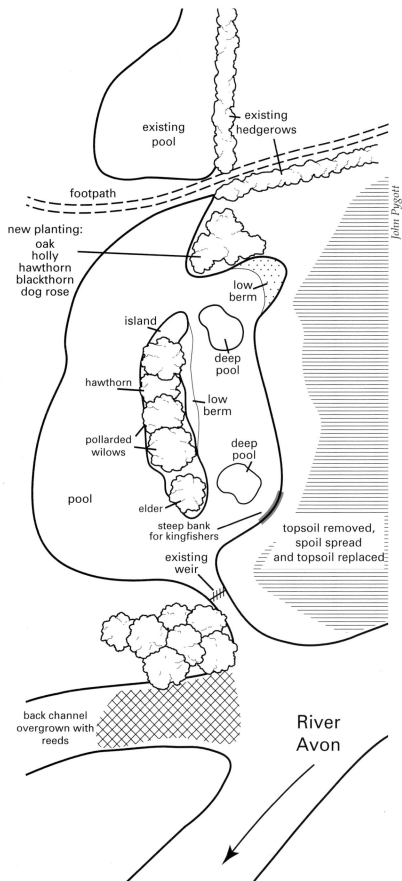

new planting:
oak
holly
hawthorn
blackthorn
dog rose

existing pool

existing hedgerows

footpath

low berm

island

deep pool

hawthorn

low berm

pollarded wilows

deep pool

pool

elder

steep bank for kingfishers

existing weir

topsoil removed, spoil spread and topsoil replaced

back channel overgrown with reeds

River Avon

Figure 5
(iii) Backwater creation at Bidford Grange, R Avon (NRA Severn-Trent region).

John Pygott

Plate 10
Creation of a floodplain backwater in a meander loop of the R Hull. Additionally the 'backwater' also acts as a flood by-pass and is designed to maintain water levels in Pulfin Bog SSSI situated in the meander loop.

Man-made features such as old mill leats (trenches for carrying water to the waterwheel) may act as artificial backwaters and can provide rehabilitation and enhancement opportunities. Rehabilitation of an old leat at Evesham on the R Avon has resulted in an excellent fish recruitment area.

Bays can also be very usefully incorporated into the design of new piped outfall structures. Figure 6 shows how an outfall could be most effectively blended into the landscape and provide ecological enhancement. Most benefits would accrue if the bay were generously proportioned. Construction of the outfall could be simplified because revetment to prevent scour is not required and installation and maintenance is undertaken without disturbance to the river. Sampling of the discharge could also be made safer and easier. A small buffer zone is created by the bay allowing potentially polluted silts to settle out clear of the river and can be easily removed before they are 'lost' downstream.

Figure 5
(iv) Backwater creation at Clifton, R Avon (NRA Severn-Trent region).

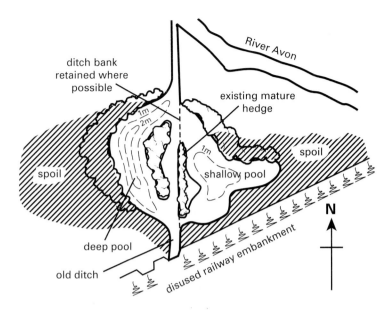

Plate 11 (below)
Floodplain backwater creation on the R Avon at Bidford Grange (Figure (iii)).

Plate 12 (bottom)
Floodplain pool/backwater creation on the R Avon at Clifton (Figure (iv)).

Bob Bishop

Liz Galloway

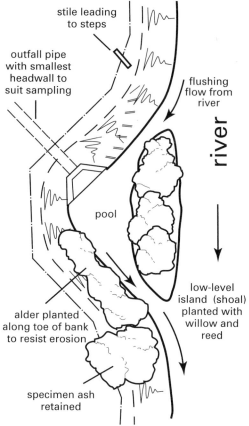

stile leading
to steps

outfall pipe
with smallest
headwall to
suit sampling

flushing
flow from
river

river

pool

alder planted
along toe of bank
to resist erosion

low-level
island (shoal)
planted with
willow and
reed

specimen ash
retained

Alistair Driver

Alistair Driver

**Plates 13 & 14
Creation of a
backwater within
the confines of
an urban area on
the R Ash**

**Plate 13 (top)
During creation**

**Plate 14 (centre)
One year after
completion of
the work**

RSPB

**Plate 15 (above)
Reconnection of a backwater to the main channel,
previously 'cut off' by a former scheme, at Olney on the
Great Ouse near Bedford.**

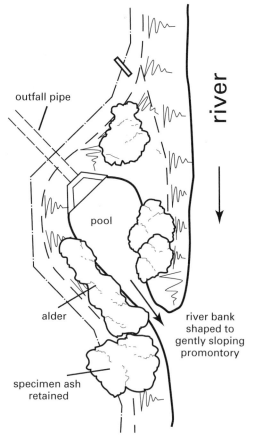

outfall pipe

river

pool

alder

river bank
shaped to
gently sloping
promontory

specimen ash
retained

**Figure 6
Two examples of off-river bays excavated to accommodate
piped outfall structures (suggested alternative to structures
built into riverbank).**

3.3.4 Multi-stage channels

**Case Studies:
R Roding
(Abridge) 3.3(d)
and R Monnow
(Maerdy) 3.3(e)**

Multi-stage channels avoid widening the riverbed yet provide significant increases in cross-sectional area. In its simplest form this concept may be visualised as the river flooding out of its dry weather flow channel to spill over a lowered part of its floodplain, excavated alongside the natural channel. Engineered multi-stage channels therefore enable the low-flow channel to remain untouched.

The natural processes that create multi-stage channels are most apparent in piedmont streams that are actively in the process of adjusting their relative position in the floodplain. The migration of such channels creates complex cross-sections which can exhibit up to four stages as illustrated in Figure 7.

The effect of multi-stage channels on flood hydrograph form are significant. Figure 8 compares theoretical hydrograph form in trapezoidal and a multi-stage channel.

(i) a natural multi-stage channel

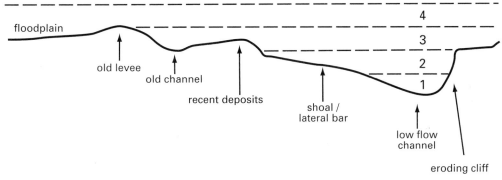

(ii) an 'engineered' multi-stage channel

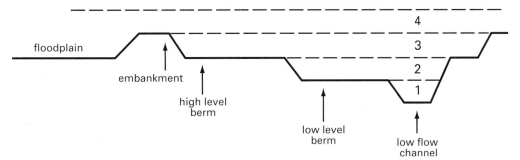

(iii) a 'naturalised' multi-stage channel

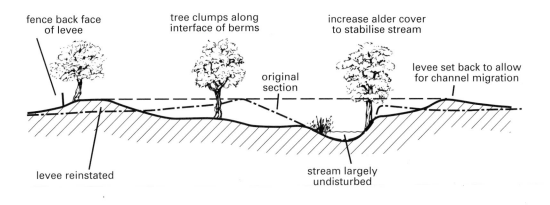

**Figure 7
Natural and engineered multi-stage channels (vertical scale exaggerated);
(i) a natural multi-stage channel;
(ii) an engineered multi-stage channel;
(iii) a 'naturalised' multi-stage channel (requires greater width than (ii) above).**

The design of multi-stage channels in lowland rivers affords considerably greater scope for environmental conservation and enhancement than is possible through the alternative of simply enlarging a

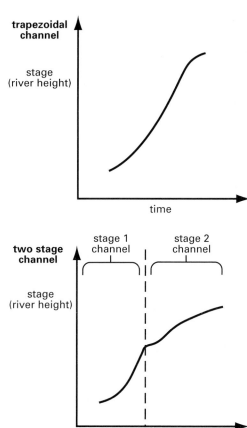

Figure 8
A comparison of theoretical hydrograph form in trapezoidal and a two-stage channel.

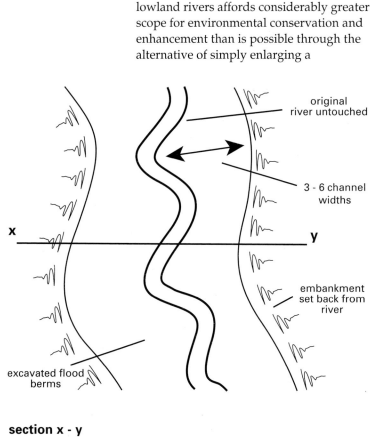

section x - y

before

after

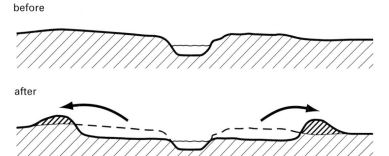

Figure 9
Multi-stage channel design

trapezoidal cross-section to gain increased channel capacity (Figure 9). However, multi-stage channels are much wider than trapezoidal channels carrying similar flows, so adequate space is crucial. Use of this option will therefore depend upon the availability of land on both sides of the channel.

Table 1: Components of an artificially created multi-stage channel

- A low-flow channel that self-sustains its width with relative freedom to adjust its form and alignment, and requiring little maintenance.
- Shoals that are sustained by stream geometry; for example localised on the inside of bends and extending under water diagonally across the channel at the exit of bends. Retained bankside features on at least one bank, including cliffs, mature trees or reedbeds.
- Low-level berms that are effectively extensions of the shoals in the vicinity of bends and may represent a degree of straightening of the channel at the second stages of flood flow. Elsewhere on 'straight' reaches low level berms may be regarded as artificial floodplains that support a variety of habitats according to design but probably need to be accessible for maintenance (including grazing where possible).
- High-level berms between the channel and any levees or artificial embankments built to simulate these. High-level berms represent the limits of the 'river corridor' created by a multi-stage design and will sensibly be aligned well clear of the overall meander width, but may nevertheless follow the mean curvature of the stream alignment. They often represent the demarcation line between starkly different land management practices such as intensive agriculture and low intensity grazing.

Multi-stage cross-sections in lowland streams have a natural precedent dating back to glacial times when many present-day landforms were first sculptured. Examples can be seen on the Stoneley Brook south of Godmanchester, Cambs. Two such cross-sections are shown in Plates 16, 17, 18 and 19 in both low-flow and flood conditions.

Table 1 gives an indication of the general form that will arise if natural principles are followed in multi-stage design.

The construction of low embankments (levees) within floodplains are an extension of the multi-stage concept that will contain all but the highest flood flows. Between the river and the levee semi-natural habitat with low intensity productivity is typical, while behind it more intensive farming is often practised. Mimicking low, flat profiles associated with natural levees affords the advantages listed in Table 2. Such embankments are common in Holland along the Rhine where inner low floodbanks give protection from summer

Plates 16–19 Naturally occurring multi-stage channels; Stoneley Brook, Godmanchester, Cambridgeshire

Plates 16 & 17 (above left and right) Upstream site in low-flow and flood-flow conditions

Plates 18 & 19 (below left and right) Downstream site in low-flow and flood-flow conditions

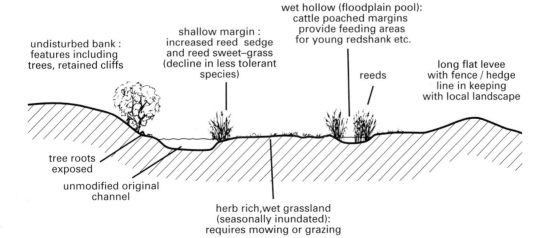

**Figure 10
Wildlife features of created two-stage channels**

Table 2: Advantages of mimicking natural levee profiles for low embankments

- Stable when overtopped by floodwater and under the weight of grazing livestock.
- Safe when mowing for hay.
- Visually less intrusive than steep-sided embankments.
- Tree stands can be planted selectively.
- Stock control fences or hedges can be accommodated above the more frequent flood levels.
- Can provide 'safe havens' for livestock during minor floods.
- Provides convenient disposal options for spoil yielded by future maintenance.

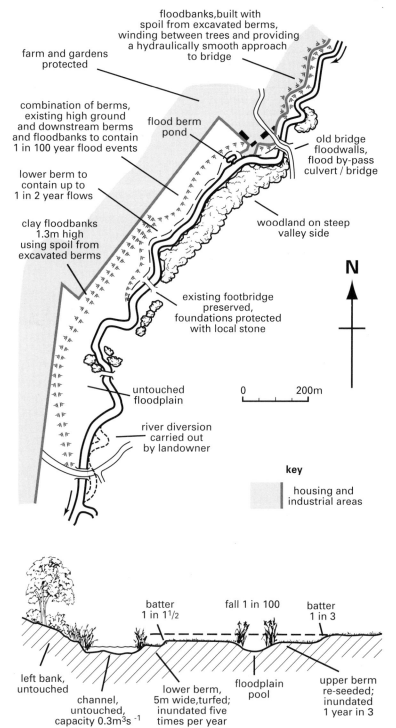

flooding. They are also used extensively both above and below Leominster on the R Lugg. (Case Study 3.4(i)).

A well-planned multi-stage channel should comprise a relatively wide corridor of land that has been carefully aligned and profiled to open out the river in a series of gentle slopes and benches that eventually build up to a smooth flood overspill onto the remaining floodplain. If levees are built, a route for re-entry of flood water back into the channel must be incorporated. Design should allow for some shoal build-up and re-working in the low-flow channel to enable natural features to develop unhindered by maintenance needs. Allowance should also be made for periodic silt deposition on the berms. Additionally, the potential effects of vegetation on flow hydraulics need to be taken into account when designing multi-stage channels. Berms need management to prevent them from becoming overgrown by scrub. Grazing enables vegetation to be kept in check, but it is dependent on the availability of suitable livestock.

Figure 11
Contrasting approaches to multi-stage channel design.
(i) R Asker, Bradpole. Serious flooding in 1970 resulted in the call for a flood alleviation scheme. The magnitude of recorded flood flows meant a 'conventional' deepening/widening and embanking scheme would not be feasible. A multi-stage scheme was therefore adopted. A low berm was created to accommodate frequently occurring floods and provide marginal wetland habitat. The wider floodplain was utilised to accommodate floods up to the predicted 1 in 100 year flood (the recorded 49 m³ s⁻¹ event), with spoil from the created berms used to create the floodbanks. The scheme has maintained in-channel interest.
Source: Lewis and Williams (1984)

There are many examples of multi-stage channels, the most studied of these being the R Roding (Case Study 3.3(d)) in Essex (Raven, 1986(a), (b) and (c)). Post-project appraisal of a number of schemes involving two-stage channels showed that major increases in reed development occurred at margins and on low second-stage channels. If the second stage is too low, even quite minor rises in discharge result in flows spilling onto berms, and insufficient velocity in the low-flow channel resulting in excessive silt deposition and marginal reed encroachment. The Monnow at Maerdy (Case Study 3.3(e)) illustrates how flood conveyance is achieved through naturally occurring two-stage channels.

Figure 10 illustrates some potential wildlife features of interest which can be associated with two-stage channel construction. Provided the low-flow channel remains self-sustaining, plant and animal richness increases on the margins, banks and floodplain.

Figure 11 (i) and (ii) shows two contrasting schemes undertaken on the R Asker and R Lugg. In the former, land on the insides of meanders was gently reprofiled to provide improved flow through the bends. In the latter, a berm on one side of the channel only provided improved conveyance along a relatively straight section. The low level and extra width of the berm on the R Asker enabled a pond to be created. Both rivers continue to fulfill the flood conveyance design standards of the schemes and have also retained in-channel interests which have been further enhanced on the R Asker by additional river corridor habitat improvements.

The design of the two-stage channel at Gillingham on the R Stour retained trees on an excavated bank creating an island at times of flood (Plates 20 and 21). The berm was seeded with a wild-flower mix, however, poor subsequent management reduced the potential wildlife interest of the site.

In 1982, works were undertaken to provide 1 in 30-year flood protection to agricultural land on the R Avon at Burlingham (Plate

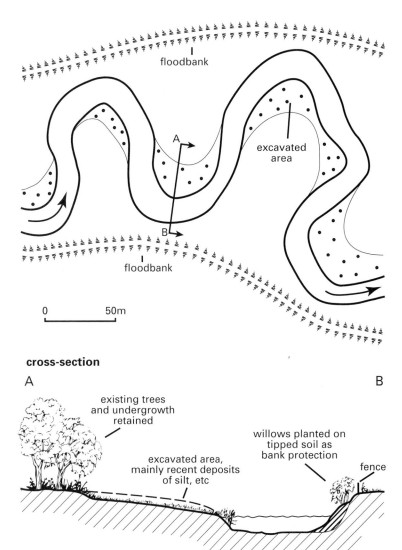

cross-section

Figure 11 (ii) R Lugg, Leominster. A multi-stage channel on the R Lugg provided enhanced flood protection yet enabled grazing to be continued within the widely spaced floodbanks (see Chapter 3.3, Figure 8; Chapter 3.4 , Figure 2). Alternate excavations on the insides of bends created a second stage to the channel, enabling floods to be 'eased' through the meanders. Spoil from these works was used to form the floodbanks, while additional bank protection on the outside of bends was provided using willows. Source: Lewis and Williams (1984)

22). Although the scheme initially led to loss of floodplain habitat, it incorporated a novel approach to two-stage channel construction, with the creation of a variety of berm profiles (Figure 11 (iii)). Appraisal of the scheme in 1992 has revealed an excellent variety of dry, wet and standing water habitats and associated wildlife at the site. Sensitive scrub management, as initially envisaged, has been essential to enable the scheme to achieve target flood defence standards. Control of extensive willow growth not only benefits flood defence but also results in a greater variety of plant communities and in turn a wider range of animals. The scheme was also successful in its objective to create suitable habitat for the marsh warbler.

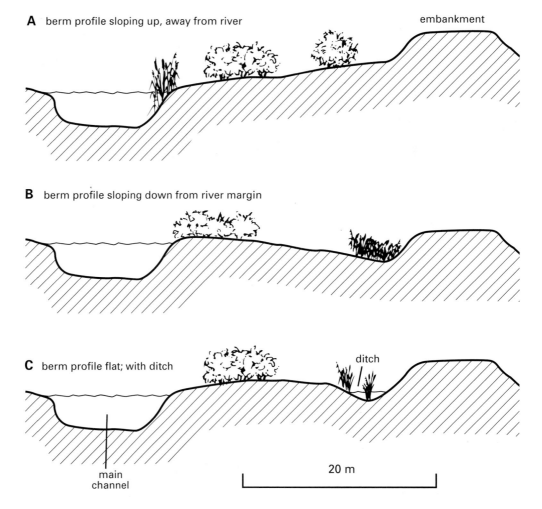

A berm profile sloping up, away from river   embankment

B berm profile sloping down from river margin

C berm profile flat; with ditch   ditch

main
channel

20 m

Figure 11 (iii) R Avon at Burlingham, two-stage channel berm profiles.

Plate 20
Two-stage channel at Gillingham on the R Stour with retained trees on an excavated bank

Plate 21
The above two-stage channel at Gillingham showing how retained trees can create an island during flood flows

Liz Galloway

**Plate 22
Wetland marginal
habitat created
during
construction of a
two-stage
channel at
Burlingham on
the R Avon**

3.3.5 Bend reprofiling

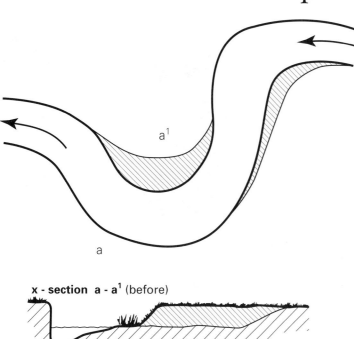

x - section a - a¹ (before)

x - section a - a¹ (after)

lowering of land
to enable grazing

lowering of land to create
extension of wetland habitat

Meanders often encompass characteristic dynamic habitats. Commonly the outside of bends contain steep, often cliff, habitats, whereas on the inside there are shoals, bars and shallow banks. Retention of such features is highly desirable because of their importance both as landscape features and wildlife habitat.

Bend reprofiling is a common practice employed to improve flood conveyance and reduce erosion. This can lead to river straightening. The problems associated with such practices are well documented (Brookes, 1990), but limited bend reprofiling may be considered permissible to check severe erosion in certain circumstances. Employed over long reaches, this may result in channel shortening, increased velocities and potentially cause greater erosion problems.

**Figure 12
Bend reprofiling. Cross-section a – a¹
retains the cliff face and channel
untouched, and the extent of wetland
habitat on the inside of the meander is
increased.
Adapted from Brandon (1989)**

Nigel Holmes

**Plate 23
Bend reprofiling
and dry by-pass
creation on R
Cam at Urgashay**

Richard Vivash

**Plate 24
Bend reprofiling
and dry by-pass
creation on the R
Dore at Pontrilas.
The shoal (bar)
has been cut to a
lower level on
the inside of the
bend. The
outside bend is
protected by
rock revetment
(Section 3.4.4)
and a single low
level deflector.
The floodplain
has been cleared
of all hedges/
bushes to
encourage flood
flows to 'by-pass'
the meanders.
The river course
follows the trees
in the
background.**

If a bend must be modified it is important to retain or re-create the natural features. If erosion is the problem soft revetment may be all that is needed and the original features of the channel can be retained (Section 3.4.4 and Hemphill and Bramley, 1989). Removing shoals from the inside of bends is likely to be ineffective and provide only temporary increased flood capacity. The shoal will be reformed during the next flood event. If some part of a shoal has to be removed, attempts should be made to retain as much as possible while reprofiling.

Figure 12 illustrates the method of bend reprofiling, which may reduce bank erosion, yet not destroy, associated habitats. Bend reprofiling should not lead to the loss of meanders. However, where

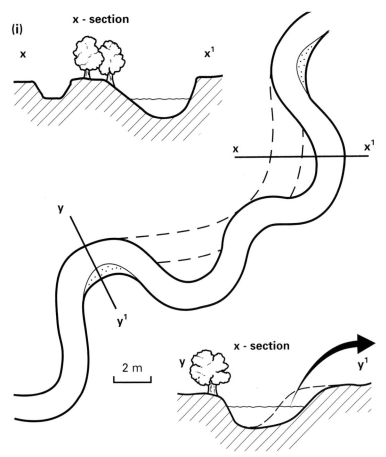

flood defence requirements deem work essential, reprofiling can be undertaken in conjunction with by-pass creation to allow meanders to be retained.

Reprofiling and by-pass creation have been used in tandem on the R Cam at Urgashay and the R Dore at Pontrilas (Figure 13 (i) and (ii) and Plates 23 and 24). The R Dore example combines the short by-pass method of protecting one meander with reprofiling the inside of another. The works have been undertaken to protect meanders and improve flood conveyance without significantly disrupting either flow regime or habitats. Where such 'dry' flood by-pass channels are employed they should have lower bed-levels at the downstream end that flood first and armouring at the upstream end to ensure low flows in the future are always directed through the meander (Section 3.4.3). If they are not carefully designed, they can lead to isolation of the original meanders as floods scour out the short cut created.

Figure 13
Bend reprofiling/by-pass creation.
(i) (above) R Cam, Urgashay, near Yeovil. Flood alleviation work was undertaken in 1984/85 to provide 1 in 50 year flood protection for adjacent properties. The approach improved capacity without deepening or significantly straightening the channel, and retained existing meanders and the tree lined character of the river. Tortuous meanders had dry by-pass channels cut across them while more gentle bends and the inside slopes were reprofiled. Loss of trees was compensated for by new planting on the redefined channel. After almost 10 years some 'brushing' of the berms and relief cuts is proposed to retard extensive scrub development. Source: Lewis and Williams (1984)

(ii) (opposite) R Dore, Pontrilas, Wales. The flood alleviation scheme in 1984 at Pontrilas on the R Dore has performed to its design standard and retained many natural channel features intact. The reprofiled bank initially had a well-developed wetland community. However, this has become dominated by tall herbaceous plants, especially Himalayan balsam. The cut-off channel has remained open and all retained trees are healthy, including those protected by block stone on the meanders.

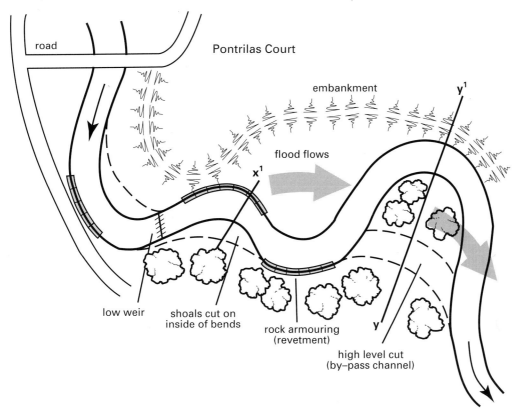

road

Pontrilas Court

embankment

y^1

flood flows

x^1

low weir

shoals cut on
inside of bends

rock armouring
(revetment)

y

high level cut
(by–pass channel)

cross sections

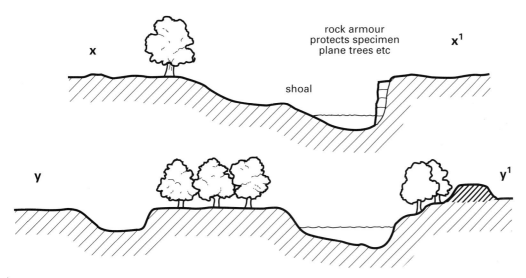

x

rock armour
protects specimen
plane trees etc

x^1

shoal

y

y^1

3.4 Construction Works

3.4.1   Introduction

3.4.2   Embankments

3.4.3   Realignments and by-passes

3.4.4   Deflectors and revetments

3.4.5   Weirs and sluices

3.4.6   Flood storage

Case Studies:
R Torne (3.4(a)),
R Lugg (3.4(b))

3.4.1 Introduction

This section includes river management works that involve defined structures, eg weirs, sluices, new flood channels, flood banks and flood storage areas. It also includes major engineering works which attempt to control or manipulate bed or bank erosion through importation of

materials, eg bank revetments and deflectors built in the channel. With all the above works the requirement for land drainage consent should be determined with the appropriate authority at the outset.

3.4.2 Embankments

RSPB

Plate 1
Ouse Washes barrier-bank

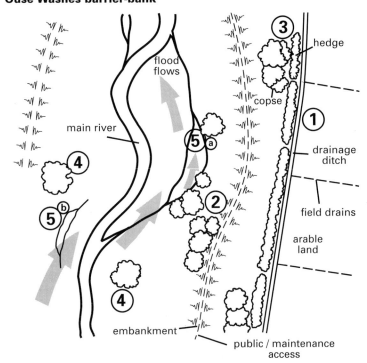

Embankments alongside rivers contain water that would otherwise spill onto adjacent land developed for agricultural or urban purposes. Embanked rivers are commonly associated with tidal estuary 'fens', low-lying 'levels' and where rivers have extensive floodplains. Embankments are also commonly used where towns and villages have properties in the river

Figure 1 (below left)
Enhancement of the environmental potential of flood embankments.

(1) Primary drainage ditch on outside of embankment. These may be major features in their own right if managed sensitively. Hedgeline incorporation adds wildlife value and helps reduce wind-generated waves, which may erode the bank.
(2) Alignment of embankment within the corridor is a matter of local judgement, but it should have numerous access ramps where trees and shrubs in clumps at ground level can be accommodated because of extra width and strength at these points. Hawthorn, maple and dogwood are ideal, but all plantings should be native to the locality and located clear of the main flood path.
(3) Extensive tree planting associated with embankments is not acceptable. This practice is discouraged in favour of seeking to establish copses in the wide corridor between the floodbank and ditch.
(4) Isolated trees, eg oak, can be features in wide sections of land between the river and embankment.
(5) The backwaters between river and embankment have been retained as valuable wildlife refuges. Backwater (a) being in almost continuous contact with the mainstream, whilst backwater (b) is periodically inundated during floods.

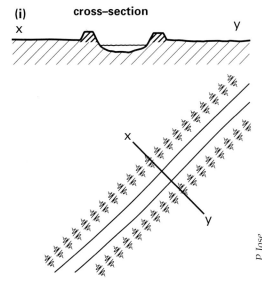

(i)

cross-section

x   y

(ii)

x¹   **cross-section**   y¹

x¹   y¹

3-6 x
channel
widths

Figure 2
Floodbanks (i) Set close to a
channelised river. (ii) Set back from an
unconfined river. Illustrates retention of
natural multi-stage channel form (see
Chapter 3.3, Figure 8).

floodplain and it is impractical to convey
high floods solely within the river.

During periods of high tides in East Anglia,
where much land is at, or below sea level,
embankments provide storage for fresh
water that is temporarily tide locked at
high tide. Fenland embankments, as on the
Ouse Washes downstream of Earith, can be
up to 7 m high (Plate 1).

Embankments maintained primarily for
flood defence purposes rarely have
significant intrinsic environmental interest.

P Jose

P Jose

Plate 2 (above)
Floodbank
situated close to
river

Plate 3 (left)
Floodbank set
back from the
river

However, by careful design it is possible to
create wildlife habitat associated with the
embankments notably establishing herb-
rich swards (Chapter 3.6), wetland habitat
(Section 3.3.3), and areas of trees and shrub
planting (Chapter 3.7).

Figure 1 shows some further aspects
related to the environmental potential of
flood embankments.

The importance of location and alignment
of floodbanks cannot be overstressed as it
affects planning decisions and land use well
into the future. Land outside floodbanks,
but within the natural floodplain, is often
seen as 'protected' and therefore suitable
for development. By contrast, the land
enclosed by floodbanks, and the riverbanks
themselves, provide opportunities for
wildlife enhancement in harmony with
flood defence and other interests.

Design and construction of river
embankments must ensure their structural
integrity during floods. For detailed design
guidelines, reference should be made to

**Plate 4
Eroding
embankment on
the Afon
Clwedog**

Richard Vivash

promotes a grass sward with strong root growth and enables regular inspection to take place. It also prevents woody growth from becoming established. Grazing can be as effective as mowing and is often better for wildlife (Chapter 3.6). Planning at the design stage should take account of whether grazing is also suitable for the bank. If grazing can be used in all areas enclosed by the floodbank, suitable habitats can be created at the outset.

technical manuals. Maintenance has to ensure that structural integrity is maintained and embankments can not be viewed as 'barren' areas ripe for tree and shrub planting. The low, flat, roll-over design of embankments used on the R Lugg (Case Study (3.4(b)) near Hereford, is an example where it was feasible to incorporate woody habitat into the design. Where the sides of low and established embankments have been used previously for disposing of dredged spoil this too may give rise to sufficient extra strength to make limited scrub growth acceptable.

Management of embankments generally consists of regular mowing or grazing. This

Alignment of embankments relative to the river is the most critical decision since this determines the extent of habitat potential. Figure 2 and Plates 2 and 3 illustrate two extremes; 1) banks situated close to the river resulting in a limited or nonexistent floodplain; 2) floodbank set back a long way from the river's edge. If a floodbank is close to a river the risk of undermining can be considerable, leading to the need for expensive revetment in the future. Plate 4 shows a riverside embankment that has eroded badly and subsequently led to it being set back from the immediate bank. Generally, embankments set close to the riverbanks require extensive revetment and

(i) narrow corridor

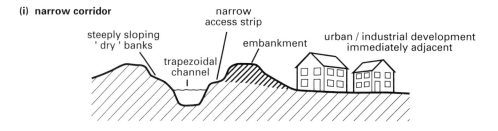

(ii) wide corridor

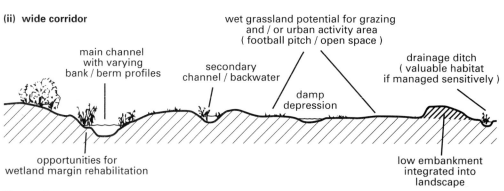

**Figure 3
Opportunities for wildlife associated with embankments located close to or distant from a riverbank. (i) Narrow corridor. Access strip too narrow to use as amenity area. No potential for grazing; mowing is the only management option.
(ii) Wide corridor. Development pressure moved away from the river's edge. Viable size for amenity area. Potential for rehabilitation/re-creation of wetland margins, backwaters and wet grassland. Potential for grazing of wet grassland.**

have to be higher and stronger than if set well back, because of lack of storage and floodplain conveyance. Maintenance requirements for the river and the embankments are greater too and no habitat enhancement for river or adjacent land is possible. Best practice is therefore to set floodbanks as far back from the bank as possible, a design which maximises habitat enhancement potential, reduces structural costs and facilitates easy future maintenance of river and floodbank.

Figure 3 introduces the concept of habitat creation potential, which is both directly and indirectly associated with embankments that are set well back from rivers. By following this method, wet grassland, scrub/wet woodland, off-river wetlands and defined public access routes are more easily accommodated. Although it is generally not practicable to incorporate all the features shown, many of them could be included when building new embankments. Public access on footpaths can also be provided along embankments without serious intrusion upon the wildlife of the wider corridor. However, this is not appropriate in areas of great wildfowl and wader interest because birds can be seriously disturbed by walkers on the skyline. The R Torne Case Study (3.4a) illustrates many habitat enhancements which can be available when raising existing floodbanks. This example also shows that when floodbanks are set well back from the edge, marginal habitats can be rehabilitated or created.

Embankments also serve as a refuge for livestock and wildlife in time of flood. This is an important aspect of the viability of the grazing regime suggested. Invertebrates are often of great interest in floodplains but little is known about how they survive periods of flooding. High spots in the floodplain, as well as the floodbanks themselves, may be important.

The need for material to build, or raise, floodbanks often provides good opportunities for wildlife enhancement. The Torne Case Study (3.4a) shows how floodplain and river margin wetlands of an almost infinite variety can be created from

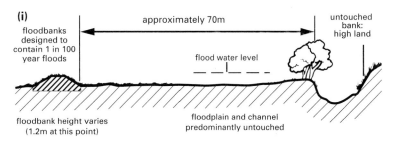

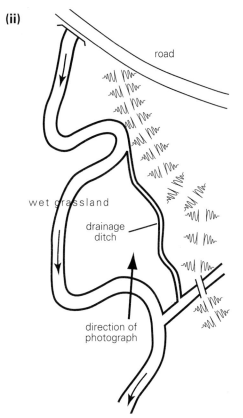

Figure 4
Examples of creating new floodbanks which protect existing river interests and maintain/enhance ecological assets of the floodplain. (i) R Asker, Bridport (1981 flood alleviation scheme). Construction of the floodbank well back from the river not only retained floodplain habitat whilst increasing flood storage capacity but also eliminated the need for extensive potentially damaging in-channel works. Adapted from: Lewis and Williams (1984)
(ii) Afon-Briant, Anglesey Dwyran flood alleviation scheme. Dwyran village had suffered from the combined effects of riverine and coastal flooding. Wet grassland in the area was of considerable importance for breeding wading birds, eg redshank and lapwing. The original design for the scheme was to site the floodbank close to the river and produce improved agricultural grassland. However, setting the floodbanks back from the river not only maintained the existing bird habitat but also provided flood protection for Dwyran to the desired standard.

impoverished wildlife habitats. This, and many other schemes combine restoration of some wetland habitats with improved angling and other recreational interests. Such opportunities may not be as great

Stuart McFadzean

Plate 5
Floodbank and drainage ditch on the Afon Briant which have been routed around an important wetland for breeding waders. The river is situated at the extreme top left of the photograph.

everywhere as they were on the R Torne, but construction of new, and raising of existing floodbanks invariably provide opportunities that must not be missed. Figure 4 (i) and (ii) illustrates two schemes where building floodbanks improved habitat diversity or led to greater protection of floodplain wetlands. On the Asker the interest developed from a two-stage channel and pool which provided some spoil for the embankment. On the Afon-Briant (Plate 5) a floodbank has been routed around a wetland important for breeding waders and this has increased its long-term prospects of remaining a site of wildlife interest.

3.4.3 Realignments and by-passes

Case Studies:
R Alne 3.4(c),
R Roding at
Passingford
3.4(d)

This section considers the opportunities for creating and enhancing river environments when constructing secondary channels or realigning existing ones. Realignments involve replacing existing channels with a completely new one. In contrast, by-pass channels complement existing channels, which are retained. The need for works of this nature most frequently results from circumstances listed in Table 1.

Realignments
The options for channel realignment as a result of the hypothetical construction of a

new road and for improvement of flood capacity as illustrated in Figure 5. New road construction along a valley floor may unavoidably coincide with the line of a meandering river. Wherever possible the road should be routed to avoid it. In circumstances where this is impossible, simply cutting off meanders and shortening river length is unacceptable because:

- this directly reduces the extent and variety of river habitat;
- and it is probable that it will cause channel instability with resultant need for additional bank protection measures.

Realignment may also be associated with flood alleviation schemes that cannot accommodate tight meanders, which cause high water levels at relatively low flows or where erosion is seriously threatening roads or buildings. A less sinuous channel is sometimes required to draw water away from towns and villages to reduce the risk of flooding through water being held back.

Figure 5 (i–iv) also shows different approaches where environmental

Table 1: Reasons for considering realignment/secondary channel options for rivers

- Capacity is too small to carry flood flows through a reach.
- Buildings or other features close to the river physically restrict options for enlargement.
- Valuable natural habitats in or near the river would be put at risk through channel enlargement.
- Other engineering proposals, most typically new road constructions, conflict with the existing alignment.
- Valuable riverside habitats, land use, flood defence or other features are threatened as river is highly active and unstable with severe erosion and meandering.
- Additional river corridor habitats and features are to be created.

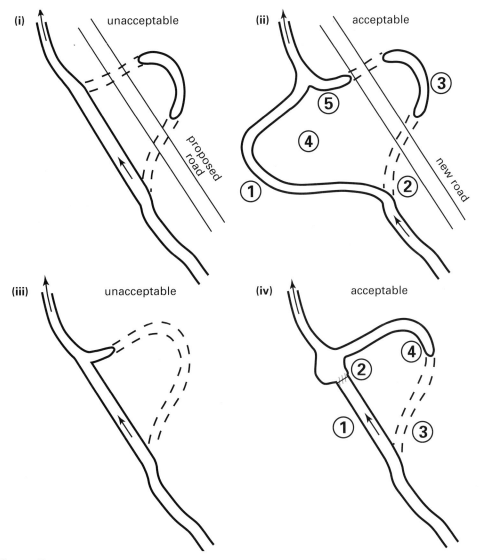

Figure 5
Acceptable and unacceptable realignment scenarios
(i) Unacceptable: realignment to avoid new highway. *Impacts*: **gradient steepened, habitat loss, erosion potential.**
(ii) Acceptable: alternative to (i)
1.Realigned channel mirror image of original
2.Spoil fills part of old channel
3.Section develops as isolated pond
4.'New' land incorporated into existing management or developed for wildlife
5.Backwaters created from redundant channel, may need deepening
(iii) Unacceptable: realignment to improve flood capacity locally. *Impacts*: **gradient steepened, habitat loss, erosion potential**
(iv) Acceptable: alternative to (iii) 1.Straight cut eliminates meander
2.Drop weir or rock armoured riffle with pool, dissipates excess energy and stabilises upstream bed levels and velocities.
3.Spoil fills part of old channel. Alternatively leave as flood/low-flow channel.
4.Old channel developed as backwater refuge.

conservation and enhancement opportunities are integrated into the design but are developed within the same constraints. The implementation of a 'mirror image' scheme (Figure 5(ii)) is often the ideal way initially to approach a realignment option. However a true mirror image often proves impracticable; land levels may be different on each side of the river, physical features may need to be avoided, soils will vary, field drainage may be affected and land ownership and

Table 2: Considerations for realignment

- Consider variations for the realigned channel – old meander traces are often evident, suggesting route options.
- The same length of channel (or more in previously shortened rivers) must be created to preserve the established mean gradient of the river and facilitate re-establishment of a regime similar to the original.
- Excavate a 'natural' channel – steep cliffs on the outside of bends, shoals on the inside, variable bed levels and few straight lines – the river will finish the job off so there is no need to leave it 'tidy'.
- Do not rush into a full programme of replanting riverside trees and other vegetation; give the river chance to settle into its new geometry. The objective is to assist natural regeneration – await sight of this, then assist when/if required.
- Exposed soils vulnerable to erosion may require some protection; flat batters are preferable to revetments.
- If revetments are required, use live timber that will grow and consolidate the bank over time, but design capacity to accommodate future growth.
- Raise bed levels locally to avoid exposing erodible sands and gravels but create shallow riffles where exposure is safe.
- Do not set out to impose a precise and fixed geometry to the river; devote time to on-site variation as work proceeds – regard each problem as an opportunity and look elsewhere to see how the river has accommodated such problems previously.

Table 3: Features that should be incorporated into new cuts

- A weir (or similar structure) to dissipate the extra energy arising from the reduced lengths. Since bed stabilisation is important, the use of rock to simulate a natural riffle is often the best approach.
- Turbulence below the weir is absorbed by excavating a scour hole or pool, but take measures to prevent the structure collapsing.
- The new cut approaching the weir is engineered to simulate the regime that exists above it.
- A backwater is created from the old abandoned natural channel. This will not retain its 'river' character forever, but progressively silt up to create marshy conditions.

Anne Skinner

management requirements may exert a strong influence. In all cases, consideration of issues in Table 2 is essential if a scheme is to be successful.

The Case Study of the R Roding at Passingford (Case Study 3.4d) provides an example where a mirror image proved impractical. This led to the adoption of a 'template' from a suitable natural section nearby. Many river realignments have been undertaken in conjunction with road building programmes since the Passingford example but few have incorporated the concepts into design and construction. However, the construction of the A543 in the Neath Valley has adopted the principle and will utilise, as realignment channels, ancient river courses discovered through field investigations and use of historical maps and parish boundaries. In general, the prevalent practice is still to minimise land areas affected resulting in relatively 'straight' cuts for both roads and rivers. Implementing more sensitive alternatives is better for wildlife and for maintaining a natural river regime but because this requires significant land-take, support from landowners and highway authorities is required.

New cuts to assist flood alleviation are a very common practice and many examples and variations exist. They often shorten river length and steepen gradients. Unless appropriate measures are taken, significant upstream scour and downstream deposition will occur. Meandering may also quickly recommence. Table 3 shows design features that aim to counter these problems. Unless new cuts incorporate or improve upon habitat features present in the original channel, and river length is maintained or increased, new cuts cannot be regarded as best practice.

New developments in highly degraded areas can provide ideal opportunities for enhancements where the developments

Plate 6
Realignment of the R Biss, Trowbridge provided the opportunity for significant habitat enhancements in the newly constructed channel.

incorporate channel realignment. The site of a Tesco superstore in the floodplain of the R Biss at Trowbridge is a typical example where the newly constructed channel incorporated significant habitat enhancements (Plate 6). Meanders were incorporated in the channel design together with berms, pool and riffle sequences, off-stream ponds and marshy areas. The whole site was landscaped using native trees. Education facilities were also incorporated to promote the scheme.

By-passes

The purpose of most river by-pass channels is to divert excess water from the main channel during flooding. In consequence, by-pass channels may be dry under low-flow conditions, although they can be designed to carry a continuous small base-flow or have the majority of flow diverted through them (Plates 7 and 8). Three such by-pass options are shown in Figure 6. If flow is split between both channels, this is more valuable to wildlife, provided there is sufficient flow to maintain habitats in the original channel.

A typical scenario is shown diagrammatically in Figure 7 where a by-pass channel affords a viable alternative to channel enlargement. The engineering objective is to convey flood water from (X) the 'overflow', to (Y) the delivery point, so that the normal rate of water-level rise in the meander is reduced. The downstream water level is the controlling factor and must be 'transferred' upstream, via the by-pass route, to point (X) as effectively as possible. Table 4 gives the key principles of this design.

Technical demands associated with some by-passes should not discourage opportunities for environmental enhancement. Figure 7 outlines the enhancement opportunities inherent in most major by-pass channel designs. An essential concept is to a create an additional river channel and a corridor of associated floodplain habitat. An island is created by a by-pass channel and this may retain its original character or provide valuable wildlife habitat with appropriate management.

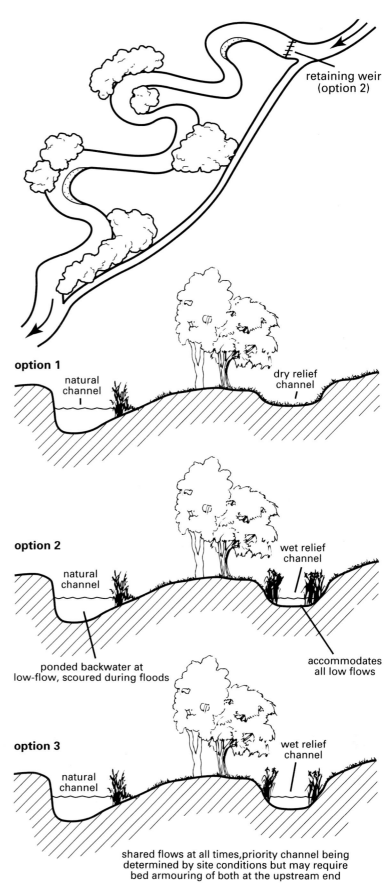

Figure 6
Three basic by-pass scenarios.

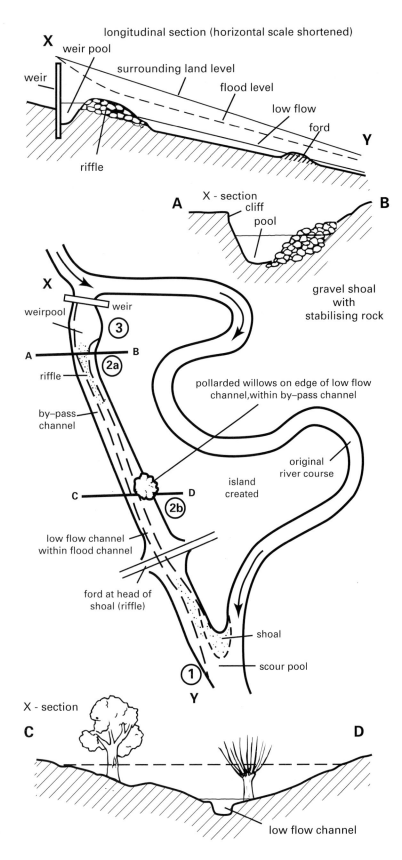

longitudinal section (horizontal scale shortened)

X

weir pool

weir

surrounding land level

flood level

low flow

ford

Y

riffle

X - section

A

cliff

pool

B

gravel shoal
with
stabilising rock

X

weirpool

weir

③

A

②a

B

riffle

by-pass
channel

pollarded willows on edge of low flow
channel,within by-pass channel

C

②b

D

island
created

original
river course

low flow channel
within flood channel

ford at head of
shoal (riffle)

shoal

scour pool

①

Y

X - section

C

D

low flow channel

By-passes can arise naturally during floods. The R Monnow at Maerdy (Case Study 3.3(e)) has a multi-stage channel that includes a natural by-pass channel, which has stabilised over many years. The stability is enhanced by self-set alders and willows on the bank.

Many examples of flood relief cut-off channels have been in place for sufficient time to illustrate problems and ecological value. Many (eg R Alne Case Study 3.4(c) and Bourne Brook) show that habitat improvements have developed from both the islands created, and additional watercourse formed. The shorter length of by-pass channels produce increased velocities, which can induce bed scour and result in the natural channel tending to function as the relief channels. Because maintaining flow through the original channel is desirable, designs need to ensure the bed of by-pass channels will not erode. Bed armouring should rarely be necessary unless the by-pass is unavoidably steep.

Figure 7
Enhancement opportunities inherent in major by-pass channel design

1. At exit of by-pass a shoal can be created on the upstream side and a scour pool on the downstream side. The stabilised channel is effected using a series of current deflectors protecting the bank from erosion and sustaining the scouring action in the pool.

2(a, b). Variable depths in by-pass channel (including low-flow channel) create a range of wet and dry habitat conditions, (sections A–B and C–D).

3. Weir pool excavated below normal ground level (scoured during flood flows). An earth cliff can be associated with the pool but care is needed to protect the weir with adequate 'wingwalls' set into the bank.

Table 4: Simple concepts and considerations for by-pass design

- A by-pass is likely to require stabilisation at its upstream end to accommodate excess energy arising from the drop in water level where the gradient is significant. A weir is normally required.
- The shortest possible route is normal, mirror image' schemes are rarely appropriate.
- Flow velocity in the by-pass can be excessive due to the shortened route and potentially increased gradients. Control is via careful design of gradients and cross-sections to limit velocities rather than providing extensive artificial revetments.
- Land use, access and maintenance of the island created by the by-pass are all important factors to be provided for in the design.
- Consider pros and cons of the by-pass channel being 'wet', ie, carry a permanent base flow, or 'dry' if summer base flows are small. Splitting flow into both the original channel and the by-pass may be detrimental to the former.

Stuart McFadzean

Nigel Holmes

Plate 7 (top)
Wet by-pass channel (left) at Worthing Mill on the Wendling Beck

Plate 8 (above)
Dry by-pass channel (left) on the Bourne Brook

3.4.4 Deflectors and revetments

Case Studies: R Clwyd catchment (3.4(e)), Broadland Rivers (3.4(f))

Maintenance of bank stability may be essential in urban areas to protect property. In rural areas this may also be the case where the channel is adjacent to roads, railways, buildings or flood defence structures. These are the key areas where deflectors and revetments are employed for bank stabilisation. However, it should be remembered that erosion is a process essential to the formation of many natural habitat features, such as backwaters, bays and bankside cliffs.

To improve bank stability, a wide range of techniques have been developed. These include the use of trees and other vegetation, the use of rock, or piling of riverbanks with steel or cement. Unless the works improve the habitat of the banks, they are not regarded as desirable for wildlife. In many instances eroding and depositing banks are preferable.

Bank protection works generally take the form of deflecting the current in the river away from the bank or reveting it so that it is resistant to erosion. Dissipation of energy is the objective of utilising both

Table 5: Typical strata, flora and revetment techniques

TYPICAL SUBSTRATES	TYPICAL ENVIRONMENT	TYPICAL ASSOCIATED FLORA	SIMULATED REVETMENT TECHNIQUE
Rock outcrop	Upland	Insignificant as aid to revetment	Quarried rock closely built and cemented
Large boulders in glacial till	Upland and piedmont	Alder securing boulders	Quarried rock in dense matrix of graded stone/ clay planted with alder saplings
Large cobbles in glacial till	Piedmont	Alder and willow binding cobbles	Crushed rock in dense matrix of graded stone/ clay. May be reinforced with open wire mesh securing willow logs and alder saplings
Cobbles in alluvial gravel/ silty clay matrix	Piedmont and lowland	Willow and alder reinforce soil	Redistributed riverine shoal material reinforced with locally cut willow and alder saplings
Sandy clay and cemented gravel lenses	Lowland shallow water	Willow and alder reinforce soil + grasses and herbage	Willow mattresses. May be reinforced with woven willow and alder saplings at toe.
Silty clays	Lowland deep water	Willow and alder reinforce soil + grasses and herbage	Sunken willow mattresses or driven willow poles supporting woven willow at toe
Soft silty clays, muds	Lowland	Reeds, grasses and herbage on slumped shelves	Reed mattresses sunk below water and extended over shallow sloping toe. May be reinforced with open mesh fabric

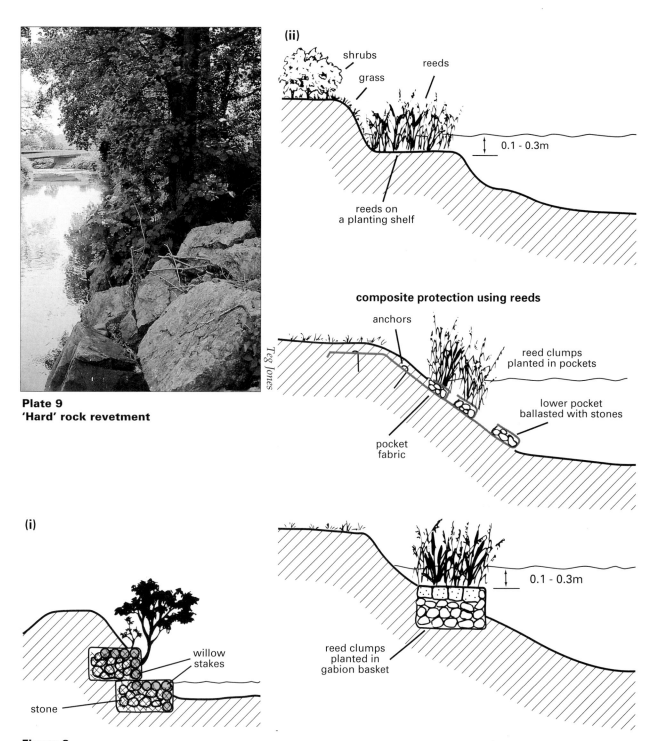

Plate 9
'Hard' rock revetment

(ii)

shrubs

grass

reeds

0.1 - 0.3m

reeds on
a planting shelf

composite protection using reeds

anchors

reed clumps
planted in pockets

lower pocket
ballasted with stones

pocket
fabric

Teg Jones

(i)

willow
stakes

stone

reed clumps
planted in
gabion basket

0.1 - 0.3m

Figure 8
Revetment examples combining trees and shrubs or other vegetation with stone or synthetic materials.
(i) R Ystrad at Brookhouse near Denbigh. Willows have matured from logs used to face gabion crates, binding the stone in a dense fibrous root system.
(ii) Examples of protection using reedbanks. Adapted from Hemphill and Bramley (1989)

Alistair Driver

Richard Vivash

Plate 10 (above) 'Soft' larch pole revetment

Plate 11 (below) The dense, strong rooting system of alders exposed at low flows

- erosion processes and instability mechanisms;
- the geomorphic (natural) process of bank erosion;
- the human impacts on the extent and rate of erosion;
- techniques for assessing and classifying erosion problems;
- management of bank erosion, eg matching solutions to problems;
- alternatives to structural intervention, eg addressing cause of problem;
- structural intervention, eg soft engineering, revetments, groynes, spurs.

The need to constrain river movement artificially can often be avoided through good management or by returning the river to a more natural regime. Revetment, therefore, often treats the symptom, not the cause of bank instability. Understanding the causes of the problem, and addressing them, should be priorities before revetment work is contemplated.

Revetments

Studying natural revetments has considerable practical application because artificial structures need to simulate the 'real thing'. Resistant substrates such as rock, boulders, cemented gravels and dense clays represent natural 'hard' revetments (Table 5; Plate 9). Trees, bushes, dense saplings, reeds, grasses and other plants constitute 'soft' revetments (Plate 10). With the possible exception of sheet rock, natural revetments are a combination of substrates reinforced by vegetation (Figure 8 (i–ii)). To identify sustainable flood defence options to protect against erosion, consideration of natural geological and vegetational aspects is essential.

Stable tree-lined upland rivers characteristically have numerous alders and other trees at the water's edge growing around exposed boulders embedded in mixed clay/gravel soils. Alder roots (Plate 11) commonly spread laterally underwater to reinforce the bed as well as the bank. 'Lowland' riverbanks are more typically characterised by willows in association with reeds, sedge, grasses and mixed herbs. Willow roots (Plates 12 and 13) spread laterally in fine soils to form an

deflectors and revetments. The two techniques can sometimes be used in combination to good environmental effect.

The purpose of this section is briefly to illustrate some of the more environmentally sensitive techniques that have proved effective. Although steel or concrete may be essential in extreme cases, they are not advocated for wildlife enhancement. A review of revetment techniques is provided by Hemphill and Bramley (1989), covering details of soil mechanics, structural considerations, and the range of proprietary revetment systems such as gabions, synthetic fabrics and articulated concrete blockwork. In addition, the final report of an NRA research and development project on bank erosion along navigable waterways provides an excellent source of information (NRA, 1993). The document includes information on the following:

excellent surface revetment, but roots will not penetrate the water table to any significant extent. Willow root 'revetment' can be very shallow at the water's edge, making large trees prone to 'wind blow'.

The value of willow for soft revetment has much to do with its remarkable ability rapidly to regenerate from even the smallest cutting and also its tolerance of frequent coppicing and pollarding. Even a fallen willow is unlikely to die because roots can strike from any point of contact with soil. The density of newly-sprouted shoots can prove invaluable in breaking up river currents that might otherwise lead to undesirable erosion.

The value of reeds and similar vegetation as a natural revetment (Figure 8 (ii); Plates 14 and 15) is associated with both the dense root structure and the tall leafy growth that absorbs energy. Species such as the common reed retain these essential characteristics through the winter season. Common reed is mainly confined to still or slow-moving waters, with fine sediment. However, reed canary-grass is common on mixed substrates where current velocity can be high, and often stabilises upland rivers, whereas reed, if well established, is tolerant of both floods and waves generated by wind and boat wash.

Case Studies 3.4(f) and 3.7(c) illustrate successful combination of trees, shrubs and other vegetation with stone and synthetic materials to revet banks so that both bank protection is achieved and wildlife benefits. Trees and shrubs can be effectively combined with gabions and bitumen mattresses (Plate 16). The R Clywd (Plates 17 and 18) is an example of a catchment where a combination of managing trees, rock and shrubs has served as an effective form of bank revetment for generations, at the same time producing a rich habitat diversity.

There are also numerous examples where herbaceous reedy vegetation or trees and shrubs are being used for bank revetment without any additional 'hard' defences. Spiling and faggoting have been extensively used in Yorkshire where mobile margins and banks are stabilised.

Richard Vivash

Richard Vivash

Examples of the successful use of the technique on lowland rivers include the Meece Brook, R Medway and Poole Harbour (Section 3.7).

Deflectors

Deflectors affect the pattern of river currents and may be installed for a variety of purposes and in a number of different forms. The prime aims are usually either to halt bank erosion or increase in-stream habitat diversity. Ecologically, current deflectors/groynes are of particular value for improving degraded sections of river in terms of fish habitat (Section 1.7.3). They provide fish with shelter from fast-flow velocities as well as improving spawning conditions in rivers suffering from low flows. In addition, they provide hard, stable substrates for colonisation by algae, mosses and their associated invertebrate communities.

Plate 12 (top) Fallen willow showing root system (1975)

Plate 13 (above) The same willow tree photographed in 1992. The trunk has been cut and has regrown. The root has split into two parts. It supports brambles and continues to stabilise the riverbank.

Stuart McFadzean

Stuart McFadzean

**Plate 14 (top)
Natural reed
margins on the
tidal R Frome
provide
protection from
boat wash and
bank erosion**

**Plate 15 (above)
Reed planting
under the
geotextile
Enkamat in the
Norfolk Broads**

The most common location for deflectors is around the outside of unstable bends, where they are used in a series, to 'nudge' the current through the required section. Flood protection work adjacent to the R Taff necessitated construction of a floodbank immediately adjacent to the river. In order to reduce the impact of erosion and mitigate any potentially adverse impact on the fishery, blockstone groynes were installed (Plate 19). The series of small groynes (and associated revetment) not only reduced scour but also provided resting pools for migratory salmonids.

For habitat enhancement purposes, deflectors are more commonly used in previously straightened reaches or where low flows are insufficient to sustain depth and velocity changes. Blockstone groynes were used at Wansford on the West Beck, a

tributary of the R Hull to alleviate the impact of low flows and associated problems of siltation of the gravel substrate. This technique has proved extremely successful (Plate 20).

Groynes were installed on the Scotsgrove Brook (Section 3.2.6) to create a self-maintaining channel, thereby reducing maintenance costs, and to enhance its degraded habitat (Plate 21). Each stone groyne deflects flow for about 5 m downstream. The work has been a success; the formerly species-poor, water-cress dominated channel now contains a range of species, including unbranched bur-reed, water-crowfoot and water-starwort; with reed canary-grass, water pepper and blue water-speedwell on the shelves.

It must be remembered also that deflectors create, as well as control scour. This means that careful thought is required before installation. The most common failure arises at the point where deflectors join the riverbank. Flood water moving over the top of the deflector at this point can scour the bank away leaving the deflector isolated and no longer serving its purpose.

True deflectors are generally shorter and/or lower than groynes and serve only to protect the base of riverbanks from direct erosion by currents and also to deflect currents in straight channels to create depth, velocity and substrate changes. When used for bank protection some revetment at the point of emergence from the bank is generally needed. In appropriate cases willow and alder may provide additional reinforcements and increase wildlife interest on the bank. Reeds often colonise the sediments deposited behind deflectors.

Deflectors, combined with revetments (Plates 17 and 18), can provide a means of influencing both river bed and bank form, affording potential for creative engineering of riverside habitat where control is essential. In most cases revetment alone is not desirable for wildlife but deflectors built to create localised scour and deposition of sediments can enhance in-stream variations in depth, water velocity

Plate 16 (top)
Gabion revetment planted with willow poles in 1977 (photographed in 1992) at Brookhouse near Denbigh on the R Ystrad. Under-cutting of the toe of a flood embankment was arrested by two tiers of stone-filled gabion crates; one below water and one above. The upper was faced with willow logs to provide root reinforcement of the stone and habitat. The works are featured on p167 of the first edition of this handbook showing early stages of growth. The works were successful with no maintenance being necessary over the succeeding 15 years. The photograph shows the maturing willow trees along the water's edge that may now benefit from selective thinning and pollarding to ensure their future security.

Richard Vivash

Plate 17 (centre)
R Clwyd at Llandynog: A small flood embankment is protected with stone revetment that incorporates deflectors. The works are approximately 10 years old in this photograph (1977).

Plate 18 (bottom)
R Clywd at Llandynog revetment/deflectors in 1992: the riverbank remaining stable 25 years after their installation.

Richard Vivash

and substrates where channel degradation has taken place. The creation of localised pools and riffles in their wake are equally beneficial to fisheries and other wildlife (Section 3.2.6). The use of deflectors in pairs, opposing each other from opposite banks, or staggered along each bank, are all variations of the basic concept. The use of larch poles driven into the riverbed at Tadcaster on the R Wharfe (Plate 22) illustrates the latter concept. The herringbone pattern of the groynes has created areas of differential flow. The groynes which show above the water level in low summer flows, are well below the surface during flood conditions. They have not only produced self-cleansing velocities but are also valuable refuges for fish fry.

To benefit wildlife, deflectors are most valuable when applied on a small scale, preferably restricted to rivers with inherently stable banks. They should be installed only when flow regimes have become altered and natural processes alone cannot reinstate the habitats that have been lost.

Richard Vivash

Table 6 lists criteria that may be regarded as good practice in simulating natural revetment and deflector techniques.

Stuart McFadzean

Plate 19
Blockstone groynes on the R Taff

Alistair Driver

Plate 21
Blockstone groynes on Scotsgrove Brook

Stuart McFadzean

Plate 20
Blockstone groynes on the West Beck a tributary of the R Hull

Plate 22
Staggered larch pole deflectors on the R Wharfe at Tadcaster

John Pygott

Table 6: Guidance for the use of deflectors and revetments

- Do not over-react to occurrences of bank instability; localised slips often settle to a new profile adding diversity; localised point erosion often has limited spread and is valuable. Migration of bends is a naturally occurring geomorphological process that is essential to sustain the overall river regime. Question whether best left alone.
- Observe the instability and seek to understand fully the mechanisms that generate it; consider action to alleviate the cause before embarking upon protective measures to treat the symptom.
- Consider removal of some energy from the river in extreme cases; eg constructions of a weir downstream of instability to flatten the gradient and reduce velocity. Design weir structure to dissipate stored energy immediately downstream via a deep, turbulent pool.
- Examine stable sections of riverbank nearby to determine the scope for simulation techniques. This includes environmentally successful engineered reaches.
- Examine the area of exposed riverbank, particularly above and below normal water level to determine whether limited toe protection will maintain support of the upper bank.
- Determine the minimum scope of works necessary to modify the regime locally and if necessary to provide some protection to the bank.
- Adopt protection techniques that break up currents attacking exposed banks rather than render the bank smooth; provide for regeneration of indigenous flora as future bank cover to further break up current and provide root reinforcement to soils and any imported revetment substrate.
- Plan and design for a specific regime with habitat development as a primary objective; do not add this later to a pre-conceived scheme.
- Augment primary features such as deep pools with secondary features to provide balanced habitat.
- Monitor performance regularly and be prepared to undertake 'first aid' as the river reacts to works carried out whilst allowing overall adjustment.

3.4.5 Weirs and sluices

Case Studies: Loughrans Weir (3.4(g)), Great Ouse at Godmanchester (3.4(h)), R Lugg (3.4(i))

Weirs and sluices are used as a means of harnessing the power of rivers to drive milling machinery, for water level/flood control and in conjunction with locks for navigation. Weirs are 'fixed structures' whereas sluices have moveable elements. Both hold back water upstream, reducing its velocity. The introduction of weirs and sluices regulates natural hydrological processes in rivers and is regarded as environmental degradation. However, where river regime has been affected by past engineering works, weirs and sluices can potentially provide either habitat protection or enhancement. This potential lies primarily in upstream retention of water and control of water levels and, to some degree, the utilisation of energy to create in-stream habitats immediately downstream.

Sluice and weir design needs reference to technical engineering manuals but should

also incorporate features noted in this section. Table 7 describes the ecological and physical impacts of weirs and sluices above, at and below the structure.

The construction of new weirs and sluices is bound to have significant environmental effects both upstream and downstream of the structure.

Minor sluices and weirs can enhance degraded in-channel habitats and floodplain wetlands. Stabilisation of an actively eroding river channel can be assisted by the construction of weirs. The effect of the weir is to flatten the gradient upstream thereby slowing the river and dissipating energy. Weirs and sluices are also used to divert flows into secondary channels, and through ditches essential for managing some wet meadows and other floodplain habitats. These structures vary from simple log weirs (Plate 23) to more

Table 7: Weirs and sluices - principal physical and environmental parameters

PARAMETER	ABOVE WEIR/SLUICE	AT WEIR/SLUICE	BELOW WEIR/SLUICE
Velocity	Slower and uniform	Rapid	Turbulent and varied
Depth	Deeper with little variation	Shallow	Very variable
Wetted area	Consistent area even at low-flow	Uniform or varied according to design; notches & fish passes reduce area at low-flow	Uniform at pool but variable at runs and other areas
Water levels	Little change (especially for automatic sluices) in response to volume increases	Change slowly in floods	Change rapidly in response to flow increases
Effect on flora and fauna	Maintained high water table for floodplain wetlands. Animals and plants favoured by ponded conditions as fine sediments pre-dominate – ie water-lily, swan mussels	Rapid velocity and smooth surfaces generally provide habitat for algal and moss growth. Where slope not steep and fissures present, rooted crowfoot. Walls favoured sites for dipper nests	Coarse substrates and tugging currents create habitat for milfoil and invertebrates such as blackflies and stoneflies

Table 8: Opportunities to restore ancient aspects of river habitat in association with weir and sluice construction

- Excavate the upstream channel to increase river width and to vary shape to promote a large pond or lake habitat.
- Vary bank profiles in the pond to provide a wide range from cliffs to shallow, multi-stage, slopes and benches.
- Create extensive shallow-water margins as a basis for wetland habitat in association with the retained level above the structure.
- Excavate bays and other sheltered water features suitable for small fish and amphibians and for mature fish in times of flood.
- Conserve existing trees and establish others, particularly where low branches can safely be allowed to extend over the river close to normal water level.
- Integrate small low-level islands clear of the main flow path as refuge for water birds, etc.
- Establish turbulent pool and riffle features immediately downstream of the structure.

Roy Stokes

Plate 23 (right) Simple log weir on the R Sowe sophisticated yet relatively low-cost structures in place on Wetmoor and Westmoor in the Somerset levels used to maintain water levels in line with ESA prescriptions (Tinkler 1993).

When unmaintained weirs collapse, major adjustments in river regime usually occur. Upstream water levels drop, flow velocities accelerate, banks may collapse and accumulated sediments are washed downstream. In time a more natural regime may be established but considerable thought is needed before a replacement is proposed. Although natural river habitats may benefit from abandonment, the previously high water

CONFIGURATION	DIAGRAMMATIC PLAN	COMMENT
1. Straight	examples common but often with downstream revetment (no pool)	Weir same width as river. Most 'efficient' layout, smallest structure for given flow , least land taken
2. Angled	typical mill head channel	Weir wider than river. Structure 'skewed' to avoid overwidening of river upstream. Creates varied downstream habitat. Common at old mills.
3. Curved	sluice e.g. Pultney weir, Bath	Weir wider than river, but 'narrowed' by curving the crest. Example is Pultney weir, Bath. Largely an amenity feature.
4. Side	old mill or generator site e.g River Monnow at Monmouth	Extreme example of skewed weir. Relatively long structure gives rise to less concentrated scour. Islands likely to form, common as 'overspills'.
5. Separate weir or weir / sluice	bridge over sluice or weir island	If built as an alternative to a single weir of greater width, this configuration considerably enhances the habitat variety of the site.
6. Below meander	low embankment e.g. upper Lugg, Leominster	This configuration stabilises the meander and gives rise to complex approach velocities. Intercepts debris and provides fish refuge and habitat variety.
7. Within meander		Weir built to simulate the 'natural' riffle arising below the bend. Stabilises bend upstream but 'develops' scour below the riffle.

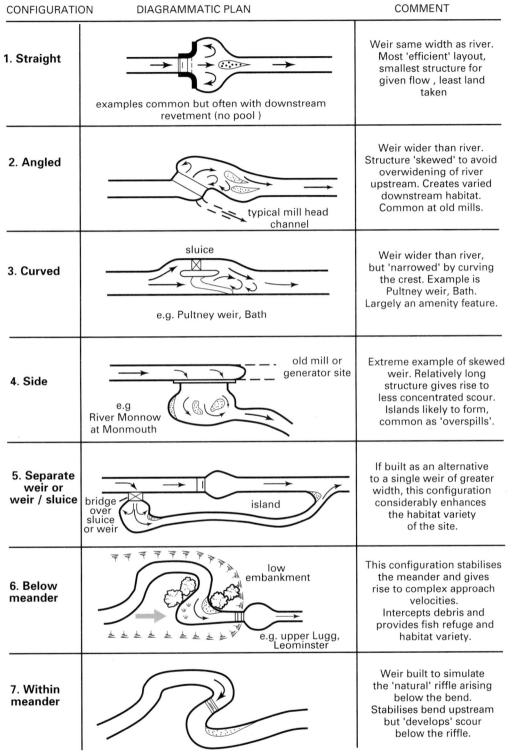

Figure 9
Alternative weir configurations

levels upstream, from the weir or sluice may have been essential for conserving wet riverside meadows and other water table or inundation-dependent habitats. If these are of great conservation value, eg Port Holme Meadow SSSI at Godmanchester on the R Ouse (Case Study 3.4(h)) then rebuilding to maintain water level control would be desirable. Regulation of flow by weirs and sluices can also be used to simulate habitats that arise naturally in rivers. The design brief for wildlife enhancement purposes should therefore include consideration of the features in Table 8.

The extent of habitat enhancement opportunities upstream is strongly influenced by the siting of the weir in relation to existing river and bankside features (Figure 9). Temptation to cut through and create a straight approach to the weir should be resisted.

Structure of weirs and sluices

A schematic weir is shown in Figure 10, which illustrates its principal technical components. Because weirs and sluices represent points of major velocity change, their viability can only be assured through the most careful process of design and construction. All new structures should enable migratory fish to pass via the structure and appropriate design should minimise loss of fish through large sluices in times of flood. Fisheries staff should, therefore, advise in the design phase.

There are two extremes of weir design. Weirs such as concrete structures with smooth crest profiles used for gauging purposes provide little environmental benefit. By contrast low crest rock structures result in greater flow variability and are generally perceived as more sensitive.

The ecological interest upstream of a weir focuses largely on the ponded habitat with features similar to backwaters. Downstream there are contrasting habitats resulting from energy dissipation that scours deep pools, typically onion-shaped in plan and section. If depth is restricted through the presence of hard rock (or rock infill) the pool elongates. The same may happen if the pool is constrained in width. The length, section and extent of the pool are thus primarily determined by:
- design of the weir or sluice;
- nature of the strata in which it is formed;
- the rate at which river level rises downstream of the structure.

If level rises are rapid, the structure soon drowns and will not create a pool.

If significant sediment is transported by the river, the pool will typically be followed by a shoal downstream. At low flows part of the shoal may be exposed and a 'run' of water over a coarse material be evident; an important feature in any river. The temptation to perceive the shoal as an hydraulic impediment is clear. However, it should be retained and left to develop.

Riverbanks around pools below structures should vary in section. Cliffs are often present as a result of active scour and benches may form from soils that have dropped following undermining. Constraining the dimensions of a scour pool reduces habitat potential. Controlling erosion will destroy the vital principle of allowing the pool to mature to create its associated wide range of habitats. In rural areas the economic value of land 'lost' to weir pools is likely to be much less than the cost of revetment to avoid the 'loss'. Engineering effort should therefore concentrate on avoiding structural damage caused by undermining.

The study of historic mill sites provides many examples of the potential to create a diverse variety of channels in combination with islands in weir design and layout. The lower reaches of the Great Ouse between St Ives and St Neots are among many examples of a lowland river that supports a multitude of secondary channels. They extend across the floodplain at several locations and, at Godmanchester (Case Study 3.4(h)), close to residential areas. They also represent significant recreation and landscape value.

In contrast, on the Bristol Avon at Chippenham, several historic sluices and

**Figure 10 (opposite)
Schematic weir structure. Side walls need careful consideration at each end. Upstream end extended to form smooth transition with stable riverbank profile. Downstream end keyed well into riverbank beyond limits of likely scour. If rock aprons are built, a 'bedding' is needed. A proprietary filter fabric is laid first protected with gravel and covered with a graded stone mix. Predominant stone size must be larger than the eventual gaps between rocks to avoid washing out.**

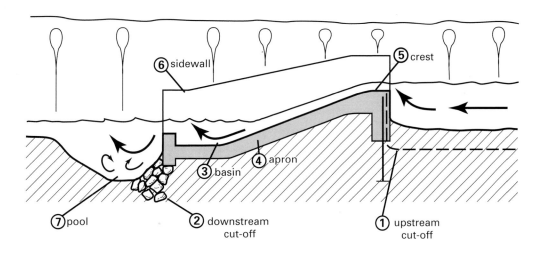

Weir component	Engineering function	Environmental consideration
1. upstream cut - off	prevents flow under and around structure	Primary component that holds water back. All others consequential to installation of cut - off. Butyl rubber sheet (dashed line) alternative to piles; extende vertically through bank
2. downstream cut - off	prevents scour undermining structure	If pool is to be developed downstream, this component most important. Trench filled with rock, alternative to piles
3. basin	energy dissipation	Can be designed to dissipate majority of energy to prevent downstream pool scouring. Can be eliminated to maximise pool
4. apron	conveyance of flow between two levels	Design critical to visual appearance and audible sound of water. Also for migratory fish. Irregular cascade over flat slope best
5. crest	controls upstream level	Horizontal over full width. Can be improved by shallow variations from horizontal to concentrate low flows
6. sidewalls	supports banks prevents scour	Height should be minimised to follow predominant flow profile over structure. Irregular stepped cross - section best
7. pool	energy dissipation	Most valuable enviromental feature. Depth and width can be calculated and structure designed accordingly. Initial excavation helpful

Richard Vivash

**Plate 24
Stone weir on
the R Lugg**

with a subsequent loss of habitat diversity and landscape interest, leaving a relatively uniform environment. Although flooding has not arisen since works were completed, it is probable that present day environmental awareness would demand a more creative scheme.

Case Study 3.4(g) illustrates how an ancient weir, which was a barrier to migrating fish, can be re-built to improve the landscape as well as facilitate fish passage. The R Lugg Case Study (3.4(i)) (Plate 24) is an example of several weirs that were installed to give greater control to the river's flow regime and incorporated features that would sustain ponded environments upstream and help develop contrasting habitats downstream.

**Case Studies:
Savick Brook
(3.4(j)), Curry
Moor (3.4(k))
and Quoile
Pondage (3.4(l))**

channels were replaced by a single large sluice in flood alleviation works in 1966. As a consequence, mill islands were removed,

3.4.6 Flood storage

Periodic inundation of floodplain land is an intrinsic feature of rivers. The term 'flood storage' is used in the context that selective flooding of land is artificially contrived. Flood storage aims to reduce the peak flow volume, which would otherwise cause flooding downstream (Figure 11). Flood storage is often required as a result

of increased run-off caused by urbanisation in the floodplain. Flood storage can be used upstream or downstream of developments to reduce flood volumes passing through channels which are too small to take the extreme flows. Flood storage areas may temporarily or permanently hold water and can serve a wide variety of uses, some of which may have nature conservation value.

River and floodplain wildlife often benefits from flood storage for two reasons: firstly, flow patterns in the river downstream of storage areas often more closely resemble those which occurred prior to catchment developments and drainage, so no further engineering works are needed to control flooding. Secondly, land within storage areas is constrained to high flood risk activities and is rarely intensively utilised. Creating and managing wildlife habitat should be an integral part of any flood defence scheme involving flood storage. A prime example is the building of Milton Keynes in the R Ouzel catchment which proceeded on the basis that there would not be a rise in flood levels downstream and the rivers would not be modified in any way. The new town is now based,

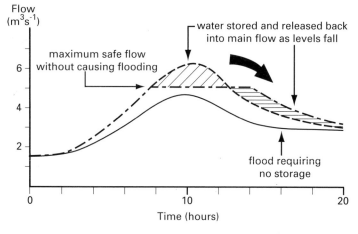

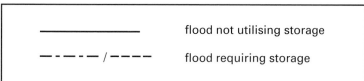

**Figure 11
The influence of flood storage on hydrograph form.**

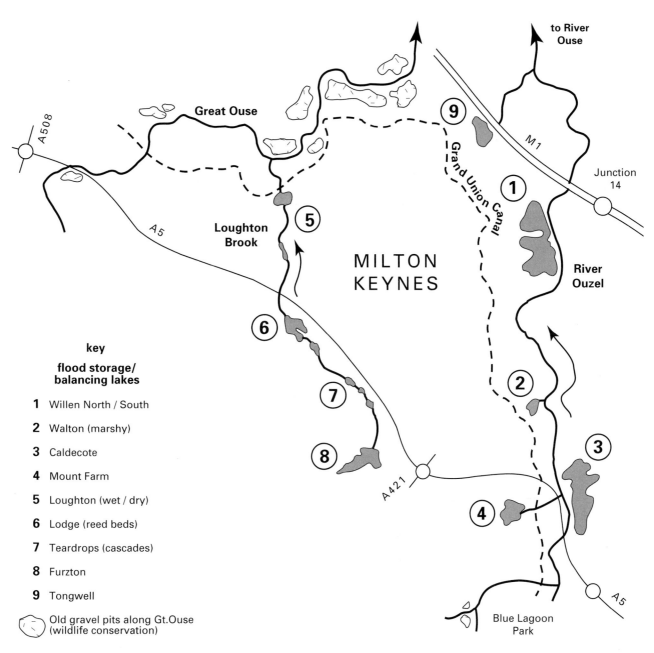

Figure 12
Flood storage at Milton Keynes, Bedfordshire.

key

**flood storage/
balancing lakes**

1 Willen North / South

2 Walton (marshy)

3 Caldecote

4 Mount Farm

5 Loughton (wet / dry)

6 Lodge (reed beds)

7 Teardrops (cascades)

8 Furzton

9 Tongwell

Old gravel pits along Gt.Ouse
(wildlife conservation)

therefore, on one of the world's largest constructed networks of flood storage reservoirs. These provide considerable public amenity and wildlife habitat. Figure 12 shows the layout of the storage lakes and some of their features.

Another form of flood storage sometimes occurs in estuaries. Rising tides hold the river water back, causing its level to rise, putting land and property at risk of flooding. River water overflows to a storage area before danger level is reached and subsequently flows back to the river as tide levels recede. The Ouse Washes in Cambridgeshire (an SSSI of RAMSAR/SPA status) have served this purpose since the 17th Century. The environmental value of the Ouse Washes is such that much of the 30 km long area is owned by conservation bodies including the RSPB, and managed almost exclusively for wildlife, while retaining their essential flood storage function.

The increasing use of flood storage areas to alleviate existing flooding problems, or mitigate the potential effects of future development, presents great opportunities for creative habitat development that fits ideally within strategic catchment planning for flood defence and environmental enhancement. There are already good examples of recent flood storage areas becoming important for wildlife. This section gives a very brief description of types of flood storage systems and highlights how some have developed valued habitats. For detailed design guidelines engineering manuals should be consulted.

Types of flood storage

Storage techniques 'mimic' naturally occurring phenomena of flooding land with varying degrees of control. Storage may be 'on-line' (ie on-stream), causing backup of levels above the control mechanism, or 'off-line', which diverts water to storage areas adjacent to the river. Figure 13 illustrates simple forms of on-line and off-line storage.

On-line storage may safeguard features downstream but can be detrimental to riverine and floodplain wildlife in the area of flooding if summer flooding, for example, inundates bird nests. On-stream storage is most commonly adopted in small-scale situations that may involve the mitigation of localised flashy run-off from new roads and industrial areas. For very small areas, storage lagoons are built into ditches and the outlet is restricted to limit the rate of discharge to the principal river system.

Off-line storage occurs where a river is embanked and flood water is diverted onto adjacent land through sluices. Evacuation of the flood water is carefully controlled and it is released only when the river downstream can cope. Such washlands may contain significant areas of permanent water, particularly if the land has been excavated to gain material for the construction of the floodbanks.

Many rivers still retain the natural characteristics of regular winter inundation

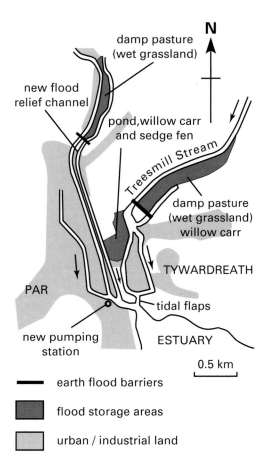

of their wide floodplains. Parts of the Yorkshire Ouse, R Wye, R Great Ouse, R Severn, R Exe and R Clwyd are good examples. The retention of these 'natural' floodplain washlands arguably contributes more to the mitigation of rapid run-off than can ever be achieved through controlled storage at specific 'problem' areas. It is, therefore, important not to lose sight of the value of natural floodplain storage in pursuit of water control measures. Such areas require none of the technology associated with controlled storage, are 'self sustaining' and of immense ecological value. The physical loss of floodplain through infilling for development and infrastructure diminishes ecological interest and often causes major flood defence problems for the future. Retaining existing floodplains as washlands is therefore of the utmost importance in considering the options for flood storage management.

In flood storage areas inundation will occur periodically and land use should therefore reflect this. Traditional low-intensity management of such wet

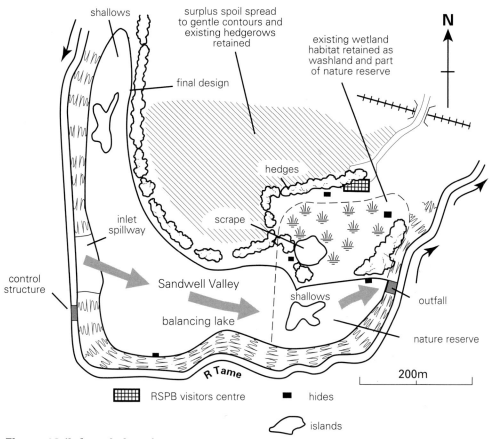

Figure 13 (left and above)
On-line and off-line storage: (i) R Par, Cornwall (opposite); (ii) R Tame, Sandwell Valley, Birmingham. Adapted from Lewis and Williams (1984)

grassland areas (as encouraged by the ESA mechanism), whether by mowing and/or grazing, enables a sustainable balance to be developed between agriculture and conservation. The RSPB has extensive experience of the management of such habitats. It runs training courses and produces advisory material on the management of this habitat (eg Tickner and Evans, 1991).

Water levels within controlled washlands can be managed to benefit wildlife. The breeding success of ground-nesting birds (eg lapwing, redshank and snipe) can be adversely affected by spring and early summer floods. This suggests that different summer and winter flooding regimes may be appropriate for flood storage areas. The diversion of flood water from the R Great Ouse to the Ouse Washes flood storage area has historically operated at a higher threshold between 1 April and 31 October. This scenario serves to protect ground-nesting birds on the washlands as well as grazing interests. Flooding of such

controlled washlands for sustained periods during the winter attracts large numbers of waders and wildfowl. Manipulation of flood level and frequency therefore enables the area to be managed to meet the habitat requirements of target species of birds. When a storage area is full, winter storms can generate significant waves that threaten embankments. Willow and poplar planted at vulnerable locations close to embankments can provide shelter for wildlife from the wind, and break up waves. On the Ouse Washes willow is maintained along the leading edge of some embankments to reduce wave-generated erosion, but the design must ensure that future maintenance access is not impeded.

Small 'on-line' storage areas receiving run-off from roads and industrial sites can also provide valuable wildlife habitat on a local scale. Benefits to wildlife are greatest if storage areas are 'oversized' so that they do not react too severely to small storms. If they are prone to high concentrations of silt, salt and oil contaminants, they may not

Pam Nolan

Plate 25 Timperley Brook flood storage scheme illustrates how flood defence schemes can create wetlands even within the constraints of urban areas.

develop great interest but will benefit the receiving watercourse. Reedbeds within the storage areas may improve water quality by trapping pollutants and also provide important wetland habitat.

Several on-line flood storage schemes including the R Par, Cornwall and off-line sites (eg Sandwell Valley, R Tame, Birmingham) illustrate how conservation can be integrated with flood defence needs in the creation of flood storage areas (Figure 13(i) and (ii)). Case Studies at Savick Brook and Curry Moor (3.4(j)and (k)) provide details of two individual schemes; the case study on the Quoile Pondage shows that ultimately many storage areas do require management to maintain their design standard.

On the R Par a series of flood storage areas were created using simple sluices and bunds. This has resulted in the floodplain being extended and protected from future developments. Marshland, wet grassland, willow carr, fen and reedbed have been protected and, as a result of increased inundation, encouraged to extend. A pond has also been developed for recreation and wildlife.

The Sandwell Valley lake provides flood protection for the Tame Valley through off-line storage. A 12-ha lake was excavated to accommodate 1 in 50-year flood flows. The engineered storage area has been developed on an existing wetland site which has been extended to include permanent areas of shallow water, islands,

shallow scrapes and hedges. It is a valued habitat within Birmingham and is an RSPB nature reserve with 'visitors' centre and associated viewing hides.

Flood storage areas on the R Wyre, Lancashire further illustrate the benefit of such areas in terms of flood defence and conservation. At Garstang, a disused railway embankment crossing the floodplain provided an ideal setting for 'on-line' storage, which will protect downstream areas and create potentially valuable wet grassland. The embankment has been adapted to form a dam for storing flood water, and control of river level is achieved by two gates. Off-line storage is also provided at Catterall, where a single gate in the embankment can be operated to divert flood flows into low lying agricultural land, which may also have the potential for wet grassland creation and rehabilitation. Additionally, such storage schemes reduce the requirement for in-channel engineering works.

The Timperley Brook flood storage scheme illustrates how flood defence schemes can create wetland habitat even within the constraints of urban areas. Situated at Broadheath, south-west of Manchester, this scheme, in the mid-1980s, aimed to alleviate flooding of residential and industrial areas with 'off-line' storage and create a valuable wetland. The results are illustrated in Plate 25.

Key References (Chapters 3.1 – 3.4)

Brookes, A (1988) *Channelized Rivers: Perspectives for Environmental Management*. John Wiley, Chichester.

Hemphill, R W and Bramley, M E (1989) *Protection of River and Canal Banks*. CIRIA, Butterworths, London.

Holmes, N T M and Newbold, C (1989) Nature conservation (A) – *Rivers as natural resources: and Nature Conservation (B)*. Sympathetic river management. In Number 8. T W Brandon (ed.) *River engineering – part II, structures and coastal defence works*. Number 8. IWEM, London

Lewis, G and Williams, G (1984) *The Rivers and Wildlife Handbook*. RSPB/RSNC, Sandy/Lincoln.

3.5 Aquatic Vegetation: Control, Establishment and Management

3.5.1.   Introduction

3.5.2.   Control of aquatic vegetation
      3.5.2.1 Mechanical control
         – Cutting
         – Desilting/dredging
      3.5.2.2 Chemical control
         – Selection of aquatic herbicides
         – Timing of treatments
      3.5.2.3 Biological control
      3.5.2.4 Environmental control
         – Shading
         – The use of straw to control algae

3.5.3.   Establishing aquatic vegetation
      3.5.3.1 Selection of materials and planting methods
         – Material selection
         – Planting methods
      3.5.3.2 Planting for different objectives
         – Habitat creation
         – Screening hard-engineering works
         – Promoting the spread of rare or declining species
         – Bank protection
         – Buffering of poor-quality run-off

3.5.1 Introduction

Aquatic plants are the primary food source in all rivers. The more varied the structure and composition of such plant communities, the greater the diversity of other wildlife it can support (Plate 1). However, in some cases aquatic plants can become so dominant that they choke

**Plate 1
Aquatic plants
greatly increase
habitat diversity**

Nigel Holmes

channels and suppress the growth of other species. In such cases these plants are regarded as weeds. Knowing the growth habits of aquatic plants, and being able to recognise potential nuisance species, is therefore vital for good river management.

Table 1 lists some of the main reasons why aquatic plants (including algae) in watercourses are controlled. For one or more of the reasons outlined weed control is carried out by most drainage authorities.

In upland rivers with few nutrients, where vegetation growth comprises mainly mosses and liverworts, there is little need for vegetation control. In addition, high velocities and coarse substrates do not favour excessive plant growth. In contrast, sluggish lowland rivers often have greater problems because suitable substrates and higher nutrient levels encourage plant growth. This problem can be exacerbated by lack of shade caused by lack of trees. Annual weed control is consequently carried out on many lowland watercourses.

During weed control operations it is often tempting to remove as much weed as possible in the interests of short-term efficiency. However, unnecessary removal not only damages the ecosystem but creates space for other troublesome species.

Weed control objectives should therefore be carefully considered and options, including 'no management', assessed on the grounds of environmental impact, and cost.

Where aquatic plant communities have adapted to a previous weed control regime, conservation may be best achieved by maintaining that management. However, where previous management has had a detrimental effect, a different form of management may bring about an improvement (Van Donk, 1990). This can involve either an increase or a decrease in the level of weed control. Changes to river ecosystems will be most severe when weed control is frequent and extensive, and

Table 1: Problems associated with excessive plant growth in rivers

- Impeded flow. Weeds can cause flooding in summer, mainly from submerged vegetation, and in autumn and winter, from dead emergent vegetation which does not die back adequately.
- Silting. Dense weed beds impede flow and cause silt to be deposited. Silt banks are then colonised by emergent species causing further siltation.
- Danger to humans and livestock. Floating weeds can disguise deep water and submerged weeds can endanger swimmers and other water users.
- Blocked pumps and sluices. Weeds and algae can block irrigation and other pumps and obstruct weirs and sluices.
- Water quality. Some algae release taints and toxins into water.
- Public health. Various water-borne pests and diseases are dependent on aquatic plants for survival.
- Deoxygenation. When large masses of vegetation die suddenly, either as a result of a weed control operation or by natural causes, the oxygen content of the water will fall and this can result in fish and invertebrate mortalities.
- Invasive aliens can cause loss of native plants.

minimal when it is localised and infrequent.

Planting vegetation in rivers has a more recent origin than weed control but has been executed with success in many situations. Five reasons for vegetation establishment are given in Table 2. There are, however, many occasions when two or more aims can be combined. Defining precise 'objectives' and suitable 'options' at the outset determines all the important decisions that need to be made concerning which species to use, the preferred location, timing, method of planting and any future maintenance needs.

Irrespective of whether management is to 'control' or to 'establish' aquatic or marginal vegetation, it is important to have a wide range of plant species appropriate to and typical of the region and river type. In this way conservation of plants and invertebrates will be encouraged.

Timescales involved in vegetation control and establishment vary considerably. As with most control measures, weed removal may have an initial adverse effect on some species, and cause loss of habitat. However, the long-term effect may be greater diversity of species and habitats. A good example is provided by a watercourse dominated by floating plants such as duckweed. Under the dense cover, light is excluded and submerged plants may die; the associated low oxygen levels may also result in fish and invertebrate mortality. When the weed is removed, the river may initially appear devoid of life. However, submerged plants will soon return to provide food and habitat for fish and

Table 2: Benefits of planting aquatic or marginal vegetation

- Provide wildlife habitat, including cover for prey.
- Create visually attractive features (and in the case of marginal vegetation, screen ugly bank structures).
- Promote the spread of a rare or declining plant species.
- Provide bank protection.
- Establish marginal buffer zones to improve water quality.
- Provide shelter for fish fry to develop (especially in early summer).

Nigel Holmes

**Plate 2
Plant species including reed sweet-grass, colonising a new channel after six months**

invertebrates. Generally, methods should either provide long-term control or enable repeat treatments to be carried out without excessive physical disturbance.

During vegetation establishment, some initial adverse disturbance may be evident and often at least one growing season is needed before conservation interest develops (Plate 2). A balanced and sustained new community structure may take years to establish. In general, aquatic plants grow quicker and establish habitats for animals more rapidly than marginal species.

3.5.2. Control of aquatic vegetation

Plants are not normally considered 'weeds' unless they interfere with flood control, human activities or with the habitat and survival of other species. For the purposes of control, five target groups of 'weed' can be identified. They are listed in Table 3. Control of bankside plants is considered in Section 3.6.

The four principal methods of control are listed in Table 4. Mechanical, chemical and biological methods tackle the symptom of a problem, whereas environmental methods tackle aspects of the cause. Environmental control often has a high capital outlay with relatively low longer term maintenance costs. The reverse is generally true for the

Table 3: Five groups of aquatic weeds and their characteristics

1. Bankside plants. Not necessarily aquatic plants but species which grow close to the water on the bank such that any herbicide applied to them could enter the water; therefore only approved aquatic herbicides should be used. Problem species often include docks, bracken, nettles and, increasingly, the introduced species, giant hogweed, Japanese knotweed and Himalayan balsam.
2. Emergent plants. Plants of shallow water which produce stems and leaves extending above water level such as common reed, sedge and rush.
3. Floating plants. Produce floating leaves which may be rooted, eg water-lily, or which are free-floating, eg duckweed.
4. Submerged plants. The majority of the plant remains under water although flowers and, occasionally, a few leaves may grow to the water surface. Most submerged plants are rooted in sediment, eg water-crowfoot, water-milfoil, but some are free-floating, eg hornwort.
5. Algae. Primitive plants growing in a number of forms, with blanket weeds often the most troublesome in rivers. These filamentous algae usually start growing attached to stones or bottom sediment but eventually break away to form floating mats or blankets.

Table 4: Methods of weed control

- Mechanical - cutting, dredging, raking and pulling.
- Chemicals - herbicides or chemicals which are not herbicides, but which may affect the availability of, for example, nutrients. The latter are not normally encountered in riverine situations.
- Biological - animal grazing, microbiological.
- Environmental control - including shading, nutrient stripping, altering the channel form to alter flow, and also no action allowing the weed growth to regain its equilibrium.

Table 5: Potential management options for weed control

GROUP	CONTROL		
	INDIVIDUAL PLANTS*	STANDS	LARGE AREAS
Emergent	Uproot Spot spray Cut by hand	Dredging Machine cutting spray	Grazing Dredging Machine cutting spray
Floating – rooted free-floating	Cut and/or rake Rake	Cut and/or rake Rake Spray	Cut and/or rake Rake Spray
Submerged	Probably invisible	Cut and/or rake Spray	Cut and/or rake Spray
Algae	Invisible	Cut and/or rake Spray	Cut and/or rake Spray

Note: the use of environmental control methods should be considered for all types of plants
*Control may not be needed unless the plant is an introduced species

other options because management effects are short-term. Table 5 shows appropriate techniques for controlling individual plants, small stands and large areas of weeds based upon growth form.

Case Study: Winestead Drain 3.5(a)

3.5.2.1 Mechanical Control

Mechanical control can be carried out in a variety of ways. The most widely used are listed in Table 6. In general, mechanical control consists of cutting, dredging or raking.

Cutting

Most emergent, rooted submerged and floating-leaved plants are effectively controlled by cutting. Depending on the depth of the water, different techniques can be used, such as hand cutting, mechanical cutting from a boat, and using a weed-cutting bucket (Plate 3).

Weed-cutting buckets cut and remove weed in the same operation but other methods of control require weed to be collected separately. Unless this is done, bridges and culverts can become blocked and deoxygenation of water occurs. Weeds may be removed either by hand rakes or by machine depending on the volume of material. Small amounts can be left on the bank but this is not appropriate because bankside plant communities can be smothered and die. Large quantities should be taken away from the river and carefully composted on sites of low conservation interest, where liquid from decomposition cannot enter the river. Weeds are usually cut in an upstream direction as this makes the operation easier and allows fragments of weed and associated invertebrates to drift downstream and recolonise.

However, where booms are used to collect the weed, the opposite direction may be preferable due to the low velocities created by the uncut downstream vegetation, aiding the trapping of cut weed.

Cutting produces an immediate hydraulic improvement but it generally stimulates regrowth. The hydraulic benefits are short-term and rarely effective for more than one season. Time of cutting is important, not only because of potential regrowth from roots and rhizomes, but also because of the potential impact on breeding birds and aquatic invertebrates. For example, on the R Mythebrooke, weed cutting was delayed in 1992 to allow the emergence of a rare dragonfly.

**Plate 3
Mechanical weed
cutting**

Stuart McFadzean

Table 6: Mechanical control methods

TECHNIQUES	APPLICATION	COMMENTS
Hand ● Scythe	Submerged, emergent, bankside	Useful in shallow water areas. and rooted floating Selective.
● Chain scythe	Emergent, rooted floating, submerged	Needs two people, not selective.
● Hand rake	Free floating algae, previously cut vegetation	Limited use for large expanses of weed, but useful in conjunction with other techniques.
Boat	Emergent, rooted and floating, submerged. Some have attachment for algae and free-floating vegetation.	Disposal of cut vegetation biggest problem. Depth of river and height of bridges may be limiting. Expensive, single purpose machinery.

Machinery
● Bucket
  - hydraulic
  - dragline
	Emergents, submerged, rooted floating	Hydraulics are more precise. Draglines have a longer reach. Access on bank required, and if wide, both banks.

● Cott rake
  - hydraulic
  - dragline
	Algae, free-floating vegetation in some circumstances and previously cut weed	Similar to above.

Flail	Bankside	Not selective

Nigel Holmes

Plate 4
A partial weed cut retains valuable aquatic habitats

Cutting periods should be selected to reflect wildlife interests and operational constraints, eg equipment availability, and the height of weed. Cutting too early in the season stimulates greater regrowth with the need for additional work later (Dawson, 1989). As a general rule, submerged plants are cut in summer and emergents are usually cut in the autumn. However, in narrow watercourses, summer reed control may be needed to keep water levels down. Some vegetation should always be retained so that uniform structure and synchronised re-growth are avoided. Under natural conditions different species grow at different times of the year and this is beneficial to both river ecology and flood control.

Plate 5
Sympathetic desilting

When flood conveyance standards are relaxed on watercourses where heavy

cutting has been undertaken in the past, changes in weed-control practice to benefit wildlife can arise (Plate 4). Case Study 3.6(c) on two drains in the Lower Trent area illustrates this point. Here sinuous cuts of only a proportion of the channel width were carried out, whereas previously the whole channel was affected. The benefits for wildlife have been so evident that this approach is now being adopted on the R Idle where the effects on conveyance of different levels of maintenance are being monitored.

Even where regular and extensive weed cutting is required, there is inevitable always some opportunity to retain patches of vegetation. This approach, if carefully planned, can enable rare species and complete communities of plants to be safeguarded. It also retains habitat structure for associated animals. This is illustrated by the Winestead Drain Case Study 3.5(a) where rotational weed cutting is now standard practice using either a boat or bucket. This involves alternating cutting from side to side and leaving one-third of the channel untouched.

Desilting/dredging

When silt accumulates around aquatic vegetation, desilting, using a mechanical excavator, restores channel capacity more efficiently than cutting. Roots and rhizomes are frequently removed with the silt so care is needed to ensure communities are not excavated along continuous lengths and complete widths of channel (Plate 5). If parts are left, plants can spread back into affected areas rapidly. Moreover, if patches of plants are left undisturbed during light dredging or cutting, invertebrate communities should recover rapidly (Pearson and Jones, 1975, 1978).

It is important to establish whether poisonous plants, such as hemlock water-dropwort, are present. If these plants are dredged out and left on the bank, they may be eaten by cattle. It is important to minimise the work undertaken both for cost and environmental reasons.

Pam Nolan

The same best-practice approaches for cutting also apply to desilting, namely:

- Alternate lengths can be desilted and left untouched, allowing rapid recolonisation by plants and animals. Fisheries will benefit where the interface between desilted and unmanaged sections provide good feeding habitat (Plate 6).

- Strips of vegetation along one or both sides of the channel are left untouched and desilting is executed through the centre only (Plate 7).

- Patches of weed can be left on the margins of the channel, or in mid-stream where structures or species dictate priority. These act both as refuges and as areas from which recolonisation can occur, whilst rare plants can be selectively avoided (Plate 8).

3.5.2.2 Chemical control

In many situations, herbicides are an effective method of aquatic weed control. The main benefits are that herbicides can be applied more quickly than mechanical methods and weeds are controlled for longer. Herbicides are often cheaper than mechanical control especially when the resultant longer period of control is considered.

Although herbicides can be applied quickly, plants may take several weeks to die completely so hydraulic benefits may be slow to materialise. Consequently, herbicides are not generally recommended for the control of weeds when a rapid response is required. For instance, when weeds blocking a channel pose a serious flood risk, herbicide usage is unlikely to alleviate the problem in time. A rapid response can, however, result if weeds such as duckweed, which float on the surface, are treated with herbicides. If spraying is initiated before the surface is blanketed, problems of deoxygenation can be avoided.

The timing of herbicide application is also important and it may be necessary to wait for the appropriate stage of growth of the

Plate 6 (top) Desilting restricted to one side of the channel

Plate 7 (centre) Desilting and weed control through the centre of the channel

Plate 8 (bottom) Marginal vegetation retained as wildlife habitat

target weeds before application can be made. Herbicide use needs careful consideration and is not always suitable. Care should be taken over the timing and extent of treatment as submerged vegetation controlled by herbicides dies back and causes deoxygenation of the water (Brooker, 1974). This applies particularly to submerged weeds and algae.

Selection of aquatic herbicides

Selection of the most appropriate chemical for a management objective requires expert knowledge of the capabilities and environmental impact of the chemical, its effectiveness against different plants, the conditions under which it is to be applied, and the nature of the watercourse. *For herbicides to be used in rivers or on banks, it is essential to use only those that are approved by MAFF for use in or near water (MAFF, 1985). Moreover, the NRA or equivalent water management body should be consulted prior to herbicide use, as the use of chemicals is inappropriate in some locations, such as sources for public drinking water supply.*

Each herbicide has a range of target weeds and situations in which it can be used most effectively. A guide to the first stage in the selection of the most appropriate product is shown in Tables 7 and 8. If plants which

should be retained are growing amongst target weeds in the same category, alternate methods of control should be adopted.

Tables 7 and 8 only help in the selection of the most appropriate product but prior to this other decisions have to be made based on management needs, environmental protection, land use and health and safety. For example:

- Identify the target weed or weeds using aquatic weed identification books and check that they are listed as susceptible to the product listed in the flow charts (See MAFF Booklet B 2078 or product labels).

- Identify any rare species that might be harmed by the use of the herbicide and, where necessary, consult country and county conservation agencies.

- Check that there are no poisonous plants (eg hemlock water-dropwort or ragwort) to which livestock have access. Such plants are normally avoided but may become more palatable to livestock after spraying yet remain toxic.

- Consult the pollution control department of the appropriate region of the NRA, River Purification Board in Scotland (RPB) and Department of

Table 7: Herbicide selection for emergent and floating weeds

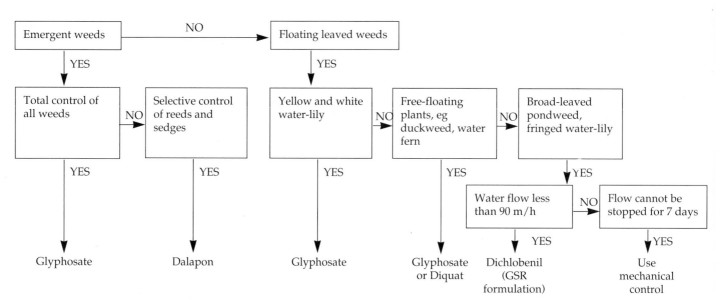

Agriculture for N Ireland (DANI) to obtain permission to use the product.

- Ensure operators are fully trained and that all applications and uses are carried out within the rules laid down under the Control of Pesticides Regulations 1986, The Control of Substances Hazardous to Health Regulations 1988, and the Wildlife and Countryside Act 1981 and subsequent amendments.

- Double-check that weed control is essential – the advice about which chemical to use is to help in the choice of the most appropriate method to safeguard the rest of the river and is *not a recommendation that herbicides should be used.*

In addition to following closely MAFF guidelines, users must also fully consider the ecological consequences of inappropriate choices of herbicides, or their use when mechanical methods would be more suitable. Cost and access are also important considerations (Brooker, 1975; Brooker and Edwards, 1973, 1974; Murphy *et al.*, 1981).

There is a safety margin between the herbicide concentration at which weeds are controlled and the concentration which is harmful to fish and other wildlife. This safety margin can be small, eg for dichlobenil GSR, and fish deaths can occur as a result of a series of complex interactions. A precautionary approach is therefore needed and 'spot treatment' is always advocated so that only a proportion of the plant biomass is treated at any one time.

Additional information on choosing the relevant herbicides and their potential ecological effects can be found in Newbold (1976), Pieterse and Murphy (1990), and Worthing (1983).

Weed control using herbicides is not widely used by the NRA, being largely confined to locations where access conditions or other reasons make it cost-effective and less environmentally damaging. The North Low/South Low system in Northumberland is a narrow low-gradient ditch (<3 m wide), which is deep and silty. It provides ideal conditions for emergent reeds and common reed is

Table 8: Herbicide selection for submerged vascular plants and algae

abundant on the banks, but bur-reed tends to choke the centre of the channel. Whenever the bur-reed extends in a thick and continuous stand right across the channel the central part is sprayed by hand (from the bank), care being taken not to affect the marginal vegetation and common reed. The annual herbicide treatment gives longer control than cutting but shorter control than desilting.

Timing of treatments

The time of year when herbicides can be applied effectively and safely is important. The correct timing for each herbicide is printed on the product label; however, for general guidance the following information may be of use.

Most emergent and floating weeds are treated by a direct spray application to the leaves. The earliest, therefore, that the spray can be applied effectively is when there is a significant amount of leaf/stem area. Mid- to late-summer spraying, like cutting, has the advantage that most birds and insects have completed their reproductive cycles and are little disturbed by the treatment.

Submerged weeds and algae are generally treated in the spring or early summer. At this time they are young and more susceptible to herbicide than later in the season. The risk of deoxygenation is also reduced because the water is relatively cold, contains high levels of dissolved oxygen and the quantity of treated plant material is small with a lower oxygen demand as it dies.

When it is necessary to treat aquatic weeds in full summer, localised control is the only acceptable approach. The use of 'spot treatment' for overgrown channels, or where only troublesome species require control, is an important advantage of herbicide usage.

3.5.2.3 Biological control

'Biological control' encompasses reduction of river vegetation by grazing animals, both managed and otherwise.

In areas of grazing marsh, water in ditches during the summer is frequently penned at an artificially high level to provide 'wet fences' for the enclosure of livestock. The browsing of marginal emergent plants by cattle helps to control excessive growth. This also produces a patchwork of open water and vegetation, which is important for many invertebrates including dragonflies. Cattle also wade into streams and rivers with shallow edges and graze both emergent and submerged plants (Plate 9). Any advantage in plant control must be balanced against disadvantages such as browsing of riverside trees and excessive trampling of banks (poaching) which encourages siltation and bank erosion. Cattle grazing cannot, therefore, be regarded as a feasible means of widespread aquatic plant control.

Ducks, geese and swans also graze aquatic vegetation and can have a significant local impact on plant communities. However, it is difficult to control them, and swans have been cited as a potential reason for the decline of crowfoot on some chalk rivers, such as the Wylye in Wiltshire.

Fish can also have an effect on aquatic plant communities. Introduced species of grass carp have been used successfully to control many species of submerged weeds as well as some floating weeds and filamentous algae (Eaton *et al.*, 1992). However, their introduction requires a licence from MAFF as well as from the NRA in England and Wales, SOAFD in Scotland and DANI in N Ireland. Their use is generally restricted to enclosed waters.

Fish, particularly carp and bream, have been shown to reduce the growth of

**Plate 9
Cattle grazing
both emergent
and submergent
plants in shallow
rivers**

Nigel Holmes

submerged macrophytes in some situations. This is considered to be the result of their benthic feeding habits, which stir up mud, increasing turbidity. Most of the evidence that these fish can affect aquatic plant communities comes from lakes and gravel pits (Giles, 1992) but it is possible that they could have the same effect in muddy lowland rivers.

Biological control, apart from introducing grass carp, is very 'hit and miss'. It is impossible to target problem species or groups, or limit the area of the channel affected, without other impacts also occurring. For this reason it remains an experimental approach to weed control.

3.5.2.4 Environmental control

Environmental control involves altering conditions to make them less suitable for plant growth. Three principal methods are: reducing nutrients, channel manipulation, and shading (Table 9). Deepening channels across part of their width can set up environmental changes that produce a rapid control response. Nutrient stripping from effluent discharges and shading take longer to achieve results.

Shading is best located on the south bank and as close to the water's edge as possible. Bur-reed, starwort, common reed, Canadian pondweed, hornwort and many other plants are very effectively controlled by shade (Plate 10). In the North Engine Drain (Lincolnshire), it has been recognised for many years that a section where trees and shrubs were established about 10 years ago needs no weed control, yet the adjacent open reaches, require regular and severe weed cutting to maintain flood conveyance. Similarly, past bankside tree planting on the North Low/South Low drainage channels in Northumberland is beginning to reduce the need for herbicide control of dense bur-reed.

Alternating shaded and open stretches creates the greatest variety of river habitats for wildlife. For instance, Lewis (1981) reported that the most species-rich sections of the R Tone in Somerset were those

where tree cover was interrupted at 40–50 m intervals, allowing direct sunlight to the channel. To establish this along open rivers, only native trees and shrubs should be used, with alder, willows and black poplar being the most suitable species. Lime, beech, oak and field maple are also suitable but grow more slowly. Where shading is required for narrow watercourses, shrubs, eg elder, blackthorn, hawthorn, are most suitable (Chapter 3.7).

The use of straw to control algae

Research by the Aquatic Weed Research Unit has shown that barley straw can reduce significantly the growth of nuisance algae. Although the exact mechanism is not yet fully established, it is known that a chemical which inhibits algal growth is

Table 9: Advantages and disadvantages of three forms of environmental control

CONTROL	ADVANTAGES	DISADVANTAGES
• Nutrient stripping	Removes phosphate and reduces excessive growth of invasive large plants and blanket weed. Long-term savings in management.	Expensive in capital outlay. Minimal short-term effects as nutrients locked in sediments.
• Channel modifications to create self-cleansing deeper channel	Deeper central channel has less silt deposition and faster velocity to create greater self cleansing and enhanced channel habitat diversity. Ideal where lower water levels are required.	Reeds may colonise 'shoulders' and create a future management need if flood conveyance compromised.
• Shading the channel	Inexpensive. Long-term maintenance minimal. When combined with open areas, in-stream habitat structure enhanced. Channel not regularly disturbed by management.	Long-establishment period to achieve desired effect. May require land owners to give up strip of land at top of bank. Limits future access for maintenance to one side. Shrubs and trees may need management in the future.

Nigel Holmes

**Plate 10
Alder shade
inhibiting fool's
water-cress
growth**

to have no adverse effect on invertebrates, fish or waterfowl and is being used increasingly as a cost-effective and environmentally friendly method of controlling algae. For example, three drainage ditches managed by an Internal Drainage Board have been treated with barley straw for over five years to control *Vaucheria dichotoma*. During this period they have required no other management, whereas before they required annual chemical or mechanical controls.

Large numbers of aquatic invertebrates in loose straw masses have also been observed. In one instance in Wales, water shrimp populations achieved levels of around 250,000/m² in straw. In trials by several water companies, algae inhibiting matting (straw between two layers of netting) has greatly improved the numbers of invertebrates (Barrett and Newman, 1993).

generated from the decomposing straw (Barrett and Newman, 1993). Trials on Chesterfield canal in 1990 showed a substantial reduction in a range of algae including the dominant filamentous green (Welch *et al,*, 1990). This technique appears

3.5.3. Establishing aquatic vegetation

An integral part of any aquatic planting scheme should be provision of enhanced in-stream and marginal habitat for wildlife. New planting should provide suitable habitat for associated species of particular conservation interest.

When considering whether planting is appropriate the following questions should be asked in relation to site-specific conditions:

- Are the species to be planted appropriate to the area and likely to benefit the desired species of wildlife in terms of cover, food or breeding sites?

- Is the water quality in the channel good enough to sustain the species to be planted?

- Is the channel of a sufficient capacity to accommodate the growth and spread of the vegetation, without requiring intensive maintenance?

- Is the planting area free from

disturbance which is likely to cause irreparable damage, eg fluvial erosion, intensive grazing, trampling, vehicle damage, herbicide drift?

If all the above criteria are satisfied, there is a sound basis for attempting a planting scheme.

3.5.3.1 Selection of materials and planting methods

Material selection

Tables 1, 2 and 3 (Section 1.4) list plants that occur in a variety of riverine habitats in much of Britain. The tables provide information about the habitat requirements of plants and therefore can be used as a guide to 'what to plant' and 'where' in river planting schemes. Mosses and liverworts are not included because it is highly unlikely that they will be included in a planting scheme.

Aquatic plants can be established 'artificially' from the following sources:

- dredged spoil containing seeds, roots and shoots from watercourses, ponds or lakes;

- individual plants taken from the wild where the species is abundant and permission has been obtained;

- plants supplied by an approved nursery;

- seeds collected from the wild from sources where the plants are common and permission has been obtained;

- seeds supplied by an approved wild-flower seed mix supplier.

Dredged spoil transfer is generally the most effective way of providing large-scale planting. Ideally, it is used where the spoil is available from dredging works close by. Unless the source is a degraded habitat in need of management, work solely to gain material for a planting scheme could be damaging; it is not good conservation practice to damage one habitat purely for the sake of re-creating it elsewhere! It is essential to ensure that it does not contain seeds, rhizomes or fragments of plants that could become troublesome. This applies particularly to species such as giant hogweed, Himalayan balsam, Australian marsh stonecrop and Japanese knotweed (NRA, 1993a), all of which are introduced invasive plants which are spreading rapidly in Britain (NRA, 1993a).

The majority of watercourse maintenance dredging nowadays is confined to 'desilting' where soft material from the river and some margins is removed. Clipping back of marginal vegetation and accompanying silt can produce spoil with a wealth of aquatic and emergent vegetation, much of which can withstand the uprooting and fragmentation caused by mechanical excavation. Spoil should be left to drain to the point where if necessary it can be transferred by non-watertight road transport without fouling the public highways. Depending on its consistency, the dewatering period can be as much as

seven days, but normally spoil is dry enough to be transported within 1–2 days of excavation. Complete drying needs to be avoided otherwise the establishment of plants is impaired.

Although the success of plant establishment from spoil transfer is high, the logistics of the exercise can be complicated. In many cases suitable material becomes available during dredging operations where access for road transport is impossible; alternatively, road access may be good but crop growing prevents the retrieval of spoil at the time of excavation. Even when all criteria are met at the donor site, similar access problems can arise at the receiver site. As a result of these constraints, keeping a short-list of suitable donor sites for future spoil transfer can be useful as part of planning programmes of planting.

Individual plants taken from the wild may also be transplanted. Under the Wildlife and Countryside Act 1981 permission must be sought from landowners prior to uprooting; moreover, specially protected plants may not be removed (see statutory protection section in Appendix II) without permission from the statutory nature conservation agencies. The occasions when it is necessary to transplant individual plants are likely to be relatively few, but may include the following circumstances:

- in amenity areas 'showy plants', eg yellow iris, may be transplanted to attract local interest;

- where works have removed unusual and/or particularly valuable plants either in wildlife or landscape terms (eg flowering-rush);

- where species enhancement through translocation is undertaken;

- where small-scale conservation work is undertaken by local interest groups (Plate 11).

Plants can also be supplied from specialist approved nurseries but care must be taken to ensure that they come from native stock, preferably from a local source. County Conservation Trusts should be approached for advice on planting and species selection. Nursery-grown common reed can be a valuable source of plant material, as pot-grown plants establish well if planted just above the water level in early summer. Ward (1992) provides further information for anyone interested in establishing common reed.

Seeds, either from a supplier or collected from the wild, are rarely used for establishing aquatic plants along rivers because virtually no information is available on their success. Sowing seed adjacent to rivers may lead to poor germination if soil-water conditions change and/or flooding occurs at critical periods. However, the use of locally gathered seed is especially recommended for species that are annuals or biennials; perennials which set abundant numbers of seed and establish rapidly from seedlings, eg rushes, flag iris, water plantain, are also ideal candidates.

Table 10 summarises the principles for successful and sensitive planting schemes. Most success is achieved when material is planted on to shelves or banks with a shallow slope where fluvial erosion is not a problem.

Planting methods

Plate 11 Small-scale planting scheme carried out by a local school

Vegetation may be planted by hand or machine. Where machinery is used, planting is rarely selective, clumps being removed from the river during dredging

Table 10: Key principles for successful aquatic plant establishment

- Use fresh, locally abundant plants
- Plant mixtures of species. Plant blocks of species so that sensitive plants can establish themselves before competing with more invasive plants.
- Check the habitat requirement of species and plant in their preferred conditions.
- Use only local stock, preferably from the same river or a tributary.
- Get permission from landowners or occupiers under Section 13 of the Wildlife and Countryside Act 1981 to remove material for planting.
- Use material from a site being disturbed as part of a management operation; otherwise take great care not to deplete the donor site of species or habitats.
- Preferably plant in early spring when the shoots are first appearing.
- When gathering seeds of annuals and biennials, scatter as soon as collected.

and then moved to the receptor site and spread using the bucket. Hand planting techniques are more precise. Plants dug out by spade in spring and planted immediately into shallow water or moist ground, often thrive best. It is vital to firm them in securely. Reed sweet-grass, greater pond-sedge, bulrush, branched bur-reed and yellow iris all transplant well using this technique.

Shoot cuttings, 5–10 cm long, may be fragile but can be planted into shallow water in spring to good effect. Greater pond-sedge, lesser pond-sedge and galingale establish well in this way, especially if they contain a short length of mature shoot (rhizome) from which they have sprouted (Plate 12). In some instances it may be necessary to protect the shoots from being washed away. In the R Medway marginal plants were successfully established in bays dug behind rows of faggots to protect against wave damage.

Common reed is difficult to establish in some situations and does best when planted into moist soil, not into water. If water levels can be controlled and gradually increased as growth proceeds,

Nigel Holmes

this is ideal (Ward, 1992). In addition to rhizome clumps and cuttings, an already established reedbed can be encouraged to expand by pegging to the ground tips of mature non-flowering shoots.

Marginal plants with soft roots that do not persist for many years can be pushed into substrates or anchored by stones. In deeper water, plants can be tied to stones, which are then released and allowed to sink to the bottom to root.

3.5.3.2 Planting for different objectives

Different planting schemes may have different objectives, depending on the type and positioning of the vegetation. The most common objective is likely to be habitat creation. However screening, buffering, bank protection and species promotion may also be objectives.

Habitat creation

The Wildlife and Countryside Act 1981 empowered Water Authorities to 'further' conservation wherever this was consistent with their other duties. Planting aquatic and marginal vegetation was rarely carried out in tandem with river engineering works prior to this but small-scale plantings began in the 1980s. Few of the early examples had details of what was planted, or the methods employed, so post-project appraisal to judge the success of establishment of individual species is difficult. However, the fact that vegetation was successfully established is evident today and is illustrated in several of the Case Studies, eg Ford Brook 3.5 (c), R Bain 3.3 (b), Project Kingfisher 3.3 (c) and Alne at Henley in Arden 3.4 (c).

Two Case Studies, R Thames at Wolvercote 3.5 (d) and R Ock at Stanford Mill 3.5 (e), illustrate successful establishment of vegetation through planting or habitat manipulation and protection to help natural establishment. In the Case Studies of the R Beult 3.3 (a), vegetation has established from in situ seedbanks and seeds, roots and shoots washed on to the marginal habitats without any planting. The plant community is now extremely diverse and provides an extensive range of

Plate 12
Mature rhizomes are often planted between stones held in place by wooden stakes

Stuart McFadzean

habitat structure at the bank/water interface that was not available before.

In more recent planting schemes, eg the R Torne and New River, details of the pre-planting conditions and exactly what was planted are available. This will allow critical assessment of transplant success to be determined (Plates 13 and 14).

In the first edition of the *Rivers and Wildlife Handbook* (1984) three planting schemes on rivers were featured. An assessment of their success is as follows:

- On the Stort Navigation, (Case study 3.5 (f)) problems of erosion occurred due to wave-wash; a clear conclusion is that planting species characteristic of the local river conditions is vital if they are to succeed.

- Planting on the Meece Brook was reported as very successful after the first two years. After more than 10 years the same species that were transplanted have continued to thrive and now grow alongside a very rich wetland community that has improved through natural colonisation from upstream.

- The Alne by-pass channel is featured as a Case Study (3.4 (c)). Vegetation was very successfully established in a new channel and has thrived. More than 10 years later many of the planted species dominate and have been augmented by natural colonisation. However, in the backwaters along the channel, silting has

**Case Studies:
3.5 (c)Ford Brook, 3.5(d) R Thames at Wolvercote, 3.5(e) R Ock at Stanford Mill, 3.5(f) R Stort Navigation**

Plate 13 (left) New River — before planting: a featureless channel with little conservation interest

Plate 14 (right) New River — after planting: habitat diversity and aesthetic value greatly increased

Nigel Holmes

occurred, and docks and nettles have replaced some reeds.

Case study 3.5(g) R Wandle

Screening hard-engineering works

When weirs and revetments are constructed and installed, or pipes cross rivers, it is often possible to incorporate measures which not only screen the visual impacts but also provide habitat. Schemes involving edge creation in front of banks are reported on in Case Studies, eg Ford Brook 3.5 (c) and R Wandle 3.5 (g). British Waterways has experimented with vegetation suspended in fabric pockets, hung over sheet piling and establishing reeds in front of vertical banks with a good degree of success (Plate 15).

The illustrations of schemes such as on the Ford Brook and Anker at Nuneaton (Plate 16) show that considerable aesthetic and wildlife value can be derived from the incorporation of vegetation planting in front of hard-engineered banks.

Case study 3.5(h) R Loddon/ R Blackwater catchment

Promoting the spread of rare or declining species

Occasionally there are opportunities to aid the recovery of these species through the introduction of not only large quantities of spoil (as described in Section 3.5.1) but also

through the careful transfer of individual plants. When removing plants for this purpose it is vital that plants are taken from the same catchment, permission from the landowner or occupier has been received, and prior consent from English Nature or the equivalent country conservation agency was sought when dealing with Scheduled or Red Data Book Species.

The Botanical Society for the British Isles also gives advice on the suitability and desirability of translocations. They keep a record of all known transplants of rare or endangered species so they should be contacted for advice and be provided with details of the completed translocations.

The Case Study of translocation of Loddon Pondweed 3.5 (h) into various sites in the Loddon catchment from a single donor site illustrates how successfully the spread of rare or declining species can be. Rare plant species have also been successfully transplanted in the R Chestle by the Warwickshire Wildlife Trust.

Bank protection

River engineering is now much more sensitive to environmental needs and, as a consequence, planting emergent vegetation to protect banks is now more commonplace. Many geotextiles are available for use in conjunction with such planting but there are still numerous pitfalls to be avoided if adequate bank protection is to be successfully achieved by 'soft engineering'. The major issues to be considered when deciding on the suitability of planting vegetation for bank protection are:

- Site conditions – are substrate and water-level conditions appropriate for the survival of marginal vegetation in the location where erosion control is most needed?

- Fluvial erosion – will the planted vegetation remain in place during floods; especially during the first year after planting, before root systems are properly established?

- Human disturbance – is the site vulnerable to trampling, eg by walkers or anglers, or to vandalism. This is important as initial damage to the geotextile can lead to total failure of a bank protection project.

- Herbivore damage – do grazing animals such as cattle and sheep, and birds such as Canada geese and ducks, have access to the planting area? If so, grazing of young shoots is likely and, in the case of cattle, serious damage to any geotextiles by poaching is possible.

Failure to address the above may lead to problems, but such biotechnical options can be very successful when used in suitable locations.

The Thames at Clifton Hampden (Case Study 3.5 (i)) which combined planting with 'Nicospan' and 'Nicobag' for bank protection, illustrates a successful application of biotechnical engineering that had some unforeseen results. British Waterways has successfully utilised reeds at Ellesmere on the Llangollen Canal to provide bank protection against boat-wash.

Stuart McFadzean

Jeremy Purseglove

Buffering of poor-quality run-off

In some cases planting marginal vegetation at or just above normal water level for any of the previously described objectives, will also provide a buffer zone which can partially trap sediment and break down pollutants before they reach the watercourse. The buffering capacity will depend on the extent of the vegetation, species present and its ability to retain the water before it enters the river. In summer, nitrate reduction may be as great as 25% if there is extensive littoral vegetation. However, the winter die-back will re-release nutrients back into the system (Haycock and Piney 1993). Similarly, in high-flow conditions the buffering effects of this marginal strip will be negligible, but in low-flow conditions, when the dilution of nutrient-rich run-off can be at its lowest, the effects can be

Plate 15 (top) Vegetation establishment using fabric pockets

Plate 16 (above) Introduction of marginal vegetation within an urban watercourse on the R Anker at Nuneaton

Case Studies: 3.5(i) R Thames, Clifton Hampden, (3.5 (j)) R Pinn

**Case study
3.5(k) R Leach**

beneficial to the watercourse. The Case Study of the R Pinn 3.5 (j) is an example where provision of a buffer to poor quality run-off was one of the key objectives. The success of the scheme illustrates that even in very localised cases, marginal planting can be of value not only for habitat creation but also potentially for the indirect benefits it provides for the aquatic communities in the watercourse. As evidence of the effectiveness of buffer strips in improving water quality is limited this is an area which needs further concerted research effort.

Key References

Barrett, P R F (1978) Aquatic Weed Control. Necessity and Methods. *Fish Mgmt*, 9, (3):93–101.

Brookes, A (1981) *Waterways & Wetlands*. British Trust for Conservation Volunteers.

MAFF (1985) *Guidelines for the use of herbicides on weeds in or near watercourses and lakes*. MAFF Booket 2078.

Worthing, C R (ed), (1983). *The pesticide manual: a world compendium*. 7th edition. British Crop Protection Council.

3.6 Bank Vegetation: Control, Establishment and Management

3.6.1.   Introduction

3.6.2.   Grazing

3.6.3.   Mowing and cutting
   – Timing of mowing
   – Pattern of Mowing
   – Disposal of cuttings

3.6.4.   Herbicides

3.6.5.   Establishing vegetation on floodbanks
   – Opportunities and options for vegetation establishment
   – Soils and seeding
   – Methods and timing of sowing
   – Use of nurse species and seed mixes
   – Post-sowing management
   – Turf transplants

3.6.1. Introduction

Management of vegetation on riverbanks and floodbanks is undertaken for numerous reasons (Table 1). Historically, management was carried out by hand or grazing, but the emphasis is now on machine cutting and brushing. Bank vegetation management can, when adapted to incorporate wildlife interest, lead to significant environmental gain through enhanced plant richness and improved habitat structure.

Grass and herb species predominate in the riparian plant communities. Plants have specific habitat requirements and different species occur as conditions change from wet to dry (Chapter 1.4). Management therefore strongly influences the overall nature conservation value of river corridors. The value of rivers is increased in urban and intensively farmed areas where they may form the only area of semi-natural habitat. The river corridor also acts as a buffer zone between the river and adjacent land. Appropriate management is very important because small changes may result in very large benefits to nature conservation without reduction in flood defence standards (Table 2).

The diverse grassland communities of floodbanks and riparian strips contain a wide array of plants, which in turn attract insects in summer and seed-eating mammals and birds in winter. Where the vegetation is tall, the structure provides habitat for nesting birds, invertebrates and small mammals. In areas of intensive arable cultivation or urban development, riverbank habitats, both dry and wet, are often the only remaining places where plants indicative of ancient habitats, eg greater burnet, cowslip and some orchids, can be found.

No single method of management will be beneficial for all types of riparian plants, so management should be appropriate to the site-specific conditions. Both nature conservation value and operational requirements are important, but in many instances flood defence needs can accommodate management practices which benefit wildlife.

It is important clearly to define operational and wildlife objectives. A combination of short and long swards on a length of river is likely to be beneficial to more species than a single length (Table 2; Plate 1). Erdhardt (1985) showed that butterfly and moth communities were richest where grassland was only lightly grazed or mown annually giving a mixed sward structure. Luff (1966) reported that a large number of beetles are associated with grass tussocks (Plate 2).

The question of whether any bank management at all is needed is important. There are many reasons why it may be necessary (Table 1). Choosing the appropriate technique is critical. The two

Table 1: Key reasons for vegetation management of riverbanks

- Minimise channel and floodplain roughness and hence maximise flood carrying capacity
- Permit floodbank inspections
- Aid structural stability of embankments (trees and shrubs on embankments are rarely encouraged as their roots may undermine structural stability; they also provide cover for burrowing animals which may also threaten stability)
- Control natural succession to scrub
- Suppress dominant rank species, especially coarse grasses and nettles
- Stimulate short, dense sward with good roots to minimise resistance
- Aesthetic reasons - to keep urban banks 'smart' and reduce 'tipping' in long grass
- Encourage specific target plant species or diverse habitat structure

Table 2: Engineering and conservation aspects of short and rough sward types on riverbanks and floodbanks

SWARD TYPE	ENGINEERING	CONSERVATION
Short	Minimises channel and floodbank roughness; maximises flow. Aids soil stability as the roots bind the soil. Permits floodbank inspections (for stability, seepage and burrowing animals.)	Provides important feeding habitat for grazing wildfowl in winter, eg wigeon and coot; used by wagtails and other birds in summer. Reduces the supply of food and shelter for other birds, small mammals and invertebrates.
Rough	Increased channel and floodbank roughness, with increased possibility of bank failure. More prone to collect flood debris and silt which reduces capacity and may lead to instability. Provides habitat for burrowing animals making them harder to detect (often local problem and may include badgers, rabbits, moles and rats).	Much greater habitat structure benefiting invertebrates, small mammals and birds, eg bumble-bee nests, butterfly colonies, bank voles, passerine birds. Tussocky areas are important as bird nesting sites, eg reed bunting and meadow pipit. Hunting areas for barn owl and short-eared owl, and for harvest mouse nest sites.
Mosaic	Generally avoided if includes shrub.	Added structure gives wider habitat for animals, eg cover for otters.

**Plate 1
The R Torne exhibiting contrasting bank swards. This situation is likely to benefit a wide range of wildlife.**

principal methods are mowing and grazing but occasionally herbicides are used. Masterman and Thorne (1992) suggest that bank vegetation may not be a serious problem for flood conveyance in many rivers. This is especially so for rivers with a width-depth ratio of >16.

This chapter considers three methods of controlling bank vegetation: grazing; mowing; and herbicides and their effects on wildlife. In addition, methods of establishment of low maintenance/high conservation interest vegetation are discussed. The type of vegetation established on a river or floodbank when engineering works are executed is an obvious determining factor for future

Nigel Holmes

interest, and will fundamentally affect the methods and cost of future maintenance.

Nigel Holmes

Plate 2
Grass tussocks provide habitats for large numbers of beetles

3.6.2 Grazing

Although both grazing and mowing can create short swards, there are areas where mowing is not practical and others where livestock for grazing are not available. A disadvantage of mowing is that it is considered as 'catastrophic' management because much of the habitat disappears instantly. Grazing, however, is a more environmentally sensitive approach.

Grazing floodbanks is a widespread practice and, where managed appropriately, is a valuable management tool, benefiting wildlife conservation and flood defence. Grazing is beneficial in flood defence terms with short swards, resulting in reduced bank roughness. In wildlife terms, grazing reduces the height of grass/herbaceous communities and maintains a varied flora. Additionally the more varied sward structure produced by grazing compared with mowing is more favourable for maintaining diverse invertebrate populations (Morris 1979 a and b).

Timing and intensity of grazing is critical, as is the choice of livestock. At moderate densities, sheep grazing results in a short, even sward. In contrast, cattle produce a more tussocky sward, whereas horses produce short sward, with tall growth in dunging areas. In general, high livestock densities produce relatively tight even swards whilst low densities tend to increase unevenness of swards.

High stocking densities, especially in wet weather, can result in poached ground, allowing weeds to colonise and increasing bank instability. Grazing limited to the summer, especially at low livestock densities, limits these effects. The benefits of trampling are that it prevents the accumulation of leaf litter and creates bare ground for invertebrates and the regeneration of wet niches for plants. Poached river edges are particularly species-rich areas, offering an interesting terrestrial-aquatic transitional habitat. Limited poaching of river margins can therefore be considered beneficial in conservation terms. However it also adds silt to the channel and can reduce cross-sectional area.

If a site requires summer grazing, cattle are preferred. Stocking before July is undesirable, especially in sites good for ground-nesting birds although very low-density grazing can be compatible with breeding waders. However, the choice of stock and the grazing regime is ultimately dependent on the landowner.

Livestock densities must be managed to ensure that overgrazing does not occur. The objective should be to graze at a level that allows banks to be inspected, to reduce the dominance of grasses, and to encourage plant richness and habitat structure for invertebrates and birds. Overstocking will adversely affect the quality and structure of the sward, thereby reducing wildlife interest.

3.6.3. Mowing and cutting

Mowing can rapidly and radically alter plant communities and therefore the habitat structure for invertebrates, birds and mammals (Plate 3). It is essential to identify the engineering and ecological management requirements for the site and ensure that these objectives are most appropriately met by mowing. The timing, frequency and pattern of cutting should be determined by these objectives.

Many of the best floodplain meadow SSSIs (eg Portholme on the R Ouse, North Meadow and Pixie Mead on the R Thames) are managed by mowing.

Nigel Holmes

Plate 3
This Lincolnshire drain has been mown to increase conveyance. However, much of the previously available habitat has now disappeared.

Case Study: North Level Engine Drain 3.6 (b)

Timing of mowing

Mowing may involve cutting either in early summer (until July) or late summer (after August). The effects of these alternatives are listed in Table 3. A pre-August cut may be necessary for areas where summer flooding is a particular problem and where maximising channel-carrying capacity and reducing roughness are priorities. Timing is critical as different flood defence and conservation objectives may have to be achieved. Moreover different plants are vulnerable at different times. The 'need' for early management must be weighed against the 'need' to retaining some habitat for invertebrates, small mammals and birds.

Autumn mowing has a number of advantages for conservation and is generally recommended. It avoids the breeding bird season, maintains abundance and diversity of herb species, and provides invertebrates with food and shelter.

Pattern of mowing

Whatever time of year mowing is carried out, it is important to avoid a 'blanket cut' of bankside vegetation. Patch cutting on a

rotation normally leads to substantial improvements in plant diversity and habitat structure, benefiting animals particularly butterflies. On riverbanks, leaving an uncut strip from the top of the bank down to the water's edge enables a representative mix of terrestrial, semi-aquatic and aquatic plants to be retained. Where this is impossible, it is important to leave the margin (at the base of the bank) unmown to retain cover at the bank/water interface. (Plates 4 & 5).

Although size and siting of each uncut patch will differ according to specific site

Table 3: Some effects of early and late mowing regimes

PRE-AUGUST CUT	POST JULY CUT
• Prevents spreading of injurious weeds	• Retains habitat structure and shelter for animals
• Reduces dominance of vigorous grasses (can be avoided by appropriate initial seeding mix).	• Seeds, etc available for birds and mammals
• Stimulates grass regrowth leading to additional cut being required.	• Avoids disturbance to late breeding birds
• Encourages tillering of grass to make a denser sward.	• Less grass production and reduced maintenance

Nigel Holmes

Stuart McFadzean

**Plate 4 (top)
A marginal strip
has been left
unmown to
retain cover at
the bank/water
interface (R Idle).**

**Plate 5 (above)
Partial bank
mowing and
channel weed
control on Spittle
Brook**

Table 4: Benefits of rotational patch cutting

- Continuation of plant species diversity through seed dispersal from uncut areas
- Food and shelter for insects and other invertebrates retained; uncut patches must be left to allow establishment of plant and animal populations into cut areas
- Small mammals (water voles, short-tailed voles and water shrews) and birds (particularly seed-eating species such as goldfinches) have habitat for shelter and feeding
- Prevents natural succession to scrub
- Reduces overall channel roughness in tandem with habitat structure (retention of isolated patches of vegetation has no significant effect in channels with a minimum 2 m bed-width

Table 5: Effects of burning

- Damage to habitats and loss of sensitive species and communities
- Erosion on banks without cover
- Release of nutrients to the soil which encourages more competitive and robust species to dominate
- May spread and burn adjacent areas of important vegetation
- Release of nutrients to the watercourse encouraging growth of aquatic vegetation (requiring additional management)
- Damage to soils, especially in peaty areas

requirements, two general guidelines should be followed:

- a minimum of 10% should be left uncut (perhaps cut on 3–7 year rotation);

- cutting patterns should be rotated, with no patch uncut for more than three years to prevent rank grasses, nettles and scrub suppressing other plants.

Table 4 lists some benefits that arise from rotational cutting consistent with flood defence needs.

Disposal of cuttings

The benefits of an appropriate mowing regime can be negated by inappropriate disposal of cuttings. When left on site, cuttings ultimately lead to suppression of

species diversity by encouraging rank species; although with fine cuttings, eg from flailing, the impact is minimised. If possible, cuttings should be mown from areas of conservation interest and heaped on dry areas of low conservation interest where they may provide hibernation and breeding sites for animals such as bumble-bees, voles, hedgehogs and snakes.

Burning as a means of controlling bank vegetation or disposal of cuttings is not recommended on either environmental or operational grounds. (Table 5).

3.6.4 Herbicides

The widespread and regular use of herbicides is not compatible with the maintenance of species-rich grasslands. The use of herbicides to spot-treat unwanted species (ie spear-thistle, ragwort, creeping thistle, Japanese knotweed and giant hogweed) may, however, be necessary, particularly on areas that are to be re-seeded.

Advice on the use of herbicides near watercourses should be sought from the NRA (or equivalent authority), IDB or ADAS. They will be able to advise on suitable products and methods of application, eg spray/wipe/spot treatment. Persons using herbicides on land which they or their employer do not

own must hold the appropriate certificate from the National Proficiency Test Council. This also applies to contractors.

Only herbicides that have been cleared for use near or in water use may be used near a watercourse (MAFF 1985). Furthermore, the NRA (or equivalent authority) must be contacted for advice prior to using herbicides near water. Spot treatment or preventing a weed problem by correct management and early remedial action is preferable to widespread herbicide use to control a problem. However, if this is imperative, Table 6 provides broad guidance on selection of appropriate herbicides.

Table 6: Herbicide selection for bankside weeds

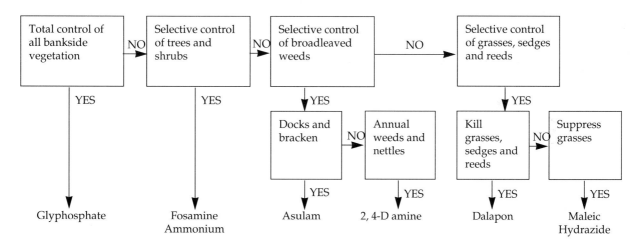

3.6.5 Establishing vegetation on floodbanks

Traditionally, new floodbanks have been sown with a grass mix dominated by rye-grass, which quickly stabilises loose soil and results in a productive sward for grazing. Grazing of floodbanks, however, is now less common and the widespread changes in farming, including reversion from arable to grassland through the set-aside initiative, mean that in large parts of

the country livestock are not readily available for grazing. Sward productivity is, therefore, no longer an asset.

It is now widespread practice to establish a sward that satisfactorily binds the soil of banks but has a short growth and low productivity. This makes sward management cheaper. 'Low maintenance'

Table 7: Advantages of low-maintenance seed mixes

- Require less mowing once established
- Often look better in amenity terms
- Are generally more tolerant of environmental stress
- Support a wider variety of wildlife
- Provide cover for ground-nesting birds, such as skylarks and partridges
- Provide a reservoir for wild flowers which are disappearing from the surrounding countryside (provided they have come from local natural stock)
- Provide more varied food and shelter for insects, such as butterflies in the larval and adult stages

Table 8: Disadvantages of low-maintenance seed mixes

- The main constituent grasses take longer to germinate and require greater care in the establishment period
- The seed is more expensive so is spread sparingly
- More thought has to be given to what mixture is used and where and how it is to be managed

Plate 6 (below) Wild-flower mix sown on a raised embankment of the R Bain

Plate 7 (bottom) Musk mallow and knapweed on the R Bain embankment

grass mixes, sometimes incorporating wild-flower seeds, can result in significant benefit to wildlife (Table 7).

Establishing a low-maintenance sward can provide great benefits to wildlife, but may also create potential problems for flood defence (Table 8). None of these problems are serious, and can be overcome, for example, by the use of 'nurse crops' initially to protect bank soils. In this respect, clear guidance on the selection of seed mixes and subsequent management is needed. Visual amenity can be greatly enhanced by low-maintenance mixes that incorporate wild flowers. On Padgate Brook, Warrington, a re-seeding scheme, which included wild flowers transplanted by the local community, thrived so much that the river is now a major focal point of interest. On the R Bain (Case Study 3.3(b)) a wild-flower mix was sown on a raised embankment used by the public (Plate 6). Within six months, spiny restharrow, yarrow, campion, musk mallow, knapweed and many other wild flowers thrived to great acclaim by local walkers (Plate 7). However, without grazing in subsequent years rank vegetation developed, to the detriment of less vigorous plants.

Low-maintenance mixes are ideal if:

- sheep or horse grazing crops the grass close to give a dense sward;

- mowing is the main form of management;

- the bank is going to be managed for amenity;

- wild flowers are to be added to the mix, and wildlife encouraged.

Opportunities and options for vegetation establishment

Seeding grass and herb species on to floodbanks is possible when new banks are being constructed or when existing banks are being raised or repaired. Both activities

Nigel Holmes

Nigel Holmes

require imported soil or the use of dredged material to form the banks. Soil pH and the level of soil fertility will affect seedling development and subsequent growth.

Low-maintenance swards can also be seeded on to existing floodbanks that require no repair or improvement. In this instance, the existing sward is stripped away and a thin layer of topsoil rotovated with subsoil before re-seeding. Where this is not feasible, the existing sward can be partially ripped out and seeded to encourage desirable species to spread into the adjacent turf.

Trials on floodbanks along the R Trent near Gainsborough (Case Study 3.6(a)) have assessed the establishment of low-maintenance swards rich in wild flowers in different soil conditions. Post-project appraisal has shown that to be satisfactory a sward needs to establish rapidly, thereby minimising the period when bank soil is unprotected and prone to erosion.

It should be remembered that floodbanks are atypical sites for grassland establishment. Banks set some distance from the river, especially those facing south and east, are often exposed to drying winds and low water tables leading to water stress. Conversely, banks facing the river may benefit from relatively moister air and nutrient input from flood water. The land between a floodbank and the river may also benefit from lateral movements of water from the river, from moister air and regular replenishment of nutrients during floods (Plate 8). Therefore, the most appropriate mixes need to be considered with respect to aspect and local conditions.

Low-maintenance grass species with herbs are generally more tolerant of low-nutrient levels and water stress and are therefore ideal for use on the top and outward faces of floodbanks. Land between the floodbank and riverbank, in contrast, is more suited to the use of a relatively unproductive strain of rye-grass, combined with marshland herbs.

If there is concern for bank integrity, a quick growing nurse crop in conjunction with a low-maintenance mixture can be used to ensure adequate protection for flood defence purposes soon after construction of the bank. For example, re-seeding experiments using low-maintenance mixes were used on the Ouse Washes Barrier Banks in 1990–1992. The Barrier Banks needed to be raised to overcome problems of rising water levels, deteriorating bank stability, bank settlement and poor access. After construction work, the banks were re-seeded using a seed mix selected to balance the need for early germination to protect the newly built bank and the long-term need to provide good grazing. The mix included annual and perennial rye-grasses and wild flowers.

Soils and seeding

Topsoil is normally high in plant nutrients and contains seeds of aggressive weed species, which germinate quickly and compete with sown seed. Putting topsoil on banks is therefore not recommended. If topsoil has to be used, for example to help establishment on impoverished clay subsoils, it should be as a thin layer, less than 10 cm thick. In this situation, clay should be roughened to provide a 'grip' for the covering topsoil to prevent it being washed off. A friable subsoil with small amounts of topsoil is ideal for establishing low-maintenance mixes.

Seedbed preparation to a fine tilth is important, particularly if wild-flower seeds are included. The seeds are generally small and if they become buried too deeply, ie

Stuart McFadzean

Plate 8
This wet shelf on the R Torne, built as part of a capital scheme, provides a wide foreshore habitat

**Case Study:
R Trent,
Gainsborough
3.6 (a)**

deeper than their own diameter, germination is poor. In such circumstances rye-grass, with its large seed, will have an advantage.

On steep slopes of riverbanks, roughening the bank surface with the teeth of an excavator bucket will help prevent seed from being washed into the channel.

Methods and timing of sowing

Damp, warm conditions are often important for successful germination. Spring sowing (April–May) is preferred as the summer growing period normally allows seedlings to become established. Low-maintenance grasses have a prolonged germination period which may extend to several weeks compared with as little as a week for rye-grass. It is for this reason, that a rye-grass nurse species is often included in low- maintenance mixes to provide early bank protection.

The simplest method of sowing is broadcasting seed, mixed with a sand or meal carrier, by hand, followed by a light raking. Broadcasting this mix on to a rough surface and allowing natural soil movements to cover it will work but decreases germination success and increases losses to birds. On large-scale works, where slopes are not steep, seed can be spread by standard farm machinery, again with a carrier, and lightly harrowed. Rolling after seeding ensures better, and more even, germination as it puts the seed in intimate contact with soil particles and moisture.

Low-maintenance seed mixes are more expensive than standard agricultural mixes and contain seeds of different size. The use of a 'carrier' (fine sand or barley meal) enables a more even and economic distribution. Where wild flowers are included in the mix, a more even distribution improves the opportunity for their establishment and subsequent spread. If enhanced erosion resistance is required, geotextile reinforcement can be used. This involves preparing the bank as previously described and sowing grass on top of a woven fabric or mat layer. On extremely steep banks, hydroseeding may be needed. This is where seed together with a binding agent and mulch are sprayed over the site. The mulch should not contain fertiliser.

Research for the NRA has indicated wide variations in sowing rates and methods. Seed may be given to farmers to apply at the agricultural rate of around 25 kg/ha. Specifications for seeding range between 13.5–55 kg/ha with the higher levels for capital works. So-called 'conservation mixes' are recommended to be sown at around 40 kg/ha and amenity grassland at 150–180 kg/ha. British Waterways specifies 340 kg/ha for urban grass areas. Rates used during low maintenance trials are provided in the Gainsborough Case Study (3.6(a)). Results suggest that rates greater than 40 kg/ha are not cost effective but the inclusion of rye-grass as a nurse crop (at 10–15 kg/ha) gives satisfactory results.

In addition to the grass mix, a variety of herb seeds can be added and sown at a rate of 3 kg/ha. This relatively low proportion of herbs has proved to be adequate in establishing a good diversity of wild flowers. Wild-flower seeds are usually smaller and lighter than grass seeds so consideration of the number of wild-flower seeds when sowing is more important than weight. Advice should be sought on which species should be included. Planting pot-grown plants after the sward is established may be more cost-effective where species that have poor germination potential are desired. To avoid disappointing results, mixes should always be selected according to site conditions.

Use of nurse species and seed mixes

Nurse species enable rapid establishment of grass cover on a floodbank but the long-term requirement is a low-maintenance sward. Named rye-grass cultivars that combine strong growth with low height (developed for sports turf), justify extra expense by germinating quickly and simplifying management in the critical establishment period.

Within six weeks, nurse crops bind the soil with a protective canopy. Cutting back to a height 5–7 cm before the sward reaches 15 cm is recommended, otherwise other seedlings will be inhibited because the nurse crop is too tall.

A nurse crop of the annual Westerwolds rye-grass has been tried in a number of places but experience has shown that the critical initial cutting is often not carried out, leading to excessive growth. Expensive hand raking of cuttings is then required otherwise the desired species are smothered. For operational reasons, therefore, a perennial nurse species is favoured.

Selection of seed mixes depends on local conditions and needs. The table of 'successful' and 'failed' plants in the Gainsborough Case Study (3.6(a)) is a helpful guide if establishment is to be on dredged silts at pH c7.2. The wild flowers that succeeded best were species with a wide tolerance of conditions. Some plants, such as yellow rattle, are parasitic, and annual, so they need to be allowed to seed before mowing. Others, such as cowslip, take several years to establish. The qualities that make a grass desirable in engineering terms may differ from those desirable for aesthetic or for wildlife reasons (Tables 7 and 8).

The Gainsborough case study suggests that grass seed mixture which combines low maintenance and quick cover while allowing wild flowers to establish and spread should be sown at 40–100 kg/ha and contain:

- crested dog's-tail   20%
- rye-grass
  (sports-turf variety)   30%
- creeping red fescue   20%
- sheep's fescue   20%
  (not required if wild flowers not included)
- chewings/hard/fine-leaved fescue 10%
  (choice of one)

Trials with wild-flower seed mix have also been carried out on the Ea Beck (Yorkshire). Sites sown in 1989 were surveyed in 1991 and 1992 to determine the germination and establishment success of

Table 9: Plants recommended for different soil types by Wells *et al.* (1981)

	SOWING RATES (kg/ha)	
	GRASS/SHORT HERB MIXTURE	GRASS/TALL HERB MIXTURE
1. Seed mixtures for sowing on heavy clay soils		
Meadow foxtail	5.0	5.0
Common quaking-grass	0.5	0.5
Crested dog's-tail	–	5.0
Red fescue *Festuca rubra* 'Cascade'	–	10.0
Red fescue *Festuca rubra* 'Highlight'	10.0	10.0
Red fescue *Festuca rubra* 'Rapid'	8.0	–
Meadow barley	1.0	1.0
Yellow oat-grass	1.0	1.0
Kidney vetch	3.0	–
Oxeye daisy	0.2	0.5
Lady's bedstraw	0.3	–
Rough hawkbit	0.5	–
Bird's-foot-trefoil	1.0	1.0
Black medick	2.0	–
Hoary plantain	0.2	–
Cowslip	0.5	–
Self-heal	0.5	–
Yellow rattle	2.0	–
Knapweed	–	1.0
Great knapweed	–	1.0
Wild carrot	–	0.9
Dropwort	–	1.0
Meadow crane's-bill	–	2.15
Common cat's-ear	–	0.3
Ribwort plantain	–	2.0
Salad burnet	–	0.3
Common meadow buttercup	–	1.0
White campion	–	0.5
2. Seed mixtures for sowing on chalk and other limestone soils		
Common quaking grass	0.5	–
Crested dog's-tail	5.0	5.0
Upright brome	–	2.0
Hard fescue	–	10.0
Sheep's fescue	–	4.0
Red fescue *Festuca rubra* 'Highlight'	10.0	10.0
Red fescue *Festuca rubra* 'Rapid'	8.0	8.0
Crested hair-grass	0.1	–
Yellow oat-grass	1.0	–
Kidney vetch	3.0	–
Clustered bell-flower	0.01	–
Harebell	0.01	–
Oxeye daisy	0.2	0.2
Lady's bedstraw	0.3	0.3
Horseshoe vetch	2.0	–
Black medick	0.2	–
Hoary plantain	0.5	–
Cowslip	0.5	–
Self-heal	0.5	–
Small scabious	0.5	0.5
Common or larger wild thyme	0.1	–
Germander speedwell	0.1	–
Knapweed	1.0	1.0
Great knapweed	–	1.0
Wild basil	–	0.1
Wild carrot	–	0.5
Bird's-foot-trefoil	–	1.0
Sainfoin	–	3.0
Wild mignonette	–	0.03
Dyer's rocket	–	0.01
Goat's-beard	–	1.0

(cont)

Table 9 (cont)

3. Seed mixtures for sowing on alluvial soils

Common bent	1.0	1.0
Meadow foxtail	5.0	5.0
Common quaking-grass	0.5	–
Crested dog's-tail	5.0	5.0
Red fescue *Festuca rubra* 'Dawson'	10.0	10.0
Red fescue *Festuca rubra* 'Cascade'	10.0	10.0
Meadow grass	3.0	3.0
Oxeye daisy	0.2	0.2
Pignut	1.0	–
Wild carrot	0.9	0.9
Lady's bedstraw	0.3	–
Common cat's-ear	0.3	–
Ragged-robin	0.0005	0.005
Black medick	2.0	–
Hoary plantain	0.2	–
Salad burnet	0.3	0.3
Cowslip	0.5	0.5
Self-heal	0.5	–
Yellow rattle	2.0	2.0
Bird's-foot-trefoil	–	1.0
Ribwort plantain	–	2.0
Great burnet	–	0.5
Pepper saxifrage	–	1.0
White campion	–	0.5

NB: Some seed may be difficult to obtain or be very expensive. In special situations plants can be grown to order by a specialist nursery

43 sown species. Problems with weeds in the sown sites were experienced, which were not evident where turfs were laid. The trials concluded that sowing seed mixes that contain native grasses and a few specific herbs was most effective and that the use of prescribed 'off the shelf' mixes was not to be recommended.

In some places extensive lengths of riverbanks are affected by saline water within the tidal reach. For example on the Arun at Arundel rye-grass strains have been virtually eliminated leaving resistant weeds to stabilise the banks. In such situations salt tolerant species such as *Festuca rubra litoralis*, a strain derived from saltmarsh turf, is more suitable. Common or sea couch-grass are ideal for saline conditions.

The wildlife value of low-maintenance mixtures is determined initially by the flowers present. These in turn create more variable habitats for animals. If the sward is short, ground-nesting birds such as skylark benefit; where grass grows taller as a result of a low-fequency cutting regime, larvae of moths and butterflies, and other invertebrates, such as grasshoppers, benefit.

A wide selection of herbs and grasses can be chosen for establishment on banks of different soil chemistry and physical character (Table 9). Guidance on suitable strains and mixes is available in STRI (1991) Wells *et al.* (1981) and Coppin and Richards (1990). Advice should be sought from conservation experts, who will be able to advise on suggest of seed and plants from reliable British stock.

Post-sowing management

It is desirable to prevent common weed species dominating the vegetation. More frequent cutting in the first two years reduces the potential weed problem, the number of cuts required being dependent on the amount of growth. Ideally swards are initially cut back to a height of 5–7 cm before reaching 15 cms. Such a regime in the first year will encourage a balanced, closed, sward with a well developed wild flower community. Grazing should not occur for at least a year. Removal of cuttings helps to reduce soil fertility and assists the development of wild-flower communities.

Establishment of low-maintenance swards should reduce the number of cuts required on a floodbank by half. Cost-savings therefore result from the reduced maintenance in the longer term. If suitable, a total cessation of cutting of a sward, once established, can be adopted for a few areas. However, the occasional cut is recommended to encourage a tight sward and richer plant and animal communities. The reduced number of cuts also benefits bank stability in drought periods as cutting retards root growth.

Turf transplants

An alternative to seeding is to transplant species-rich turfs from an existing site on to a newly prepared floodbank. The donor site should be one that is under threat and may be lost altogether. Habitat transplantation projects are not always successful. Where only minor patching repairs are needed, turfs may be taken from the back (outward face) of the floodbank and some seed scattered in their place.

Turf transplantation should be carried out in winter and early spring when vegetation is dormant and there is little invertebrate activity. Turfs should be damp but not wet; in this state they will hold together better. The receiving area substrate should be prepared in a similar way as a seedbed. Commercial turf-cutting machinery is the most efficient for taking material from the donor site. Not only is it quicker, but it also produces much more regular turfs which are easier to lay and take hold more readily. However, if transplants involve moving deep-rooted species this method is not recommended.

Turfs should be as deep and as large as possible and their prolonged storage should be avoided; a few weeks will cause disintegration of the turfs and bare patches upon re-establishment. If necessary, for a short period, turfs can be stored in 1 m high stacks and kept moist. Donor and receiver sites should have similar soils and aspect for best results.

Gaps between relaid turfs should be filled with soil from either the donor or recipient site and seeded with a low-maintenance grass/herb mix. An even surface is essential for continuing management. Herb-rich turfs can be laid in patches to maximise their benefit so they act as sources for colonisation over the rest of the bank, which is sown with a low-maintenance mix. Once turf is established, grazing or mowing should be resumed as soon as possible.

The Case Study on the R Avon at Barton (3.6(b)) indicates that turfing is a viable approach to establishing rich swards in the long-term. When rich turfs are in short supply, they can be used in conjunction with low-maintenance grass mixtures to gain maximum value.

The 200-year-old floodbank on the site of a floodbank improvement scheme on the R Nidd, Yorkshire had a rich meadow flora. In order to retain conservation interest 100 m2 of turfs cut from the original bank were transplanted on to the new floodbank after it had been raised.

Turfing on floodbanks on the Ea Beck in Yorkshire in 1989 indicated, a year after the transplantation, that a wide range of species had taken at the new site. However, common spotted orchid failed to grow. This may be because orchids require a greater depth of turf to be transplanted than other species. Turfs moved at this site were around 20 cm deep. In contrast, orchids moved at a building site at Thurrock near London, using a tractor-mounted post-hole borer taking 25–30 cm cores centred on the orchid plants, did establish successfully.

Key References

Dickinson, N M and Polwart, A (1982) The effect of mowing regime on an amenity grassland ecosystem: above- and below-ground components. *J. of Applied Ecology.* 19:569–77.

Hemphill, R W and Bramley, M E (1989) *The protection of river and canal banks.* A guide to selection and design. Construction Industry Research and Information Association. Butterworths.

MAFF (1985) *Guidelines for the use of herbicides on weed in or near watercourses and lakes.* Booklet 2078.

National Rivers Authority (1988, 1989, 1990 and 1991) *Establishing low maintenance swards with wild flowers on river banks.* NRA

Wells, T, Bell, S and Frost, A (1981) *Creating attractive grasslands using native plant species.* Nature Conservancy Council, Peterborough. 2078.

National Rivers Authority (1988, 1989, 1990 and 1991) *Establishing low maintenance swards with wild flowers on river banks.* NRA

Wells, T, Bell, S and Frost, A (1981) *Creating attractive grasslands using native plant species.* Nature Conservancy Council, Peterborough.

Case Study: R Avon, Barton 3.6 (b)

3.7 Tree and Scrub Establishment and Management

3.7.1 Introduction

Woody vegetation is used by many forms of wildlife. Landscape, amenity value and other factors including bank stability are also affected by trees and scrub. The species present, their growth pattern, structure, extent and age all influence the range of wildlife in the riverine habitat. A wider variety of birds, mammals and invertebrates will occur where a range of trees and scrub offers different sources of food, shelter and breeding cover. (RSPB 1978a and b, 1979; Hawkins *et al.*, 1982; Macdonald and Mason, 1983; Mason *et al.*, 1984).

Trees and scrub along the riverbank and within the floodplain are significant landscape features. They create a stable environment in terms of light, shelter and

temperature within the river corridor and thereby provide habitats for a range of animals and plants that would not otherwise find suitable conditions. Trees and scrub also provide a link to other terrestrial habitats in and beyond the river valley. Copses may be remnants of former extensive ancient woodlands. Wet woodlands, hydrologically connected with the river, are known as carrs and are dominated by alder and willow, and often contain remnants of the ground flora and fauna associated with ancient floodplain wetlands.

Table 1 lists some key aspects of trees and scrub which make them important for river wildlife. For example, shade cast by trees and scrub can provide moist conditions in

Table 1: Key aspects of trees and scrub that make them important for wildlife

Underwater fine roots	feathery roots important habitat for invertebrates (Smith *et al* 1991).
Overhanging trees and roots over water, eg willow	fish refuges.
Cavities in bank under large tree roots, eg ash, oak, sycamore	potential otter holts.
Fine tree roots through bank soils, especially fine, friable soils and sandy gravels	bind soil – help stabilise bank and reduce erosion.
Bushy growth of scrub with variety of species	cover for many birds, eg tits, warblers and gamebirds, and mammals, eg dormice, hedgehogs. dense cover provides nest sites for many birds, eg moorhen, and lying up area for otters and cover for voles.
Mature and dead tree trunks	cavities for nesting goosander, woodpeckers and owls, breeding and roosting sites for bats. pollards provide safe nest-sites for duck and have rich invertebrate communities. old bark, especially in wetter parts of the country supports rich fern, lichen and moss communities and everywhere is important for fungi and insects. dead wood under water important for invertebrates such as cranefly.
Leaves, buds, flowers and fruits	huge variety of animals feed on trees – oak, willow, alder and birch are the richest (Kennedy and Southward, 1984). Leaf fauna taken by birds. Insects falling from leaves into water are food for fish (Hawkins *et al.*, 1982; Mason and MacDonald 1982; Mason *et al.*, 1984). Seeds and fruits important in winter, eg siskin and redpoll feeding on alder.

which delicate ferns, mosses, liverworts and lichens can thrive (Plate 1). Tree-less sections lack such plants, whilst opening up the tree or scrub canopy, often results in their demise. Aquatic plants may also dramatically increase if tree or scrub shade is removed.

Nigel Holmes

Plate 1
Shading on the R Tawe results in damp conditions in which ferns, mosses, liverworts and lichens thrive

3.7.2 Management decisions

If trees and scrub are to continue to make important contributions to river corridor wildlife, river management techniques must either:

- work around existing trees managing them with care and sensitivity to meet engineering needs; or

- provide replacement trees or scrub through replanting, or extend habitat by new planting.

The first option is always preferable. Ancient woodland is irreplaceable, and new planting cannot re-create it. Impacts on both landscape and wildlife can be dramatic even when removed trees and scrub are replaced. Tree planting must therefore be regarded as a bonus, not an alternative to careful management of existing trees. However, new planting is always worth considering as it can enhance most river environments. A combination of both options may be appropriate. Sections 3.7.2 to 3.7.5 consider the management of existing scrub, management of trees, and the planting of trees and shrubs.

The value of riverside scrub and trees for wildlife, visual amenity and practical management of rivers for flood defence is paramount and in this last respect, their

use for erosion control is highlighted in Section 3.7.6.

Considerations before management

To make informed decisions about management it is essential to examine the reasons for undertaking maintenance of trees and shrubs.

Flood defence reasons may dictate the need for tree management because a tree, or parts of a tree, may be impeding flow or obstructing bridges or other structures. For example, a tree may prevent machine access for dredging operations. Scrub within a channel increases roughness, reduces conveyance and increases the risk of blockage. The potential impact of tree and scrub growth on flow hydraulics should be allowed for within the design calculations.

There may be good ecological reasons why tree management is desirable. For example, an even-aged stand of alder may benefit from selective coppicing to create greater structural diversity. A combination of both engineering and ecological needs may prompt management action; coppicing and re-pollarding come into this category. Regular pollarding will prevent a tree from collapsing, with the consequent loss of wildlife habitat and the increased risk of channel blockage.

However, wise judgement is often required for effective tree management. Some tree species can naturally look unstable, eg the arching habit of black poplar, but this does not necessarily mean they are unstable and need to be managed by cutting.

To maintain the continuity of tree and scrub habitat, a policy of 'little and often' management is usually best. The complete removal of one component of habitat can be significant for wildlife. For example, removing all branches that dip low over a river may remove safe nesting sites for moorhens. Removing only those limbs which are causing a problem, is ecologically acceptable and (Figure 1 and Plate 2) the temptation to remove more should must be resisted.

Wherever possible, all tree maintenance should be carried out between October and March, outside the bird breeding season and when invertebrates are largely inactive. Most sap is down at this time, therefore trees have a better chance of survival, especially if large limbs are removed. If management is carried out in spring and summer, only the lightest maintenance should be undertaken and the site searched for nests. Large trees with significant fissures and cavities will require prior survey for bats prior to management or felling.

Tree management is a skilled job and a well-trained work-force is essential for sensitive management. Such training should include safety aspects as well as how to coppice, pollard and prune trees without damaging them and how and where to dispose of material.

Regrowth

In deciding on a preferred management option, it is important to know what species are involved and how they respond

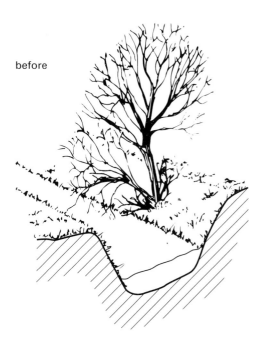

before

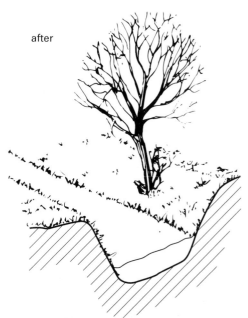

after

Figure 1
Trimming of overhanging branches.
Source: Newbold *et al.* (1989)

Plate 2
Acceptable
overhanging
branch removal

Nigel Holmes

to cutting. A few broadleaved species will not resprout if felled. However, most do so readily and will respond to coppicing or pollarding.

If a continuous line of riverbank trees is cut down, it is likely to regrow to produce a line of bushy shrubs, which may create more of an obstacle to high river flows than the original trees. Alternatively, it may allow modification of the habitat to benefit wildlife and allow machine access for management. Similarly, with some coppiced trees it is possible to cut away regrowth to retain single stems to grow on as a tree.

Grazing of cut stems often prevents regrowth and therefore after coppicing there may be a need to protect shoots from grazing livestock (Figure 2i).

Disposal of material

Cut material should be disposed of with care. For example, there have been instances where fires have been badly sited, such as under the canopy of mature trees.

Fires should not be lit on rock faces as lichen, moss and liverwort flora will be irreparably damaged. Similarly, herb-rich vegetation and communities on river shingle can be damaged by bonfires and the original vegetation structure rarely returns. The number of fire sites should be restricted to the absolute minimum, and fires should not be allowed to spread. In some cases it may be necessary to remove the material from site altogether. Burning on dry peat and on rare habitats should not occur. An alternative to burning, currently gaining favour, is chipping surplus woody material. Woodchips can be used on site as a mulch for tree planting areas or for the surface of informal paths.

Practical use of cut material not only reduces the amount of material to be disposed of, but also provides opportunities. Spiling, faggots and live stakes are all examples whereby both dead and live material may be used on site for bank protection. Examples are given in the section on 'revetments' (3.4.4) and in Section 3.7.6. Opportunities to enhance sites by using cut material to generate new pollards and coppices are numerous. A supply of willow stakes, 20 cm or more in diameter, sharpened at their basal end and driven into the ground will rapidly sprout shoots and roots in spring. In dry soils they

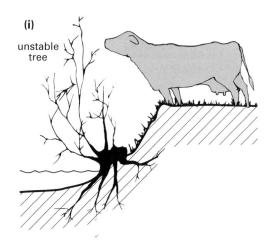

(i)

unstable tree

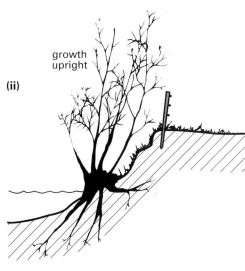

(ii)

growth upright

Figure 2
The need for fencing. (i) Browsing restricts the growth of vertical shoots, to outward curving shoots become the main growth, perhaps causing instability in later years. (ii) Fenced from browsing, the main growth is upright. Source: Lewis and Williams (1984)

stage 1 build basic structure

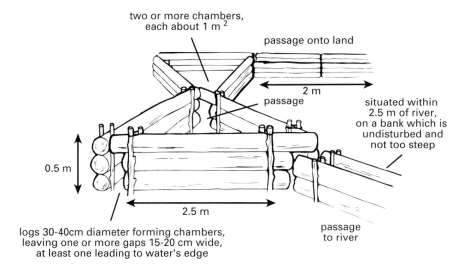

two or more chambers,
each about 1 m ^{2}

passage onto land

2 m

passage

situated within
2.5 m of river,
on a bank which is
undisturbed and
not too steep

0.5 m

2.5 m

logs 30-40cm diameter forming chambers,
leaving one or more gaps 15-20 cm wide,
at least one leading to water's edge

passage
to river

stage 2 lay small branches to form roof

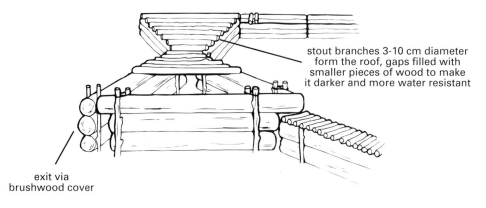

stout branches 3-10 cm diameter
form the roof, gaps filled with
smaller pieces of wood to make
it darker and more water resistant

exit via
brushwood cover

stage 3 cover with branches / branchings
and stake down

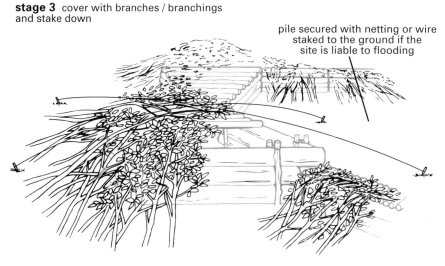

pile secured with netting or wire
staked to the ground if the
site is liable to flooding

Figure 3
**Log-pile holts should imitate the flood debris piles often used by otters for lying up. They should usually
be sited where there is little natural cover, and if not used by otters still provide useful habitat for other
wildlife which like rotting wood. Source: NRA (1993)**

should be driven in deeply to the level of the water table.

Larger material and brashings can, in agreement with landowners, be stacked as log piles above the flood level to rot and provide a temporary home for birds and mammals. For invertebrates it is preferable for material to be in close contact with the ground in shade or dappled sun to aid rotting. Otter holts, made from cut tree material, are simply 'structured log piles'. Figure 3 illustrates how a log pile holt may be constructed. Land drainage consent may be required from the appropriate authority to construct an artificial holt.

Piles of timber and brash, which have been secured to the ground if necessary, can be particularly valuable for wildlife in providing cover where a lot of scrub has been removed. It is only a temporary measure, however, and is not an alternative to retaining woody cover.

Fencing

Where trees and scrub are removed because they obstruct flow, some attention should be given to creating space for future regrowth. Coppice and scrub growth within channels is often caused by grazing where the only growth is beyond the reach of livestock. Cutting down all bank trees and scrub removes woody wildlife habitat, but does not solve a long-term management problem as it will regenerate and re-create the same problem in a few years' time. Fencing the bank will not only encourage the main growth to be vertical (Figure 2ii) but also allows space for trees and scrub to develop on the bank top. Shade from growth on the top of the bank will also reduce growth at the base of the slope. Fencing is discussed further in Section 3.7.5.

3.7.3 Management of bank scrub

Working through scrub

The simplest option for conserving continuous low scrub is to ignore it. A tracked machine can drive over low scrub without permanently damaging it. Recovery is quick but fencing may be needed for protection against livestock damage. This technique is only suitable for species with soft stems like bramble, rose and small sallows. As with maintenance of trees, minimal disruption to associated fauna will result if work is confined to autumn and winter.

Machines should be able to work through hedges and scrub less than 2 m high, although on small watercourses the vision of the machine driver may be obstructed. Dense, woody scrub can be coppiced and then fenced where livestock are present. On the Driffield Canal, Yorkshire, 30% of a hawthorn scrub hedge which was preventing access of a dredging machine

was cut but not fenced. The coppiced regrowth has been grazed and further regrowth prevented due to lack of fencing.

Scrub growth can be tolerated on at least one side of many floodbanks and sometimes both. Maintenance on floodbanks to protect marginal land (itself often of conservation value for breeding waders) can be designed to provide a succession of scrub. At Newlands Beck, Cumbria, gorse was left on the landward side of the bank, thus protecting the bank from cattle damage. The top and riverside of the bank are cut on roughly a six-year cycle to restrict extensive scrub growth in order to enable inspection for vermin. Limited grazing of adjacent land was cited as the main reason for relaxing the standard of maintenance on the floodbanks. Such standards allow for the creation and maintenance of a diverse linear habitat, in stark contrast to the closely cut or grazed floodbank grassland.

**Plate 3
Selective
thinning on the
Old Bedford
River,
Cambridgeshire**

Stuart McFadzean

In the Bristol Avon catchment, many small rural rivers where the watercourses are in a tunnel formed by a canopy of scrub are treated in this way. Management takes place from boats punching small holes through the scrub at approximately 100-m intervals to enable removal and disposal of cut branches. Only low branches, which collect trash, are removed. This treatment is almost invisible outside the channel, and is particularly useful in areas of high amenity or landscape interest. It also retains natural shade control of in-stream vegetation (Section 3.5.2.4) and a moist shaded micro-climate for plants such as ferns, mosses and liverworts.

Selective thinning

On the Old Bedford River in Cambridgeshire (Plate 3) control of the dense willow growth that had encroached from one bank into the channel was required. A management strategy was adopted whereby patches of overhanging osiers were retained but the remainder were cut back to the bank, an operation carried out from boats. This diversified the previously uniform densely shaded stands of willow, whilst retaining sufficient cover for nesting moorhens and coots. The resultant extra light at the water margin allowed marginal and submerged aquatics to thrive and increase diversity of the habitat.

Tunnelling through continuous scrub on both banks

Trimming scrub from within the channel will restore flood capacity without opening the channel to too much light or removing significant wildlife habitat. Retention of shade vasting vegetation inhibits in-channel and bankside vegetation growth, thereby reducing the potential requirement for management in such areas.

3.7.4 Management of trees on riverbanks

Trees on riverbanks can create flooding hazards as well as obstructions to machinery necessary for river management works. The emphasis of tree management work should be on tree maintenance rather than tree clearance. Removal of trees with their roots should be regarded as a 'last resort', in part because of their value in stabilising banks.

Working around trees

In many situations, trees (and isolated patches of scrub) make machine access to the channel difficult or complicates the design of new structures, such as floodbanks. However, there are good reasons for attempting to conserve woody vegetation, whether in a remote, rural situation or in a highly developed urban area.

It may be quicker to cut a tree down than for an excavator to work around it, but this should never be the sole reason for removal. Mature trees are the major structural element of riverbank woodland and cannot be readily replaced. They should, therefore, be retained wherever possible.

The extent to which dredging machines can work around bankside trees varies according to bank profile and height, the type of machine, size of trees and the operator's skill. In practice, most machines can work around bankside trees 10 m apart but this may limit their effectiveness and increase time taken to complete dredging work. Newly planted trees should be spaced far enough apart to allow for future machine access.

There are several 'best practice' principles to follow when working around established trees. The base and area under the canopy of trees should remain as undisturbed as possible. Tree bark is not waterproof; banking soil around it will often cause decay leading to the death of the tree. Similarly, roots need to breathe; compaction or raising the land level can suffocate roots. Increasing soil height also impedes water reaching the roots. Oaks are particularly susceptible to changes in soil aeration and drainage patterns.

Protecting individual trees from damage can be achieved through conditions being applied to consents. For example, during flood protection works at Sturminster Marshall, Dorset, consent conditions specified that all riverside trees be protected by chestnut paling fence, located 1 m beyond the line of the canopy or at a radius of 5 m from the trunk, whichever was the greater. Within that area, all excavations had to be undertaken by hand to protect the tree roots.

It is feasible to retain trees within embanked channels and when constructing new floodbanks. Constructing a sinuous floodbank or wall to avoid trees is also possible. Trees will not present a flood hazard provided the design and maintenance take account of the increased

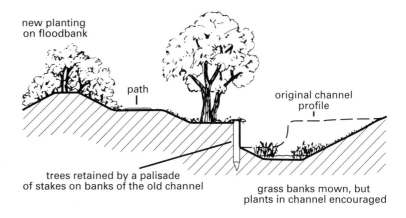

view from channel

Figure 4
Retention of trees using a palisade of stakes at Spittle Brook, Warrington.
Source: Lewis and Williams (1984)

roughness within the flooding area. On the Spittle Brook at Warrington, widening and embanking works resulted in the removal of all the original plant cover on the riverbank except for two clumps of trees, which were conserved by constructing a palisade of stakes on the riverside to support the soil around the roots and prevent the trees slipping into the river (Figure 4). The retained trees gave maturity to the landscape and acted as a refuge and food source for invertebrates and birds.

Another method of protecting individual trees has been tried on the R Avon in Warwickshire. Here the trunk of a mature ash stands in an 'alcove' with the sides protected by stone revetment (Figure 5).

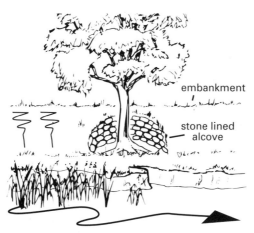

Figure 5
Use of stone revetment for retaining an ash tree on the R Avon, Warwickshire. Source: Lewis and Williams (1984)

A different approach was taken on the Bentley barrier bank in Yorkshire. Here, the floodbank was raised and rebuilt alongside the old one so that it was possible to retain mature hawthorn trees on the top and one side of the old bank.

Marking trees to be managed

There may be considerable value in marking individual trees where coppicing, pollarding or limb removal is being undertaken. Indeed, this is essential practice when a workforce is unfamiliar with the location or working method. It is even more important when there are specific trees which must not be disturbed, such as those where there are otter holts or bat roosts. Standard codes such as 'C' for coppice, 'P' for pollard and 'SR' for selective removal of limbs are desirable.

Individual branch removal

Lopping branches that obstruct machinery, or are a potential flood hazard because they are collecting trash, is a routine, but skilled job. As for scrub management, only those branches which are causing a flood hazard should be removed and, ideally, some overhanging branches should be left.

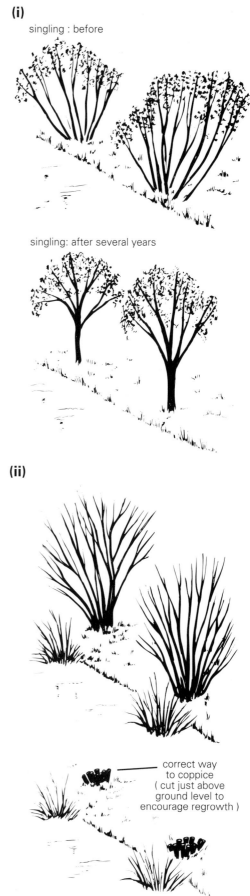

Figure 6
(i) Partial coppicing or singling : the selection of single coppice stems to form trees.
(ii) Rotational coppicing.
Source: Newbold *et al.* (1989)

Dead trees can be lopped and topped and allowed to remain standing as valuable habitat for wildlife that depends on dead wood.

If machinery has to work close to trees, vulnerable branches are better trimmed or removed before work starts. This is preferable to risking more extensive damage during the work.

The use of sealing compounds on cut surfaces is now regarded as inadvisable. A healthy tree is capable of quickly producing a healing callus over cut surfaces. Cavities in old trees should never be filled.

Coppicing

Coppicing is a traditional method of managing trees so that the stump (known as the stool) and roots remain alive and provide a basis for the periodic harvesting of the stems that grow from the stool. The principle of coppicing is based on the natural ability of some trees to send up multiple stems after cutting. In the past, many riverside trees would have been coppiced to provide timber for firewood, poles, hurdles and basket making.

If coppice is not regularly harvested, it continues to grow, creating a multi-stemmed tree. The wildlife associated with coppiced trees depends on maintaining a diversity of areas of light and shade, so some trees should be cut regularly. This is especially true where riverside coppice is a remnant of ancient woodland, and will benefit plants such as the bluebell, wood anemone and primrose, small mammals and butterflies such as the pearl-bordered and small pearl-bordered fritillaries.

There are two principal coppicing regimes for riverbanks. In each case, stems are cut just above ground level to encourage regrowth.

- *Partial coppicing or singling.* The recognised practice is to promote coppice by retaining one stem and cutting the rest (Figure 6i). The retained stem is usually vertical and of good form. However, removing only the

Figure 7 Spiling and coppice willow stumps protecting a cliff on the R Lugg. Source: Lewis and Williams (1984)

problem stems of a coppice stool may shift its centre of gravity and thus render the tree unstable. Careful judgement is therefore required before partial coppicing.

On extensive sections of the R Okement in Devon, alders were partially coppiced for the first time for many years. Regrowth was rapid. Continuity of mature tree cover was retained and the mass of young shoots now deflect high river flows away from the mature trunks and help to protect the bank. Full coppicing of blocks of alders would have been an alternative, but in this case would have failed to provide the desirable structural variety and a rich mixture of shade and light.

- *Rotational coppicing.* Traditionally, blocks of woodland were cut on a rotation over a number of years. This technique can be adapted to produce a good structural range of growth in riverbank trees. Utilising this technique all the stems of a stool are cut in rotation, leaving no 'leaders' (Figure 6(ii)). It is a method used on the wide sections of the R Severn where alder, willow and ash are cut on a 10–15 year cycle and the bushy regrowth maintains a dense, vigorous bank-protecting cover. Willows and alder may be planted to provide bank protection (Figure 7).

In this example, a combination of spiling, the use of willow logs (and adequate fencing) gives good bank

**Plate 4
'Laying' of trees
on the Cwm y
witham (Upper
Severn
catchment)**

Stuart McFadzean

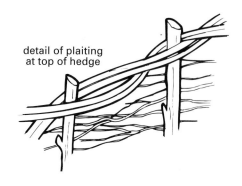

detail of plaiting
at top of hedge

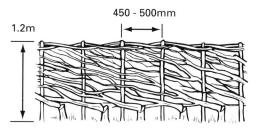

1.2m

450 - 500mm

**Figure 8
The laying of channel-side hedges in the
traditional fashion.
Source: Newbold *et al.* (1989)**

protection and good bank habitat for
wildlife. A short coppice cycle of up to
six years stops development of mature
trees, encourages vigorous root growth
and provides the light and shade
required by specialist flora and fauna.
Heavy browsing of a newly coppiced
stool will kill it, so retaining a barrier of
bramble or providing fencing will help
to encourage growth.

**Plate 5
Traditional
pollarding**

The traditional technique of 'laying' trees
and shrubs, normally associated with
hedges, is a form of coppicing (Plate 4 and
Figure 8). Few hedges run parallel to rivers

but lines of scrub along banks can be
converted to a hedge by laying. On the R
Rhiw, in Wales, a small, gravelly upland
river, a landowner coppiced riverside alder
and willow. After about seven years the
regrowth was laid facing downstream.
Erosion was arrested on this bank, in
contrast to the grazed unprotected banks,
which continued to erode. A laid hedge
requires regular trimming if this technique
is to be successful. Wildlife benefits lie
largely in the creation of a scrubby
hedgeline, despite the initial treatment of
trees, which is quite severe. If long lengths
are to be laid, some 'standard' upright trees
should be retained. This technique is
applicable on rivers of similar character
where fencing is difficult or costly to install
and maintain.

Pollarding

Pollards are trees which have been
traditionally cut about 2 m above the
ground (Plate 5). Pollarded trees, like
coppice,. produced rods, poles, firewood
and fence posts.

Most broadleaved trees can be pollarded,
but willows, oak, ash and beech are the

Alistair Driver

most common examples. Regular pollarding prolongs the life of trees and the bole (trunk) may become hollow and weaken with age (Plate 6). Regular pollarding prevents crowns becoming overgrown and vulnerable to splitting.

Pollards can be exceptionally rich wildlife habitats. Leaf litter accumulates under mature crowns, forming soil into which bramble, honeysuckle and rose may grow and provide ideal breeding and resting places for a wide variety of animals, such as owls, bats and ducks. Many insects feed within the canopy foliage and are themselves fed upon by birds. Very old tree trunks are often covered in lichens, and can be particularly important habitat for a number of rare invertebrates.

The frequency of pollarding depends on the type of tree and the potential use to which the timber is put. A 5–10-year cycle may be appropriate for firewood, whereas a 10–20-year cycle may be required to produce timber for fence posts. If the development of the rich crown community is of paramount importance, 20–30 years may be required. It is good practice to stagger the timing when pollarding large numbers of trees because simultaneous cutting would create a significant loss of habitat and adversely affect the landscape.

The whole crown should be pollarded at the same time and not just problem limbs. Partial pollarding can cause the tree to become unbalanced and split, thus exacerbating potential flooding problems or leading to the loss of the entire tree. Pollarded trees, unlike multi-stemmed coppices, rarely collect trash during floods. However, the bank can scour out behind the bole if the pollard is growing on a relatively soft bank.

Poles and whips from the cut limbs can be used to propagate trees elsewhere on the bank (Figure 9).

Pollards do not require protection against livestock grazing provided the crown is high enough. For sheep or cattle the crown needs to be at least 2 m from the ground, or 3–4 m for horses (Plate 7).

**Plate 6
Old pollard. Less than 100% pollard may severely weaken such a tree further**

Stuart McFadzean

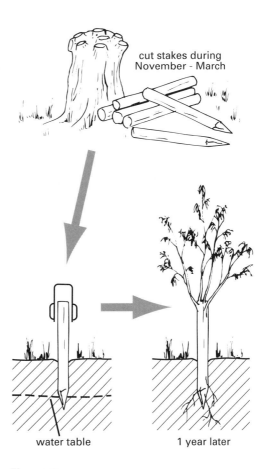

cut stakes during November - March

water table

1 year later

**Figure 9
Willow poles used for tree propagation. Adapted from Newbold et al. (1989)**

Stuart McFadzean

**Plate 7
Pollards do not
require
protection
against stock
when crown is
high enough**

is therefore largely confined to the river corridor. After years of neglect, many previously pollarded riverside willows have developed a crown growth of epiphytic scrub including blackthorn, hawthorn, buckthorn, dog rose, bramble, guelder-rose and elder. Along many sections of riverbank this is the best dense scrub habitat available, because riparian fields have been ploughed right up to the top of the bank.

Pollards may be successfully started by 'beheading' trees at the correct height when the trunk is up to 0.3 m in diameter. However, poplars up to 1 m in diameter have been successfully converted to pollards on the R Stour at Longham (Dorset).

The R Ock in Oxfordshire runs through a landscape dominated by large, open arable fields separated by poor-quality, over-managed hedgerows. Good wildlife cover

Thinning and cleaning

Thinning and cleaning of riverside trees is rarely either practical or desirable. There are rarely sound engineering reasons for not retaining single-stemmed trees (Plates 8(i) and (ii)) but brashing their lower branches to restore flood conveyance standards is acceptable. Climbers like ivy and honeysuckle should be retained as there is no evidence that they kill healthy trees. Ivy, in particular, provides vitally important evergreen cover, early nectar and late berries for insects and birds.

Dead and dying trees, whether standing or fallen, provide habitat for fungi,

Nigel Holmes

Nigel Holmes

**Plates 8(i) and (ii)
Tree retention on Ellington Brook where its impact on conveyance is negligible
(a) (left) during low flows (b) during flood**

invertebrates, bats and birds. Unless they are obviously in danger of falling into the river and creating a flood risk, or there are safety reasons for removing a tree, such as nearby footpath, dead trees should be left standing. Thinning is best restricted to sites where a more diverse structure and range of species is desirable or where alien species have invaded and are threatening the integrity of a native stand.

3.7.5 Planting trees and shrubs

Reinstatement of tree and scrub cover is such a long process that replanting should always be considered an inferior option to conserving existing woody vegetation. Planting may take place for the same reasons as retaining existing trees: for wildlife, landscape, timber, and provision of shelter, cover, bank protection and shade. Where the long-term aim is to provide a woodland wildlife habitat, tree planting should strive to achieve structural diversity. Because woodland is not just a collection of trees, creating woodland requires a different strategy from tree planting. Although it may take 50 years for a tree to mature, woodland habitat will not develop in the same timescale. Barrell (1993) provides a useful method of assessing the life expectancy of existing trees, which can be used to help to choose new trees when planting.

Choosing suitable planting areas

The choice of site for planting is important, as planting in some areas will reduce existing wildlife or landscape value. For example, wetland, grassland, reedbed and tall herb communities are irreparably damaged by tree planting. Large numbers of trees may also be inappropriate in the open landscapes of areas such as Romney Marsh, the Somerset Levels and the Fens, although pollarded willows were formerly typical of these areas. These characteristic landscapes attract breeding waders and large flocks of wintering birds, which are discouraged from using areas enclosed by trees.

Tree planting should only be carried out when establishment of other vegetation, such as tall herbs, has been rejected as less valuable. To achieve maximum benefit planting should be considered on a

catchment basis. Ideally, planting should be linked to existing features to increase their value for wildlife along the river corridor. Suitable sites may include the junction of hedges with streams or ditches, or where there are existing otter holts, areas of scrub or small copses (Figure 10). Tight meanders are often a favoured area for planting and when wet, these create wet woodland.

Where rivers are treeless, wildlife will benefit most from planting on, rather than away from the bank. The wildlife interest of the river will be increased by the input of leaves and other organic matter and a greater variety of physical structure and micro-climates will be created (Mason *et al.*, 1984). Suitable trees, eg ash and oak, may

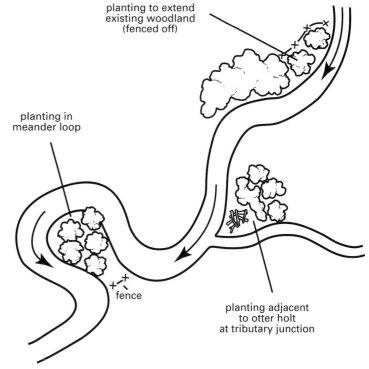

**Figure 10
Suitable planting sites.**

shade in larger channels

where trees shade the
watercourse, leave gaps
of variable width

where trees only give partial shade,
a continuous line is acceptable

shade in smaller channels

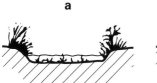
a
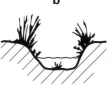
b

c

the effect of shade on aquatic plants as the channel
width reduces.
In **'c'** the channel is completely shaded
even if orientated in a north - south direction

Figure 11
Manipulation of shade: the use of shaded and unshaded sections of bank, to depress or eliminate aquatic plant growth in the shaded sections and encourage plant growth in the unshaded section. Source: Newbold *et al.* (1989)

Table 2: Typical native species

Ash
Aspen
Beech
Birch, silver
Birch, hairy
Blackthorn (s)
Buckthorn (s)
Alder Buckthorn(s)
Cherry, wild
Dogwood (s)
Elder (s)
Guelder-Rose (s)
Hawthorn (s)
Hazel (s)
Holly (s)
Hornbeam
Lime, small-leaved
Maple, field
Oak, pedunculate
Poplar, white
Poplar, black
Privet, wild (s)
Rose, dog (s)
Rowan
Wayfaring-tree
Willow, crack
Willow, grey (s)
Willow, white
Willow, goat (s)
Willow, osier (s)
(s) = shrub/small tree

provide otter holts in the future if planted close to the water's edge.

Shade depresses plant growth, and this in turn affects assemblages of invertebrates and plants. Consequently, selection of the location and density of planting is important (Figure 11). Low scrub will densely shade a small ditch, but will have little effect on a wide river. As more sunlight reaches a north–south orientated ditch than one lying east–west, orientation of the stream will determine the precise nature of planting schemes. If planned correctly, habitat enhancement from tree planting may also, through shading, reduce the need for weed management (see Chapter 3.5). Details of the effect of shade on plants in lowland streams are summarised by Dawson and Kern-Hansen (1979).

Preparation for planting and selecting species

- Tree planting adjacent to 'main' river or sea defences requires land drainage

Table 3: Native species to be encouraged throughout England, Scotland and Wales; local stock is always recommended. Source: Soutar & Peterken (1989)

LARGE AND MEDIUM-SIZED TREES	SMALL TREES AND SHRUBS
Alder	Blackthorn
Ash	Broom
Aspen	Gorse
Birch, silver	Guelder-rose
Elm, wych	Hawthorn, common
Rowan	
Willow, eared	Hazel
Willow, goat	Holly
Willow, grey	Rose, dog
Willow, osier	

consent from the NRA in England and Wales.

- Planting should be of native species suited to the area, soils and conditions.

Table 4: Native species to be encouraged within Soutar and Peterken's 10 planting zones

LARGE AND MEDIUM-SIZED TREES	ZONES									
	1	2	3	4	5	6	7	8	9	10
Apple, crab			S	S	S	S	S	S	S	S
Beech						S	S	S		
Cherry, bird	S	S	S	S		C				
Cherry, gean		S	S	S	S	S	S	S	S	S
Hawthorn, midland					C	C	C	C		
Hornbeam						S	S			
Lime, small-leaved				C	C	C	C	C	C	
Lime, large-leaved				C	C		C			
Maple, field				C	S	S	S	S	S	S
Oak, common	S	S	S	S	S	S	S	S	S	S
Oak, sessile	S	S	S	C	C	C	C	C	C	S
Pine, Scots	C									
Poplar, black					C	C	C	C	C	
Poplar, grey					S	S	S	S	S	
Service-tree					C	C	C	C	C	C
Whitebeam		C		C			C	C		
Willow, crack			S	S	S	S	S	S	S	S
Willow, white			S	S	S	S	S	S	S	S
Yew				C			C	C		

SMALL TREES AND SHRUBS	1	2	3	4	5	6	7	8	9	10
Box							C	C		
Buckthorn, alder				S	S	S	S	S	S	S
Buckthorn				S	S	S	S	S		
Butchers-broom						S	S	S	S	S
Dogwood				C	S	S	S	S	S	S
Elder		S	S	S	S	S	S	S	S	S
Juniper	C	C	C	C			C	C		
Privet				S	S	S	S	S	S	S
Rose, field				S	S	S	S	S	S	S
Spindle				S	S	S	S	S	S	S
Spurge-laurel				S	S	S	S	S	S	
Wayfaring-tree					S		S	S	S	
Willow, almond				S	S	S	S	S		
Willow, bay			S	S						
Willow, purple			S	S	S	S	S	S	S	S

Note: S = suitable species; C = suitable species, but take the greatest care to use local stock.
Source: Soutar and Peterken (1989)

The native species already present in an area usually define the character of a particular landscape, and invariably are suitable in planting schemes. However, there may be opportunities in degraded areas to re-create past landscapes with appropriate species that have been lost (Tables 2–4 and Figure 12).

New planting schemes should be flexible enough to allow for planting around existing clumps of bramble, scrub and trees, and also leave open areas to create glades. In some areas removal of existing trees can be acceptable, for example an ageing plantation of hybrid poplars was felled along the R Thames in West Oxfordshire in 1988 to enable the planting of substantial numbers of native trees and shrubs. The poplars had little conservation value and their removal facilitated the establishment of native trees. Natural regeneration of wild flowers such as cowslip, dog violet and self-heal occurred in response to increased light.

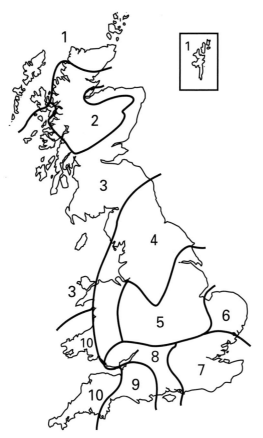

Figure 12
The 10 planting zones in Great Britain.
Source: Soutar and Peterken (1989)

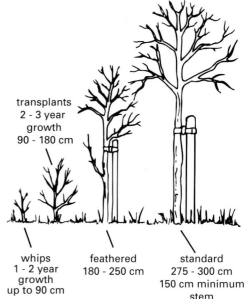

Figure 13
Typical tree sizes (recommended sizes are covered in Part I of BS 3936).
Source: Soutar and Peterken (1989)

Planting schemes should be kept simple with a mixture of trees and shrubs to give maximum structural diversity; two or three tree species and four or five shrub species is an ideal mix. Edging with short shrub species also helps to create shelter at ground level. Grouping single species prevents fast-growing species from dominating others. Approximately five shrubs to every tree is recommended in dense plantings. In each case a carefully prepared planting plan should be drawn up.

In urban situations, integrating wildlife and visual amenity may result in native shrubs and trees being interplanted with exotic species. On the Spittle Brook in Warrington, native hawthorn, dogwood and gorse were mixed with non-native cotoneaster, berberis and rambling rose. These provide berries for songbirds and act as effective barriers for sensitive areas. Evergreens such as native holly, box, wild privet or broom and non-natives such as pyracantha provide good winter cover and some food for birds and mammals.

Planting stock shouldd be healthy, disease-free and vigorous. Stock should be obtained from a reputable nursery and conform to the relevant British Standard (3936). Root-balled plants should have the roots supported in a hessian bag. 'Transplants' have had a minimum of one year in a seed bed and two years in nursery lines, and may be 0.3–2.5 m tall. 'Whips' are 0.9–2.5 m tall. Standards generally exceed 2.5 m (Figure 13).

Small trees are easier to transplant than larger ones, as they better withstand transplant shock and drought. Using whips and transplants is also much cheaper, as survival rates are good;
small trees grow faster, and are less often vandalised than larger, staked trees.

The use of live willow stakes to create pollards has been referred to in Section 3.7.2; faggoting and spiling for bank protection relies on an abundant supply of live willows, and occasionally alder; see Section 3.7.6.

Practicalities
Planting, like tree management, should be carried out when the ground is free from frost and waterlogging during the period

from October to the end of March. The only exception to this is container-grown stock but they also do best when planted in the same period.

Protecting trees from damage by frost and drying out before planting is vital. Drying out is a principal cause of failure or poor performance and can occur very rapidly in wind or still cold air. Therefore stock should not be left outside overnight before planting with their roots exposed.

Adequate site preparation is very important and the ground should be cleared of vegetation using where appropriate a herbicide approved by ADAS and pollution control staff. Turf removal is an alternative. Increased chances of success for planting on poor soils will be achieved by incorporating some moist, non peat-based, compost. In areas where moisture content is likely to be low water retention can be improved by using a root dip.

Fencing is often a vital part of any successful planting scheme. All timber used should be tanalised softwood. Posts should be at least 80 mm in diameter, spaced 3 m apart, and strained at 50-m intervals or at changes of direction. When stock are not present, a nominal fence is still worthwhile to prevent accidental damage. Where cattle graze, the fence should have three strands of barbed wire. This should be augmented with wire netting if sheep are present. A half round top rail and plain wire should be substituted where horses are pastured.

In wadeable rivers livestock damage can be prevented by fencing off the planted area. On Deddington Brook in North Oxfordshire, tree planting in a fenced-off meander loop suffered severe grazing damage from sheep, which by-passed the fence by entering the stream during low flows.

Another example of the need to provide adequate fencing is illustrated by a case on the R Mole in Surrey. Expensive standard trees died within a year of planting because a gap was left between the fence and the river and the trees were eaten. On the R Teme in Herefordshire, sheep damaged trees that were not protected by wire netting whereas trees fenced by netting thrived.

Planting methods and spacing

Trees and shrubs in plots should be spaced no farther than 1.5 m apart. A typical specification for a hedge is two staggered rows, 0.25 m apart with plants 0.5 m apart. This helps to suppress weed growth and create early shrubby cover. Plants up to 0.9 m high can be planted in a V notch dug into the ground but taller trees should be planted in a pit large enough to accommodate the full spread of the roots.

Protection of trees and shrubs from rabbit or deer browsing is also important. Guards should be of a type and height sufficient to protect the growing point but allowing free growth. Shrubs with a bushy growth are better protected within mesh netting, supported by two canes, or a special shrub shelter. Tree shelters, 0.75 m high, supported by an adequate stake, are good protection against rabbits, but should be 1.2–1.5 m tall where deer graze. Spiral rabbit guards, cut to an appropriate size, represent another option.

Although stakes are not necessary for plants less than 1.5 m high, marker canes may help in locating smaller whips for maintenance purposes and to help support spiral guards. Standard trees will need a short stake, buckle tie and buffer on the windward side of the trunk.

Adequate maintenance in the first two, or preferably three years (five for standard trees) is essential. The vegetation around the base of each shrub or tree to a radius of 0.5 m must be impeded to give the growing shoot a chance and prevent smothering by tall weeds. This can be effectively achieved using an approved herbicide. Cutting can stimulate grass growth and increase competition for water so mulching with wood chip to a minimum depth 50 mm helps both to suppress weed growth and to retain moisture.

Finally it is worth remembering that the lowest price may not be the cheapest in the long term. Poor-quality stock, lack of care in planting, poor standards of fencing and inadequate maintenance are often major reasons for the failure of tree planting schemes.

3.7.6 Bank revetment using willows, alders and other trees

Live trees and shrubs, as well as dead trunks and brushwood, have been very successfully used to protect banks from erosion. The benefits of using woody material compared with 'hard' defences such as rock and man-made materials is that the woody material creates 'natural' habitats for riverbank plant species to establish themselves. Trees and shrubs can also be effectively used in conjunction with hard defence materials, particularly where additional protection is needed or where high standards of protection are needed before the trees and shrubs have fully established (Section 3.4.4).

The most typical forms of bank protection using woody material are: faggoting (brushwood or brashings tied in bundles); and spiling (weaving of typically willow withies around willow stakes). Other techniques include using logs and brush. Chapter 5 in Hemphill and Bramley (1989) provides an excellent summary of natural bank protection using many of the techniques briefly described below.

**Plate 9
Use of willow
tree trunk to halt
erosion**

Logs and brush

Very large tree trunks can be used to halt erosion by laying them along the riverbank, half submerged (Plate 9). If they are willows, sprouting will occur along the trunk and additional protection and habitat is thus provided in the future by the root system and shoots, eg R Ouse at Hemingford, Huntingdon.

Trunks and large branches can also be used to fill scour holes between other trees to

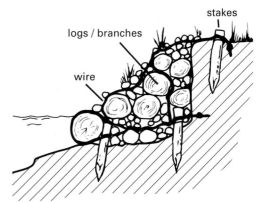

**Figure 14
Bank protection on the Afon Clwyd
using logs and branches.
Source: Lewis and Williams (1984)**

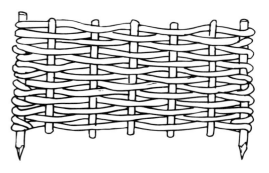

**Figure 15
A woven hazel hurdle.
Source: Lewis and Williams (1984)**

Nigel Holmes

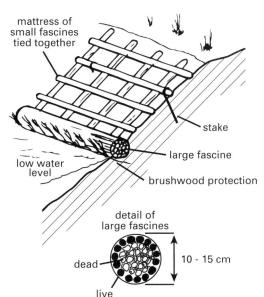

Figure 16 Fascine (faggot) mattresses used to protect the lower bank from erosion due to high velocity flow or boat wash.
Source: Hemphill and Bramley (1989)

construction

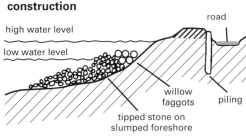

established

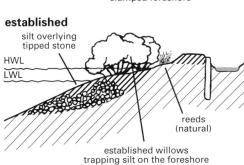

Plates 10 (i) and (ii)
Use of faggots for bank/bed stabilisation in tidal waters
(i) (above) R Ouse at Cleere Hall, Yorkshire
(ii) (left) Poole harbour

Figure 17 Willow faggoting on the tidal Ouse at Barlow Grange, downstream of Selby. Source: Lewis and Williams (1984)

provide immediate protection and good submerged habitat. As with smaller logs used as bank protection, they need to be firmly wired in place, attached to stakes driven deeply into the edge of the river and bank (Figure 14). These areas provide habitat for water voles and otters as well as channel edge refuges for fish fry.

Alder logs and brashings wired into a scour hole on the R Bride, Dorset, during

maintenance work in 1981 are still in place in 1993. They have not only successfully maintained channel stability but also provided excellent habitat.

Hurdles

Woven 'hurdles' (Figure 15) are a traditional means of providing initial protection until living plant cover has re-established. Usually made of hazel, hurdles will not grow, but will protect a regraded bank from wash and scour while a natural riverbank plant community grows up through the basket weave. Over a period of 10 years or so, the wood will rot, but by

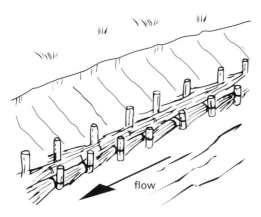

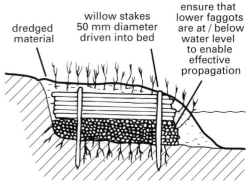

osier faggots (fascines), 2 m long,
30 cm diameter
(placed in 2 layers at right angles to each other)

Figure 19
Faggots used to fill in an eroded area in an existing bank or reinforce a new bank.
Source: Hemphill and Bramley (1989)

Figure 18
(i) R Ure: faggot staked parallel to the bank, butt end pointing upstream.
(ii) R Ure: In the case of deep erosion, additional faggots may be laid at right angles to the bank.
Source: Lewis and Williams (1984)

this time the plants should have developed well enough to ensure the bank remains stable.

Faggoting

The purpose of faggoting is to trap silt and sediment as the flow of water is retarded by the loose twigs and branches. The bank becomes consolidated through accretion and any subsequent scour is prevented by the woody branches buried in silt. Faggots can also be bound together to produce fascine mattresses and then sunk with stones on to the channel bed to prevent scour (Figure 16). They are usually used to stabilise eroding tidal rivers (Plates 10i and 10ii). On the embanked tidal R Ouse below Selby at Barlow Grange, willow faggots were used in 1981 to protect the base of the floodbank (Figure 17). Inspection in 1993

revealed well-established cover of willow at the site and that the technique continues to be successful in preventing erosion.

Faggots can be made of any brashings that are available. However brashings of fresh willow are likely to take root and grow, especially if cut in winter. A considered choice has to be made between using willow or non-willow faggots for different situations. In small watercourses (<5 m wide) growth of willow from even a single bank may cause an unacceptable flood hazard, and alternative materials should be used. In larger channels, growing willows may be beneficial – their roots helping to stabilise bank material and their shoots providing a first line of defence against bank scour. For example faggoting was used in 1981 on the R Ure at Middleham in Yorkshire in the 20 m wide braided channel to prevent undercutting and slumping (Figure 18). Figure 19 shows a cross-sectional profile of faggots used for bank repair and reinforcement.

Spiling

A variation on the use of willow for faggots for bank protection is the craft of 'spiling' or weaving willow withies around fresh winter-cut willow stakes (Plate 11 and Figure 20). The technique requires more skill than faggot work, but has the advantage that it uses less material. It is appropriate for the protection of steep or vertical banks.

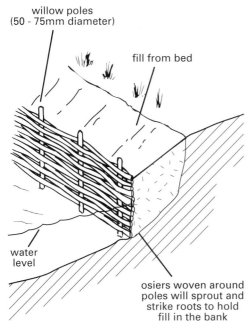

willow poles
(50 - 75mm diameter)

fill from bed

water
level

osiers woven around
poles will sprout and
strike roots to hold
fill in the bank

Figure 20
Protection by spiling.
Source: Hemphill and Bramley (1989)

Plate 11 (left)
Spiling on R Ogmore at Bridgend

Plate 12 (below)
Spiling on R Medway

Stuart McFadzean

Ideally, the willow stakes will take root and sprout to provide living, permanent protection. Fencing of the bank top to prevent grazing of the new growth by stock will encourage successful establishment because without it, the stakes will die and eventually rot.

Spiling was used in 1981 to protect eroding outer meander bends on the Meece Brook at Norton Bridge, Staffordshire. Sharpened willow stakes were driven into the riverbed at the bank toe, and withies wound around them. The area behind was then back-filled and the upper bank graded. Examination of the site in 1993 revealed established bankside willows which had developed from the spiling since there was no evidence of artificial planting.

Plate 12 shows one of six sites identified by the Medway river project as requiring bank protection. Spiling using willow stakes and sweet chestnut faggots was successfully undertaken.

Stuart McFadzean

Key References

Emery, M (1986) *Promoting nature in cities and towns. A practical guide.* Croom Helm.

Newbold, C, Honnor, J and Buckley, K (1989) *Nature Conservation and the management of drainage channels.* NCC/ADA.

Smart, N and Andrews, J (1985) *Birds and broadleaves handbook.* RSPB.

Part 4
CASE STUDIES

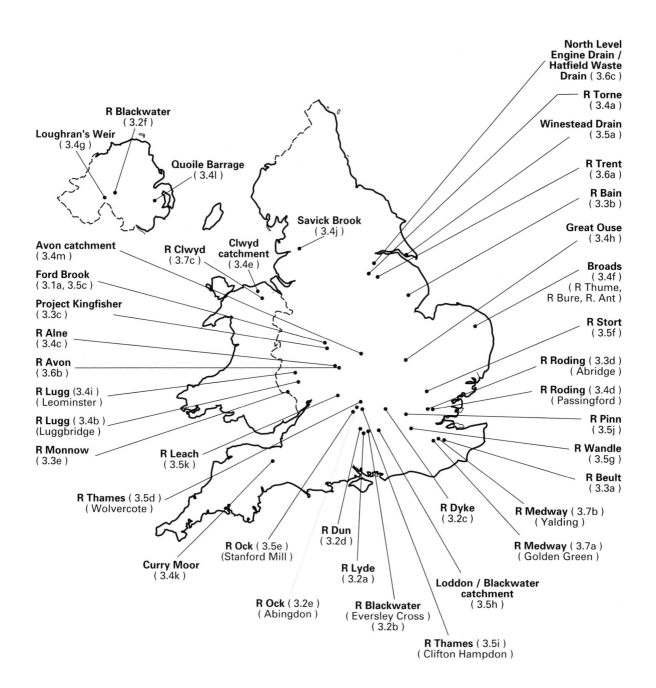

North Level Engine Drain / Hatfield Waste Drain (3.6c)

R Torne (3.4a)

Winestead Drain (3.5a)

R Trent (3.6a)

R Bain (3.3b)

Great Ouse (3.4h)

Broads (3.4f) (R Thume, R Bure, R. Ant)

R Stort (3.5f)

R Roding (3.3d) (Abridge)

R Roding (3.4d) (Passingford)

R Pinn (3.5j)

R Wandle (3.5g)

R Beult (3.3a)

R Medway (3.7b) (Yalding)

R Medway (3.7a) (Golden Green)

R Blackwater (3.2f)

Loughran's Weir (3.4g)

Quoile Barrage (3.4l)

Savick Brook (3.4j)

Avon catchment (3.4m)

R Clwyd (3.7c)

Clwyd catchment (3.4e)

Ford Brook (3.1a, 3.5c)

Project Kingfisher (3.3c)

R Alne (3.4c)

R Avon (3.6b)

R Lugg (3.4i) (Leominster)

R Lugg (3.4b) (Luggbridge)

R Monnow (3.3e)

R Leach (3.5k)

R Thames (3.5d) (Wolvercote)

Curry Moor (3.4k)

R Ock (3.5e) (Stanford Mill)

R Dun (3.2d)

R Lyde (3.2a)

R Ock (3.2e) (Abingdon)

R Blackwater (Eversley Cross) (3.2b)

R Dyke (3.2c)

Loddon / Blackwater catchment (3.5h)

R Thames (3.5i) (Clifton Hampdon)

Location map for case studies

Introduction

This part of the handbook contains a series of case studies which illustrate the environmentally sensitive use of the river management techniques presented in Part 3. To merit inclusion all schemes have been in place for approximately five years. The case studies follow a standard format:

- *General information*
  Provides location, date of work/scheme and techniques utilised with cross-referencing to Part 3 of the handbook

- *Objective*
  Provides details of engineering/ conservation objectives

- *Background*
  Explains situation that led to the work/scheme being proposed.

- *Scheme approach*
  Provides details of design and implementation of the scheme

- *Scheme appraisal*
  Provides evaluation/appraisal of scheme success in environmental and engineering terms, based upon best available information. The section is not intended to provide definitive post-project appraisal.

The map opposite shows the location of the case studies. The case study numbering enables easy cross-referencing with the techniques sections.

Ford Brook

Walsall Borough Council

Location:	Walsall to Rushall in R Tame catchment north of Birmingham OS 1:50,000 No 139, Grid Ref SK 0200
River type:	Urban and semi-rural river with pebble/gravel bed and local silt and clay
Size:	3–5 m bed width with design capacity of *c* 22 m³s⁻¹
Length affected:	2 km
Date:	1985/86

Techniques/Features:
River diversion (3.4.3)
Creation of wetland edge habitat (3.3.2)
Habitat creation on concrete sill of deepened channel (3.2.3)
Bridging flows to feed original channel and protect wetland

Objective:
Achieve design standard for urban flood alleviation scheme, while protecting a wetland potentially at risk and creating extensive habitat improvements to the river.

Background

In 1971 Walsall Borough Council (WBC) began the task of attempting to alleviate the extensive flooding problems in their area. Work on Ford Brook had three phases. Phases 1 and 2 involved improvements to open channels and culverts as well as new culverting. Phase 3 primarily involved improvements to open channel and alleviating constrictions at river crossings and near properties. Original plans proposed a gabion-lined trapezoidal, deepened and widened channel through meadowland bordered by a wetland. Grant-aid was deferred by MAFF subject to a re-design which would satisfy the Urban Wildlife Group (UWG) and the then Nature Conservancy Council (NCC). A re-designed scheme integrated flood defence requirements with both habitat protection and channel enhancement.

Scheme approach

Many new features were created as well as retaining the majority of the original channel even though the scheme had to provide efficient discharge of flood water from upstream with a bed level around 2 m below that of the pre-scheme condition. The original channel retained its bed and water levels, being fed by the Rough Brook, a tributary not requiring improved conveyance. The scheme included the following components:

- Concrete-lined channel, bed level lowered by >2 m at Station Road with a pre-cast sill on the inside of the bend incorporating a trough planted with wetland vegetation.

- A long by-pass channel for Ford Brook across the floodplain (bed level of c 2 m below the existing Ford Brook) which incorporated a narrow low-flow channel and shelves, creating extensive new wetlands within the floodplain). Channel confinement and prevention of erosion was effected by use of vertical elm boarding (400 x 50 mm retained by 75 mm stakes backed by puddled clay).

- The majority of the old channel retained in its entirety and unmodified, now being fed by water from Rough Brook which was bridged over the new channel of the Ford Brook; the retained level of water ensured the wetland habitat was unaffected by the scheme.

- Extensive planting of wetland shelves by the UWG (see Case Study 3.5 for details).

Scheme appraisal

Work was completed in 1985 and over a period of eight years hydraulic performance has been equal to other sections with no additional maintenance costs. The scheme was heralded by WBC as being a great success not least because it proves that major civil engineering works and environmental safeguards are not incompatible (Heath, 1989). The establishment of vegetation has been very successful but more importantly the habitats created have enabled extensive natural recolonisation to occur. Kingfishers, herons and water voles are regularly seen in the area.

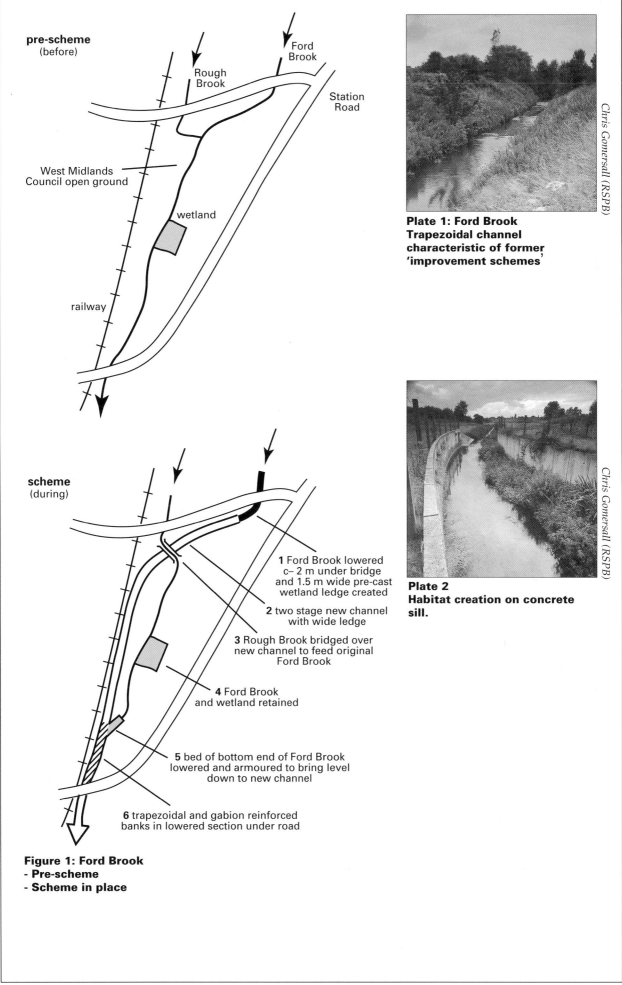

pre-scheme
(before)

Ford
Brook

Rough
Brook

Station
Road

West Midlands
Council open ground

wetland

railway

**Plate 1: Ford Brook
Trapezoidal channel
characteristic of former
'improvement schemes'**

Chris Gomersall (RSPB)

scheme
(during)

1 Ford Brook lowered
c– 2 m under bridge
and 1.5 m wide pre-cast
wetland ledge created

2 two stage new channel
with wide ledge

3 Rough Brook bridged over
new channel to feed original
Ford Brook

4 Ford Brook
and wetland retained

5 bed of bottom end of Ford Brook
lowered and armoured to bring level
down to new channel

6 trapezoidal and gabion reinforced
banks in lowered section under road

**Figure 1: Ford Brook
- Pre-scheme
- Scheme in place**

**Plate 2
Habitat creation on concrete
sill.**

Chris Gomersall (RSPB)

R Lyde

Thames Water/NRA Thames Region

Location:	Hartley Wespall, Basingstoke, Hants OS 1:50,000 No 175 Grid Ref SU 696 554
River type:	Chalk stream (silted), calcareous nodules
Size:	2–5 m wide up to 750 mm deep Flow range 0.1 to 10 m^{3}s^{-1}
Length affected:	850 m over three weeks
Date:	July 1987

Techniques/Features:
Partial dredging (3.2.2)
Installing stone to create pools and riffles (3.2.6)
Replacing bed material to create islands and shoals (3.2.5)

Objective:
Improve conveyance to reduce upstream water level by 200 mm; improve the stream as a fishery; improve habitat diversity of channels and margins.

Background

Due to low flows and past insensitive management the natural chalk-stream character has changed to a heavily silted, shallow, uniform channel with bur-reed dominating the margins. Dredging to reduce water levels upstream enabled fishery and conservation staff to input into the design to enhance the limited wildlife interest.

Scheme approach

- Retain important natural features such as long, flat riffles, deep pools, etc.

- Creation of deeper pools on meanders, and islands to increase velocity and induce cleansing of gravels.

- Open up densely overgrown sections by some brush cutting and pollarding of willow.

- Installation of in-stream devices such as gravel deflectors, large boulders and groups of stone to increase habitat potential.

- Dredging removed bed material in asymmetric manner; where gravel riffles had to be lowered they were replaced at a lower level.

Scheme appraisal (1993)

- All flood defence objectives were achieved with lowering of water levels, future maintenance of bur-reed not required.

- The islands, gravel riffles and boulders are still in place enabling faster flowing water with improved clarity.

- Biological investigation in 1986 and 1990 showed marked improvements in invertebrates.

- Bur-reed has been significantly reduced and typical chalk-stream species such as crowfoot and cress have been established.

David Van Beesten

Plate 1: R Lyde
Before partial dredging operation

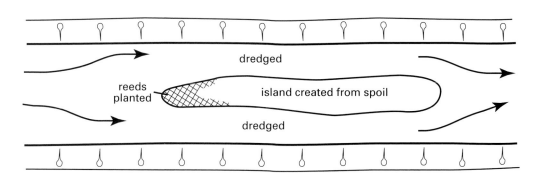

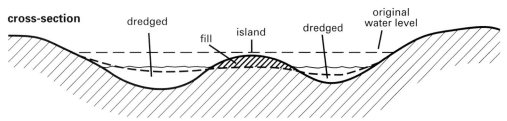

Figure 1: R Lyde
Light maintenance dredging undertaken in
1987 to lower water levels and to improve
wildlife habitat

Plate 2
After dredging. Creation of an island using
the spoil

R Blackwater
at Eversley Cross

Case Study 3.2 (b)

Thames Water/NRA Thames Region

Location:	South of Wokingham on Surrey/Hants border OS 1:50,000 No 175, Grid Ref SU 800 622
River type:	Substrate-gravel/silt
Size:	10–20 m wide, 150–1200 mm deep. Flow range, 0.5–5 m^3s^{-1}
Length affected:	1 km
Date:	September 1988

Techniques/Features:
Dredging to deepen only part of the channel (3.2.2)

Objectives:
Reduce water levels, reduce weed growth; enhance in-stream habitats.

Background

The R Blackwater is a heavily engineered river which suffers from major weed growth including fennel, broad-leaved pondweeds and unbranched bur-reed, which raise summer water levels to an unacceptable degree.

Scheme approach

- The existing channel was generally wide and shallow, approximately 12 m wide by 500 mm deep. The need to improve the diversity of the habitat while reducing the aquatic weed growth led to the following dredging proposals:

- Dredge a meandering central channel 3–4 m wide with a minimum depth of 1 m, to reduce the water level.

- Working from downstream, any riffles that were formed by the dredgings were to be left and possibly extended to produce long riffle beds.

- Banks to remain untouched and margins to be left at a minimum width of 1 m. In places this margin to be reinforced by planting.

- Bank vegetation was to be retained as far as possible. Mature trees were retained.

- Only one bank to be used, the dredgings to be placed at least 2 m back to form an access route about 3 m wide.

- The above parameters indicated that the only machine capable of meeting the requirements was a VC 15 long-reach excavator Great attention was paid to ensure an adequate depth of dig as previous attempts showed that lack of boldness at this stage left the channel too shallow allowing weed growth to return.

Scheme appraisal 1993

Water levels have been reduced at the critical location by 450 mm but with no adverse effect on bankside vegetation. Reduced weed growth has resulted in no requests for cutting since 1988 (previous regime was annually). Channel features such as meanders, cliffs over the channel and marginal vegetation are still in place.

Increased diversity of channel habitats including pools, riffles, and shallow berms has resulted in, with the creation of distinctive wide margins with rich emergent vegetation and a central fast-flowing channel with contrasting flora, and firmer substrate. Fish populations have increased since the work was undertaken.

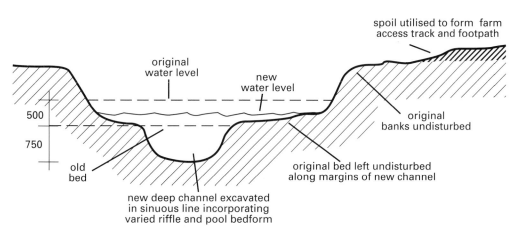

original
water level

new
water level

spoil utilised to form farm
access track and footpath

500

750

original
banks undisturbed

old
bed

original bed left undisturbed
along margins of new channel

new deep channel excavated
in sinuous line incorporating
varied riffle and pool bedform

Figure 1: R Blackwater at Eversley Cross
Deep channel excavated to reduce water levels and
to reduce weed growth obstruction of normal flows

David Van Beesten

Plate 1: R Blackwater at Eversley Cross
partially dredged in 1988 to provide 1m depth in
middle one-third of channel. A typical reach with
banks and margins undisturbed by dredging

David Van Beesten

Plate 2
Riffles and pools were retained where they
existed. Note upstream reach is clear of weed in
central dredged section

The Dyke

Case Study 3.2 (c)

Thames Water/NRA Thames Region

Location:	High Wycombe, Bucks OS 1:50,000 No 175, Grid Ref SU 876 921
River type:	Chalk stream
Size:	*c* 4 m bed width, *c* 75 m deep Mean flow = 50 l s^{-1}
Length affected:	100 m over three weeks
Date:	July 1987

Techniques/Features:
Channel narrowing to create self-sustaining low flow channel (3.2.4)

Objectives:
Retain water level but increase depth and velocity in self-sustaining narrower channel to improve habitat for crayfish.

Background

Ecological interest had declined due to reduction in flow and consequent silting and shallowing. The small stream supported native crayfish which were under threat from the changed regime.

Scheme approach

- Narrow one side of channel by importing limestone blocks which provided suitable habitat for the crayfish.

- On opposite side abutting park 750 mm `Netlon' was used behind which stone and pipes were placed to also provide crayfish shelter.

- Remove silt from central channel and place at edges, stabilise new bed regime with gravel.

- A JCB 3CX and a three-man gang using hand tools executed the work for £5,000 at 1987 prices.

Scheme appraisal 1993

- The chalk stream channel has become silt-free and has maintained required depth.

- Rockwork has remained intact and was initially used by crayfish; some blocks have been dislodged for use in rockeries. More than 80% is now covered by plant growth (including reed canary-grass and reed sweet-grass)

- Due to settling of fill behind the Netlon, posts and netting now stand proud; it is felt that they should have been only temporary measure and moved after two years to leave a self-supporting bank. The bank is now self-supporting but the posts and mesh are unsightly in an otherwise attractive river landscape.

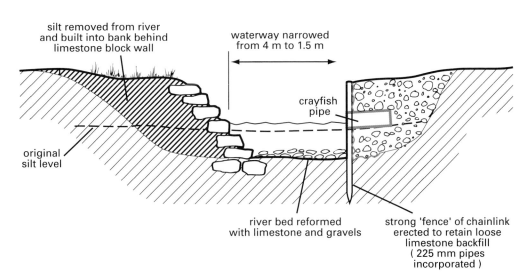

Figure 1: R Dyke
River narrowed to improve crayfish habitat (1987)

Labels in figure:
- silt removed from river and built into bank behind limestone block wall
- waterway narrowed from 4 m to 1.5 m
- crayfish pipe
- original silt level
- river bed reformed with limestone and gravels
- strong 'fence' of chainlink erected to retain loose limestone backfill (225 mm pipes incorporated)

David Van Beesten

Plate 1: The Dyke
Placing stones and pipes behind 'Netlon' to provide crayfish shelter

David Van Beesten

Plate 2
Narrowed section with improved regime and crayfish habitat

R Dun

Thames Water/NRA Thames Region

Case Study 3.2 (d)

Location:	Freemans Marsh SSSI; Hungerford in the Kennet Catchment, Berks OS 1:50,000 No 174, Grid Ref SU 328 686
River type:	Chalk substrate, gravel, pebbles and some silt.
Size:	4 m–10 m wide 0–600 mm deep Flow range = 0.05–0.7 m^3s^{-1}
Length affected:	700 m over 4 weeks
Date :	August 1986

Techniques/Features:
Deliberate narrowing of channel to induce self-cleansing regime (3.2.4)
Substrate redistribution to improve habitat (3.2.6)
Island creation from spoil (3.2.5)

Objectives:
Narrow channel to enable flora and fauna lost through diminution of flows to return to the river.

Background

The Dun is a classic case of a chalk stream suffering from low flows. Previously the wide, shallow channel had sufficient flow to keep the natural gravel-bed clean; before the scheme these gravels had become silty. The once prevalent water-crowfoot had given way to starwort and reeds and the channel no longer had sufficient depth or velocity to support the indigenous population of brown trout.

Scheme approach

- Minimise disturbance to Freeman Marsh SSSI – use wide-tracked vehicle and limit access to dry parts of site only.

- Dredge from within channel, leaving rich margins, banks and adjacent habitats untouched.

- Dredge narrow section within the section; close supervision to ensure individual plants saved in places to aid recolonisation.

- Dredged material redistributed within the channel to increase habitat diversity.

Scheme appraisal (1993)

- Improved self-sustaining and cleansing ability of channel enabled return of crowfoot where narrowing greatest.

- Emergent weed growth no longer needs maintenance but not reduced as much as desired.

- Substrate diversity increased, and in parts returned to closely mimic the condition prior to low flow problems with coarse gravels and pebbles.

- The island created has developed an extremely rich flora, including marsh orchids.

- Post-project appraisal indicates that a bolder approach of narrowing by more than 50% (instead of 40%) would have created a regime more capable of keeping coarse substrates clean and encouraging greater growth of crowfoot.

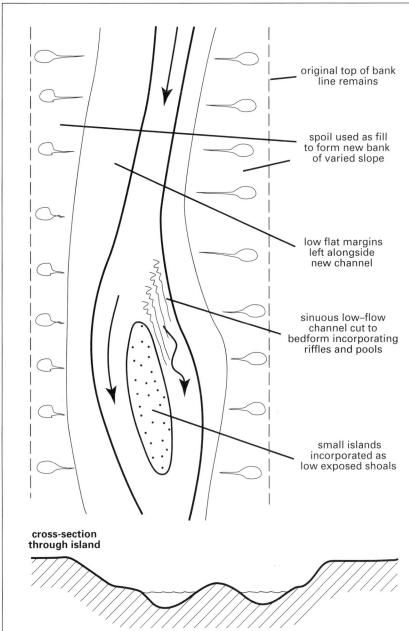

**cross-section
through island**

**Figure 1: R Dun
River narrowing to induce self-cleansing flow regime**

original top of bank
line remains

spoil used as fill
to form new bank
of varied slope

low flat margins
left alongside
new channel

sinuous low–flow
channel cut to
bedform incorporating
riffles and pools

small islands
incorporated as
low exposed shoals

Stuart Mcfadzean

**Plate 1: R Dun
Narrowing to accommodate summer low flows.
Note the shallow bay creation**

Alistair Driver

**Plate 2
Recolonisation of margins and
bank by vegetation including
marsh orchids**

R Ock, near Abingdon

Case Study 3.2 (e)

Thames Water/NRA Thames Region

Location:	Rural area west of Abingdon, Oxon OS 1:50,000 No 175, Grid Ref SU 456952
River type:	Clay
Size:	Dry weather flow 0.3 m^{3}s^{-1} and mean annual flood 13 m^{3}s^{-1}
Length affected:	Approximately 1 km
Date:	1981/82

Techniques/Features:
Introduction of gravel and limestone to improve speed of recovery following dredging (3.2.6)

Objective:
Increase opportunities for natural regeneration of river flora and fauna following major works by importing suitable substrates and increasing variations in flow patterns.

Background

A major land-drainage scheme was executed on the Ock catchment during 1981/82. Although the river suffered a severe pollution incident in 1979 the Ock was held in high esteem by local anglers as a very good coarse fishery. The proposals to deepen and widen the channel were expected to have major adverse environmental impacts so various methods were tried to minimise damage and encourage natural regeneration.

Scheme approach

The deepening and widening of the Ock removed virtually all the plants and animals with the natural gravels and silts. A uniform bare bed was created, comprised primarily of clay. Since smooth hard surfaces such as this discourage recolonisation by plants, and no other habitat cover was available for invertebrates and fish, ameliorative measures were taken. These included:

- Replacing an old retaining sill (which had created a holding pool) with a submerged gabion structure at a lower depth.

- Over-deepening areas of channel to improve selected reaches or reinstate pools.

- Where uniform clay was exposed, a l km stretch of river had gravel and limestone spread on the bed.

- Where a new cut was made, limestone was spread on the bed and six deflectors of various types were built, to create pools and eddies (bare sections were left as controls).

Scheme appraisal

The recolonisation was monitored very closely by Thames Water Authority Fishery and Biology staff in the early years following completion (Jenkins and Magrath; 1984). This involved comparing sites where substrates had been modified to improve habitat and where no such changes had been made. In the year following the works the numbers of invertebrates and animals present in the dredged section, where no bed material had been imported, were far lower than the improved sections respectively. The speed of colonisation by a variety of plants was markedly improved where bed materials had been imported. The three-year monitoring illustrated that this technique accelerates recovery of macrophyte and invertebrate communities following dredging so that more diverse and productive communities are sustained than in untreated exposed clay beds. The modifications represented 0.64% of the scheme costs.

Immediately after the works fish recovery was slow due to pollution. Later surveys provided evidence that substrate improvements had enhanced both numbers of fish and population structure (E Hopkins, pers comm).

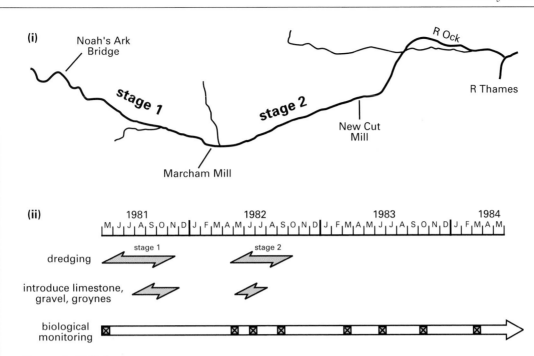

(i)

Noah's Ark
Bridge

R Ock

R Thames

stage 1

stage 2

New Cut
Mill

Marcham Mill

(ii)

	1981		1982		1983		1984
	M J J A S O N D	J F M A M J J A S O N D	J F M A M J J A S O N D	J F M A M

dredging

stage 1

stage 2

introduce limestone,
gravel, groynes

biological
monitoring

Figure 1: R Ock
Introduction of gravel and limestone to improve
speed of recovery following dredging

Vaughan Lewis

Plate 1: R Ock
Placement of gravel and limestone on riverbed

305

R Blackwater, Northern Ireland   Case Study 3.2 (f)

Department of Agriculture Northern Ireland (Watercourse Management Division)

Location: Catchment south-west of Lough Neagh, Northern Ireland
N I Discovery No 19

River type: Moderate to high energy rivers through clay, gravels and cobbles.

Size: All rivers up to 15 m wide x 3 m deep.

Length affected: 350 sites selected for rehabilitation over 5 years.

Date: River works 1984–1992; rehabilitation began in 1990; 150 sites by May 1993

Techniques/Features:
Rehabilitation of riffles and Pools (3.2.6)
Low weirs (3.4.5)
Deflectors, boulders (3.4.4)

Objective:
To re-establish fisheries in the Blackwater system to at least pre-drainage scheme numbers, comprising extensive spawning and nursery beds as well as pools.

Background

Between 1984 and 1990 a major scheme was carried out in the upper catchment of the R Blackwater to improve the drainage of agricultural land. Many such drainage schemes throughout the UK have come under criticism from environmental groups because of the damage to important conservation interests, notably the loss of fishery status and drainage of associated wetlands. Since then in Northern Ireland, as a result of the experience gained, significant improvements have been made in environmentally sympathetic river management policies and practices. An example is the maintenance through co-operative management of a high water table in Annaghroe, an important wetland area within the catchment.

The Blackwater scheme incorporated substantial channel resectioning and regrading, giving rise to a number of adverse effects on the area including a deterioration of fishery quality (Williams, Newson and Browne 1988).

The need for rehabilitation work was therefore widely accepted, including restoration of the rivers fishery aspect. The potential for substrate rehabilitation and introduction of in-channel structures to vary flow characteristics for fishery enhancement proposals was therefore researched. On the basis of such research a scheme was prepared.

Scheme approach

- Target species; primarily migratory salmon and indigenous trout.

- Extensive consultation with DANI Fishery Division, Fishery Research Laboratories, Fisheries Conservancy Board for Northern Ireland.

- Provide habitat for all stages of salmon life cycle (spawning, nursery and holding), with aim to increase habitats for other river plants and animals.

- Works to be cost effective on a site by site basis but be assessed also on benefits for whole river.

- Performance monitoring to commence immediately each element of rehabilitation is complete, supported by selective pre-works monitoring.

- Lessons learnt from monitoring to be incorporated in further rehabilitation works.

- Work undertaken from upstream end of system moving down river to avoid silting.

- Tree cover and bank vegetation to be reinstated where critical to fishery habitat.

The general approach was to simulate the previously occurring natural pool–riffle–pool sequence as far as possible. Particular attention was paid to variations in water depth and velocity and bed diversity through import of materials. Gravel sizes, mix and distribution were carefully selected with rock structures used to stabilise gravels or create localised diversity.

Scheme appraisal

Following the initial period of works, results are encouraging with fish spawning in newly created beds. Problems overcome, or being addressed, include migration of gravel with floods, silting in gradients below 1 : 1,000, and achievement of optimal depth/velocity.
The effects on water levels and channel conveyance are being monitored.

The attention being paid to monitoring the performance of this comprehensive scheme and the refinement of designs as work proceeds can be expected to yield information of widescale value.

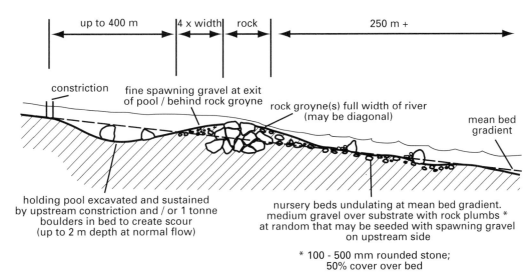

up to 400 m   4 x width   rock   250 m +

constriction

fine spawning gravel at exit of pool / behind rock groyne

rock groyne(s) full width of river (may be diagonal)

mean bed gradient

holding pool excavated and sustained by upstream constriction and / or 1 tonne boulders in bed to create scour (up to 2 m depth at normal flow)

nursery beds undulating at mean bed gradient. medium gravel over substrate with rock plumbs * at random that may be seeded with spawning gravel on upstream side

* 100 - 500 mm rounded stone; 50% cover over bed

Figure 1: R Blackwater
Schematic longitudinal section showing
typical sequence of pools, spawning gravels
and nursery areas on a rehabilitated reach

Plate 1: R Blackwater
Fishery rehabilitation on the Ballygawley
Water (Oct 93)

Plate 2
Replacement of nursery gravels on the
Ballygawley Water.

Joe Nicholson

Joe Nicholson

R Beult

Case Study 3.3 (a)

NRA Southern Region

Location:	Yalding in the Medway catchment, Kent OS 1:50,000 No 188, Grid Ref TQ 701 496
River type:	Lowland clay river
Size:	Bed width 12–15 m depth >1 m
Length affected:	2 km
Date:	1984

Techniques/Features:
Reprofiling steep riverbank to create wetland edge habitat (3.2.2)

Objective:
Provide improved wildlife habitats at the bank/water interface whilst undertaking a maintenance dredging operation

Background

In 1984, the RSPB was responsible for funding a number of River Corridor Surveys (RCS) with a view to providing management advice to the Water Authorities on alternative methods of maintenance dredging. Southern Water Authority in the Kent area welcomed such inputs, with the Beult being an example. At the time of survey (winter) dredging had already begun and banks were being resectioned to form steep, smooth slopes extending to well below the water line. The local landowner was keen to promote a more varied bank profile to benefit wildlife and enable him to gain better access to the water for fishing. For such benefits he was prepared to forego almost 2 m of land along the riverside.

Scheme approach

River corridor survey team, machine driver, supervisor and landowner worked closely on an alternative management strategy which involved re-sectioning the banks to create 1–1.5 m wide wetland ledges about 20 cm above normal water level along the working bank. The scheme proposals were made in the light of:

• Valued marginal wetland habitats were limited along the lower Beult due to the height and steepness of the banks.

• Creation of the habitat alone would be sufficient to elicit a beneficial ecological response since natural establishment should be good due to a rich mix of suitable species being present within the catchment.

Scheme appraisal

The banks were resectioned in spring, thus creating wetland shelves which were inundated several times before early summer. Within the first four months colonisation was rapid, with a varied and rich community developing. Reeds and rushes (branched bur-reed, reed canary-grass, hard rush) grew from both seeds and shoot/root fragments. Rapid early colonisers were annual wetland species such as brooklime, blue and pink water-speedwell, water forget-me-not, water-cress, marsh yellow-cress and the alien Indian balsam. Common perennials which rapidly colonised were purple-loosestrife, great willowherb, gipsywort, marsh woundwort, meadowsweet and water-mint. After more than eight years the community remains very rich but annuals are much rarer with perennials dominating. The ledge had merged with the emergent flora of the channel to create a wide `toe' to the bank which superficially appears to be natural.

The resectioning has been regarded as a valued ecological enhancement for both bank and marginal flora. The habitat structure created is also likely to have benefited fauna but no supporting data exist. The work did not compromise the required hydraulic conveyance and the works facilitated better angling access for the landowner. The need to resection steep and stable banks at all as part of maintenance dredging has to be questioned, however in this Case Study the willingness of the landowner to give up almost 2 m of land along the river enabled potential ecological degradation to be turned to advantage.

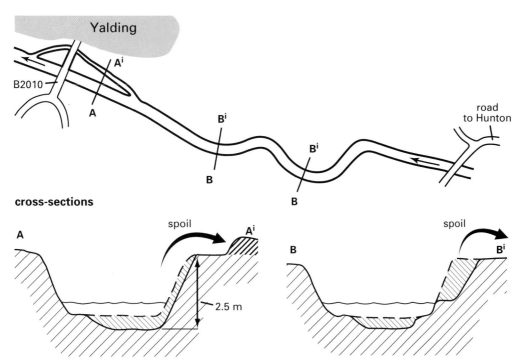

**Figure 1:R Beult
Reprofiling steep riverbank to create wetland
edge habitat**

**Plate 1: R Beult
Reprofiling work in progress**

**Plate 2:
Established marginal vegetation**

R Bain

Anglian Water/NRA Anglian Region

Case Study 3.3 (b)

Location:	Edge of village in rural area. Coningsby, Lincolnshire OS 1:50,000 No 122, Grid Ref TF 220 581
River type:	Lowland river receiving highland water in the fenland catchment; clay also present
Size:	Bed width 10 m
Length affected:	500 m
Date:	1984

Techniques/Features:
Reprofiling banks with poor interest to win material for floodbanks (3.4.2). To create habitats at the river's edge for wetland plants (3.3.2). Translocation of plants from old watercourse into resectioned edge (3.5.3)

Objective:
Enhance bank and marginal habitat in conjunction with provision of material to enable an existing floodbank to be raised. Maximise the ecological interest of the marginal habitat by transferring vegetation from the old river course

Background

The original scheme design proposed to win material for raising the floodbank from the narrow strip of grazed land between the Bain and the floodbank. This was intended to be the most sympathetic approach since guidelines on best practices generally recommend that banks should be left untouched wherever possible. A river corridor survey (RCS) contracted by the RSPB revealed that the bank was of minimal interest, being very steep and clothed in nettle, great willowherb, tall grass and little else. The RCS also indicated that behind the floodbank the old course of the Bain was still present; it was also rich in rushes, reeds, and wetland plants, but very overgrown. The scheme design was thus altered to take advantage of the opportunities the floodbank improvement provided.

Scheme approach

- Material for the floodbank was obtained from the bank of the river, the edging being reprofiled to create a 1 m wide ledge at just above normal water level.

- At approximately 15 m intervals over two-thirds of the scheme length, small hollows were excavated into the new berm so that vegetation could be planted into them to help colonisation.

- The course of the old river was re-opened to enable aquatic plants to re-establish; some of the plant material was carted to the Bain and planted into the hollows dug in the new berm.

- Since the floodbank is a popular footpath the new surface was re-seeded using a wild-flower mix.

Scheme appraisal

Rapid establishment of vegetation occurred on the berm where the following species thrived; reed canary-grass, reed sweet-grass, floating sweet-grass, hard rush, brooklime, water-cress, water forget-me-not and water-mint. Plants such as ragged-robin, fleabane, pink water-speedwell and meadowsweet were also recorded. The majority of the vegetation, in terms of both cover and species, was new to the bank and present as a direct result of the scheme. Within two years the marginal reed fringe had extended into the river and provided new habitat and dense cover for fish and invertebrates. The constant use of the footpath along the bank top and dogs swimming in the river, meant that the habitat potential for nesting birds in the reed fringe was not utilised.

The scheme was heralded a success by the community and featured in the local weekly paper soon after its completion. Establishment of the wild-flower mix was generally poor, although species such as musk mallow, oxeye daisy, bird's-foot-trefoil, knapweed, spiny rest-harrow, field scabious and campion thrived. Part of the problem was rank growth due to the floodbank not being grazed. In the winter of 1992/93 the Bain was dredged and much of the created ledge was inadvertently removed. Some vegetation remained however, and recovery is likely to be good with improved potential for the less invasive species to thrive due to removal of much of the reed sweet-grass.

Nigel Holmes

**Plate 1: R Bain
Reprofiling work in progress, 1984**

Nigel Holmes

**Plate 2: Established marginal
vegetation, 1990**

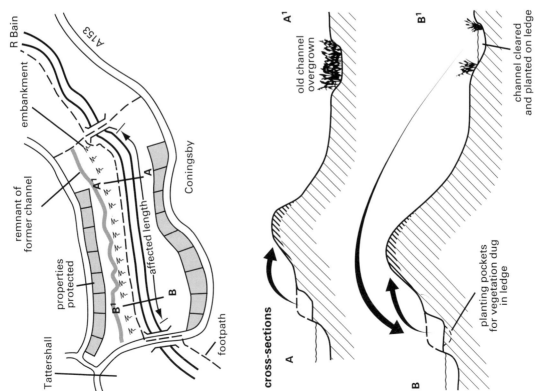

**Figure 1: R Bain
Reprofiling of banks with little conservation
interest to win material for floodbanks and create
marginal wetland habitat**

Project Kingfisher

**West Midland Borough Council
(WMBC), Birmingham City Council,
Solihull Borough Council**

Case Study 3.3 (c)

Location:	R Cole catchment east of central Birmingham OS 1:50,000 No 139, Grid Ref SP 182 879
River type:	Pebble/gravel-bed with steep earth banks
Size:	6–10 m bed width
Length affected:	7 km of river
Date:	Work began in 1985, extensions and new ponds more recently undertaken

Techniques/Features:
Creation of on-line pools and wetlands; re-creation and establishment of new floodplain pools and wetlands (3.3.3)

Objective:
Create a series of pools and wetland habitats within the Cole valley to restore lost habitats for wildlife and provide visual amenity, passive recreation and education benefits for the densely populated community

Scheme approach

In the early 1980s WMBC acted with the local City and Borough Councils and Severn Trent Water Authority in promoting an ambitious scheme to improve habitats and the landscape along 7 km of the R Cole to benefit wildlife and people. Part of the proposals included wetland habitat rehabilitation and creation. The RSPB was involved in the project alongside other conservation bodies and provided information on river corridor habitats and made recommendations regarding wetland habitat creation. Project Kingfisher was launched officially in early summer 1985 with the ceremonial breaching of the R Cole into one of two backwater pools. Both pools were created as shallow backwaters open to the river; the openings were made at an angle facing downstream to ensure flood debris and silt would not be washed into them. During construction aquatic and marginal vegetation was transplanted and a record kept of the species to enable post-project appraisal of colonisation.

The pools had an established appearance within a few months of their creation and were deemed a success on wildlife and landscape grounds. The pool at Bordesley Green has not been changed since being constructed but extensions and modifications were made to the pool above the M6 motorway. A pipe was installed to provide better circulation of water; to avoid debris getting into the pool the pipe was laid below the surface of the water at low-flow periods. This element of the scheme was appraised as providing such great value for money that extensive areas of open water were created in the Chamberlain Playing Fields area. A total of four large water bodies have been formed and reprofiled in the last four years. In addition to this the old R Cole has been managed by a local conservation group who have maintained open water areas and structural habitat.

Scheme appraisal

All aspects of the wetland habitat creation programme have been successful. No 'vegetation control' has been required in the original pools and improved circulation has resulted from the introduction of the piped feed. The planting schemes were successful, with plants such as greater pond-sedge, yellow flag, flowering rush, kingcup, and yellow water-lily thriving in and around the pools. The much larger new water bodies were not planted and have very poor floral communities. This confirms that in impoverished catchments open water habitat creations need to be supplemented by suitable aquatic and marginal planting schemes to maximise their wildlife and landscape interest. Both the original pools were created at a cost of less than £500 each and less than £2,000 has been spent on the extensive new ponds.

Nigel Holmes

Plate 1: Project Kingfisher, R Cole M6 backwater viewed from upstream (April 1993)

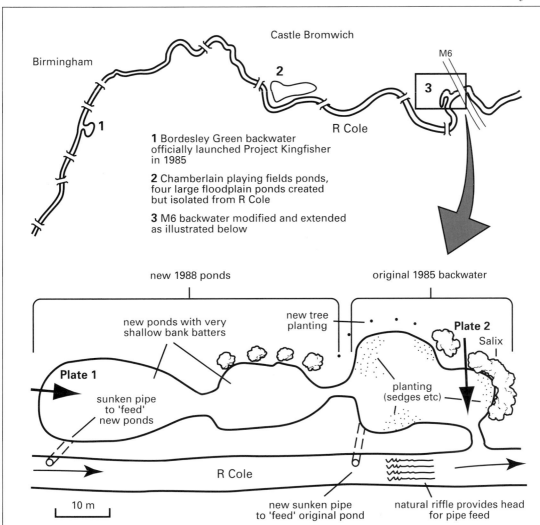

Castle Bromwich

Birmingham

M6

2

3

R Cole

1

1 Bordesley Green backwater officially launched Project Kingfisher in 1985

2 Chamberlain playing fields ponds, four large floodplain ponds created but isolated from R Cole

3 M6 backwater modified and extended as illustrated below

new 1988 ponds

original 1985 backwater

new ponds with very shallow bank batters

new tree planting

Plate 2

Salix

Plate 1

sunken pipe to 'feed' new ponds

planting (sedges etc)

R Cole

10 m

new sunken pipe to 'feed' original pond

natural riffle provides head for pipe feed

**Figure 1: Project Kingfisher; R Cole
Creation of on-line pools and wetland areas**

Nigel Holmes

**Plate 2
Connection of M6 backwater with main channel (April 1993)**

R Roding at Abridge

Case Study 3.3 (d)

Thames Water/NRA Thames Region

Location:	Village of Abridge, near Loughton, Essex OS 1:50,000 No 4177, Grid Ref TQ 461 968
River type:	Gravel and clay with gravel bed and pool and riffle sequences
Size:	2–4 m wide; 150–1,500 mm deep Flow = 0.2–7.0 m³s⁻¹
Length affected:	3 km
Date:	1979

Techniques/Features:
Two-stage channel (3.3.4)

Objectives:
Flood alleviation for Abridge using a method of channel construction not involving trapezoidal sectioning.

Background

This pioneering scheme attracted considerable research attention and modelling. Raven (1986 a,b,c) investigated birds and plants pre-and post-scheme and compared communities on the different treatments. Wojick (1981) described the scheme in his thesis and Sellin and Giles (1985) and others studied the flow characteristics, habitats and flora.

Scheme approach

Retain the meandering channel but excavate land on one or both banks to provide flood capacity. The width of excavation varied from 30–50 m with lowering to 500 mm above low water level (during construction a major flood washed topsoil from this second stage and lowered it to below design level). Vertical cliffs were given some protection from erosion by larch poles. Grazing of the berms by cattle was to take place as part of the overall scheme design to ensure a relatively unobstructed flood path.

Scheme appraisal (1992)

A striking feature of the Roding is the extent to which tall reeds have colonised the wide, low-level berms. The `engineered' appearance is more characteristic of some fenland rivers than of the incised tree-lined brooks common to Essex. The wide fringes are now valued habitats for reed warblers and reed buntings but species-richness of plants is limited on the banks due to the extent of reed growth. Within the channel a diverse community and habitat structure remains.

In some respects, the Roding has become a victim of its own success. Freedom from flooding, which the scheme brought to adjacent land, resulted in a conversion from grazing to arable so cattle were no longer available to graze the berm. Cutting is now required to maintain capacity but the aforementioned erosion of topsoil resulted in parts of the second-stage channel being too wet for machine access.

A study of hydraulic performance before and after cutting has concluded that the scheme is significantly below design capacity. This is due to a combination of impedance to flow by reeds over the berms, and to complex eddying effects associated with the physical geometry, particularly where the original streamway meanders laterally across the berms.

An outstanding achievement of the design is the establishment of a broad river corridor (lacking upstream) through an area of intensive agriculture. Reprofiling of the berms is being considered to bring the scheme closer to its hydraulic design objectives and to provide improved machine access and maintain wildlife interest.

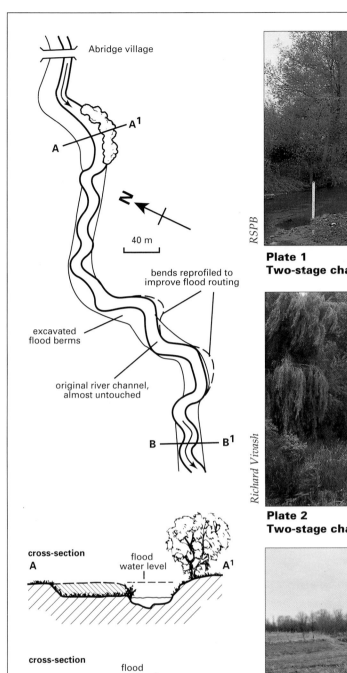

Figure 1: R Roding
Plans and cross-sectional diagrams of the two-stage channel below Abridge

RSPB

Plate 1
Two-stage channel in May 1981

Richard Vivash

Plate 2
Two-stage channel in 1991

Richard Vivash

Plate 3: R Roding, Abridge
Berm at meander 0.5 km downstream of Abridge. This small section has been cleared of reed by hand cutting due to poor access for plant.

R Monnow

Case Study 3.3 (e)

Welsh Water/NRA Welsh Region

Location:	Maerdy between Llangua and Alltryrynys, Herefordshire OS 1:50,000 No 161, Grid Ref SO 3725
River type:	Steep catchment with active regime variation and transportation of gravel
Size:	Up to 30 m wide
Length affected:	6 km
Date:	1976

Techniques/Features:
Maintenance of a natural multi-stage channel (3.3.4) including
Shoal reinforcement (3.2.5)
Willow brushing (3.7)
Alder bank protection (3.7)

Objectives:
Maintain the natural multi-stage character of the Monnow for the benefit of efficient hydraulic performance and retention/enhancement of ecological and fishery interests.

Background

This reach of the Monnow follows the A465 Hereford to Abergavenny road where it forms a 'mobile' border between England and Wales. The reach affords an easily accessible and excellent example of an active piedmont river that displays natural multi-stage characteristics.

Scheme approach

This comprised partial excavation of shoals to rebuild actively eroding riverbanks and the extensive use of willow cuttings and alder trees to reinforce these. Shoals were also carefully manoeuvred (but not removed) to retain habitat features such as islands and major fishing pools without radically altering the established regime. Skilled labour combined with excavators and bulldozers utilised local materials to check the river's tendency towards dramatic fluctuations.

Scheme appraisal

The channel gives the appearance of being natural and 'unmanaged' with considerable diversity of habitat. In essence as much habitat value is present after the operation as before. The photographs, cross-section and plan show a reach with a natural island and associated by-pass at Maerdy. This scheme suggests that management operations which maintain adequate capacity can also help retain important wildlife features. The incorporation of meanders, islands and multi-stage by-passes into new designs are shown to have naturally occurring precedents.

The reach described is valuable to those who seek to gain a visual appreciation of the natural power of a river to create and sustain habitats. In particular the reach demonstrates the ability of trees to hold banks in place, and the use of wide, complex channels as alternatives to uniform trapezoidal sections. The success of the works more than 15 years after construction is an important illustration of how design standards can be met and maintained by options which work with, not against, natural river processes.

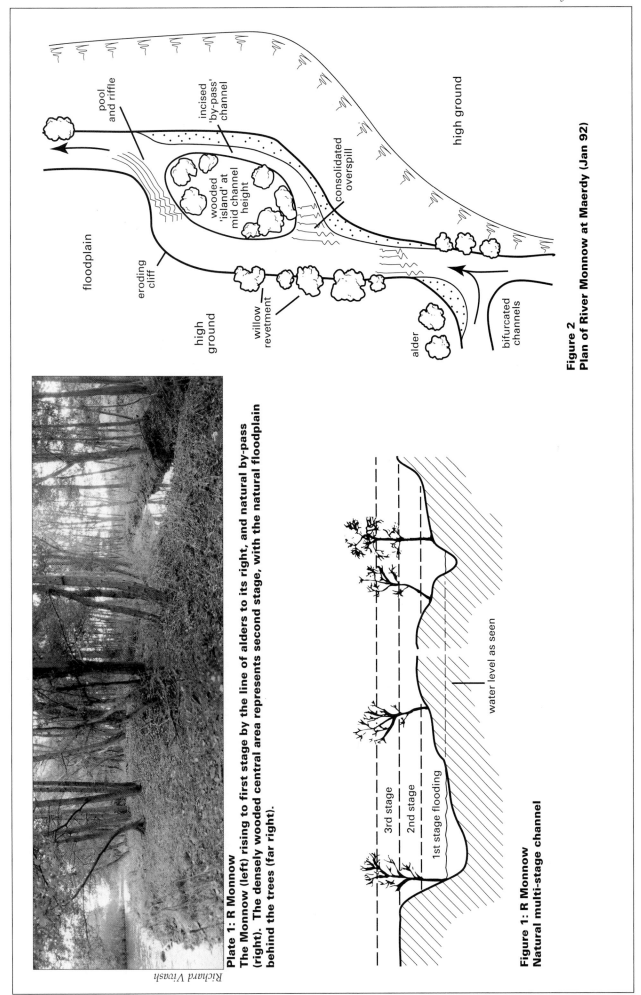

Figure 2
Plan of River Monnow at Maerdy (Jan 92)

pool and riffle

incised 'by-pass' channel

consolidated overspill

high ground

wooded 'island' at mid channel height

floodplain

eroding cliff

high ground

willow revetment

alder

bifurcated channels

Plate 1: R Monnow
The Monnow (left) rising to first stage by the line of alders to its right, and natural by-pass (right). The densely wooded central area represents second stage, with the natural floodplain behind the trees (far right).

Richard Vivash

Figure 1: R Monnow
Natural multi-stage channel

3rd stage

2nd stage

1st stage flooding

water level as seen

317

R Torne

Case Study 3.4 (a)

Severn Trent Water/NRA Severn-Trent Region

Location:	Hatfield Chase, Doncaster OS 1:50,000 Nos 111 and 112, Grid Ref SE 676 035 to SE 742 041
River type:	Low gradient, artificial straight channel through fenland
Size:	*c* 8–10 m bed width with embankments *c* 2 m high
Length affected:	*c* 7 km
Date:	1985–1990

Techniques/Features:

In-stream and in-corridor habitat creation to win spoil for embankment

Planting of created habitats

Objective:

Change of approach to spoil winning for flood embankment maintenance in order to maximise potential for habitat creation and enhanced recreation.

Background

The R Torne is a tributary in the extensive lowland Trent area near the Humber estuary. Much of its lower reaches are in the form of an historical straight, artificial and embanked channel bordered by valued farmland on peat which requires pumped drainage into the river.

In the late 1970s it was decided that maintenance of the floodbanks was required. Under-drainage of the land (much of it below sea level) over many years had resulted in peat shrinkage and a severe drop in the height of parts of the floodbanks. The original proposal and initial work gained material from the bed of the river to raise the height of the floodbanks. When this work began in the mid-1980s little attention was paid to river habitat restoration.

Scheme approach

Major changes in approach occurred half way through the project, co-ordinated by the Area Conservation and Recreation Officer. These plans were the subject of detailed consultation with external bodies with interest in the river, including angling, recreation, rambling and horse-riding interests, as well as statutory and voluntary landscape and wildlife bodies.

Instead of gaining material for raising the banks by merely deepening the river, the majority of spoil was taken from the edges or from land between the river and the floodbank. This had the potential of transforming previously monotonous steep trapezoidal banks into diverse and attractive habitats. Shallow underwater shelves were constructed between low wet banks so that both river and wetland plants could thrive and provide the ideal environment for a diverse range of animals. Where space allowed, pools and wetlands of varying sizes and depths were created by winning material for the floodbanks.

Some areas were left for natural recolonisation to occur, whilst in others planting of a wide range of aquatic and wetland plants took place.

Scheme appraisal

The wetland and marginal habitats created have all rapidly established the character intended and colonisation by plants and animals has exceeded all expectations. Many plants and animals rarely, if ever, seen along this stretch previously have already become commonplace. Local people were also quick to acknowledge the resounding improvement in the corridor environment for wildlife and their passive recreational activities. Planting of aquatic and wetland plants has established species known to have occurred previously but which may not have been able to recolonise naturally. A major ecological post-project appraisal is being undertaken to determine more precisely the value to wildlife of these habitat enhancement works, achieved at no extra cost, whilst providing material to bring the floodbanks back to their design standard.

Plate 1: R Torne
Shallow underwater shelves

Nigel Holmes

Plate 2
Isolated pools

Nigel Holmes

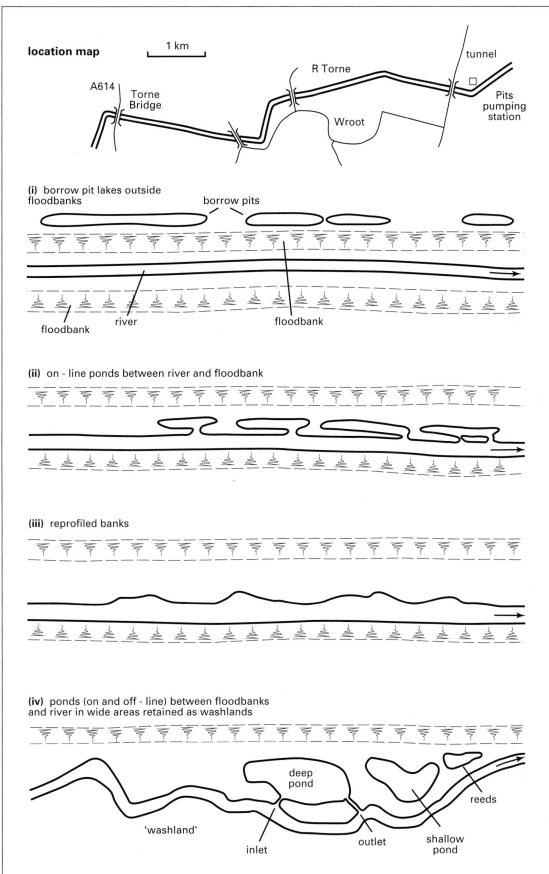

location map

1 km

A614

Torne
Bridge

R Torne

tunnel

Wroot

Pits
pumping
station

(i) borrow pit lakes outside
floodbanks

borrow pits

floodbank

river

floodbank

(ii) on - line ponds between river and floodbank

(iii) reprofiled banks

(iv) ponds (on and off - line) between floodbanks
and river in wide areas retained as washlands

deep
pond

reeds

'washland'

inlet

outlet

shallow
pond

Figure 1: R Torne
The range of habitat creation options undertaken on the outside (option i) and inside
of the floodbank (options ii, iii and iv)

R Lugg at Lugg Bridge

Welsh Water/NRA Welsh Region

Location: From Lugg Bridge on A465 upstream to Moreton on Lugg, NE of Hereford
OS 1:50,000 No 149
Grid Ref SO 512459

River type: Lowland through alluvial clays/silts/gravels

Size: *c* 15 m wide x 3 m deep

Length affected: 6 km

Date: 1978–1981

Techniques/Features:
Low, flat `roll-over' flood embankments set well clear of established meanders (3.4.2)

Objective:
Control the frequency of flooding over the rural floodplain of the Lugg and maintain a relatively natural channel.

Background

The Lugg floodplain to the north and east of Hereford is generally up to 1 km wide and is predominantly grassland. Frequent and prolonged flooding of this land limited its productive potential, giving rise to some requests in the mid-1970s for engineering control works.

Scheme approach

The concept adopted for flood control was based upon establishing low flat roll over embankments on both sides of the river at sufficient distance from the natural bank to meet the following criteria:

- Allow for migration of meanders without significant risk of undermining the embankments.

- Gain sufficient spoil for embankment construction through reprofiling the intervening land up to the riverbank.

- Provide sufficient cross-sectional area between embankments to convey the 1 : 5 year design flood before over-topping.

- Facilitate continued grassland management over the whole embankment and riverside area.

By realigning and strengthening natural levees a significant increase in flood conveyance was achieved without direct physical disturbance of the river channel itself. It also established a substantial corridor of land along the river that could not be farmed intensively.

The approach described was not adopted universally on the Lugg, with areas of high ecological interested excluded from the scheme and others receiving greater standards of protection to enable greater flood control.

Scheme appraisal (1993)

The scheme objectives have been achieved with flooding frequencies greatly reduced behind the floodbanks. No major changes in regime, due to this form of embanking, are evident and it remains a river with high ecological and aesthetic value. The embankments have over-topped occasionally without undermining their stability but this did lead to the addition of floodgates to allow water to return to the river as the flood subsides. The hydraulic performance of the scheme has been studied on behalf of MAFF as part of two research and development projects to improve knowledge of environmentally sensitive methods of flood control. (MAFF/UEA 1991); (MAFF/HR Ltd FR312 – November 1992).

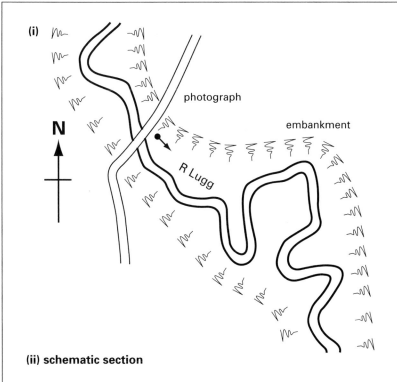

(i)

photograph

embankment

N

R Lugg

(ii) schematic section

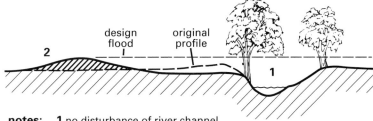

2

design flood

original profile

1

notes: 1 no disturbance of river channel

2 a) embankments formed from reprofile
of riverside land.Max slope both sides 1:7

b) no freeboard on embankments
-design for overtopping

Figure 1: R Lugg
(i) Flat, 'roll-over' flood embankments, set clear of established
meanders at Wergin's bridge, Sutton St Nicholas
(ii) Schematic section, NE of Hereford

Richard Vivash

Plate 1: R Lugg
Grazing of berms excavated to form low 'roll-over' embankments

R Alne

Case Study 3.4 (c)

Severn Trent Water/NRA Severn-Trent Region

Location:	Beaudesert Street, Henley in Arden, Warwickshire OS 1:50,000 No 151, Grid Ref SP 153 659
River type:	Clay
Size:	2–6 m width
Length affected:	Part of a larger scheme. By-pass approximately 300 m long
Date:	1979/80

Techniques/Features:
Wet and Dry by-pass channels (3.4.3)

Objectives:
Provide additional flood capacity without significant disturbance to the established river by use of two by-pass channels.

Background

Capital works were undertaken to alleviate flooding problems at Henley in Arden in 1979/80. The scheme resulted in the R Alne being deepened (by up to 1 m) and in some places widened. At Beaudesert Street, capacity was increased by use of two by-pass channels with different low-flow characteristics.

Scheme approach

The by-pass downstream of Beaudesert Street was constructed following the principles set out in Table 4 Chapter 3.4. The weir height at the start of the by-pass was set to allow a base flow to be shared by both channels. The new by-pass channel incorporated variable bank slopes and tree planting on the south side. In contrast the upstream by-pass was designed to be dry except during floods, leaving the entire base flow within the original waterway.

Scheme appraisal 1993

No major channel maintenance work was required until 1992, over 10 years after construction. A new river regime has established and no property flooding has occurred.

The downstream by-pass channel has now become the principal waterway leaving the original channel without flow during dry periods. It has developed some of the characteristics of a flashy upland stream with a natural, multi-stage cross-section. A shallow 'low flow' channel meanders through gravel shoals giving rise to pool and riffle characteristics. A rich aquatic and marginal plant life has developed and the bankside trees and the newly created island have formed a valued wildlife refuge.

The by-pass channel above Beaudesert Street reacted similarly becoming the main waterway, with the original channel developing a substantial gravel shoal just at the point of bifurcation. This occurred very soon after construction and forced base-flows into the by-pass. Careful dredging re-established the design standard which has remained stable. The porosity of the gabion control weir initially led to loss of base flow into the by-pass channel but this has been reduced significantly following the accretion of sediments.

Both by-passes have proved to be technically efficient while adding to habitat diversity, locally.

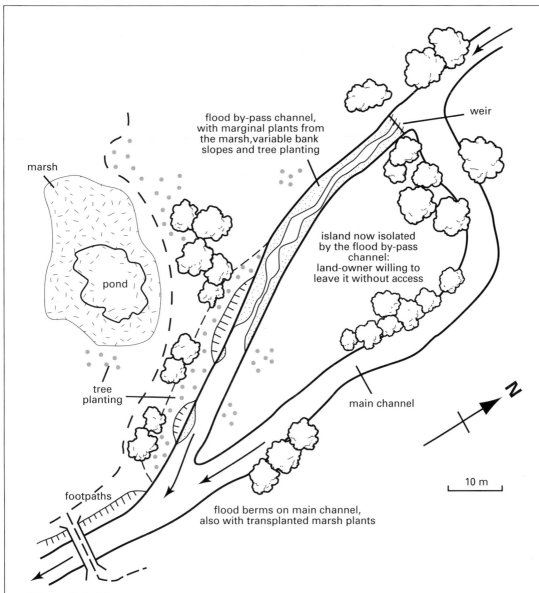

Figure 1: R Alne
By-pass and island creation. Source: Lewis and Williams (1984)

Plate 1: R Alne
Upstream section of by-pass after maintenance cut of woody vegetation in December 1991

Plate 2
Downstream section of by-pass December 1991

R Roding at Passingford

Thames Water/NRA ThamesRegion

Location:	Adjacent to M25 approximately 500 m upstream of Passingford, Essex OS 1:50,000 No 177, Grid Ref TQ 508 975
River type:	Lowland through alluvial clays and silts
Size:	*c* 1.4 m width Flow 0.2–6.0 m³s⁻¹
Length affected:	150 m
Date:	1982

Techniques/Features:
Whole river realignment (3.4.3)
Incorporating meanders and various revetments (3.4.4) With pools and riffle construction and imported substrates (3.2.6).

Objective:
River diversion to accommodate construction of the adjacent motorway while conserving essential riverine characteristics appropriate to the reach.

Background and scheme approach

These works were detailed in the first edition of this handbook (p.142). The river was realigned utilising the layout of a nearby reach as a `template', resulting in gentle meanders being incorporated into the new cut with revetment at points of potential erosion. The revetments specified were stone-filled gabion mattresses laid over the exposed fill at each end of the cut with stakes and alder on the outside of each newly excavated bend. Pools and riffles were incorporated into the designed bed profile and gravel introduced.

The approach was innovative for its time as it contrasted markedly with initial proposals for a straight cut revetted with concrete blocks.

Scheme appraisal

Ten years after construction the river appears to have established a regime in keeping with former conditions and there are few signs of it having been engineered. The cut is stable and has required no special maintenance. Figure 1 shows the layout and highlights the following observations derived from site inspection in 1992.

- The realignment is devoid of any trees, although some low bushes of mixed species have established at the downstream end of the cut. This is possibly accounted for by the grazing of land on both banks; without protection, young trees will only survive if they are beyond the reach of livestock.

- The introduction of gravel to the bed has been beneficial to invertebrates and fish but no true pool and riffle sequence has been achieved. This is a low energy reach with sluggish characteristics.

- The only clear evidence of revetment remaining are two short runs of close piled fencing stakes standing approximately 500 mm above ground level. These are both sited where the bank is closest to the motorway and probably served to support the bank against collapse under the weight of passing agricultural machinery. There is no sign of the river eroding or undermining, the piles and gabion mattresses are no longer in evidence, having been covered with soil.

- In general the riverbanks appear to have naturalised under the influence of grazing cattle with localised stands of rush and reed, poached strips, shelves and favoured drinking places. Ruderal plants are evident in the few stony places along the more disturbed north bank close to the motorway.

- The objectives of the work have been achieved. The reach has environmental value which is immeasurably greater than anything likely to have been derived without the attention to detail given. The approach merits far wider application than has been evident in different parts of the country.

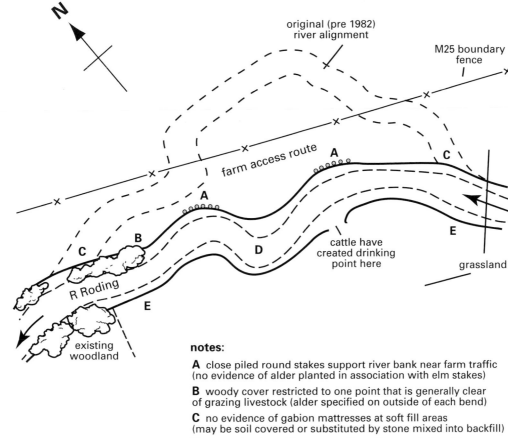

notes:

A close piled round stakes support river bank near farm traffic
(no evidence of alder planted in association with elm stakes)

B woody cover restricted to one point that is generally clear
of grazing livestock (alder specified on outside of each bend)

C no evidence of gabion mattresses at soft fill areas
(may be soil covered or substituted by stone mixed into backfill)

D water depth and flow generally uniform and sluggish ;
typical of the reach (no evidence of pool and riffle specified)

E south bank supports reed and rush marginal plants and is
profiled by poaching of cattle
North bank more stoney with some ruderal plants

**Figure 1: R Roding. Passingford
Whole river realignment**

**Plate 1: R Roding
Downstream view over entire realignment**

**Plate 2
Upstream view of part of reach**

325

R Clwyd Catchment

Welsh Water/NRA Welsh Region

Case Study 3.4 (e)

Location:	Main river plus tributaries of catchment south of Rhyl, Clwyd, NE Wales OS 1:50,000 No 116 Grid Ref SJ 069657
River type:	High energy from Denbigh Moors down to low energy approaching coastal marshes.
Size:	All sizes up to 20 m wide
Date:	Since early 1960s

Techniques/Features:
Bank protection and shoal management utilising: brush bundles, log/brush revetments (3.7.6); stone gabions, (with or without willow stakes) and deflectors and revetments (3.4.4); shoal management (3.2.5)

Objectives:
To maintain conveyance within a natural stable regime without removal of sediments.

Background

The central catchment feature is the pastoral Vale of Clwyd into which several large tributaries flow from rocky uplands. The Clwyd meanders through the Vale northwards to the flat tidal reaches associated with the historic Rhuddlan marshes. The rivers are strongly characterised by gravels over varied substrates. The rivers are largely unimproved in the rural areas since the last century. Alder and willow are prevalent along the banks which are prone to erosion where trees are absent. Flood routing is generally effected by embankments at a few, mainly urban, areas but otherwise the Vale is allowed to flood freely.

Scheme approach

Riverbank maintenance is central to the NRA's management strategy, the objective being to ensure that the channel regime established over many years is sensibly sustained. No sediments are removed from the river, even through towns, although any extensive shoals associated with major instability may be partially redistributed and utilised in the protective works.

Operations involve regularly cutting excessive brushwood from trees at the water's edge, some of which is utilised in bundles to reinforce the banks between mature trees. Logs are utilised as deflectors. Regeneration of riverside trees is a key feature of all maintenance work.

Stone is utilised as a revetment if an embankment is adjacent. However, here too willow and alder are integrated into the design to provide long-term stability. Gravel shoals are also redistributed if they are encouraging undesirable erosion on the opposite bank.

The plates show a sample of the techniques utilised in the Vale.

Scheme appraisal

The maintenance strategy employed has proved successful over many years, resulting in a river system that has abundant wildlife and is scenically attractive. It represents an excellent example of man working with nature towards a situation that is representative of co-existence.

Plate 1: Clwyd catchment - Installing deflectors/revetment Reconstructed riverbank nearing completion with series of log deflectors (R Clwyd Llannerch 1992)

Phil Weaver

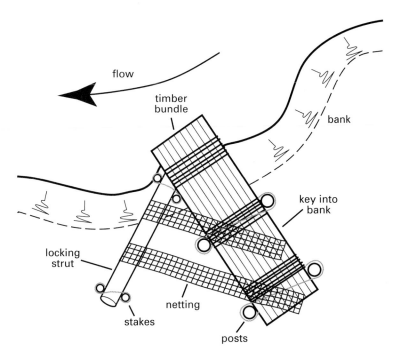

Figure 1: R Clwyd
Positioning of typical 'bundle' type groyne or deflector

Plate 2
Five willow log deflectors with one year's growth (Pont Clwyd)

Plate 3
Bank revetment close to flood embankment utilising willow bundles laid under blockstone (R Elwy St Asaph)

Phil Weaver

Phil Weaver

Broads Reed Revetment

Case Study 3.4 (f)

Anglian Water/NRA Anglian Region

Location:	• R Bure, left bank at Thurn Mouth TG 398 152 • R Thurne, right bank at Thurn Mouth TG 400 153 • R Ant, left bank above Hunsett Mill TG 362 242 OS 1:50,000 No 134, Norfolk
River type:	Slow-flowing through peat deposits
Size:	Around 30 m wide. Navigable depths.
Length affected:	Many sites with a programme of trials continuing.
Date:	1991

Techniques/Features:
Revetment of eroding peaty banks using geotextiles and indigenous Norfolk reeds(3.4.4).

Objectives:
To alleviate the risk of flood embankments being undermined and to reinstate wildlife habitat.

Background

The banks of the R Bure and its main Broadland tributaries the Ant and Thurne, are extensively supported by sheet piling. Since1983 trials have been undertaken to develop techniques that rely upon the colonisation of the riverside margins by reeds and sedges to protect the banks from erosion. Boat wash is a primary cause of erosion.

Scheme approach

The aim of the works is to simulate the naturally occurring reaches of reed-fringed river where waves are observed to be absorbed within the biomass of the reed stands. Both the roots (rhizomes) and stems (fronds) are important. A fringe at least 2 m wide has generally been sought, through experience and limited research.

The simple expedient of introducing reed rhizomes to the river margins that are eroding is not a viable option since reed would inevitably have established naturally had conditions been suitable. It has been necessary to engineer a suitable substrate profile within which an adequate width of reed fringe can be introduced, and to reinforce the substrate to ensure the stability of the proposed reedbed.

The most successful trials have all involved reprofiling of the riverbank utilising fill (or by cutting it back where space permits) and then reinforcing it with a proprietary geotextile. Reed rhizomes are introduced to the top layer of profiled fill prior to laying the geotextile which is carefully selected to ensure that reed can penetrate it without difficulty. The references given above locate the most successful trials.

Reed growth close to, and above, the normal water line can be fairly rapid but is generally much slower at depth. Underwater planting is rarely effective, since the reed frequently dies. Norfolk reed is known to grow in up to 1.5 m of water and it is this characteristic that is important in gaining the required revetment mechanisms of energy absorption both at the surface and below. The geotextile used under water may need to be different from that above because it is likely to be the primary revetment medium for some time before being supplemented by reed growth.

Scheme appraisal

Geotextiles that incorporate asphalt have proved to be most successful on the Broadland rivers although others are known to have proved useful in less demanding situations. The NRA has commissioned research into development of semi-natural revetments of the type described, because much has yet to be learned before techniques can be introduced with confidence. Reed establishment is best above normal water level with early observations indicating that rhizomes spread down the bank into the water to provide the strongest underwater growth. Where reed has established well, reed warblers breed in good numbers.

John Ash

Plate 1: Broadland Rivers
R Thurne. Reed cover was achieved within two years, above normal water level, on this tidal river, giving the traditional reed fringe to the waterway.

John Ash

Plate 2
R Ant. Erosion control using natural vegetation. Sedge grew within three months and the embankment face was covered by sedge and grass within two years.

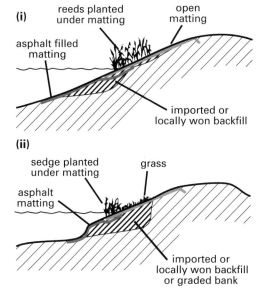

(i)

reeds planted under matting   open matting

asphalt filled matting

imported or locally won backfill

(ii)

sedge planted under matting   grass

asphalt matting

imported or locally won backfill or graded bank

Figure 1: Broadland Rivers -
Revetment of eroding peaty banks
(i) R Thurne.
Floodwall erosion by boatwash, checked by regrading embankment with imported material, planting reed rhizomes and covering with an asphalt filled geotextile to below water level
(ii) R Ant.
Poor-quality peat floodwall eroded by scour. Bank regraded, old locally won sedge placed at toe, upper wall seeded with grass. Floodwall face covered with an asphalt filled geotextile.

Loughrans Weir Fish Pass

Case Study 3.4 (g)

Department of Agriculture Northern Ireland (Watercourse Management Division)

Location:	On Ballygawley Water at Ballygawley, Co Tyrone, Northern Ireland N I Discovery Series No. 19, Grid Ref 575 630
River type:	Moderate energy river through clay/silt/stone substrate
Size:	Weir 14.5 m wide x 2.5 m high.
Length affected:	One of a series of three ancient weirs near the town.
Date:	Rebuilt 1988

Techniques/Features:
Weir reconstruction: cemented block stone in a tiered cascade to re-establish fish migration (3.4.5)

Objectives:
To protect the established river regime through substantial reconstruction of an ancient vertical drop weir and to provide passage for migratory fish.

Background

To enable the passage of migratory fish to valuable spawning areas in the head waters of the Ballygawley Water, fish passes were built on each of three weirs adjacent to the village of Ballygawley. The middle weir called Loughrans was built about 100 years ago and was in fact used for generating the first electricity in the village. It consisted of a vertical masonry wall measuring 3 m in height and stretching 15 m across the channel. It constituted a barrier to migratory fish and was in danger of collapse necessitating major reconstruction works to protect the established river regime.

Scheme approach

In Northern Ireland three basic types of fish pass are now commonly installed: the 'pool and traverse' type with notched overflow weirs, the 'diagonal baffle' on the apron of a weir and a 'multiple cascade' type. This study highlights the last.

Design considerations were to:

- Control water velocity to a speed which enabled fish to swim up the weir.

- Avoid rapid changes in flow pattern.

- Provide resting areas for fish within the structure of the weir.

- Possess a well-located fish entrance.

- Be economical to construct and maintain.

- Be able to operate without interference by sediment and debris.

- Be environmentally attractive in appearance.

Following consultations with DANI Fisheries Division a series of four blockstone cascades with concrete infill were built immediately downstream of the weir. The cascades were slightly tapered towards the centre to concentrate the flow. Pools varying from 1.0 m depth at bankside to 1.2 m in the centre of the channel were formed behind each cascade. This allows fish to rest as necessary before attempting further jumps.

To take account of the aesthetics of the site special care was taken to integrate blockstone bankside revetment into the new structure.

Scheme appraisal

The reconstructed weir is a most attractive feature that suits this urban fringe environment. Fish have successfully migrated upstream of the weir and the long-established river regime, both upstream and downstream, has been conserved.

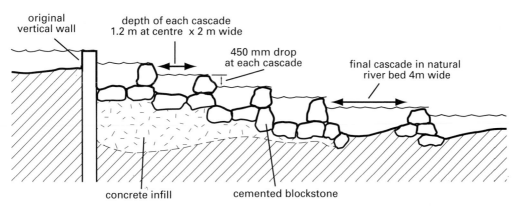

Figure 1: Loughrans Fish Pass, Ballygawley Water Weir reconstruction to re-establish fish migration facility

**Plate 1
Ballygawley Water
before rebuilding**

Joe Nicholson

**Plate 2
Ballygawley Water
Completed weir 14.5m
wide; each cascade
crest forms a shallow
dish to concentrate
flow towards the
centre.**

Joe Nicholson

Great Ouse

Anglian Water/NRA Anglian Region

Location:	Godmanchester, Cambridge OS 1:50,000 No. 153, Grid Ref TL 243 705
River type:	Slow river through alluvial clay/silt/gravel
Size:	30 m wide; 1.2 m minimum navigable depth
Length affected:	Around 3 ha of land and waterways
Date:	Historic mill location

Techniques/Features:
Weirs and Sluices (3.4.5) A complex of river channels and islands featuring weirs and open flood meadow, sluices and pools providing habitat diversity, recreation and amenity

Objective:
Illustrate functional control of water levels for navigation and flood alleviation purposes with diverse water and land interests.

Background

Godmanchester is one of many ancient mill sites on the Great Ouse. In addition to the main navigable channel used by pleasure boats, the river system comprises numerous overspill channels and by-passes; some traverse the extensive floodplain providing considerable variation to the wildlife habitat of the river corridor between St Ives and Bedford, a distance of some 45 km. Other significant local mill sites include St Ives, Houghton, Brampton and Paxton.

The schematic plan of the Godmanchester site shows the layout of weirs, sluices and channels as they are today although little trace of the mill remains.

Scheme approach

Each of the key elements highlighted on the plan are briefly described below. Photographs show the contrasting scour pools at A and C providing wildlife or amenity interest.

A Three automatic sluices serve to control upstream water levels by lifting in response to increasing flood flows. Lack of a stilling basin within the structure gives rise to a large scour pool downstream.

B The remains of the old mill sluices pass a small flow into a smal scour pool that is formed by the flow of floodwaters over an adjacent high-level weir which is normally dry.

C Two narrow weirs cascade a permanent flow of water into fully developed scour pools that lead into the nearby navigation channel through shallow marshy reedbeds. These are immensely valuable `off river' habitats.

D The navigation lock which can also pass flood waters, downstream of which is a secure landing stage and a quiet backwater in normal conditions.

E Part of the upstream channel that runs between the lock (D) and the old mill site (B) is a wide expanse of water that abuts the main thoroughfare through the old part of the town. It has considerable landscape value and supports a diverse wildfowl population that provides an invaluable introduction to `wildlife' for local children.

The islands of land between the channels are maintained by the Town Council to provide a football pitch and childrens' play area as well as a wildlife refuge. A riverside path leads to the lock and the SSSI floodplain meadow of Port Holme which depends on periodic flooding. The whole area is critical for carrying flood water clear of the town.

Scheme appraisal

The site highlights the potential for diversity of rivers and wildlife habitat associated with weirs and sluices given imagination and foresight whenever such structures are planned.

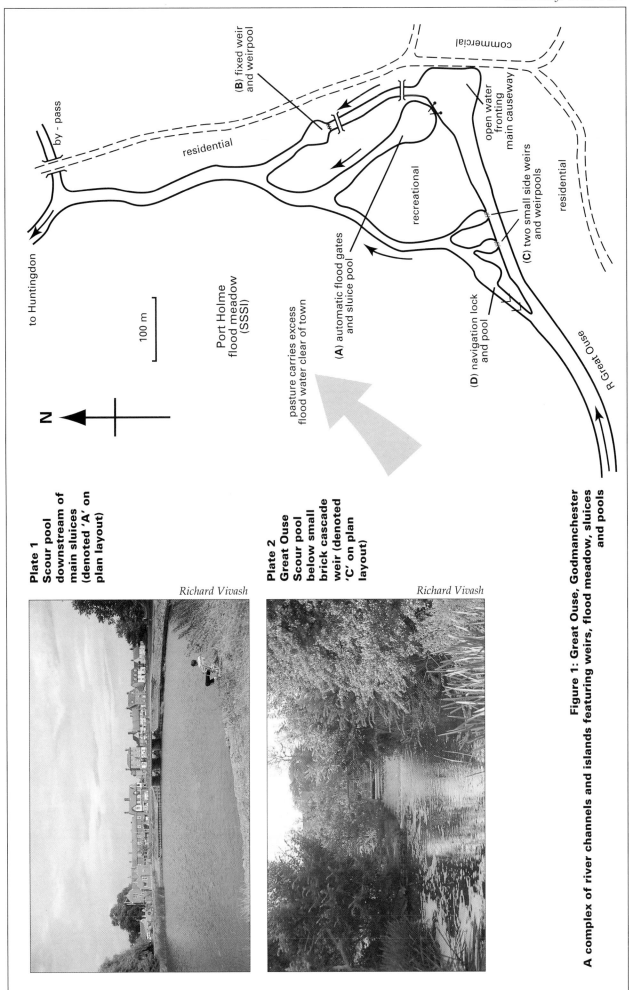

Plate 1
Scour pool
downstream of
main sluices
(denoted 'A' on
plan layout)

Richard Vivash

Plate 2
Great Ouse
Scour pool
below small
brick cascade
weir (denoted
'C' on plan
layout)

Richard Vivash

Figure 1: Great Ouse, Godmanchester
A complex of river channels and islands featuring weirs, flood meadow, sluices
and pools

to Huntingdon

by - pass

residential

100 m

N

Port Holme
flood meadow
(SSSI)

pasture carries excess
flood water clear of town

(B) fixed weir
and weirpool

commercial

open water
fronting
main causeway

recreational

(C) two small side weirs
and weirpools

residential

(A) automatic flood gates
and sluice pool

(D) navigation lock
and pool

R Great Ouse

R Lugg near Leominster

Case Study 3.4 (i)

Welsh Water/NRA Welsh Region

Location:	North-west of Leominster to Kingsland, Herefordshire OS 1:50,000 No 149, Grid Ref SO 4860 to 4561
River type:	Medium energy river through clay and gravel
Size:	*c* 12 m wide
Length affected:	4.5 km
Date:	1978–1980

Techniques/Features:
Drop weirs for flood alleviation and river stabilisation. Works also included regrading (3.2.3) embankments (3.4.2) and willow revetments (3.7.4).

Objectives:
Reduce frequency of flooding over whole floodplain and stabilise an eroding river regime.

Background

This reach of the Lugg was marked by very active meanders resulting in significant loss of farmland annually and inundation of crops during both summer and winter. The resultant sediment load was high leading to siltation at Leominster where conveyance is critical because of the number of properties at risk of flooding. The active regime is largely attributed to the natural adjustments associated with a steep increase in the gradient of the floodplain from 1:600 above the town to 1:2,000 below Leominster

Scheme approach

The scheme concept was to dissipate energy at seven drop weirs, each approximately 1.5 m high and to regrade the riverbed between each. At the upper end three concrete weirs with fish ladders were built and the channel straightened to long sinuous curves in trapezoidal cross sections.

Over the lower section a `soft' approach was used. Four weirs were constructed entirely of rock with relatively flat aprons and only short basins for energy dissipation within the structures. No meanders were removed but the inside of each was reprofiled to a natural shoal to provide material for the construction of embankments set well back from the river (See Case Study 3.4 (b)). Embankments start at each weir and extend upstream with reducing height to follow the design flood levels. Willow was used to revet some exposed banks and assist habitat regeneration.

Scheme appraisal (1993)

The primary aim of reducing flood frequencies have been fully realised over both the upper and lower section described but the environmental value of each stands in marked contrast. In the upper section the channel, banks and weirs remain featureless and the fish ladders are prone to blockage with debris.

The lower section displays major pools below each weir with attendant riffle regime over the immediate, downstream reach. Here, natural processes create and maintain small cliffs and deposit gravels to form the riffles and shoals (although some removal of shoals has been considered necessary). Upstream of the weirs a great habitat variety exists with reed and `withy' beds, marginal wetlands and numerous sheltered backwaters. Wildlife interest is high over the entire lower section and one part has been designated a SSSI; essentially this is because the scheme and its maintenance allows the natural development of habitats.

The capital costs of construction works in the upper and lower sections were similar, with no additional costs attaching to the environmental enhancement achieved. However, the area of land required to engineer the lower section was much greater.

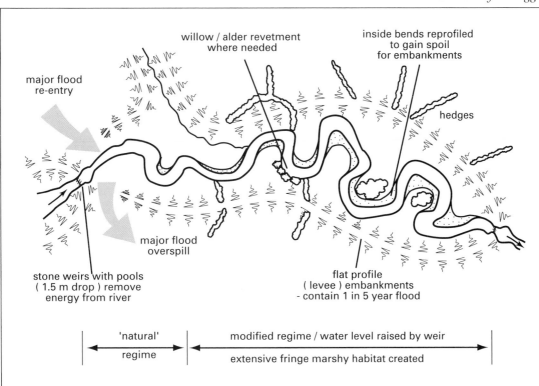

major flood
re-entry

willow / alder revetment
where needed

inside bends reprofiled
to gain spoil
for embankments

hedges

major flood
overspill

stone weirs with pools
(1.5 m drop) remove
energy from river

flat profile
(levee) embankments
- contain 1 in 5 year flood

'natural' regime ←→ modified regime / water level raised by weir

extensive fringe marshy habitat created

note; land drainage via separate arterial drains along edge of flood plain connected
to main river below weirs

**Figure 1: R Lugg, Leominster
Flood alleviation work combined with channel
stabilisation activities**

**Plate 1
R Lugg**
One of four rock weirs built over
the lower reaches of the scheme,
following construction of three
concrete weirs. A scour pool has
been built in and the weir
designed to avoid the need for
fish ladders

Richard Vivash

**Plate 2
The river upstream of a rock weir
showing habitat diversity**

Richard Vivash

Savick Brook

NRA North West Region

Case Study 3.4 (j)

Location:	Highgate Park, Fulwood, Preston, Lancs OS 1:50,000 No 102, Grid Ref SD 5432
River type:	Urban watercourse
Size:	*c* 3 m
Length affected:	1 km
Date:	1991

Techniques/Features:
On-stream flood storage (3.4.6) associated with recreation, amenity and wildlife habitat creation.

Objective:
To reduce peak flood flows through an urban suburb which previously suffered from flooding.

Background

Flooding at Fulwood, an urban suburb of Preston, has been alleviated by damming the Savick Brook at nearby Highgate Park to create a flood storage area. A valuable wildlife park has been developed as part of the scheme.

Scheme approach

The Savick Brook at Highgate lies in an incised valley with a floodplain that is about 80 m wide. This historical washland has been utilised as a flood storage area by damming of the Brook, enabling flood waters to be regulated by a control sluice incorporated into the dam. The temporary lake created during floods extends to nearly a kilometre upstream of the dam. Built in 1991, the dam is constructed of earth and incorporates a hard surface overspill to ensure its stability when flood levels exceed the dam's capacity.

The recreational and wildlife potentials of Highgate Park were examined in relation to the scheme which led to a number of environmental developments, the most notable being the enhancement of a naturally wet corner of floodplain near the dam. This area now incorporates a pond of about 1,000 m² with an island and fringe marshes. Elsewhere the park exhibits deciduous woodland, a shrub layer of bramble and elder as well as a brookside meadow planted with native flowers.

These developments were all promoted by the NRA as part of the Flood Alleviation Scheme. The British Trust for Conservation Volunteers and nearby schools also played an active role, ensuring `ownership' of the park by local children and teenagers from the outset. An ongoing educational study area has also been incorporated.

The plan shows the layout of the newly enhanced Highgate Park as depicted by the Science Department of the nearby William Temple High School staff and pupils. The flood storage zone covers the entire area east of the A6 extending eastward for approximately 1,000 m. The photograph shows Highgate Park in summer 1992.

Scheme Appraisal (1993)

This particular scheme effectively combines the engineering of flood alleviation with wildlife enhancement in the context of an urban environment. In the longer term the engineering of the scheme should ensure that a kilometre length of the river corridor is protected from the ever present pressures for more intensive land use and developments.

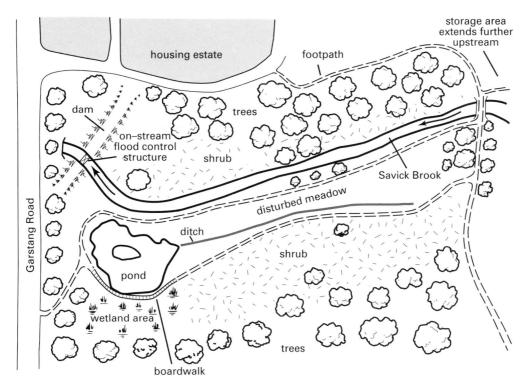

Figure 1: Savick Brook
On-stream flood storage in an urban area

David Porter

Plate 1
The valley of the brook has been dammed
to provide flood storage, and Highgate Park
developed as a wildlife area. Photograph taken
in July 1992, the year following construction of
the dam

Curry Moor

Wessex Water/NRA South-Western Region

Case Study 3.4 (k)

Location:	North of R Tone, North Curry, Nr Taunton, Somerset OS 1:50,000 No 193, Grid Ref ST 3227
River type:	Tidal/fluvial interface
Size:	Embanked river approximately 10 m wide.
Length affected:	600 ha of meadow land including Curry and Hay Moors
Date:	Flood storage established in 14th Century; first pumps installed 1864

Techniques/Features:
Flood Storage (3.4.6)
River management features control of both summer and winter water regimes through the meadowlands.

Objectives:
To ensure efficient operation of the flood storage system in co-existence with sustainable agriculture and wildlife habitat.

Background

The R Tone flows from the hills to the south and west of Taunton to join the R Parrett before flowing north to Bridgwater. Both are embanked to contain high spring tides. Downstream of Taunton flood waters from the R Tone spill onto Curry Moor where the water builds up to depths of 3 m behind a Barrier Bank. The figure shows the layout.

Scheme approach

The overspill of flood waters on to Curry Moor is via a fixed spillway within the banks of the R Tone (see plan). Flood waters stored in Curry Moor may initially discharge back into the Tone by gravity but most is pumped out from close to the Barrier Bank. Up to three weeks' pumping is required after the cessation of overspill to restore the winter regime of water levels in the extensive system of rhynes serving the Moor.

Farming on Curry Moor's 600 ha is centred on grass with some withy plantations that support the local basket trade. Grassland management is generally of low intensity and is dependent on fluctuations in water levels that are maintained in the drainage system. Although generally flat, sufficient relief exists to allow cutting for silage and hay on the `higher' fields, whereas some remain damp all year.

The drainage and surface ditch system is fed with fresh water from a small upland catchment at the western end of the moor but this is heavily supplemented by drawing water from the Tone above the tidal sluice during the drier months. This gives rise to rich plant and animal life in the ditches.

Assessment and potential

The potential exists to raise the environmental value of the Curry Moor flood storage areas further through a small shift in the sensitive regime of water level control towards conditions ideally suited to wildlife habitat

associated with winter wetlands. This cannot be achieved without affecting the viability of the farming enterprises and MAFF has designated the area as an Environmentally Sensitive Area. Working with the NRA and conservation bodies (including the RSPB), the MAFF designation will help realise the full environmental potential of Curry Moor in tandem with its vital role as a flood storage area.

Photographs (June 1992) show land on Curry Moor under the present regime. Similar land on the nearby West Sedgemoor RSPB reserve has been systematically inundated for longer periods over winter and is subject to higher summer retention levels in the drainage Rhynes. The aerial photograph shows Curry Moor in full flood during 1978 when water levels were exceptionally high and overspilled into North Moor via the Barrier Bank.

Richard Vivash

Plate 1: Curry Moor
Some of the lowest land on Curry Moor, subject to low intensity grassland management; recently harvested

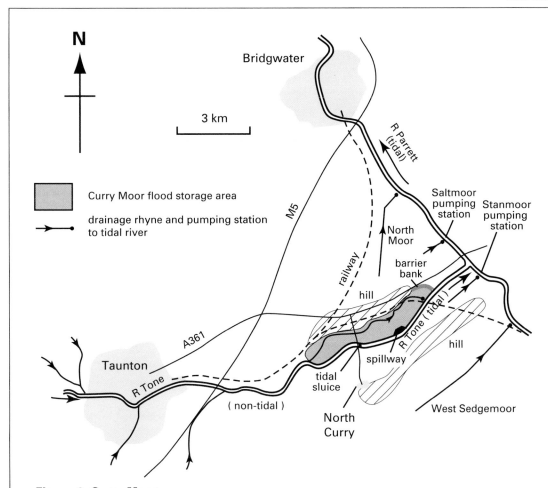

**Figure 1: Curry Moor
Flood storage**

**Plate 2
Aerial view of Curry Moor in flood**

Quoile Pondage

Case Study 3.4 (I)

**Department of Agriculture Northern Ireland
(Watercourse Management Division)**

Location:	North of Downpatrick on Quoile River, Northern Ireland N I Discovery Series No 21, Grid Ref 505 495
River type:	Impounded river behind tidal flood barrier
Size:	7 km long, 80 ha
Length affected:	4.5 km
Date:	Barrier built 1950s – Desilting 1991 – 1992

Techniques/Features:
Flood storage (3.4.6) – desilting of storage basin with minimum disturbance to the substantial waterside habitat that has developed over 40 years.

Objective:
To maintain the flood storage capacity of the pondage and the conveyance of the Quoile River

Background

Prior to building the Quoile Barrier in the 1950s the town of Downpatrick suffered regular inundation from the sea and also from the Quoile River. This occurred when heavy rainfall within the catchment coinciding with high tides. The barrier is situated 4 km downstream of Downpatrick on the Quoile River near its confluence with the sea and comprises 16 tidal flaps, two of which provide passage for fish.

The Quoile River pondage basin upstream of the Barrier is an integral part of the flood defence system for the town which must be periodically desilted to maintain the level of protection to an acceptable standard. The area has since been designated as a National Nature Reserve (carrying out maintenance desilting is therefore a particularly sensitive operation requiring special measures).

The margins locally support species-rich stands of emergent vegetation, including locally scarce species such as flowering-rush. It is also an important site for wintering and breeding wildfowl.

Scheme approach

Desilting work was carried out by long reach dragline so as to retain as much marginal vegetation as possible and was limited to the narrow reaches where conveyance is critical. This was achieved by:

- Working directly from the bank over narrow fringes of vegetation.

- Building temporary access ramps through wide fringes of vegetation, to work in front of it. Spoil was spread back behind the inundation zone, and ramps were removed when works were completed. The diagram shows a typical working arrangement.

Work was executed outside the bird breeding season.

Scheme appraisal

Approximately half of the upper pondage has been desilted, with minimal loss of emergent vegetation and no disturbance to breeding wildfowl. Areas disturbed by the access ramps quickly recovered.

**Plate 1
Quoile Pondage. View of Quoile Pondage, Downpatrick, with extensive marsh vegetation.**

Joe Nicholson

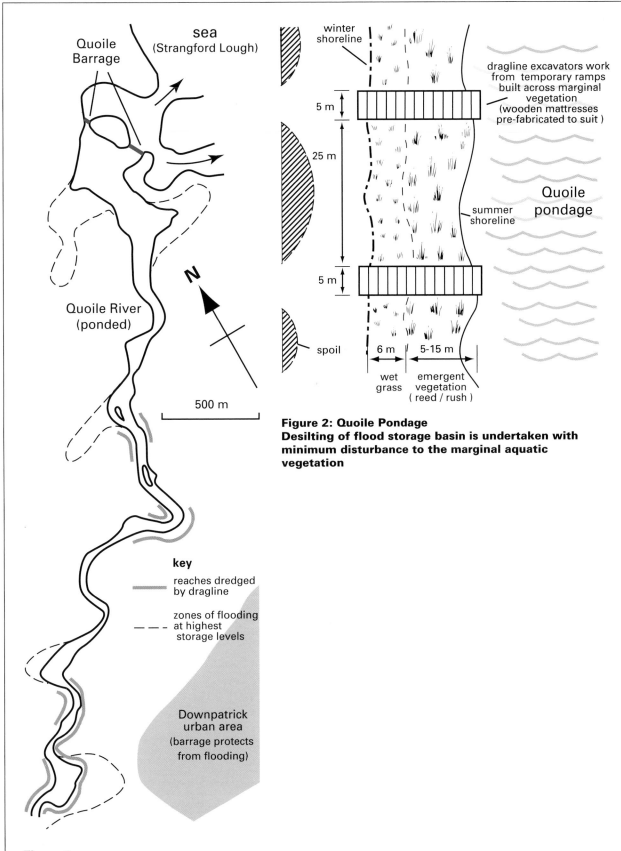

Figure 2: Quoile Pondage
Desilting of flood storage basin is undertaken with minimum disturbance to the marginal aquatic vegetation

Figure 1
Plan of Pondage under normal flow conditions. Dredging operations undertaken without damage to the extensive marginal vegetation

Avon Catchment

Severn Trent Water/NRA Severn-Trent Region

Case Study 3.4(m)

Location:	Upper Avon and Claycoton Brook from Yelvertoft to confluence, Warwickshire OS 1:50,0000 No. 140, Grid Ref SP 153 659
River type:	Clay
Size:	3–10 m width
Length affected:	Upper Avon 9 km Claycoton Brook 3 km
Date:	1987–94

Techniques/Features:
Creation of pools and riffles (3.2.6)
Bays and backwaters (3.3.3)
Wetland rehabilitation (3.4.7)
Planting schemes – trees and shrubs (3.7.5)

Objectives:
Catchment approach to rehabilitation of wildlife interest in tandem with landscape and cultural heritage.

Background

Past land drainage schemes on the Upper Avon and its `main river' tributaries had been effective in creating improved agricultural output but resulted in considerable degradation in wildlife, fisheries, landscape and archaeological interest. A series of enhancements began in the late 1980s which planned to have local benefit, with strategic value to the whole upper catchment.

The Figure shows 10 significant environmental initiatives and the date of their commencement. These were also supported by other projects of a less major nature.

Scheme approach

During the late 1980s opportunities for rehabilitation were assessed on the basis of their benefit locally and how individual schemes would complement and enhance the value of other works being carried out to the Upper Avon. Some of the key enhancement works include the following.

- Planting to increase scrub and taller vegetation by planting up small pockets in meanders and field corners at 2, 5, 7, 8, 9 and 10. This is to combat the overall loss of trees, bankside vegetation and habitat, largely by agricultural practices.

- Habitat creation – riverside marsh and reedbed at 1; restoring original water levels and controls to damp woodland and hazel coppice at 4 (SSSI); rehabilitation of fishery by creating pools and moving gravels at 5; marshy meander and bay at 7, pools at 8 and 9.

- Structures – reinstatement of sluice control to lake and turbine feeding canal at 3.

- Landscape quality – replanting of willows to form riverside pollards at 2 and reinstatement of river corridor landscape generally; enhancement of water landscape features, eg Serpentine Lake at Stanford Hall at 4.

- Recreation – improvement of facilities at Stanford Hall (4) and for disabled, particularly angling at 9 .

Scheme appraisal

The environmental initiatives taken within this Case Study area have been broadly grouped under five headings but in practice, most projects incorporate many aspects. Post-Project Appraisal concluded that the scheme had been very successful, and as a consequence of this individual conservation/enhancement initiatives have to date been evaluated in relation to current policy and environmental practice on an informal, and subsequently, more formal basis. Opportunities for future work have already been identified at 1, 2, 3, 4, 6, 9, and 10.

In reflection of the strategic approach to this enhancement project the identified opportunities will be assessed not on their individual merits on a local scale but considered in relation to catchment needs within the framework of the Avon Catchment Management Plan.

The Case Study demonstrates one of the earliest applications of landscape planning techniques to develop a long-term environmental strategy. This was in the mid-1980s and was similar to that now being developed on an inter-functional basis by the NRA for catchment planning purposes, incorporating a range of disciplines from archaeology to water quality.

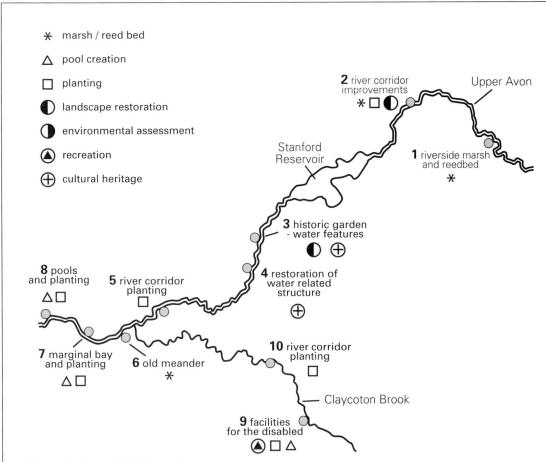

Legend:

✳ marsh / reed bed

△ pool creation

☐ planting

◑ landscape restoration

◐ environmental assessment

▲ recreation

⊕ cultural heritage

2 river corridor improvements ✳ ☐ ◑

Upper Avon

Stanford Reservoir

1 riverside marsh and reedbed ✳

3 historic garden - water features ◑ ⊕

8 pools and planting △ ☐

5 river corridor planting ☐

4 restoration of water related structure ⊕

7 marginal bay and planting △ ☐

6 old meander ✳

10 river corridor planting ☐

Claycoton Brook

9 facilities for the disabled ▲ ☐ △

Figure 1: Avon Catchment
Catchment approach to rehabilitation and restoration

Paul José

Plate 1: Avon Catchment
Restoration of sluice structure

Liz Galloway

Plate 2
Rehabilitation of turbine canal

Winestead Drain

NRA Northumbria and Yorkshire Region

Location:	Winestead Drain in Hull catchment at Patrington, Yorkshire OS 1:50,000 No 107, Grid Ref TA 392 207
River type:	Minimal gradient drain on alluvial silt and sand
Size:	6–8 m wide, banks 2–3 m high
Length affected:	30–60 m lengths
Date:	Continuous from 1988

Techniques/Features:
Rotational weed cutting (3.5.2)

Objective:
Modify previous weed control to save money, retain required conveyance and provide environmental gain through reedbed habitat creation

Background

Winestead Drain is a pumped system which has been heavily maintained in the past. It has an important flood defence function and is popular as a fishery. Common reed and reed canary-grass dominate the margins. The drain demonstrates how to maintain standards of service while providing environmental benefits through a less intensive annual cutting regime.

Scheme approach

The previous annual reed cut from bank to bank has been discontinued in favour of retaining marginal fringes on a rotational basis. Strips 1–2 m wide in 30–60 m lengths are left uncut for one or two years so that rotational cutting allows reed stands to remain to provide cover.

Scheme appraisal

The reduction in cutting has lowered management costs but not compromised the required conveyance of the channel. Risk of debris being caught in the channel or choking the screens to the pumps has not been increased. Emergent stands of reed have increased winter cover and provided new spring habitat used by nesting warblers.

The less intensive management of reed on the Winestead Drain has provided direct benefits for wildlife on the Drain itself and other similar local watercourses. It is now the preferred management prescription which, where possible, aims to integrate the needs of flood defence, land drainage, wildlife conservation, fisheries and visual aesthetics.

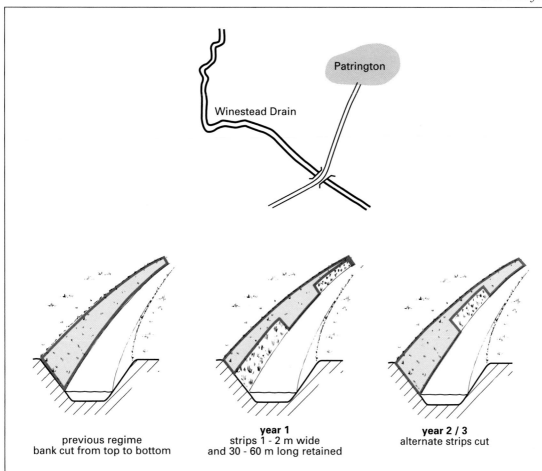

previous regime
bank cut from top to bottom

year 1
strips 1 - 2 m wide
and 30 - 60 m long retained

year 2 / 3
alternate strips cut

**Figure 1: Winestead Drain
Rotational weed cutting**

Ford Brook
Walsall Borough Council

Case Study 3.5 (c)

Location:	Walsall to Rushall in R Tame catchment north of Birmingham OS 1:50,000 No. 139, Grid Ref SK 0200
River type:	Urban and semi-rural river with pebble/gravel bed and local silt and clay
Size:	3–5 m bed width with design capacity of *c* 22 m^{3}s^{-1}
Length affected:	2 km
Date:	Scheme completed 1986, vegetation planted 1987

Techniques/Features:
River diversion (3.4.3)
planted with wetland vegetation.
Concrete troughs in deepened channel (3.2.3)
planted with marginal plants (3.5.3)

Objective:
Achieve design standard for urban flood alleviation scheme while creating marginal wetlands in a by-pass channel. Habitat creation for natural plant regeneration and initial planting were key elements of the scheme. Illustrate that even in constrained situations some vegetation establishment can be accommodated

Scheme approach

The capital flood alleviation scheme (see Case Study 3.1 (a)) incorporated a new by-pass channel, which featured a low-flow channel (confined by elm boarding) and extensive wetland habitats which function as a second-stage channel as flow volumes increase. The second-stage channels were created at around 15–25 cm above the low-flow water level and planted with a variety of wetland plants by the Urban Wildlife Group (UWG). The planting of vegetation on the berm was to help initial stabilisation of the soils so that the habitat could be colonised naturally by the rich array of species identified from within the catchment by the UWG in pre-scheme river corridor surveys. On the berms were planted yellow flag, soft rush, common reed, branched bur-reed, purple-loosestrife, water-mint, meadowsweet, kingcup and ragged-robin.

Under Station Road, Ford Brook had to be lowered by 2 m and constraints of space precluded any widening of the river for habitat enhancement. Even though a vertical sided concrete channel had to be built the design incorporated a low-flow channel and a marginal trough on the inside of the meander which was planted with vegetation. The ledge is less than 20 cm above the low-flow water level and so remains moist at all times. Soft rush, reed canary-grass, branched bur-reed and yellow flag were planted.

Scheme appraisal

After six years, the establishment of planted vegetation and natural colonisation has exceeded all expectations. The only planted species which did not thrive was common reed; this species is notorious for poor establishment unless all factors are right. The low-flow channel has been maintained and the vegetation on the berm has not become over-rank due to low intensity horse grazing. From spring through to summer the wet ledges turn yellow through a succession of kingcup, yellow flag and great yellow-cress. Interspersed with these species are water forget-me-not, water stitchwort, water-cress, fool's water-cress, brooklime, reedmace and many other wetland species which have colonised naturally because the habitat created has a high water table but is not water-logged. In winter the stands of reed sweet-grass provide edge habitat and winter-green food for animals. Even in the linear trough created in the concrete-lined section the majority of the cited species thrive and form a vegetated habitat throughout the year. In spring 1993 water voles bred on the ledge amongst dense vegetation given additional protection by surface flood debris.

Initially some slight scour at the beginning and end of the ledges occurred in response to increased velocities; however this problem was not evident in 1993 because the vegetation had become so established that it bound the soil effectively and precluded this happening. The same problem initially occurred at the top end of the `trough' but this too stabilised over the first two years.

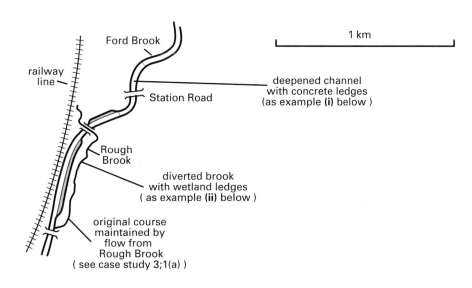

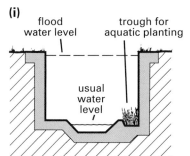

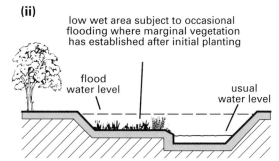

(i) flood water level   trough for aquatic planting

usual water level

(ii) low wet area subject to occasional flooding where marginal vegetation has established after initial planting

flood water level   usual water level

**Figure 1: Ford Brook
(i) Planting of concrete ledges with marginal vegetation;
(ii) Planting of wetland feature.**

**Plate 1: Ford Brook
Planting of concrete ledge with marginal vegetation**

Chris Gomersall

**Plate 2
Planting of wetland feature**

Chris Gomersall

R Thames
at Wolvercote

Case Study 3.5 (d)

Thames Water/NRA Thames Region

Location:	Wolvercote near Oxford, Oxfordshire OS 1:50,000 No 164, Grid Ref SU 480101
River type:	Navigable Thames with silt substrate
Size:	20 m width; 5–2 m deep
Length affected:	80 m
Date:	1986

Techniques/Features:
Protecting a section of bank and open water from boat-wash, using a boom(3.5.3)

Objective:
Habitat enhancement through encouraging the development of marginal vegetation

Background

The banks in the middle reaches of the R Thames are extensively affected by boat wash. This led to a reduction in marginal reedbeds and associated habitat loss. An experimental attempt was made to redress this by encouraging the development of marginal flora in a wide bay on the Thames at Wolvercote.

Scheme approach

A floating boom was installed across the bay and aquatic and marginal vegetation was planted within the protected area. The boom was constructed from sections of capped PVC 200 mm diameter plastic pipes shackled together and attached to galvanised posts driven into the riverbed. The 80 m long boom protected a substantially longer length of riverbank and aquatic river habitat. The planting was designed to complement and extend the existing narrow (1 m wide) marginal fringe of reed sweet-grass and reed canary-grass. Branched bur-reed was transferred with some soil in plastic sacks from a nearby dredging site and heeled into shallow water (0-300 mm deep). Yellow water-lily was transferred from the R Mole during a flood alleviation scheme and dropped into the silt in weighted gabion baskets.

Scheme appraisal (1993)

The results of the experiment showed:

- Bur-reed took very successfully initially but during subsequent years erosion caused by eddying within the river reduced this growth at the downstream end of the section.

- The water-lilies failed to become established. This could have been a result of the depth of soft silt or inadequate weighting of the large plants which may have been carried away as river flows increased.

- Within the major part of the boom protected area, the indigenous marginal vegetation spread extensively outwards from the bank and within three growing seasons a marginal fringe of 3-5 m had been established. Beyond this, clumps of self-seeded branched bur-reed and flowering-rush appeared.

In 1991, it was considered that the marginal fringe was sufficiently extensive to be self supporting. As originally planned, the boom was removed for use at another location. Two years later, with no boom protection, the established vegetation has declined slightly from when the boom was in place. Lack of recent cattle poaching at the downstream end has resulted in a rich new fringe of reeds developing here.

Plate 1: R Thames at Wolvercote
Floating boom and planting of vegetation

Alistair Driver

Plate 2
Established vegetation behind boom

Alistair Driver

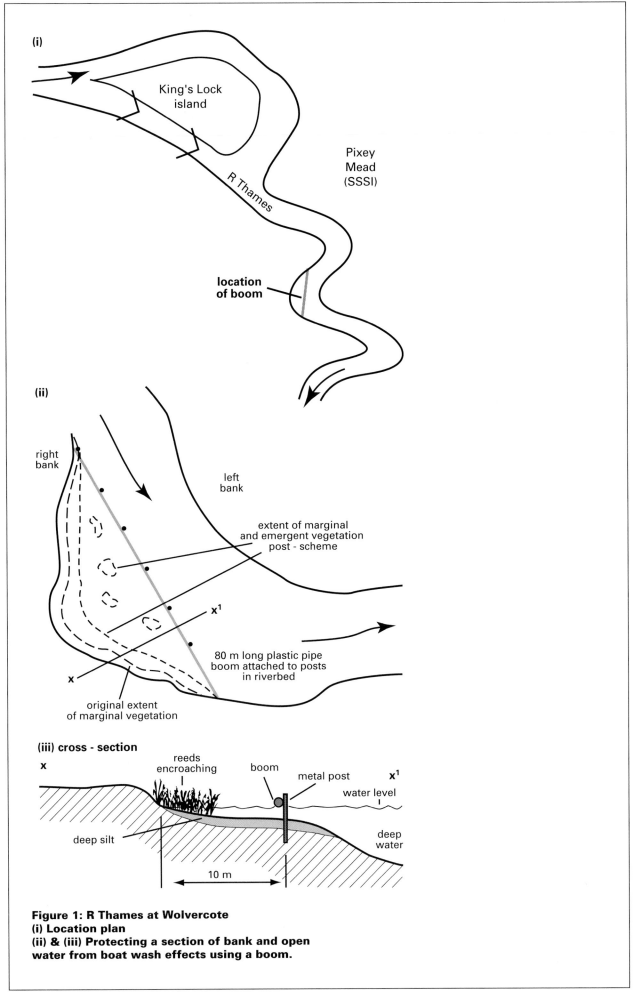

(i)

King's Lock island

R Thames

Pixey Mead (SSSI)

location of boom

(ii)

right bank

left bank

extent of marginal and emergent vegetation post - scheme

x¹

80 m long plastic pipe boom attached to posts in riverbed

x

original extent of marginal vegetation

(iii) cross - section

x

reeds encroaching

boom

metal post

x¹

water level

deep silt

deep water

10 m

Figure 1: R Thames at Wolvercote
(i) Location plan
(ii) & (iii) Protecting a section of bank and open water from boat wash effects using a boom.

R Ock at Stanford Mill

Thames Water/NRA Thames Region

Location:	R Ock at Stanford-in-the-Vale, Oxon OS 1:50,000 Grid Ref SU 343927
River type:	Clay river with natural gravels exposed.
Size:	2–3 m bed width with variable depths from 0.2–1.5m
Length affected:	100 m
Date:	1987

Techniques/Features:
Two-stage channel (3.3.4) and marginal planting (3.5.3)

Objective:
To provide suitable habitats for wetland plants to colonise the exposed bank of a two-stage channel created during flood alleviation works.

Background

Channel enlargement works were required on the R Ock by-pass channel at Stanford Mill and presented an opportunity to create in-channel and bankside habitat diversity. Because the flora and fauna of the river was known to be rich in other parts of the Ock, a decision was made that extensive planting of the newly created habitats would not be worthwhile. Instead it was decided to allow the majority of these to establish naturally, with only some initial planting.

Scheme approach

Enlargement works deliberately created a two-stage channel with a berm approximately 50 mm above mean water level. The design was for inundation to be frequent. The British Trust for Conservation Volunteers carried out limited hand planting on the edge of the bare berm immediately after completion of the engineering work in May 1987. Various common marginal species were planted, including branched bur-reed and water plantain to provide an immediate 5% vegetation coverage which would help to entrap shoots, roots and seeds carried down by rising river flows.

Scheme appraisal (1993)

- By September of the first year (four months) the berm had a 90% coverage of marginal vegetation dominated by branched bur-reed but also numerous other species including water-cress and water forget-me-not.

- The rapid cover which developed in the first summer came primarily from seeds and root fragments swept down from densely colonised margins upstream.

- The extent of deposition of seeds, roots and other material on the muddy shelf, which led to such a rapid colonisation, suggests that the initial planting effort was unnecessary. Where ample material is available from upstream, such planting is no longer executed on similar schemes because of the lessons learned.

- After six years the shelf has developed a stable community which looks natural and has created a new and valued habitat structure, used by river animals too.

- Shading by adjacent trees has reduced some vegetation but comfrey, teasel, purple-loosestrife and other species have developed well.

- The landowner is delighted by the improved wildlife and aesthetic aspects of the channel and the two-stage channel is maintenance-free with a retained design capacity.

**Plate 1: R Ock at Stanford in the Vale
Habitat creation in progress; December 1986**

Alistair Driver

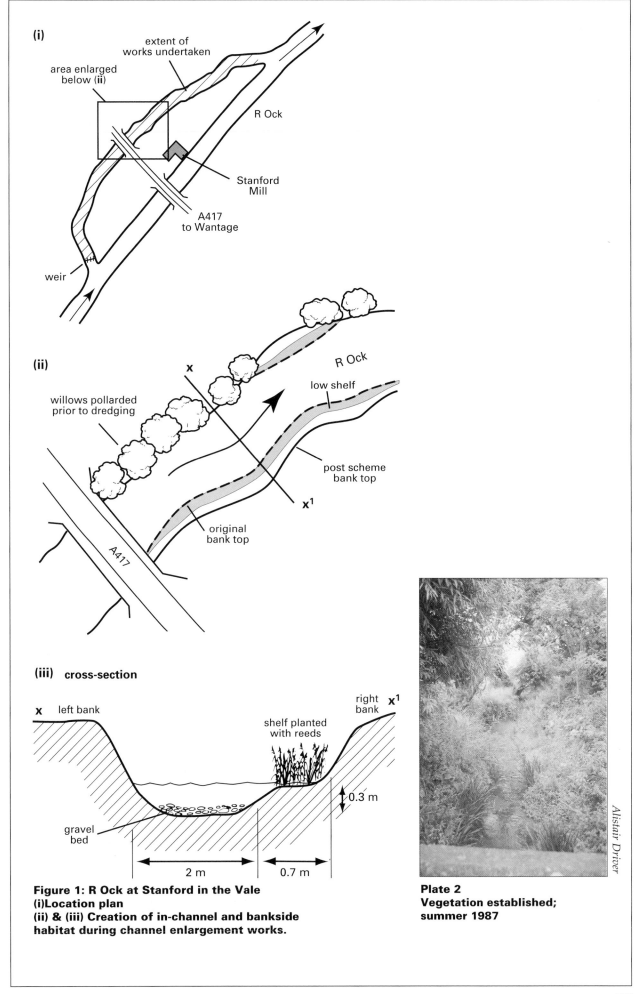

(i)

extent of
works undertaken

area enlarged
below **(ii)**

R Ock

Stanford
Mill

A417
to Wantage

weir

(ii)

willows pollarded
prior to dredging

R Ock

low shelf

post scheme
bank top

original
bank top

A417

x

x¹

(iii) cross-section

x left bank

right
bank x¹

shelf planted
with reeds

0.3 m

gravel
bed

2 m

0.7 m

**Figure 1: R Ock at Stanford in the Vale
(i)Location plan
(ii) & (iii) Creation of in-channel and bankside
habitat during channel enlargement works.**

**Plate 2
Vegetation established;
summer 1987**

Alistair Driver

R Stort Navigation
Research Project

Case Study 3.5 (f)

Location:	Stort at Bishops Stortford, Hertfordshire OS 1:50,000 No 167, Grid Ref TL 490 212 – TL 494 192
River type:	Slow channelised river on clay
Size:	10–15 m width; bed 1.5–2.5 m below water level
Length affected:	150 m of bank along 3.3 km of river works
Date:	1980

Techniques/Features:
Creation of shallow water berms (3.3.2) and transplantation of marginal river plants (3.5.3)

Objectives:
Assess the re-establishment of marginal plant species from transplanted material on reprofiled banks following river channel excavation

Background

Between 1978 and 1980 the R Stort Navigation was subject to a capital flood alleviation scheme. The scheme included deepening and widening the channel. These works removed wide fringes of marginal vegetation. A research studentship with University College London enabled the re-establishment of vegetation to be studied.

Scheme approach

During the scheme experimental enhancement works included the construction of shallow-water berms which were planted with marginal species using a range of propagative materials.

The established cross-section of the navigation channel consisted of steep banks above the water level and a shallow shelf sloping to a silt channel bed. The new berms (150 m in total), were constructed to re-create the removed shelf. The berms were divided into plots and each planted with a single marginal species. Twelve species were selected for trial, some previously found along the channel margins, others occurring in adjacent wetlands, ditches and slow-flowing waters.

Most species were transplanted using small clumps of rhizome and shoot material or young individual plants. Propagation by shoot cuttings was also trialled. All were planted at the water's edge and at a depth of about 0.25 m, depending on the depth in which the species were generally observed. Planting was carried out in 1980 at the onset of the growing season of each species, covering a period from March to May.

Scheme appraisal

The shallow-water berms did not fully replicate the original channel conditions because they had a clay substrate lacking an established silt cover, were subject to subsidence as the channel stabilised and initially were open to wave wash from boat traffic. The more steeply graded banks also resulted in tall herbaceous vegetation developing above the berms, which subsequently collapsed and smothered plants at the water's edge. Allowance is therefore needed for these factors and so a wider berm with a very gentle slope is required.

Initially most planted species performed well across the range of propagation techniques. (See table). Only common reed had a poor survival rate (30–40%), and many species had no losses. By the second summer colonisation (measured as the length of berm occupied by shoots) had increased from 20–50% for most species. Greater pond-sedge and bulrush showed the greatest rate of colonisation from their ability to produce long underground rhizomes. Tussock forming species such as hard rush spread less effectively.

Many species were grazed by waterfowl and water voles and this probably weakened colonisation, but did not affect survival in the early years. The most susceptible species were common reed, reed sweet-grass and yellow iris.

After 13 years nearly half the species had entirely died out and two others survived only as small clumps in their original plots. Those species originally widespread along the navigation tended to perform best. Sweet flag was the only species that had not originally been widely present along the navigation to now occur abundantly within a plot. Outside the specially created berms little marginal vegetation had re-established save for a few small stands confined to the bank edge.

The study demonstrates the long-term advantage of planting primarily with species found along the river in similar habitats to those created. It also shows that steep channel excavations can result in the elimination of marginal vegetation, with no natural recolonisation if the original habitats are not re-created.

Table 1: Establishment of marginal plant species in declining order of performance

PLANTS (AND LOCAL STATUS) (see notes below)		PLANTING MATERIAL	COMMENTS ON BERM COLONISATION (i) in 2nd summer (ii) in 13th summer
Greater pond-sedge	(A)	Rhizome and shoot clumps	(i) No losses; near complete colonisation (ii) Complete colonisation
		Shoot cuttings	(i) No losses; 86% colonisation (ii) 80% colonised.
Lesser pond-sedge	(A)	Rhizome and shoot clumps	(i) No losses; 70% colonised (ii) Complete colonisation and localised branched bur-reed
		Shoot cuttings	(i) 80% survival; 67% colonised (ii) Complete colonisation with lesser and greater pond-sedges
Sweet flag	(C)	Rhizome and shoot clumps	(i) No losses; 56% colonised (ii) 80% colonised and widespread bulrush
Bulrush	(B)	Rhizome and shoot clumps	(i) 90% survival; 91% colonised (ii) Widespread within complete colonisation by greater pond-sedge and localised lesser pond-sedge
Common club-rush	(C)	Rhizome and shoot clumps	(i) No losses; 40% colonised (ii) 40% colonised and very locally branched bur-reed
Yellow iris	(B)	Rhizome and shoot clumps	(i) No losses; 51% colonised (ii) Localised within complete colonisation by greater pond-sedge
Branched bur-reed	(A)	Rhizome and shoot clumps	(i) 90% survival; 42% colonised (ii) Very localised within near complete colonisation by greater pond-sedge.
Galingale	(C)	Shoot cuttings	(i) No losses; 71% colonised (ii) Failed; no colonisation
Hard rush	(B)	2-year-old plants	(i) No losses; 37% colonised (ii) Failed; no colonisation
Reed canary-grass	(B)	2-year-old plants	(i) 80% survival; 40% colonised (ii) Failed; complete colonisation by greater pond-sedge
Reed sweet-grass	(B)	Rhizome and shoot clumps	(i) 70% survival; 70% colonised. (ii) Failed; no colonisation
Common reed	(B)	Rhizome and shoot clumps	(i) 30% survival; 11% colonised (ii) Failed; no colonisation
		Shoot cuttings	(i) 40% survived; 13% colonised (ii) Failed; 90% colonised by branched bur-reed

NOTES:
(A)   Species originally widespread along navigation channel
(B)   Species occurring in adjacent wetlands/ditches
(C)   Species from slow waters elsewhere in area

Footnote: Research undertaken by Douglas Kite (EN Dorset) at University College London

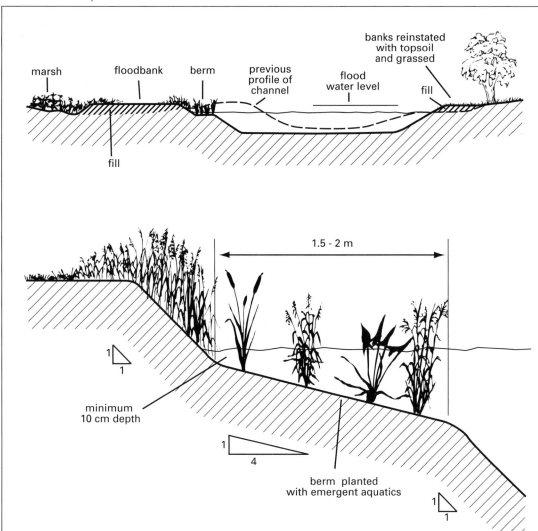

Figure 1: R Stort, Bishops Stortford: Creation of shallow water berms
(i) Typical cross-section in bermed reach.
(ii) R Stort showing the berm on the left, with well-established emergent aquatic
plants. In contrast, the far bank graded 1 in 1.5, with almost no emergents.
Source: Lewis and Williams (1984)

Plate 1
Shallow water berm recently planted with vegetation; 1980

Plate 2
Established vegetation

R Wandle
Thames Water/NRA Thames Region

Case Study 3.5 (g)

Location:	R Wandle at Carshalton, South London OS 1:50,000 No 176 Grid Ref TQ 284 655
River type:	Urban catchment, clay with substrates of silt and ballast
Size:	*c* 15 m width, 1–2 m depth
Length affected:	65 m
Date:	1988

Techniques/Features:
Channel dredging to create shelf (3.3.4) into which reeds were planted to screen piling (3.5.3)

Objectives:
Screen sheet piling with vegetation and provide a semi-natural toe habitat to the bank; minimal wildlife habitat was available..

Background

The branch of the R Wandle requiring maintenance dredging is subject to heavy accumulation of silt and urban debris because of a weir, a short distance downstream. The reach is flanked on the left bank by Wilderness Island, a London Wildlife Trust nature reserve, and on the right bank by an industrial estate with a river frontage of steel-piled hard standing. In view of the ugly appearance of the right bank, and the extreme contrast which it provided with the left, a scheme proposed a shelf alongside the piled bank to enable vegetation to be established for screening purposes.

Scheme approach

Dredging was undertaken from within the channel since the reach could be de-watered by utilising the sluice. A shelf was constructed by installing a 65 m length of Nicospan geotextile, supported by galvanised scaffold poles, at a distance of approximately 2 m from the riverbank. The area between the Nicospan and the steel piling was then backfilled using a combination of firm silt and ballast dredged from the silted channel. The Nicospan was installed up to a height of only 150 mm above mean water level to create damp substrates for wetland plants. In the autumn large quantities of emergent vegetation were transferred by hand from Wilderness Island, which required management, by London Wildlife Trust volunteers. Three species; yellow flag (60%), sedge (30%) and reedmace (10%) were planted. All were dug manually and planted into the soft mud surface of the new terrace.

Scheme appraisal (1993)

Within two years the terrace had developed to such an extent that the flourishing reed mace and yellow flag were screening much of the unsightly piling; nesting moorhens were also present. After five years, habitat and screening has developed still further. The piling is totally screened, and colonisation by other plants such as gipsywort and purple-loosestrife has taken place. The poles and Nicospan are no longer visible. The shelf neither helps nor hinders flood defence needs as it is located on a retained reach above a weir.

Screening a limited section of unattractive bank may appear extravagant, however the cost, at only £2,000, was accommodated within the maintenance dredging budget because there was a saving on off-site removal of dredged silt.

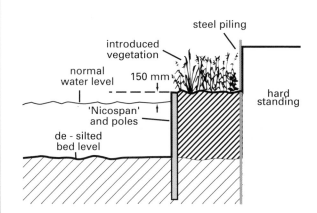

Figure 1
River Wandle: Screening of sheet piling using vegetation.

Alistair Driver

Plate 1
Channel dredgings used to provide material for shelf creation.

Alistair Driver

Plate 2
Vegetation successfully established after planting of artificial shelf.

R Loddon and R Blackwater Catchments

Case Study 3.5 (h)

Thames Water contract to an environmental consultant

Location:	5 sites in the lower reaches of the R Loddon catchment and extending 4 km up the R Blackwater/R Whitewater, Surrey/Hants OS 1:50,000 No 175 Grid Ref SU 7463
River type:	Clay rivers, both with considerable gravel substrates with Blackwater receiving heavy urban run-off and the Loddon with good groundwater base-flow.
Size:	Sites were 8–15 m wide with depth varying from 0.5–1.5 m
Length affected:	6 sites <50 m long
Date:	1987/88

Techniques/Features:
Transplanting a single rare species in new sites using a variety of methods and into a range of substrates (3.5.3)

Objectives:
Determine if Loddon pondweed could be successfully translocated from one site to another and document success and failure so that future efforts could be refined and improved upon.

Background

Loddon pondweed is rare in Britain, being present in just a handful of rivers such as the R Thames, R Loddon, Bristol Avon and Dorset Stour. The primary aim of the study was to see how feasible it was to remove this rare plant from a threatened site and locate it in more protected areas. An additional objective of the study, to spread the species within the catchment in which it has a stronghold, was deemed worthwhile in its own right.

Scheme approach

Subterranean turions and living shoots were taken from a donor site on the R Loddon in June and stored in water tanks over winter. Plants were transplanted by hand to five new sites in the R Loddon catchment in June the following year. In addition to planting vegetative material that had been stored for a season, some plants were also translocated from the donor to the recipient sites on the same day.

A variety of planting methods were experimented with, in a variety of substrates and at contrasting water depths and velocities. Planting in clay was carried out by digging a narrow V with a spade into which plants were firmly heeled in. Planting on coarse gravel was carried out by excavating a trench with a heavy duty fork. A third method involved plants being tied to bricks to weigh them down to the substrate.

Regular observations were made each month in the first year. Assessments were also made and reported to the NRA Thames Region during 1989 and 1990.

Scheme appraisal (1993)

At most sites the transplants established rapidly and most spread widely from their initial planted areas. From the study, various conclusions were drawn, including the following:-

- Loddon pondweed can be removed from a river, stored and replanted successfully in a suitable location.

- The type of substrate into which the material is planted is usually not as critical as other factors which influence the overall suitability of the site (eg physical disturbance, competition with other plants, grazing by swans).

- Generally, clay mixed with fine gravel proved to be the most suitable substrate and coarse pebbles and gravel were totally unsuitable.

- Depth of water was not critical with success achieved over the range 0.2 m–1.25 m.

- The method of planting did not greatly affect success but of all methods heeling into the bed worked best.

- On the R Blackwater, a tributary with no previous Lodden pondweed present, plants spread to compete with other aquatics and now cover >100 m^2.

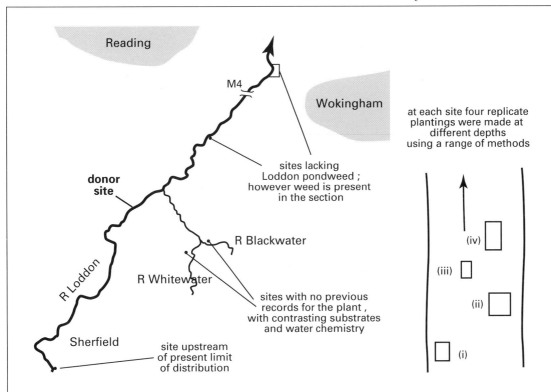

Reading

M4

Wokingham

at each site four replicate
plantings were made at
different depths
using a range of methods

**donor
site**

sites lacking
Loddon pondweed ;
however weed is present
in the section

R Blackwater

R Loddon

R Whitewater

sites with no previous
records for the plant ,
with contrasting substrates
and water chemistry

(iv)

(iii)

(ii)

(i)

Sherfield

site upstream
of present limit
of distribution

**Figure 1
R Loddon and Blackwater catchments. Transplanting Loddon pondweed into new
sites.**

Nigel Holmes

**Plate 1
Plant material tied to bricks to
weigh them down to the
substrate.**

Nigel Holmes

**Plate 2
Successful establishment of
Loddon pondweed on the
R Blackwater.**

R Thames at Clifton Hampden

Case Study 3.5 (i)

Thames Water/NRA Thames Region

Location:	R Thames at Clifton Hampden, Oxon. OS 1:50,000 No. 164 Grid Ref SU 546947
River type:	Navigable river, mixed geology with silt and ballast bed.
Size:	>15 m wide; 1–2 m depth
Length affected:	50 m
Date:	1988

Techniques/Features:
Planting behind `Nicospan' (3.4.4/3.5)
`Nicobags' with reeds (3.5.3)
utilising Nicobags to create a protected underwater ledge (3.4.4)
to encourage natural regeneration

Objective:
Protect a riverside towpath utilising reeds `Nicospan' and `Nicobags'.

Background

Immediately downstream of Clifton Hampden Lock on the R Thames, in the lock cut itself, the channel is relatively narrow and deeply incised. As a result, the banks are liable to undercutting and slippage with resultant impact on towpath safety.

Scheme approach

Bank repair and long-term protection works were carried out using a combination of geotextile and emergent planting. Nicospan was used to retain the bank, with planting inside Nicobags. These large (2.0 m x 1.0 m x 0.5 m deep) non-degradable fabric bags were filled with a mixture of silt and ballast dredged from the adjacent bed of the R Thames and placed at the foot of the vertical bank to provide toe protection. Three 25 mm incisions were made in the upper surface of the bags and rhizomes of common reed, reed mace and greater pond-sedge planted by hand into each of the incisions and firmly heeled down.

Scheme appraisal (1993)

Since 1988, growth of the planted vegetation within the Nicobags has been successful, but it has been unexpectedly overshadowed by the extensive spread of reed along the Nicobag-protected underwater shelf.

The stability of the substrate resulting from the presence of the Nicobags has enabled the reed to spread from a sparse stand approximately 15 m long and 0.5 m wide to a dense stand almost 30 m long and 1.5 m wide. Sedge and reed warblers now breed in the continuous bed of reeds. Much of this reedbed had developed from the natural spread of rhizomes and shooting has taken place around the margins of the bags. Some growth has occurred through the bagwork itself but this has been limited. The growth in front of the bags, combined with the growth of the planted reed mace, provides total vegetation cover at the water's edge.

Some bags are exposed above water level and the reedmace and pond-sedge has been supplemented by natural establishment of water-mint, great willowherb and purple-loosestrife. These bags initially provided ideal `fishing platforms' for anglers, and trampling and physical uprooting delayed complete cover by reeds and other bank vegetation.

Now the reeds are so well established that they completely screen the Nicospan, and accrete river sediments as they continue to spread as a fringe along the river.

Plate 1
Manoeuvring Nicobags

Alistair Driver

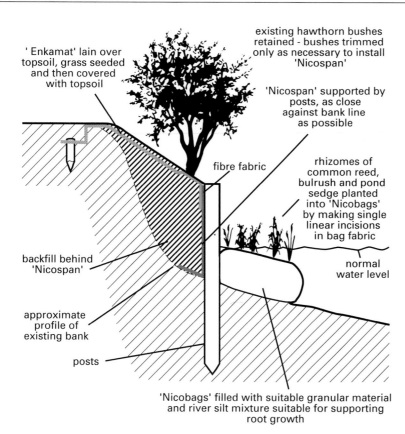

'Enkamat' lain over topsoil, grass seeded and then covered with topsoil

existing hawthorn bushes retained - bushes trimmed only as necessary to install 'Nicospan'

'Nicospan' supported by posts, as close against bank line as possible

fibre fabric

rhizomes of common reed, bulrush and pond sedge planted into 'Nicobags' by making single linear incisions in bag fabric

normal water level

backfill behind 'Nicospan'

approximate profile of existing bank

posts

'Nicobags' filled with suitable granular material and river silt mixture suitable for supporting root growth

Figure 1
R Thames at Clifton Hampden. Planting in association with Nicospan/Nicobags.

Plate 2
Nicobags in place

Plate 3
Vegetation established

Alistair Driver

Alistair Driver

R Pinn

Thames Water/NRA Thames Region

Location:	R Pinn at Eastcote, Ruislip, West London OS 1:50,000 No 176, Grid Ref TQ 105387
River type:	Urban watercourse with silt and ballast bed 4 m wide deepened channel
Length affected:	50 m
Date:	1988

Techniques/Features:
Planting on a ledge (3.5.3)
to create a screen to piling, wildlife habitat and outfall effluent filter

Objective:
Marginal shelf creation as part of a channel enlargement scheme.

Background

To reduce flooding and erosion a series of flood alleviation works were executed in the 1980s. They included channel realignment and bank protection works in the section through Eastcote, during 1988.

Scheme approach

At one point where the channel runs immediately alongside a main road, channel widening and deepening was required in addition to toe protection for the concrete retaining wall for the road. Steel piling was required for strength and stability but it was set 1.5 m out in the channel to enable the creation of a strip of marginal vegetation to serve the following purposes.

- Soften the ugly nature of the retaining wall.

- Provide habitat of local importance for plants and invertebrates.

- Act as a seed source for other suitable marginal areas downstream.

- Be a `natural' filter for run-off discharging from several land drains set in the retaining wall. (No attempt was made to calculate required volumes of filtration material).

The spoil used for the planting was dominated by greater pond-sedge, but it also contained several other common wetland species including great willowherb and water-mint. Pond-sedge was chosen because its roots form a dense mat which tolerates inundation under storm-flow conditions. This sedge-rich spoil was spread in a layer 225 mm thick on top of a net of Wyretex which was folded over the top of the shelf and pinned down. This type of geotextile is a tough woven mesh of polypropylene and wire fabric designed to provide long-lasting protection for vegetated banks.

Scheme appraisal (1993)

The growth of plants on the regularly inundated shelf has been extremely good with a variety of plant communities developing on the shelf. At the upstream end, away from land drains, Himalayan balsam and nettle have spread. Where shaded, by trees, the locally common, shade-tolerant pendulous sedge has naturally colonised; where less shaded, yellow flag, purple-loosestrife, tufted hair-grass and reed canary-grass are present. In the central sections alongside the land drains the shelf is dominated by the luxuriant growths of wetland plants. The truly aquatic flora of the river has also benefited from the creation of this strip; water-crowfoot and starwort now grow alongside the previously recorded curled pondweed and Nuttall's pondweed, in a self-cleansing channel. When viewed from the road the piling is obscured totally by vegetation and the wire is buried by silt and matted shoots. The vegetated shelf appears to be serving a useful purpose as a 'biological filter' for run-off issuing from the land drains.

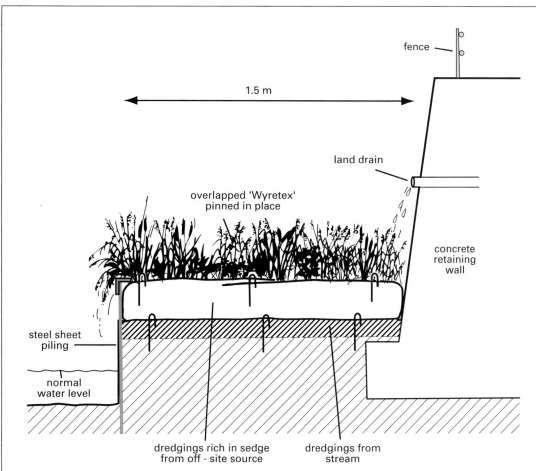

fence

1.5 m

land drain

**overlapped 'Wyretex'
pinned in place**

**concrete
retaining
wall**

**steel sheet
piling**

**normal
water level**

**dredgings rich in sedge
from off - site source**

**dredgings from
stream**

**Figure 1
R Pinn, Eastcote. Planting to screen sheet piling**

Alistair Driver

**Plate 1
Work in progress**

Alistair Driver

**Plate 2
Vegetation established on ledge**

363

R Leach
Research Project

Case Study 3.5 (k)

Location: Eastington, Northleach in the
Cotswolds, Gloucestershire
OS 1:50,000 No 163
Grid Ref SP 128 132

River type: Limestone

Size: 2 m bed width, 40 cm depth

Length affected: 1 km

Date: 1988

Techniques/Features:
Buffer zone for nutrient retention (3.5.3)

Objectives:
To evaluate the success of buffer zones by establishing the nutrient retention characteristics of a) a 17-year-old grass sward buffer zone (*Lolium perenne L.*), b) an 18-year-old poplar buffer zone (*Populus italica*)

Background

The R Leach is a headwater tributary of the R Thames. In 1970 near-saturated non-agricultural land adjacent to the river was planted with perennial grass and poplar trees to provide cover in the river valley. The site was never drained, either with ditches or tile drains. The site when planted was not envisaged as a buffer zone but exhibits the characteristics of a well-established nutrient buffer.

Previous research in USA, New Zealand and France suggested that buffer zones reduce agriculturally derived nitrate prior to the run-off entering the river environment.

The project, utilising the established buffer zone, primarily sought to evaluate how much nitrate was retained in the strips adjacent to the river.

Research approach

In 1988 sections of the flood plain (16–25 m wide) were monitored (network of piezometers and water samplers) to determine the shallow groundwater chemistry of the site. Monitoring focused on the winter period, but sampling was for 18 months. All water flowing through the site from agricultural land was via sub-surface routes. There was no overload flow.

Results and recommendations

Essentially, all nitrate was retained in the buffer strips. The grass site was 85% efficient and the poplar site 99% efficient. Hence negligible proportions of the original loading reached the river, irrespective of season, flow velocity or air temperature.

It is recommended from the study that if buffer zones are engineered the following should be considered as possible guidelines.

- Small ditches and streams are a priority to be buffered because collectively they influence the river water quality of the whole catchment.

- Width – For every 1 m of stream width there should be 10 m of buffer zone up to a limit of 50 m, to provide adequate protection to the river environment.

- Hydrology – In winter the site should be near saturation (water table within 10 cm of the surface).

    – In summer the water table should be within 1–1.5 m of the soil surface (flow in this case should only be sub-surface).

- Vegetation – For nitrate reduction the only requirement is stable vegetation (namely non-rotational). Trees are generally better but grass performs well.

Once established, estimated time until the zone becomes functional is up to three years. MAFF are currently undertaking a three-year project to establish design and management guidelines for the implementation of buffer zones.

Footnote: Research undertaken by Dr Nick Haycock (Silsoe College, Cranfield University) at Oxford University

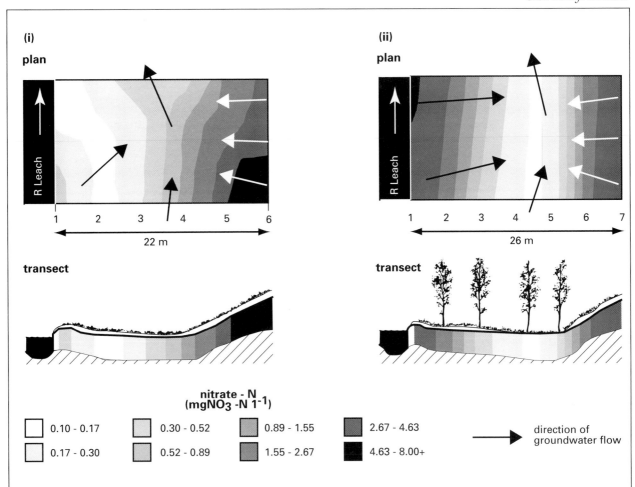

nitrate - N
(mgNO$_3$ -N l^{-1})

0.10 - 0.17	0.30 - 0.52	0.89 - 1.55	2.67 - 4.63
0.17 - 0.30	0.52 - 0.89	1.55 - 2.67	4.63 - 8.00+

direction of groundwater flow

Figure 1: R Leach, buffer zones.
(i) The mean concentration of groundwater nitrate, in a grass vegetated floodplain, during January 1990.
(ii) The mean concentration of groundwater nitrate in a poplar vegetated floodplain during January 1990

Nick Haycock

Plate 1
Sampling site on the R Leach

365

R Trent
Severn Trent Water/NRA Severn-Trent Region

Location:	R Trent, Beckingham, Gainsborough, Nottingham OS 1:50,000 No 112 Grid Ref SK 806 903
River type:	Tidal lowland reach
Size:	>50 m wide
Length affected:	200 m
Date:	1986–91

Techniques/Features:
Establishment of trial low maintenance seed mixes (3.6.5)
post-project appraisal of their success and assessment of maintenance demands of resulting swards

Objectives:
Experimental establishment of low-maintenance grass mixes and wild-flower seed mixes to determine what succeeds where, and why; precursor to reduction in the management of the floodbanks and ecological and aesthetic enhancement.

Background

In the early 1980s, Jeremy Purseglove promoted the idea that 'the banks of the Trent should flower by the year 2000'. In tandem with this vision, flood defence needs suggested that sea-level rises and general wear and tear of the banks would necessitate future floodbank repair and raising. To gather objective data on how successfully low-maintenance grass mixes and wild-flower seeds could become established, experimental plots were set up to record the success and failure of species and methods.

Experimental approach

A stretch of floodbank and foreshore was sprayed with herbicide and rotovated to give bare ground, representing a newly created floodbank.

The original trial consisted of four contiguous blocks, of 30 x 20 m, the long axis of each block running north/south. Within each block there were six plots, of 5 x 20 m, the long axis of each extending over the steep west facing slope across the flat top and down the east face and foreshore. Six grass mixtures were allocated at random to the six plots within each block. Each block was divided in half, one half having 19 species of wild flowers added to the grass mixture.

The grass mixture was sown at 150 kg/ha (15 gm²) as recommended for amenity grassland and the wild-flower mixture at 3.19 kg/ha (0.319 gm²) to give 10 seeds of each species/m². The plots were sown in autumn without a nurse crop.

The second trial copied the original format but with four blocks of four plots. This trial gave a comparison with the original trial by sowing the grass mixture at the conservation rate (recommended by NCC) of 40 kg/ha. The plots were sown in spring with a nurse crop of Westerwolds rye-grass at 10 kg/ha. Extra low-maintenance grass species were included and the wild flowers were sown at twice the rate to see if there was a noticeable increase compared with the original trial.

The productivity of the plots was checked by taking mean heights and comparing the results with the original sward farther along the bank. A cutting regime was superimposed upon the trials, cutting 3/4/5 times a year and the results monitored.

Project results and appraisal

An abnormally cold autumn left the original trial bare and vulnerable to winter floods, and a drought summer left the second trial bare and vulnerable also. Both eventually produced a short, herb-rich sward. The different rates of grass seeding made little significant difference. Use of a nurse crop did not work as anticipated because it was not cut soon enough, resulting in shading of the desirable species. Doubling of the seeding rate of the herbs made no significant difference. Some grass species did noticeably better than others in what was a very stressed environment.

The floodbank trials helped to determine which species would establish best, according to environmental factors. This resulted from three distinct community types developing in three areas of the bank:

- very water-stressed west-facing bank where growth was shortest;

- less stressed, east-facing bank with higher humidity (due to the river) and less intense exposure to sunlight;

- foreshore, enriched by river (nitrates, phosphates), not water stressed and where vigorous grasses and broadleaved weeds soon almost completely replaced the low-maintenance grasses and flowers.

Species that thrived, and those that failed or did badly, are listed in the Table. The key finding was that certain species would thrive only in one location. More importantly, the trials suggested that low-maintenance grasses with wild flowers can adequately bind floodbank soils to satisfy flood defence needs. Although floodbank mowing is not yet reduced to the proposed twice per year, the foreshore has been allowed to develop a diverse community structure through a single autumn mowing regime. Waders and other ground-nesting birds now thrive where previously they had not.

Relative performance of species germination and establishment in seed mixtures sown on a flood

SCIENTIFIC NAME	SPECIES	BROAD-LEAVED HERBS			GRASSES	
		Good	Fair	Poor	Good	Poor
Achillea millefolium	Yarrow	X				
Bellis perennis	Daisy	X				
Centaurea nigra	Knapweed	X				
Hypochoeris radicata	Common cat's ear	X				
Leontondon taraxacoides	Hairy hawkbit	X				
Leucanthemum vulgare	Oxeye daisy	X				
Medicaga lupulina	Black medick	X				
Primula veris	Cowslip	X				
Prunella vulgaris	Selfheal	X				
Ranunculus acris	Meadow buttercup	X				
Sanguisorba minor	Salad burnet	X				
Trifolium dubium	Suckling clover	X				
Galium verum	Lady's bedstraw		X			
Leontodon hispidus	Rough hawkbit		X			
Lotus coriculatus	Bird's-foot-trefoil		X			
Rhinanthus minor	Yellow rattle		X			
Pimpinella saxifraga	Burnet saxifrage			X		
Plantago media	Hoary plantain			X		
Silene dioica	Red campion			X		
Stachys officinalis	Betony			X		
Anthorxianthum odoratum	Sweet vernal grass				X	
Cynosurus cristatus	Crested dog's-tail				X	
Lolium perenne	Perennial rye-grass				X	
Trisetum flarescens	Yellow oat-grass				X	
Festuca ovina	Sheep's fescue				X	
Festuca rubra ssp Commuta	Chewings fescue				X	
Festuca rubra ssp Pruimosa	Creeping red fescue				X	
Festuca longifolia	Hard fescue				X	
Festuca tennifolia	Fine-leafed sheep fescue				X	
Agrostis capillaris	Common bent-grass					X
Agrostis castellana	Highland bent-fescue					X
Agrostis stolonifera	Creeping bent-grass					X
Lolium perenne 'Lorina'	Rye-grass					X
Pheleum pratense	Timothy					X
Poa compressa	Flattened meadow grass					X
Poa trivialis	Rough meadow-grass					X

Note: The species that performed well were able to cope with a very stressed environment, exposure to intense sunlight, low soil moisture and competition. The pH of the soil was around 6.

R Avon

Severn Trent Water/NRA Severn-Trent Region

Case Study 3.6 (b)

Location:	Left bank of navigable Avon at Barton, Bidford on Avon, Warwickshire OS 1:50,000 150, Grid Ref SP 109 512
River type:	Clay
Size:	>10 m width, 1–2.5 m depth
Length affected:	Two 25 m lengths of floodbank
Date:	1981

Techniques/Features:
Turfing of new floodbank and seeding of low-maintenance grasses (3.6.5)

Objective:
Establish a herb-rich, low-maintenance, sward on a new floodbank constructed to protect the village of Barton

Background

An ecologically diverse and visually attractive bank design was promoted when a new bank was built in 1981. The design would not compromise flood defence needs and would require less management in the future. An unimproved pasture grazed by horses provided turfs for the new floodbank as the grazing regime was not appropriate for its long-term safeguard. Benefits from the turfs would be evident to the general public since a public footpath runs close-by and the bank backs on to a caravan park.

Scheme approach

- A 2.5 m high floodbank was constructed away from the edge of the river, with side-slopes of 1:1.5–1:3

- Turfs were hand cut by conservation volunteers and laid chequerboard fashion in two areas 25 m long; this method allowed limited material to influence a large area of new ground.

- The rest of the area was sown with Mommersteeg International's fine grass mixture.

- After compaction and bedding-in, the area was mown annually with removal of cuttings to reduce fertility; cutting is in late summer to enable seeds to be set and dispersed.

Scheme appraisal

Initially the turfs transplanted were rich in cowslip, oxeye daisy, lady's bedstraw, quaking grass and scabious. More than 10 years later the majority of the original complement of species laid down are still there but adder's tongue was not found in 1991. Cowslips abound and these and other herbs have spread from the original loci of the turves to the grass sward established alongside them. The management of banks was originally an annual late summer/autumn cut only, with cut material removed from the bank.
In recent years the vegetation has become rank due to less cutting and lack of material removal. Invasion by tall grass and rank ruderals could reduce the interest of an essentially grazed/cut meadow flora, the owner also wishes to have more regular cuts and material carted away to reduce the fire risk at the caravan park.

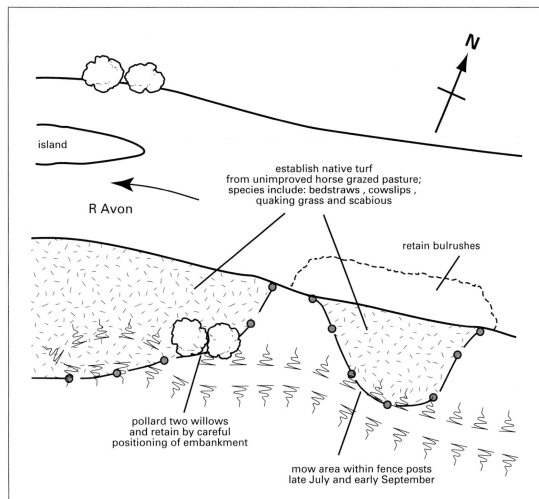

island

R Avon

establish native turf
from unimproved horse grazed pasture;
species include: bedstraws , cowslips ,
quaking grass and scabious

retain bulrushes

pollard two willows
and retain by careful
positioning of embankment

mow area within fence posts
late July and early September

**Figure 1: R Avon, Barton.
Turfing a new floodbank.**

North Level Engine Drain/Hatfield Waste Drain

Case Study 3.6 (c)

Severn Trent Water/NRA Severn-Trent Region

Location:	West of Belton Grange, Crowle, Humberside OS 1:50,000 No. 112, Grid Ref SE 765103
River type:	Man-made drainage channels
Size:	*c* 5 m bed width, 1–1.5 m depth
Banks:	1: 2 side slopes, silt at base
Date:	Historical management practices

Techniques/Features:
Contrast of mowing regimes and their effects on habitat structure and floral richness of banks (3.6.3)

Objectives:
Illustrate the ecological effects of two different bank management regimes on two watercourses running side by side

Background and Management

North Level Engine Drain and Hatfield Waste Drain are watercourses running side by side which provide functions and accordingly receive differing maintenance regimes. Both are of a similar size and trapezoidal cross-section. The Hatfield Waste Drain is a pumped drainage system in which a high carrying capacity is required. A short grass sward is preferred to minimise channel roughness; hence the banks receive close cuts with a flail mower several times a year. Marginal fringes are partially retained with yellow flag and sedge patches deliberately avoided.

In contrast, the North Level Engine Drain now receives a much reduced run-off discharge from Hatfield Chase since the steam-driven Dirtness pumping station has been replaced by a modern pump serving 2,000 ha. The maintenance requirements are now much less intense than they were; as a result one bank is grazed by cattle and the other bank receives only an occasional cut at the end of August.

Appraisal

The banks of the Hatfield Waste Drain have little structural variation and a poor plant community. Coarse grasses dominate and only common herbs such as meadowsweet and great willowherb are obvious. In contrast, the banks of the Engine Drain have greater habitat structure due to cattle trampling and the greater plant richness. An NRA survey in May 1993 showed a richer community on the Engine Drain banks, supporting bank plants such as meadow-rue, lady's smock, Nottingham catchfly, field scabious, cowslip, adder's tongue and valerian, which were not found on the adjacent banks of the Waste Drain. In the channel water-starwort, broad-leaved pondweed, water dock, fennel pondweed and curled pondweed were recorded in the same survey in the Engine Drain but not in the Waste Drain.

The surveyor in 1993 noted for the Engine Drain `Extremely rich bankside flora ... also high faunal interest – very rich in insects with some interesting specimens ... rich marginal vegetation supports varied birdlife'. Reed buntings, sedge and reed warblers nest in the reeds, sedges and rushes . No such statements were made for the Waste Drain which was described as `steep-sided with short, cropped sward'.

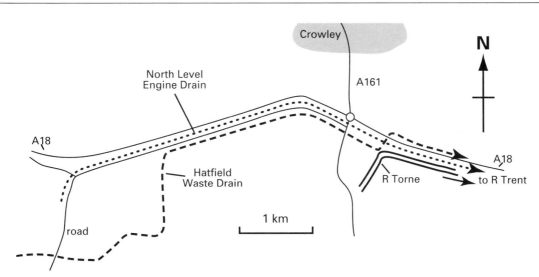

Figure 1
North Level Engine Drain/Hatfield Waste Drain. Location of drains.

Val Holt

Plate 1
North Level Engine Drain, with a rich bankside flora and fauna as a result of reduced levels of maintenance.

Val Holt

Plate 2
Hatfield Waste Drain, showing the effects of a high level of maintenance.

R Medway at Golden Green

Medway River Project staff and volunteers

Location:	Hartlake Bridge, Golden Green, Tonbridge, Kent, OS 1:50,000 No 188, Grid Ref TQ 628 473
River type:	Lowland river, water levels artificially maintained for navigation. Coarse gravels overlain by 1–2 m of alluvial clay
Size:	*c* 20 m width, 0.5–2.0 m depth
Length affected:	40 m
Date:	September 1988–November 1988. Additional works May 1990

Techniques/Features:
Nicobag retaining wall backfilled with river dredgings and batter stabilised by Enkamat (3.4.4). Faggots used to repair failures of technique above (3.7.6)

Objectives:
Restore original line of riverside footpath, lost through severe erosion following 1987 storm. Protect adjacent woodland and reinstate bankside and emergent vegetation

Background

The R Medway navigation is a popular and intensively used recreational resource. The angling rights on this section are controlled by Tonbridge Angling Society. The bank, situated mid-way through a series of bends, suffered severe erosion in the high flows which followed the October 1987 storm, exacerbated by the flow being diverted by fallen trees.

Scheme approach

- A retaining wall, 40 m long x 2 m high, was formed from 350 Nicobags filled with gravel extracted during navigation maintenance. The bags formed a near vertical wall up to 3 m from the existing bankface.

- Backfilling behind the retaining wall, to water level, with river gravel.

- Formation of bank above water level, comprising river dredgings, compacted to form a stable gradient of 1:2. Approximate height 2 m.

- Protection of graded bank with Enkamat, pegged with metal spikes at 1 m intervals, and covered with 50 mm of soil.

- Planting of locally acquired emergent vegetation (bur-reed and flowering-rush) into the top course of bags.

Scheme appraisal

- Enkamat was not strong enough to withstand spate flows during the following winter and in places was damaged by anglers scrambling down the bank.

- Failure of the Enkamat at the upstream end of the site enabled spate flows to wash gravel from behind the Nicobags, destabilising the retaining wall, and eventually leading to the collapse of parts of the restored bank.

- Recolonisation of emergent and bank vegetation was very poor, primarily due to the nutrient deficient nature of the river dredgings, disturbance by anglers and shading from the adjacent wood.

In May 1990, following the loss of 10 m of the top course of the Nicobag wall, volunteers constructed a 10 m x 1.5 m retaining wall of sweet chestnut faggots. The faggot wall was built at a gradient of 1:2 and secured with stakes to the lower courses of Nicobags, which had remained stable throughout the spate flows. The faggots have withstood three winters of spate flows and are successfully accumulating silt and vegetation.

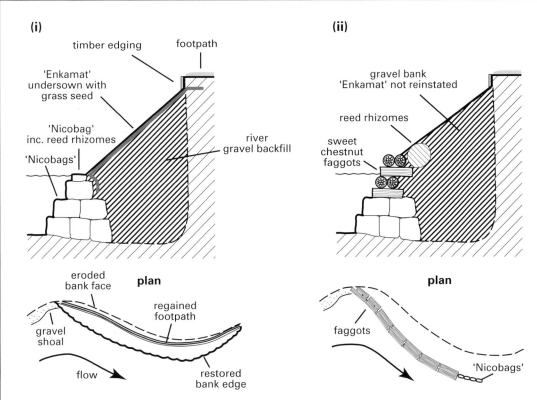

Figure 1: River Medway at Golden Green. Restoration of riverside footpath:
(i) Original scheme, Sept 1988; Nicobag retaining wall backfilled with river dredgings
(ii) Faggots used to repair failures of above techniques

Plate 1
Faggoting undertaken in May 1990

Plate 2
Vegetation growth after three years (May 1993)

373

R Medway at Yalding
Medway River Project staff and volunteers

Case Study 3.7 (b)

Location: South bank of Medway, approx 200 m upstream of the Twyford Bridge, Yalding, Kent.
OS 1:50,000 No 188
Grid Ref TQ 688 496

River type: Lowland river. Water levels artificially maintained for navigation. Coarse gravels overlain by 1–2 m of clay.

Size: 15–30 m width; 0.5–2.0 m depth

Length affected: 100 m

Date: 1989–1991

Techniques/Features:
Protective bund using sweet chestnut faggots (3.7.6) up to 1 m from bank, backfilled with soil and planted with branched bur-reed (3.5.3)

Objectives:
To reduce erosion at head and toe of timber revetments and to provide habitat in an otherwise poor river environment

Background
The riverside path at Twyford Bridge, Yalding, is probably the most heavily used section of the River Medway. Initial works, involving timber revetments, were intended to ensure long-term access for pedestrians and anglers and to facilitate overnight mooring by boat users. Concern was expressed that the toe of the timber sections would be prone to erosion, undermining the structure and resulting in the loss of safe access. To reduce this effect the project has established a series of narrow reed fringes, between the revetments, to trap silt and stabilise the bank during spate flows.

Scheme approach
- The river channel had a natural ledge, approximately 1 m from the existing bank on which a protective wall of faggots was built. The faggots were not laid in the traditional manner of alternating layers but in continuous linear fashion, parallel to the bank, to a height of approx 200 mm above normal summer water level (to protect plants from boat wash).

- The ledge behind the faggots was backfilled with soil to approx 150 mm below water level and planted with branched bur-reed. Plant material was obtained from extensive beds downstream and planted within one hour of being removed from the original site.

Scheme appraisal
- Faggots have established well and accumulated considerable amounts of silt.

- Bur-reed has established a very dense cover, now used by some birds (mainly mallards and moorhens) for nesting, as well as providing good initial dissipation of wave energy.

- Erosion of the revetments has been minimal, except where damage has been caused by anglers using the ledges for improved access to the water.

**Plate 1
Sweet chestnut faggots backfilled with soil.**

Brian Smith

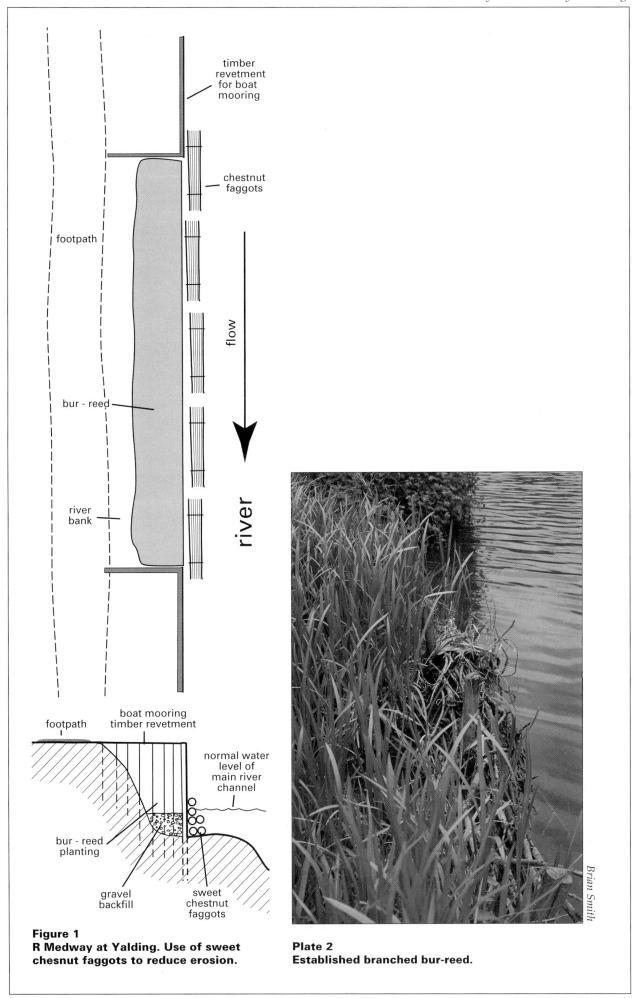

Figure 1
R Medway at Yalding. Use of sweet chesnut faggots to reduce erosion.

Plate 2
Established branched bur-reed.

Brian Smith

R Clwyd

Welsh Water/NRA Welsh Region

Case Study 3.7 (c)

Location:	Pont-y-Cambwll, near Denbigh, Clwyd OS 1:50,000 No 116 Grid Ref SJ 075 709
River type:	Gravel bed
Size:	Approximately 8 m wide; 1.5 m deep on bend
Length affected:	One bend
Date:	1976

Techniques/Features:
Bank revetment using willow stakes and sheep netting (3.4.4/3.7.6)

Objectives:
To reinstate an eroding bend to its prior regime at minimum cost.

Background

In 1976 a large willow growing on the inside of a bend in the river fell across the apex, causing it to act as a current deflector. Erosion of the outside of the bend rapidly followed as the river sought a new alignment. Stability was successfully restored by utilising the fallen willow to revet the eroding bank.

Scheme approach

- Restore previous regime and alignment.

- Use tree cover as primary revetment, simulating conditions elsewhere.

- Maximise use of local materials; minimise imports; minimise land disturbance.

- Minimise costs.

The method developed is indicated in the figure. Fencepost-size stakes were cut from the fallen willow and stapled to sheep netting to form flexible mattresses. The mattresses were floated on the river and held at right angles to the bank before soil was dropped on to the bankside end causing the mattress to sink under the weight. The re-formed bank was roughly profiled before pulling the free end of each mattress out of the water and over the face of the fill. The mattress ends were secured by anchoring to stakes driven in to trenches cut back in firm ground, and backfilled.

Works were undertaken close to, or during the growing season enabling the willow logs to shoot rapidly and root in the critical damp zone near the water's edge.

Scheme appraisal (1992)

The river remains stable and the bend supports a dense run of willows that have not required maintenance, although routine thinning and pollarding is now carried out.

The technique is suitable for relatively deep-water situations. Pollarding of nearby willows provides material, as well as encouraging habitat regeneration.

The need for works arose from the fall of a mature willow, which highlights the importance of regular maintenance to reduce such risks.

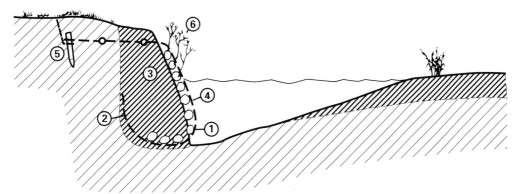

construction technique

1 willow stakes fixed to sheep netting to form mattresses
2 mattresses floated and held at right angles to eroding bank
3 fill sinks mattress against river bank
4 free end of mattress pulled over face of fill
5 mattress secured to buried stakes by twisted tie wires
6 willow growth above water level

note :
The river will adjust it's profile along the face of the fill causing the fill to settle. The continuation of the mattressing under the fill (**2**) should ensure security of the revetment after settlement

Figure 1
R Clwyd at Pont-y-Cambwll. Bank revetment using willow stakes and sheep netting.

Richard Vivash

Plate 1
Willow growth three months after bank reconstruction in 1976.

Richard Vivash

Plate 2
The entire river protected by maturing willows. However, selective thinning and pollarding is required to prevent them falling; the cause of the original erosion.

Appendix I: Health and Safety

Introduction

Working close to rivers, streams or any other body of water can be potentially dangerous.

The Supervisor in control of on-site activities should be responsible for ensuring that all field workers are aware of potential dangers and the correct procedures to adopt in case of accidents or dangerous occurrences.

Health and Safety should be an integral part of any training programme provided for field workers and every effort should be made to minimise risks in the field, by identifying hazards, assessing risks and deciding on the appropriate precautions.

Possible hazards when working in or adjacent to rivers

Leptospirosis (Weil's disease)

Weil's disease is the most serious form of an illness called Leptospirosis. Rats, cows and other animals can carry different types of leptospira bacteria. However, in Britain Weil's disease is most commonly associated with rats. Although not affected themselves, infected animals excrete the bacteria in their urine. The bacteria can survive in fresh water for about four weeks, and people can become infected through contact with infected urine, contaminated water or muddy soil.

Leptospira bacteria can enter the human body through:
- cuts, grazes and sores on the body or in the mouth;

- mucous membranes such as those which line the nose and eyes.

Simple precautions to reduce the chances of contracting the disease are:
- Ensure cuts, scratches or skin abrasions are thoroughly cleansed and covered with a waterproof plaster.

- Avoid rubbing your eyes, nose and mouth during work.

- Clean protective clothing, footwear and equipment after use.

- After work, and particularly before taking food or drink, wash hands thoroughly.

Lone working

This is a common feature of many organisations' operations, where people working in remote locations on their own face particular problems due to the nature of their work.

Some sites present more of a danger to the lone worker than others and full consideration must be given to the hazards when carrying out risk assessments.

Sites that may be dangerous include:
- construction sites
- marsh/swamp areas
- remote/isolated locations
- coastal cliffs, steep slopes and banks
- culverts and manholes
- active/disused lagoons

Efforts should be made to minimise the risks to lone workers by training good communications and by adopting an efficient and disciplined reporting procedure.

Electric fishing

Electric fishing is an essential and effective technique for fishery management of lakes and rivers but the combination of electricity and water makes it a potentially hazardous activity.

Under the Electricity at Work Regulations 1989, electric fishing falls into the category of working near live conductors and as a consequence, it is a requirement that suitable precautions are taken to prevent injury.

Electric fishing is a specialist activity,

which should be carried out by competent persons using properly designed and tested equipment.

The National Rivers Authority has produced a Code of Practice for Safety in Electric Fishing Operations. It is commended as the most informative and up to date document covering this type of work activity.

Use of hazardous substances

The use of hazardous substances at work is mainly governed by the Control of Substances Hazardous to Health Regulations 1989 (COSHH) and the Control of Pesticides Regulations 1985 (CPR).

The four stages for prevention of occupational health hazards and protection of workers are:
- the provision of instruction and information on occupational health hazards, precautions and personal hygiene;

- removal or substitution of an 'unhealthy' process, eg where a potentially toxic chemical is being used, it may be possible to substitute a less toxic material that will do the same job;

- segregation of processes so that only those immediately involved are in contact, eg arc welding may be carried out behind screens or enclosures away from casual passers-by;

- personal protection – being the last resort in employee protection.

Blue-green algae

Blue-green algae are natural inhabitants of many inland waters, estuaries and the sea.

In fresh waters, they are found in suspension and attached to rocks and other surfaces at the bottom of shallow waters and along the edges of lakes and rivers.

For reasons that are not yet fully understood, bloom and scum forming blue-green algae in fresh water, brackish water and sea water are capable of producing toxins.

These toxins have caused the death of wild animals, farm livestock and domestic pets in many countries, including farm animals and dogs in the UK in 1989. In humans, rashes have occurred following skin contact, and illnesses have occurred when blue-green algae have been swallowed.

A report *Toxic Blue-green Algae* has been produced by the National Rivers Authority copies of which can be obtained from the Anglian Region, Kingfisher House, Orton Goldhay, Peterborough PE2 5ZR.

Water safety

Working over, on or near to water presents a number of potential problems, in particular:

- the ever present risk of persons falling into water;

- the complexity of the legal obligations, which can vary from district to district.

Detailed safe working procedures should be developed for each individual project in the light of prevailing conditions.

Before starting any project which is over, on or near water and involves the use of any kind of craft, the person in control of operations is strongly advised to obtain the fullest information on local bye-laws and conditions.

In cases of doubt the nearest Marine Office of the Department of Trade and Industry (DTI) or the Health and Safety Executive (HSE) area office should be contacted.

Common sense precautions

- Avoid steep or unstable banks.

- Avoid rivers during spate conditions.

- Do not enter the water if the riverbed is not visible.

- Work in pairs if river channels need to be crossed.

- Wear the appropriate protective clothing and equipment for the job and weather conditions.

- Carry a basic first aid kit.

- Establish an agreed system of emergency action in case anyone fails to report in or sign off at the end of the day.

- Wear an approved life jacket where a danger of drowning exists.

Sources of further advice and information

Organisations

National Rivers Authority – Health and Safety Department
Royal Society for the Prevention of Accidents – Water Safety Department
Health and Safety Executive – Local Area Office
British Red Cross
English Nature – Health and Safety Department
Department of Trade and Industry

Information

National Rivers Authority – Code of Practice for Electric Fishing
National Rivers Authority – Marine Safety Policy
Control of Substances Hazardous to Health Regulations 1989
Health and Safety at Work Act 1974
Management of Health and Safety at Work Regulations 1992
BS 3680 Part 3Q 1993 – Measurement of liquid flow in open channels
Provision and use of Work Equipment Regulations 1992
Manual Handling Operations Regulations 1992
Workplace (Health, Safety and Welfare) Regulations 1992
Personal Protective Equipment at Work Regulations 1992
Construction Safety – Published by the Building Advisory Service
The Construction Regulations 1961, 1966 and 1989
The Electricity at Work Regulations 1989
Noise at Work Regulations 1989
Control of Pollution Act 1974
Environmental Protection Act 1990

Appendix II: Statutory Protection

Introduction

This Appendix is divided into two sections, presenting information on the statutory protection mechanisms in the UK for wildlife habitats and individual species of flora and fauna. The first section includes an overview of international conventions and legislation which apply to wetland habitats including those associated with rivers. The second section has been adapted, with minor modifications, from Boon *et al.*, 1992.

Section 1
Habitat Protection

Introduction

This section highlights the following issues:
- why conserve wildlife habitats;
- the international context;
- the application of international conventions and EU Directives in the UK;
- the habitat protection network;
- consultation procedures over operations in or likely to affect SSSIs/ASSIs.

It has been written to:
- inform river engineering and conservation staff;
- explore the key areas where consultation is required both within the river engineering bodies and with external nature conservation bodies;
- point to sources of further guidance and information.

The river engineer has a vital role in contributing to the protection and sympathetic management of wetland habitats through a consideration of the need for engineering works and the manner in which they will be carried out.

Why conserve wildlife habitats?

There are a number of reasons why consideration is given to wildlife conservation, including:

- scientific and ecological considerations – the maintenance of biodiversity, that is the preservation of our current range and diversity of species and habitats and the genetic resources that they contain;

- moral considerations – it can be argued that all plants and animals have a right to exist and that we have a duty to ensure their survival;

- cultural considerations – society places a value on wildlife for reasons including the pleasure that we derive from their existence and their use as an educational resource.

Species cannot be considered in isolation from their habitat. As a consequence, legal measures have been introduced to protect habitats in parallel with those produced to protect individual species (detailed in the accompanying section to this Appendix 'Species Protection in the United Kingdom').

Wildlife conservation is not confined to the UK. It is not practical to conserve migratory wildlife just by measures taken in one country. As a consequence, measures have been taken to conserve wildlife throughout the world through international treaties and in the European Union (EU) through binding legislation agreed by all member countries. These treaties (Conventions) and EU legislation (Directives) have to be examined to give the context within which specific UK legislation has been introduced to conserve wildlife.

This new edition of *Rivers and Wildlife* is published at a time of change within UK legislation. In particular, the precise legislative mechanisms by which the EU Habitats and Species Directive will be introduced in the UK have not been decided. The scope and intention of this legislation can be highlighted by examination of the Directive itself.

The international context

Some species, particularly birds, migrate long distances between suitable habitat in different countries. It is therefore essential for habitat protection to be considered within an international framework. There are a number of international agreements which seek to protect habitats either throughout the world, in specific geographic regions or for distinct classes of wildlife. An outline of the most relevant provisions is given in Tables 1 and 2. Of particular relevance to anyone considering activities within wetland habitats, such as river engineering works, is The Convention on Wetlands of International Importance especially as Waterfowl Habitat, which was drafted at Ramsar, Iran in 1971. The Ramsar Convention, as it is commonly known, aims to conserve wetlands and promote their wise (sustainable) use. The UK Government ratified this Convention in 1976. Recent resolutions and recommendations of the Conference of Contracting Parties have included the need for the adoption of an integrated catchment planning approach to all wetlands and for management plans to be developed for protected sites (Ramsar Convention Bureau 1993).

These concepts have been extended to all habitats within the EU through two Directives, one specifically upon bird conservation and the second upon the conservation of all habitats and upon non-bird flora and fauna.

- The EU Directive on the Conservation of Wild Birds (79/409/EEC), referred to as the Birds Directive in this Appendix, requires Member States to safeguard the habitats of migratory birds and certain particularly threatened birds (listed on Annex 1 to the Directive).

- The EU Directive on the Conservation of Natural Habitats and of Wild Fauna and Flora (92/43/EEC), referred to as the Habitats and Species Directive in this Appendix, requires Member States to safeguard the habitats of certain particularly threatened species and to take positive conservation actions throughout their country.

These international commitments require measures not only to classify and protect sites, but also to promote the incorporation of conservation measures in land and water policies and in decision making procedures. This is essential for the maintenance of many wildlife populations, particularly widely dispersed species. The conservation of such species is dependent upon the sympathetic management of the whole of the river system. The river engineer has a vital role to play in contributing to this sympathetic management through a consideration of the need for engineering works and the manner in which they will be carried out.

Application of International Conventions and EU Directives in the UK

The international agreements and directives are implemented in the UK through a combination of specific wildlife protection legislation, general statutory duties upon a wide range of bodies and policy and other guidance upon decision making procedures from central Government.

In Great Britain, the legislation intended to allow implementation of the site protection requirements of the Birds Directive is incorporated into the Wildlife and Countryside Act 1981. The Northern Ireland equivalent is the Nature Conservation and Amenity Lands Order 1985. This legislation will require amendment to bring it into accordance with the requirements of the Habitats and Species Directive. The UK Government has stated that in order for it to be able to comply with the Birds Directive requirement for site protection, all sites of international importance are, or will be, notified as Sites of Special Scientific Interest (SSSIs) in Great Britain or Areas of Special Scientific Interest (ASSIs) in Northern Ireland.

At the end of 1993, a total of 77 sites had been designated in the UK as Special Protection Areas (SPAs) under the Birds Directive and a total of 69 internationally important wetlands designated under the Ramsar Convention. Many of these sites are designated under both the Directive and the Convention. Some of these sites include within them riverine wetlands. Examples include Lough Neagh and Lough Beg in Northern Ireland (Ramsar only), Loch Ken and River Dee Marshes in Scotland (Ramsar and SPA), Cors Caron in Wales (Ramsar only) and the Ouse Washes in England (Ramsar and SPA). A list of the sites which qualify for designation under the Birds Directive and brief details of the habitats and birds which occur within those sites can be found in Pritchard *et al.* (1992). A description of those Ramsar sites that were designated up to 1 March 1993 can be found in Jones (1993). A list of those sites which qualify for designation as SACs under the Habitats and Species Directive will be available from the statutory nature conservation bodies in due course.

The habitat protection network

The network of protected sites which represents the best examples of our natural heritage of wildlife habitats, geological features and land forms consists of the SSSIs in Great Britain and the ASSIs in Northern Ireland. This network represents the basic minimum area of habitat which needs to be conserved if we are to maintain the current range and distribution of our wildlife. The sites are identified using a set of well established scientific criteria by the relevant statutory nature conservation body in each country of the United Kingdom (English Nature, Department of the Environment for Northern Ireland, Scottish Natural Heritage and the Countryside Council for Wales). These bodies have produced information documents upon the site protection system (eg English Nature, 1992; DoE(NI) Environment Service, 1993).

Once sites have been identified they are notified to the owner and/or occupier, the relevant local planning authorities and the relevant Secretary of State. This notification includes information upon the site boundaries, why the site is of special interest and a list of potentially damaging activities about which the statutory conservation body should be consulted. The site is also registered as a local land charge (or appropriate national equivalents) so that persons who may be considering acquiring an interest in the

land can also be informed. In England and Wales this notification extends to the National Rivers Authority and Internal Drainage Boards so that they shall consider how their activities might affect the SSSI and be carried out in a manner which 'furthers' nature conservation.

Consultation procedures over operations in or likely to affect SSSIs/ASSIs

Specific consultation procedures set out in the relevant legislation apply to owners and occupiers, local planning authorities and certain statutory bodies. The bodies with powers to regulate river engineering works through the granting of consents and to undertake such works themselves fall into this latter category. The statutory consultation process permits the statutory conservation bodies to provide site specific advice and, to assist owners and occupiers, financial support.

Owners and occupiers are required to give four months notice in writing if they intend to carry out, or cause or permit to be carried out, any of the listed potentially damaging operations. This initiates a period of negotiation which can be extended by agreement between the parties and also by order of the relevant Secretary of State (a 'Section 29 Order' in Great Britain). When such an order is in place, its legal requirements not to carry out specific operations can be applied to any person. The statutory conservation body is able to offer the owner or occupier a payment in return for a management agreement which will protect the nature conservation interest. Failure to inform the statutory conservation body can lead to a fine. Owners or occupiers are not liable for the unauthorised actions of third parties such as trespassers or vandals.

Consultation is required between the statutory conservation body and the planning authority before a decision is taken upon applications received for planning permission. Where a particular development is authorised by the relevant local planning authority this overrides the need for the owner or occupier to consult with the conservation body.

Consultation is required in England and Wales between the statutory conservation body and with those bodies undertaking or consenting river engineering works under section 17 of the Water Resources Act 1991 (a statutory duty upon the NRA) and section 13 of the Land Drainage Act 1991 (a statutory duty upon internal drainage boards). The consultation has to be upon proposed works or consents likely to affect a SSSI. As a consequence it should include works or consents outside the boundaries of the SSSI, that is elsewhere in the catchment, which could affect, for instance, water tables or flooding frequency in the SSSI. An exception to prior consultation is given for emergencies but the statutory conservation body still has to be informed of what has been done as soon as possible. Further information upon the procedures to be followed are given in the relevant guidance documents (MAFF/DoE/WO, 1991; MAFF/EN/NRA, 1992). This guidance advocates early consultation and that such consultation should be with both the statutory bodies and voluntary nature conservation bodies such as the RSPB and county wildlife trusts.

Consultation is also advocated by the relevant Government Country Offices and Departments as good practice to be undertaken where statutory provisions do not apply. Instances include local

Table 1: International Conventions

Convention on Wetlands of International Importance especially as Waterfowl Habitat (the 'Ramsar Convention')

The importance of wetlands has been recognised by the adoption of this Convention at a meeting of countries concerned with wetland and waterfowl conservation held at Ramsar, Iran, in 1971 (Carp 1972). A copy of the full text of the Convention can be found in Pritchard, *et al.* (1992). The preamble to the Convention refers to the contracting parties' desire 'to stem the progressive encroachment on and loss of wetlands now and in the future'. The UK Government signed the Convention in 1973 and Parliament ratified it in 1976. The key provisions of the Convention are:

- Each Contracting Party to designate suitable wetlands within its territory for inclusion in a list of wetlands of international importance.

- Contracting Parties to formulate and implement their planning so as to promote the conservation of wetlands included in the list and also, as far as possible, the 'wise use' of all wetlands in their territory.

- Contracting Parties to promote the conservation of wetlands and waterfowl. Where a Contracting Party, in its own urgent national interest, deletes or restricts the boundaries of wetlands included in the list, it should compensate for any loss of wetland resources.

Regular conferences of the Contracting Parties consider matters relating to the Convention. The 1987 Conference at Regina in Canada (Ramsar Convention Bureau 1988) defined 'wise use' thus: 'The wise use of wetlands is their sustainable utilisation for the benefit of humankind in a way compatible with the maintenance of the natural properties of the ecosystem'. Natural properties of the ecosystem were defined as its 'physical, biological or chemical components, such as soil, water, plants, animals and nutrients, and the interactions between them'.

The Convention on the Conservation of European Wildlife and Natural Habitats (The 'Bern Convention')

This Convention encourages the promotion of co-operation between European countries in their conservation efforts, especially with respect to migratory species. The UK is a party to this Convention, having ratified its provisions in May 1982. A summary of the Convention has been prepared by the Council of Europe (1991). The key provisions of the Convention are:

- Contracting Parties are obliged to conserve wild plants and animals with an emphasis upon endangered and vulnerable species and their habitats.

- Contracting Parties undertake to give special attention to the protection of areas that are of importance for specified migratory species.

authorities in England and Wales (MAFF/DoE/WO, 1991), organisations carrying out works in or adjacent to watercourses in Scotland (Scottish Office, 1993) and Watercourse Management Division in Northern Ireland (DANI, 1991)

Such bodies may also find themselves to be an owner or occupier of a SSSI/ASSI in which case the separate consultation provisions set out above also apply to that area of land which is in their ownership or occupation.

Table 2: European Union Legislation

Directive on the Conservation of Wild Birds (79/409/EEC)
Emphasis is placed in the Directive on the need to conserve bird habitats as a means of maintaining populations. In part, such habitat protection is to be achieved by the establishment of a network of Special Protection Areas (SPAs) throughout the Community. As well as SPAs, the Birds Directive also indicates that other means of protecting populations are necessary, especially where these populations are vulnerable and dispersed. These 'wider countryside' conservation measures are a necessary complement to site-based conservation. A full text of the Directive can be found in Pritchard *et al.* (1992). The key provisions for habitat conservation of this Directive are:

- Member States to take requisite measures to preserve, maintain or re-establish a sufficient diversity and area of habitats for all the species of birds naturally occurring in the wild state

- Member States to apply special conservation measures, including the classification of SPAs, to two groups of birds. These are vulnerable species which are listed in Annex 1 and all other regularly occurring migratory bird species.

- In respect of SPAs, economic and recreational requirements must be considered only after ecological, scientific and cultural requirements except in the urgent national interest and where no alternative options exist.

Directive on the Conservation of Natural Habitats and of Wild Fauna and Flora (92/43/EEC)
Emphasis is placed in the Directive on actions to conserve habitats and to restore populations of plants and animals (other than birds) to a favourable conservation status. In part, such habitat protection is to be achieved by the establishment of a network of Special Areas of Conservation (SACs) throughout the Community. As well as SACs, the Directive also indicates that other means of protecting populations are necessary, especially where these populations are not in a favourable conservation status. The Directive requires 'wider countryside' measures as well as site-based conservation. The key provisions for habitat conservation of this Directive are:

- Member States to take requisite measures, including the designation of SACs, to conserve the habitats listed in Annex 1.

- Member States to take requisite measures, including the designation of SACs, to conserve the habitats of the species listed in Annex II.

- In respect of SACs, economic and recreational requirements must be considered only after ecological, scientific and cultural requirements except in the urgent national interest and where no alternative options exist.

Like all Directives under the Treaty of Rome, the above two Directives describe what needs to be achieved; but the manner in which these objectives are to be attained is left to individual Member States. The European Commission has a monitoring role and can initiate court proceedings against Member States for failure to comply with the Directives.

References

Carp, E (1972) *Proceedings of the international conference on the conservation of wetlands and waterfowl. Ramsar, Iran, 30 January – 3 February 1971.* Slimbridge, IWRB.

Council Of Europe (1991) *The Bern Convention on Nature Conservation.* Council of Europe, Strasbourg.

DA(NI) (1991) *Drainage works carefully planned and executed minimise environmental damage and encourage regeneration.* Department of Agriculture (Northern Ireland) Watercourse Management Division, Belfast.

DOE(NI) Environment Service (1993) *Target 2001 – A programme for the survey, declaration and monitoring of Areas of Special Scientific Interest in Northern Ireland.* DoE (NI) Environment Service, Belfast.

English Nature (1992) *What you should know about Sites of Special Scientific Interest.* English Nature, Peterborough

Jones, T A (Compiler) (1993) *A Directory of Wetlands of International Importance, Part Three: Europe.* Ramsar Convention Bureau, Switzerland.

MAFF/DoE/WO (1991) *Conservation Guidelines for Drainage Authorities.* MAFF, London.

MAFF/EN/NRA (1992) *Environmental Procedures for Inland Flood Defence Works: A guide for managers and decision makers in the NRA, IDBs and local authorities.* MAFF. London.

Pritchard, D E, Housden, S D, Mudge, G P, Galbraith, C A and Pienkowski, M W (eds.) (1992) *Important Bird Areas in the UK including the Channel Islands and the Isle of Man.* RSPB, Sandy.

Ramsar Convention Bureau (1988) *Convention on Wetlands of International Importance Especially as Waterfowl Habitat. Proceedings of the third meeting of the Conference of Contracting Parties. Regina, Saskatchewan, Canada; 27 May to 5 June 1987.* Ramsar Convention Bureau, Switzerland.

Ramsar Convention Bureau (1993) *Convention on Wetlands of International Importance Especially as Waterfowl Habitat. Draft proceedings of the fifth meeting of the Conference of Contracting Parties. Kushiro, Japan: 9–16 June 1993.* Ramsar Convention Bureau, Switzerland.

Scottish Office (1993) *Conservation, access and recreation – Code of practice for Water and Sewerage Authorities and River Purification Authorities.* Scottish Office, Edinburgh.

Section 2: Species Protection

(Adapted with minor modifications from Boon, P J, Morgan, D H W and Palmer, M A (1992) Statutory Protection Of Freshwater Flora And Fauna In Britain. *Freshwater Forum* 2 (2): 91–101)

Introduction

The conservation of freshwater habitats and the species they harbour demands a diversity of approaches. Over the past 50 years, the emphasis of conservationists in general has gradually changed from one merely of preservation to one of active management and habitat restoration. Even where such measures are successful, threats to individual species may remain; for example, from wilful destruction or commercial exploitation. In these cases, legislation designed to protect habitats, whether nationally (such as the provisions for Sites of Special Scientific Interest (SSSIs)), or internationally (such as the designation of sites under the European Community Habitats and Species Directive and the Ramsar Convention), cannot be wholly effective.

Duties are laid on the NRA and the IDBs under the Water Resources Act 1991 and the Land Drainage Act 1991 to 'further the conservation of flora, fauna and ...' and on DANI under the Nature Conservation and Amenity Lands (Northern Ireland) Order 1985 'to have regard to the need to protect...flora and fauna' which do not specify the need for protection by any other legislation. Additionally, the Land Drainage Improvement Works (Assessment of Environmental Effects) Regulations 1988 require that projects likely to have significant effects on the environment are subject to an environmental assessment which helps to identify both potential opportunities for positive conservation measures as well as potentially adverse effects.

The aim of this component of the appendix is to summarise the present legislation aimed at protecting freshwater species in Britain, and briefly to review its effectiveness. Some areas have been deliberately omitted, such as fisheries legislation designed to conserve stocks. Interested readers are referred to other publications such as those by Howarth (1987) and Jones (1991).

Species rarity

Species protection legislation is naturally focused on those species which are rare or endangered. Rarity may arise for different reasons. Some species have very specific ecological requirements and are unable to adapt and colonise other areas. Some have become rare either as a result of exploitation or due to the destruction or degradation of their habitats. Rarity thus becomes an important criterion in the assessment of conservation value (Ratcliffe 1977), but does not necessarily qualify species as appropriate candidates for statutory protection, although it does in the case of birds. As the coverage, intensity and frequency of freshwater survey and monitoring increases, so the status of individual species becomes clearer. The rarest species are listed in British Red Data Books; those including freshwater species are now available for vascular plants (Perring and Farrell 1983), charophytes (Stuart and Church 1993), insects (Shirt 1987), other invertebrates (Bratton 1991) and birds (Batten, *et al.*, 1990) with volumes covering bryophytes, lichens, fish and other vertebrates in preparation. Other reviews of the status of particular groups include Palmer and Newbold (1983) for wetland and riparian plants, Wallace (1991) for Trichoptera, Foster (in preparation) for the Coleoptera, and Maitland and Lyle (1991) for fish. We have not attempted to provide a complete list of rare British freshwater species as there is no straightforward way of deciding what should or should not be included, and the amount of information available for some groups is far greater than for others.

National Legislation - The Wildlife and Countryside Act 1981

General provisions for species protection
This Act is the main instrument for species protection in Great Britain. Parallel arrangements apply to Northern Ireland and the Isle of Man under separate legislation.

Animals other than birds. Section 9(1) of the Act states that:
'Subject to the provisions of this Part, if any person intentionally kills, injures or takes any wild animal included in Schedule 5, he shall be guilty of an offence.'

It is also an offence under Section 9(4) to '... damage or destroy or obstruct access to any structure or place which any wild animal included in Schedule 5 uses for shelter or protection, or disturb any such animal while it is occupying a structure or place which it uses for that purpose.'

Section 9(2) makes an offence of the '... possession or control of any live or dead wild animal included in Schedule 5 or any part of, or anything derived from, such an animal.'

Plants. The protection of plants is contained within Section 13, where:
'Subject to the provisions of this Part, if any person intentionally picks, uproots or destroys any wild plant included in Schedule 8, or not being an authorised person intentionally uproots any wild plant not included in that schedule, he shall be guilty of an offence.'

Section 9 and 13 also include prohibitions on a wide range of activities relating to the sale and commercialisation of wild specimens of certain scheduled species and their derivatives.

Section 28 allows the statutory conservation agencies to designate Sites of Special Scientific Interest (SSSIs) on the strength of flora and fauna.

Freshwater species of animals (other than birds) and plants listed on Schedules 5 and 8.

Table 1 gives details of all freshwater plants and animals (other than birds) currently protected under the Act (including some which only spend a part of their life-cycle in water, eg *Aeshna isosceles*).

Birds. Under the Act all wild birds, their nests and eggs (with few exceptions) are protected. For riverine species it is an offence intentionally to:

- kill, injure or take any wild bird;

- take, damage or destroy the nest of any wild bird whilst it is in use or being built;

- take or destroy the egg of any wild bird;

- disturb any wild bird listed on Schedule 1 of the Act (see below) whilst it is nest building or at a nest containing eggs or young; or disturb the dependent young of such a bird.

Riverine birds, on Schedule 1 of the Act, are listed in Table 2.

Section 14 covers the prohibition of the introduction of non-native species of plants and animals into the wild by unlicensed persons. A number of these, for example, giant hogweed, Japanese knotweed and coypu, have already posed problems.

The Wildlife and Countryside Act contains provisions for a regular review of scheduled species. Section 22(3) empowers the Secretary of State, on a representation made to him by the Joint Nature Conservation Committee (JNCC) (acting on behalf of the three statutory successor bodies of the NCC: the Nature Conservancy Council for England, Scottish Natural Heritage, and the Countryside Council for Wales) to add to Schedules 5 or 8:

> '... any animal or plant which, in his opinion, is in danger of extinction in Great Britain or is likely to become so endangered unless conservation measures are taken.'

There are similar provisions for removing from the Schedules species no longer endangered. The JNCC may make representations at any time but is in any event bound to make a review of protected species every five years under the terms of Section 24(1) of the Act.

The first review of Schedules 5 and 8 was in 1986 and the second was in 1991. The review procedure covers species themselves threatened in Great Britain. However, there is a need for Great Britain to accept the wider responsibility of affording protection to species that may not be under threat nationally but are considered vulnerable at a European or global level by international forums in

which we participate. Thus, Section 22(4) of the Act provides for the Secretary of State to protect any animal or plant for the purpose of complying with an international obligation.

Defences and exemptions. There are provisions contained within the Act which, under certain circumstances, afford a defence against actions which would otherwise be illegal. For example, under Section 10 an otherwise unlawful act with respect to a protected animal species is not illegal if the person shows that it was the incidental result of a lawful operation and could not reasonably have been avoided. Whether any particular action was incidental and whether it could reasonably have been avoided is a matter for the Courts, but as an example a fisherman who unintentionally catches a powan or a vendace (Table 1) while fishing for other species, or a contractor who destroys a reed warbler's nest may not have committed an offence, although in the case of the fish there would be a presumption that it would be returned to the water unharmed. Section 13(3) makes a similar exemption for plants uprooted or destroyed during an otherwise lawful operation. Similarly the possession or control of a protected species is not an offence if the person involved shows that the specimen in question had not been taken or killed illegally. An important provision under Section 16 allows licences to be granted by the 'appropriate authority' to permit otherwise illegal activities if they are being undertaken for purposes such as scientific research, education, or photography. For information on licences contact EN, CCW or SNH. Licences may also be granted under the same section by MAFF/SOAFD to permit killing to preserve public health, to prevent the spread of disease or to prevent serious damage to livestock or fisheries.

In the case of birds exceptions also exist for the control of pest species (Table 3) and sporting birds (Table 4), shot during the open season. Pest species may be killed, or eggs taken under general licence by authorised persons (landowners or persons with their permission).

It should be noted that in respect of plants and all animals including birds, the Act only related to wild specimens; that is to say specimens which were living wild before they were killed, taken, uprooted, or picked. In any court proceedings, however, the specimen will be assumed to be wild unless the contrary is shown.

Effectiveness of Legislation in the Protection of Freshwater Species

It is not easy to quantify the success (or otherwise) of an individual legal instrument, such as the Wildlife and Countryside Act, in the conservation of a particular species. This clearly depends upon a combination of factors, including the extent and quality of the habitat, and the intensity of the threat. Nevertheless, there are a number of benefits (and problems) which can be readily identified, associated with the statutory protection of freshwater species.

Benefits

Although birds are an exception (being fully protected in Britain) it would be inappropriate and impractical to attempt to add all threatened species of other animals and plants to Schedules 5 or 8. In considering its advice to Government, the JNCC (and NCC before) has sought to propose only species whose direct legal protection would potentially bring tangible conservation benefits to the species concerned. In many cases (especially where there are insidious threats such as habitat loss or pollution), with the provisions of the Act as they are, no significant benefits are likely to accrue by scheduling species.

Once a species is scheduled, however, some secondary benefits become evident, such as increasing public awareness of its importance, encouraging positive habitat management, and devoting increased resources to study the species.

There may be additional benefits as planning authorities are made aware of the presence of scheduled species within an area proposed for development. This proved to be the case at a Public Inquiry held in February 1988 to consider a development proposal for Greatstone Gravel Pit, part of the Dungeness SSSI. This site is believed to contain the largest population of the medicinal leech (*Hirudo medicinalis*) in Britain, and possibly in the whole of western Europe (Wilkin 1987). *H. medicinalis* is listed in the IUCN Invertebrate Red Data Book for Invertebrates (Wells, *et al.*, 1983), as it is now threatened in many of the 26 countries it once inhabited. In Britain, too, it has progressively declined, and its status is given as 'Rare' in the recently published British Red Data Book for Invertebrates (Bratton 1991). The need to conserve the medicinal leech throughout its range has been recognised by its inclusion on Appendix III of the Bern Convention, Annex V of the EC Habitats and Species Directive, by international trade regulations, and (in November 1987) by adding it to Schedule 5 of the Wildlife and Countryside Act (see Table 1).

The subject of the Public Inquiry for Greatstone Pit was the proposed development of a windsurfing and watersports centre. Both the Nature Conservancy Council (NCC) and the Royal Society for the Protection of Birds (RSPB) opposed the scheme on the grounds of nature conservation. Apart from the direct threat to important bird populations from recreational disturbance, the remainder of the evidence centred on the potential impact of the development on the medicinal leech. Factors such as the extent of marginal vegetation, host availability, water movement and temperature regime are all important to this species, and the NCC considered that these were all liable to alteration if the development were to proceed (Boon 1988).

Following the Inquiry, the Inspector stated that: 'Dungeness is acknowledged as being of international importance as a wetlands area and for migratory birds, and Greatstone Pit is now known as a habitat for the medicinal leech, which is to be protected nationally and internationally'. He also concluded from the evidence produced at the Inquiry that activities such as windsurfing and angling would be likely to have indirect detrimental effects on medicinal leeches through their direct impact on birds and amphibia (letter from the Departments of the Environment and Transport, 2.6.88). The Secretary of State accepted the Inspector's recommendation and refused to grant planning permission. While there were several factors that ultimately influenced the outcome of the Inquiry, the statutory protection of *H. medicinalis* certainly played a part in the final decision in favour of conservation.

In a similar case in 1985, proposals for increased recreational activity on a lake in Worcestershire were rejected after a Public Inquiry, partly because this is the only site in Britain for ribbon-leaved water-plantain, *Alisma gramimeum* – a Schedule 8 plant.

As far as birds are concerned, the main benefits from the legislation for riverine species is the prevention of nesting site destruction. For Schedule 1 species (such as the kingfisher) this is absolute and it is an offence under any circumstances to kill the bird or damage/destroy its nest. For other protected species, although there is a defence against killing or destroying (if it was the incidental result of an otherwise lawful operation), it is hoped that workers consider delaying damaging operations (such as silt dredging) until the end of the breeding season.

Problems

Some threatened species may be natural candidates for scheduling, owing to pressures from collection or exploitation, but such pressures only account for a part of the overall threat. For example, the native Atlantic stream crayfish *Austropotamobius pallipes* has suffered a drastic decline in Britain over the past decade (Holdich and Reeve 1991), a decline that has continued despite the addition of the species to Schedule 5 (Table 1). Apart from problems of physical habitat degradation, and a general decline in water quality, much of the harm to this species is caused by the spread of crayfish plague, a fungal disease particularly associated with the introduction of a plague-resistant, non-native species of crayfish. Although the statutory protection afforded to the native species is valuable in highlighting its importance and in controlling some

activities, it can do little to reduce the threat from disease. Other mitigating action has been taken in this case, including the addition of non-native species to Schedule 9 of the Wildlife and Countryside Act, thus making illegal their release into the wild.

One of the most recent species to be granted statutory protection in Britain is the freshwater pearl mussel (*Margaritifera margaritifera*). This species illustrates another problem of scheduling: that of enforcement. Populations of the freshwater pearl mussel have continued to decline throughout its range, and in Britain this has largely been due to a combination of organic pollution and overfishing (Young 1991). The need to protect this species has been recognised internationally by its inclusion on Appendix III of the Bern Convention and Annex V of the EC Habitats and Species Directive. *M. margaritifera* was added to Schedule 5 on 27 March 1991 (Statutory Instrument 367), thus making it illegal to kill or injure it, but not to examine a mussel for pearls and return it unharmed to the river as has been the traditional practice of professional pearl fishermen. Unfortunately, evidence suggests that a great deal of damage is done to mussel populations each year by collectors who either do not know how to inspect mussels without harming them, or are unconcerned at the consequences of their actions. However, many of the sites where healthy populations still remain and where damage is occurring are situated in the remoter parts of Scotland, and in these areas enforcement of the legislation will be difficult (Young 1991).

Future Requirements

The protection of freshwater species through concerted efforts at maintaining and improving habitat quality must remain a top priority. There is little point in focusing all the attention on legal implements applied to individual species if nothing is done to reverse declines in water quality and quantity, or in safeguarding physical habitat structure. However, alongside such measures, legislation for protecting endangered species forms an important second thread.

To be effective, statutory methods require three fundamentals. First, there must be adequate, up-to-date information on the distribution of species populations so that their status can be accurately assessed. There are still many groups of freshwater organisms where this knowledge is inadequate. Second, resources should be directed towards regular monitoring of threatened species. Only then can recommendations be made to government for adding other species to Schedules or, if appropriate, removing species no longer considered endangered. It also provides a means of evaluating the effectiveness of the legislation itself. Third, for those species which do enjoy protected status the legislation must be used to full advantage. This may entail programmes of education to increase general awareness of the importance of certain species and their habitats. It may also require improved methods of detecting infringements of the laws and better ways of enforcing it.

Northern Ireland

Birds, certain mammals, reptiles, amphibians, butterflies and plants are protected under the Wildlife (Northern Ireland) Order 1985. The provisions of this Order are similar to those in force in the remainder of the United Kingdom, although the species listed within the schedules differ, reflecting their distribution within Northern Ireland. Further information is available from the Department of the Environment (Northern Ireland) Countryside and Wildlife Service, Calvert House, Castle Place, Belfast B21 1FY.

References

Boon, P J (1988) Town and Country Planning Act 1971, section 35: Local Inquiry Application for Planning Permission by Jonathan Finn-Kelcey to Develop a Windsurfing and Water Sports Centre at the Greatstone Pit, Leonard Road, Lydd-on-Sea, Kent. Proof of Evidence.

Batten, L A, Bibby, C J, Clemont, P, Elliott, G D and Porter, R F (1990) *Red Data Birds in Britain*. NCC and RSPB, London.

Bratton, J H (ed.) (1991) *British Red Data Books: 3. Invertebrates other than Insects*. Joint Nature Conservation Committee, Peterborough.

Department of Environment (NI) (1985) *The Wildlife Law and You*. DoE (NI), Belfast.

Holdich, D M and Reeve, I D (1991) Distribution of freshwater crayfish in the British Isles, with particular reference to crayfish plague, alien introductions and water quality. *Aquatic Conservation: Marine and Freshwater Ecosystems*, 1:139–158.

Howarth, W (1987) *Freshwater Fishery Law*. Blackstone Press Ltd, London.

Jones, A (1991) British wildlife and the law. A review of the species protection provisions of the Wildlife and Countryside Act 1981. *British Wildlife*, 2:345–358.

Maitland, P M and Lyle, A A (1991) Conservation of freshwater fish in the British Isles: the current status and biology of threatened species. *Aquatic Conservation: Marine and Freshwater Ecosystems*, 1:25–54.

Palmer, M and Newbold, C (1983) Wetland and Riparian Plants in Great Britain. *Focus on Nature Conservation*, No. 1. Nature Conservancy Council, Peterborough.

Perring, F H and Farrell, L (1983) *British Red Data Books: 1. Vascular Plants. 2nd ed*. Royal Society for Nature Conservation, Lincoln.

Ratcliffe, D (ed.) (1977) *A Nature Conservation Review*. Cambridge University Press, Cambridge.

Royal Society for the Protection of Birds (1993). *Wild Birds and the Law*. Sandy.

Shirt, D B (ed.) (1987) *British Red Data Books: 2. Insects*. Nature Conservancy Council, Peterborough.

Stewart, N F and Church, J M (1993) *Red Data Books of Britain and Ireland: Stoneworts*. Joint Nature Conservation Committee, Peterborough.

Wallace, I D (1991) A review of the Trichoptera of Great Britain. *Research and survey in nature conservation*, No. 32. Nature Conservancy Council, Peterborough.

Wells, S M, Pyle, R M and Collins, N M (1983) *The IUCN Invertebrate Red Data Book*. International Union for Conservation of Nature and Natural Resources, Gland.

Wilkin, P J (1987) A study of the medicinal leech *Hirudo medicinalis* (L.) with a strategy for its conservation. Unpublished Phd thesis, Wye College, University of London.

Young, M R (1991) Conserving and Freshwater Pearl Mussel (*Margaritifera margaritifera* L.) in the British Isles and Continental Europe. *Aquatic Conservation: Marine and Freshwater Ecosystems*, 1:73–78.

Table 1: A list of freshwater organisms (excluding brackish-water and estuarine species) protected (+) under Schedules 5 and 8 of the Wildlife and Countryside Act 1981, with note of their status under the EC Habitats and Species Directive (Annex II, IV or V) and the Bern Convention (Appendices I-III).

Offences covered under Schedules 5 and 8 are killing and injuring (K/I), taking (T), possessing (P), disturbance at and damage to place of shelter (D/D), picking, uprooting and destroying (P/U/D), sale (S).

COMMON NAME	K/I	T	P	D/D	S	EC	Bern
Schedule 5							
Medicinal leech	+	+	+	+	+	V	III
Apus	+	+	+	+	+	-	-
Fairy shrimp	+	+	+	+	+	-	-
Atlantic stream crayfish	-	+	-	-	+	II,V	III
Fen raft spider	+	+	+	+	+	-	-
Norfolk aeshna dragonfly	+	+	+	+	+	-	-
Water beetle (*Graphodurus zonatus*)	+	+	+	+	+	-	-
Water beetle (*Hydrochara caraboides*)	+	+	+	+	+	-	-
Water beetle (*Paracymus aeneus*)	+	+	+	+	+	-	-
Freshwater pearl mussel	+	-	-	-	-	II,V	III
Glutinous snail	+	+	+	+	+	-	-
Common frog	-	-	-	-	+	V	III
Common toad	-	-	-	-	+	-	III
Natterjack toad	+	+	+	+	+	IV	II
Great crested newt	+	+	+	+	+	II,IV	II
Palmate newt	-	-	-	-	+	-	III
Smooth newt	-	-	-	-	+	-	III
Burbot	+	+	+	+	+	-	-
Allis shad	+	+	-	-	-	II,V	III
Sturgeon	+	+	+	+	+	V	III
Vendace	+	+	+	+	+	V	III
Whitefish (Powan)	+	+	+	+	+	V	III
Otter	+	+	+	+	+	II,IV	II

	P/U/D	S	EC	Bern
Schedule 8				
Bearded stonewort	+	+	-	-
Derbyshire feathermoss	+	+	-	-
River jelly-lichen	+	+	-	-
Tarn lecanora	+	+	-	-
Creeping marshwort	+	+	-	-
Strapwort	+	+	II,IV	I
Pigmyweed	+	+	-	-
Welsh mudwort	+	+	-	-
Adder's-tongue spearwort	+	+	-	-
Ribbon-leaved water-plantain	+	+	-	-
Floating-leaved water-plantain	+	+	II,IV	I
Slender naiad	+	+	II,IV	I
Starfruit	+	+	-	-
Holly-leaved naiad	+	+	-	-

Footnotes

1. Bats - although not strictly freshwater animals regularly use bankside trees for roosting. They are fully protected at all times.

2. For a full list of species protected under the Wildlife (Northern Ireland) Order 1985 see *The Wildlife Law and You* published by DoE (NI).

Table 2: Birds protected by special penalties under Schedule 1 of the Wildlife and Countryside Act

The species listed are only those associated with rivers and their environments:

Barn owl
Bearded tit
Bewick's swan
Bittern
Black-tailed godwit
Cetti's warbler
Garganey
Harrier (all species)
Kingfisher
Little bittern
Little ringed plover
Marsh warbler
Osprey
Purple heron
Ruff
Savi's warbler
Spotted crake
Temminck's stint
Whooper swan

also: (between 1 Feb and 31 Aug)
Goldeneye
Greylag goose (in Outer Hebrides, Caithness, Sutherland and Wester Ross only)
Pintail

Table 3: Birds classed as pest species under the Wildlife and Countryside Act

Collared dove
Crow
Feral pigeon
Great black-backed gull
Herring gull
House sparrow
Jackdaw
Jay
Lesser black-backed gull
Magpie
Rook
Starling
Wood pigeon

Table 4: Birds that may occur in or near riverine habitats and which may be killed or taken under Schedule 2, Part 1 of the Wildlife and Countryside Act

SPECIES	CLOSE SEASON
Canada goose	1 Feb – 31 Aug
Coot	"
Common snipe	1 Feb – 11 Aug
Gadwall	1 Feb – 31 Aug
Golden plover	"
Goldeneye	"
Greylag goose	"
Mallard	"
Moorhen	"
Partridge	2 Feb – 31 Aug
Pheasant	2 Feb – 30 Sept
Pink-footed goose	1 Feb – 31 Aug
Pintail	"
Pochard	"
Shoveler	"
Teal	"
Tufted duck	"
Wigeon	"
White-fronted goose (in England and Wales only)	"
Woodcock	1 Feb – 30 Sept (England and Wales) 1 Feb – 31 Aug (Scotland)

Table 5: A list of freshwater organisms (excluding brackish-water and estuarine species) recorded in Britain, not scheduled under the Wildlife and Countryside Act, but listed in the EC Habitats and Species Directive (EC, Annexes II, IV or V) and the Bern Convention (Appendices II, III).

COMMON NAME	EC	Bern
Orange-spotted emerald dragonfly	II,IV	II
Southern damselfly	II	II
Water beetle	II,IV	II
River lamprey	II,V	III
Brook lamprey	II	III
Sea lamprey	II	III
Twaite shad	II,V	III
Grayling	V	III
Salmon	II,V	III
Barbel	V	-
Spined loach	II	III
Bullhead	II	-
Houting	II,IV	III
Plants		
Bog moss	V	-

Appendix III: Abbreviations used in text

ADAS	Agricultural Development and Advisory Service	HSE	Health and Safety Executive
		IDB	Inland Drainage Board
ASSI	Area of Special Scientific Interest (NI)	IFE	Institute of Freshwater Ecology
ASPT	Average Score Per Taxon	IH	Institute of Hydrology
BGS	British Geological Survey	ISR	Invertebrate Site Register
BMWP	British Monitoring Working Party	ITE	Institute of Terrestrial Ecology
BSBI	Botanical Society of the British Isles	JNCC	Joint Nature Conservation Committee
BTO	British Trust for Ornithology	MAFF	Ministry of Agriculture, Fisheries and Food
CCW	Countryside Council for Wales	NCC	Nature Conservancy Council
CIRIA	Construction Industry Research and Information Association	NI	Northern Ireland
		NRA	National Rivers Authority
		NWC	National Water Council
COSHH	Control of Substances Hazardous to Health Regulations	OS	Ordnance Survey
		PCB	Polychlorinated biphenyl
		PHABSIM	Physical HABitat SIMulation
CPR	Control of Pesticides Regulations	RCS	River Corridor Survey
		RHS	River Habitat Survey
CPUE	Catch Per Unit Effort	RDB	Red Data Book
DANI	Department of Agriculture for Northern Ireland	RIVPACS	River Invertebrate Prediction and Classification Scheme
DoE	Department of the Environment	RPB	River Purification Board
DOE(NI)	Department of the Environment (Northern Ireland)	RSPB	Royal Society for the Protection of Birds
		SOAFD	Scottish Office Agriculture and Fisheries Department
DTI	Department of Trade and Industry	SNH	Scottish Natural Heritage
		SPA	Special Protection Area
DWF	Dry Weather Flow	SRPB	Scottish River Purification Board
EN	English Nature		
EQI	Index of Environmental Quality	SSSI	Site of Special Scientific Interest
EU	European Union	STRI	Sports Turf Research Council
FBA	Freshwater Biological Association	UK	United Kingdom of Great Britain and Northern Ireland
GIS	Geographical Information System	WOAD	Welsh Office Agriculture Department

Appendix IV: Scientific names of species referred to the text

PLANTS

Adder's tongue	*Ophioglossum vulgatum*
Alder	*Alnus glutinosa*
Alga	*Chladophora glomerata*
red	*Hildenbrandia rivularis*
Angelica, wild	*Angelica sylvestris*
Apple	*Malus sylvestris* spp *sylvestris*
Arrowhead	*Sagittaria sagittifolia*
Ash	*Frangula alnus*
Aspen	*Populus tremula*
Avens, water	*Geum rivale*
Balsam, Indian	*Impatiens glandulifera*
Barley, meadow	*Hordeum secalinum*
Basil, wild	*Clinopodium vulgare*
Bedstraw, lady's	*Galium verum*
Beech	*Fagus sylvatica*
Bell-flower, clustered	*Campanula glomerata*
Bent, common	*Agrostis tenuis*
creeping	*A. stolonifera*
Birch, hairy	*Betula pubescens*
silver	*B. pendula*
Bird's-foot-trefoil	*Lotus corniculatus*
greater	*L. uliginosus*
Bistort, amphibious	*Polygonum amphibium*
Bitter-cress, large	*Cardamine amara*
Bittersweet	*Solanum dulcamara*
Blackthorn	*Prunus spinosa*
Bladder-sedge	*Carex versicaria*
Blinks	*Montia fontana*
Bogbean	*Menyanthes trifoliata*
Box	*Buxus sempervirens*
Brome, upright	*Bromus erectus*
Brooklime	*Veronica beccabunga*
Broom	*Cytisus scoparius*
Buckthorn	*Rhamnus catharticus*
Bulrush, common	*Typha latifolia*
Bur-marigold	*Bidens cernua*
Bur-reed, least	*Sparganium minimum*
branched	*S. erectum*
unbranched	*S. emersum*
Burnet, great	*Sanguisorba officinalis*
salad	*Poterium sanguisorba*
Butcher's-broom	*Ruseus aculeatus*
Butterbur	*Petasites hybridus*
Buttercup, common	*Ranunculus acris*
meadow	
Campion, white	*Silene alba*
Canary-grass, reed	*Phalaris arundinacea*
Carrot, wild	*Daucus carota*
Cat's-ear, common	*Hypochoeris radicata*
Celery-leaved buttercup	*Ranunculus sceleratus*
Cherry, bird	*Prunus padus*
wild	*P. avium*
Club-rush, common	*Scirpus lacustris*
floating	*Eleogiton fluitans*
wood	*Scirpus sylvaticus*
Colt's-foot	*Tussilago farfara*
Comfrey	*Symphytum officinale*
Cowslip	*Primula veris*
Crane's-bill, meadow	*Geranium pratense*
Crowfoot, round-leaved	*Ranunculus omiophyllus*
ivy-leaved	*R. hederaceus*
Daisy, oxeye	*Leucanthemum vulgare*
Dog's-tail, crested	*Cynosurus cristatus*
Dogwood	*Cornus sanguinea*
Dropwort	*Filipendula vulgaris*
Duckweed, fat	*Lemna gibba*
common	*L. minor*
Dyer's rocket	*Reseda luteola*
Elder	*Sambucus nigra*
Elm, wych	*Ulmus glabra*
Fern, Royal	*Osmunda regalis*
Fescue, red	*Festuca rubra* var. 'Cascade'
	'Dawson'
	'Highlight'
	'Rapid'
Flowering-rush	*Butomus umbellatus*
Fox-sedge, false	*Carex otrubae*
Foxtail, marsh	*Alopecurus geniculatus*
meadow	*A. pratensis*
orange	*A. aequalis*
Frogbit	*Hydrocharis morsus-ranae*
Gipsywort	*Lycopus europaeus*
Goat's-beard	*Tragopogon pratensis*
Gorse	*Ulex europeus*
Guelder-rose	*Viburnum opulus*
Hair-grass, crested	*Keoleria cristata*
Hairy sedge	*Carex hirta*
Harebell	*Campanula rotundifolia*
Hawkbit, rough	*Leontodon hispidus*
Hawthorn	*Crataegus monogyna*
Hazel	*Corylus avellana*
Hemp-agrimony	*Eupatorium cannibinum*
Holly	*Ilex aquifolium*
Hornbeam	*Carpinus betulus*
Hornwort, rigid	*Ceratophyllum demersum*
Horsetail, marsh	*Equisetum palustre*
water	*E. fluviatile*

Iris, flag	*Iris pseudacorus*	lesser	*C. acutiformis*
yellow	*I. pseudacorus*	Pondweed, bog	*Potamogeton polygonifolius*
Juniper	*Juniperus communis*	broad-leaved	*P. natans*
Knapweed	*Centaurea nigra*	Canadian	*Elodea canadensis*
great	*C. scabiosa*	curled	*Potamogeton crispus*
Lady's smock	*Cardimine pratensis*	fennel	*P. pectinatus*
Lime, large-leaved	*Tilia platyphyllos*	flat-stalked	*P. friesii*
small-leaved	*T. cordata*	horned	*Zannichellia palustris*
Liverworts	*Chiloscyphus polyanthos*	opposite-leaved	*Groenlandia densa*
	Marsupella emarginata	perfoliate	*Potamogeton perfoliatus*
	Nardia compressa	shining	*P. lucens*
	Pellia epiphylla	small	*P. berchtoldii*
	Scapania undulata	Poplar, black	*Populus nigra*
	Solenostoma triste	grey	*P. canescens*
Loosestrife, yellow	*Lysimachia vulgaris*	white	*P. alba*
Maple, field	*Acer campestre*	Privet, wild	*Ligustrum vulgare*
Mare's-tail	*Hippuris vulgaris*	Purple-loosestrife	*Lythrum salicaria*
Marsh marigold	*Caltha palustris*	Quaking-grass, common	*Briza media*
Marsh-bedstraw, common	*Galium palustre*	Ragged-robin	*Lychnis flos-cuculi*
Mat-grass	*Nardus stricta*	Ragwort, marsh	*Senecio aquaticus*
Meadow-grass	*Poa pratensis* 'Baron'	Rattle, yellow	*Rhinanthus minor*
Meadow-rue	*Thalictrum flavum*	Reed, common	*Phragmites australis*
Meadowsweet	*Filipendula ulmaria*	Reedmace	*Typha latifolia*
Medick, black	*Medicago lupulina*	narrow-leaved	*T. angustifolia*
Mignonette, wild	*Reseda lutea*	Rose, dog	*Rosa canina*
Monkeyflower	*Mimulus guttatus*	Rowan	*Sorbus aucuparia*
Moor-grass, purple	*Molinia caerulea*	Rush, bulbous	*Juncus bulbosus*
Mosses	*Brachythecium rivulare*	hard	*J. inflexus*
	Bryum alpinum	jointed	*J. articulatus*
	Calliergon cuspidatum	sharp-flowered	*J. acutiflorus*
	Cinclidotus fontinaloides	Sainfoin	*Onobrychis viciifolia*
	Dichodontium pellucidum	Saxifrage, pepper	*Silaum silaus*
	Dicranella palustris	Scabious, small	*Scabiosa columbaria*
	Fontinalis antipyretica	field	*Knautia arvensis*
	Fontinalis squamosa	Sedge, bottle	*Carex rostrata*
	Hygrohypnum ochraceum	common	*C. nigra*
	H. luridum	hairy	*C. hirta*
	Hyocomium armoricum	pendulous	*C. pendula*
	Philonotis fontana	water	*C. aquatilis*
	Polytrichum commune	Self-heal	*Prunella vulgaris*
	Racomitrium aciculare	Service-tree	*Sorbus torminalis*
	Rhynchostegium riparioides	Sharp-flowered rush	*Juncus acutiflorus*
	Schistidium agassizii	Shoreweed	*Littorella uniflora*
	Sphagnum spp	Sneezewort	*Achillea ptarmica*
	Thamnobryum alopecurum	Soft-rush	*Juncus effusus*
Moss, willow	*Fontinalis antipyretica*	Spearwort, greater	*Ranunculus lingua*
Nottingham catchfly	*Silene nutans*	lesser	*R. flammula*
Oak, pedunculate	*Quercus robur*	Speedwell, germander	*Veronica chamaedrys*
sessile	*Q. petraea*	Spike-rush, common	*Eleocharis palustris*
Oat-grass, yellow	*Trisetum flavescens*	Spindle	*Eonymus europaeus*
Pignut	*Conopodium majus*	Spurge-laurel	*Daphne laureola*
Plantain, hoary	*Plantago media*	Stitchwort, marsh	*Stellaria palustris*
Plantain, ribwort	*Alisma plantago lanceolata*	Sweet-flag	*Acorus calamus*
water	*A. plantago-aquatica*	Sweet-grass, floating	*Glyceria fluitans*
Pond-sedge, greater	*Carex riparia*	plicate	*G. plicata*

reed	*G. maxima*	grey	*S. cinerea*
small	*G. declinata*	purple	*S. purpurea*
Teasel	*Dipsacus fullonum sylvestris*	white	*S. alba*
Thyme, common large	*Thymus drucei*	Willowherb, hairy	*Epilobium hirsutum*
wild	*T. pulegioides*	Woundwort, marsh	*Stachys palustris*
Tormentil	*Potentilla erecta*	Yellow-cress, creeping	*Rorippa sylvestris*
Tufted-sedge	*Carex elata*	great	*R. amphibia*
Tufted-sedge, slender	*C. acuta*	marsh	*R. palustris*
Tussock-sedge, great	*C. paniculata*	Yew	*Taxus baccata*
Valerian	*C. valeriana officinalis*		
Vetch, horseshoe	*Hippocrepis comosa*	**FISH**	
kidney	*Anthyllis vulneraria*	Atlantic salmon	*Salmo salar*
Violet, marsh	*Viola palustris*	Brown trout	*S. trutta fario*
Water chickweed	*Myosotum aquaticum*	Rainbow trout	*S. gairdneri*
Water dock	*Rumex hydrolapathum*	Pike	*Esox lucius*
Water figwort	*Scrophularia auriculata*	Common carp	*Cyprinus carpio*
Water forget-me-not	*Myosotis scorpioides*	Crucian carp	*Carassius carassius*
Water-mint	*Mentha aquatica*	Goldfish	*C. auratus*
Water-cress	*Nasturtium officinale*	Barbel	*Barbus barbus*
fool's	*Apium nodiflorum*	Gudgeon	*Gobio gobio*
Water-crowfoot, brook	*Ranunculus calcareus*	Tench	*Tinca tinca*
common	*R. aquatilis*	Silver bream	*Blicca bjoerkna*
fan-leaved	*R. circinatus*	Bream	*Abramix brama*
pond	*R. peltatus*	Bleak	*Alburnus alburnus*
river	*R. fluitans*	Minnow	*Phoxinus phoxinus*
stream	*R. penicillatus*	Rudd	*Scardinius erythrophthalmus*
thread-leaved	*R. trichophyllus*	Roach	*Rutilus rutilus*
Water-dropwort, hemlock	*Oenanthe crocata*	Chub	*Leuciscus cephalus*
river	*O. fluviatilis*	Orfe	*L. idus*
Water-lily, fringed	*Nymphoides peltata*	Dace	*L. leuciscus*
white	*Nymphaea alba*	Spined loach	*Cobitis taenia*
yellow	*Nuphar lutea*	Stone loach	*Noemacheilus barbatulus*
Water-milfoil,		Eel	*Anguilla anguilla*
alternate	*Myriophyllum alterniflorum*	Three-spined	
spiked	*M. spicatum*	stickleback	*Gasterosteus aculeatus*
Water-parsnip, lesser	*Berula erecta*	Nine-spined stickleback	*Pungitius pungitius*
Water-speedwell,		Perch	*Perca fluviatilis*
blue	*Veronica anagallis aquatica*	Ruffe	*Gymnocephalus cernua*
pink	*V. catenata*	Zander	*Stizostedion lucioperca*
Water-starwort,		Bullhead	*Cottus gobio*
blunt-fruited	*Callitriche obtusangula*		
common	*C. stagnalis*	**AMPHIBIANS**	
intermediate	*C. hamulata*	Common frog	*Rana temporaria*
Water-starwort,		Common toad	*Bufo bufo*
intermediate	*Callitriche hamulata*	Natterjack toad	*B. calamita*
Waterweed, Canadian	*Elodea canadensis*	Smooth newt	*Triturus vulgaris*
Nuttall's	*E. nuttallii*	Great crested newt	*T. cristatus*
Wayfaring-tree	*Viburnum lantana*	Palmate newt	*T. helveticus*
Whitebeam	*Sorbus aria*		
Whorl-grass	*Catabrosa aquatica*	**REPTILES**	
Willow, almond	*Salix triandra*	Grass snake	*Natrix natrix*
bay	*S. pentandra*	Adder	*Vipera berus*
crack	*S. fragilis*	Smooth snake	*Coronella austriaca*
eared	*S. aurita*	Common lizard	*Lacerta vivipara*
goat	*S. caprea*	Sand lizard	*L. agilis*

BIRDS

Great crested grebe	*Podiceps cristatus*
Little grebe	*Tachybaptus ruficollis*
Grey heron	*Ardea cinerea*
Mute swan	*Cygnus olor*
Mallard	*Anas platyrhynchas*
Wigeon	*A. penelope*
Teal	*A. crecca*
Tufted duck	*Aythya fuligula*
Goosander	*Mergus merganser*
Red-breasted merganser	*M. serrator*
Water rail	*Rallus aquaticus*
Moorhen	*Gallinula chloropus*
Coot	*Fulica atra*
Oystercatcher	*Haematopus ostralegus*
Little ringed plover	*Charadrius dubius*
Golden plover	*Pluvialis apricaria*
Lapwing	*Vanellus vanellus*
Redshank	*Tringa totanus*
Common sandpiper	*Tringa hypoleucos*
Snipe	*Gallinago gallinago*

Kingfisher	*Alcedo atthis*
Sand martin	*Riparia riparia*
Pied wagtail	*Motacilla alba*
Grey wagtail	*M. cinerea*
Yellow wagtail	*M. citreola*
Reed warbler	*Acrocephalus scirpaceus*
Sedge warbler	*A. schoenobaenus*
Dipper	*Cinclus cinclus*
Reed bunting	*Emberiza schoenoclus*

MAMMALS

Water shrew	*Neomys fodiens*
Daubenton's bat	*Mysotis daubentoni*
Whiskered bat	*M. mystacinus*
Natterer's bat	*M. nattereri*
Pipistrelle	*Pipistrellus pipistrellus*
Otter	*Lutra lutra*
Mink	*Mustela vison*
Water vole	*Arvicola terrestris*

Appendix V: Glossary

aggressive weed species A species that competes so effectively that it can eliminate others.

algae A diverse group of simple aquatic plants, some microscopic, which may grow in rivers in great profusion (blooms).

alien Plant or animal not native to the country concerned.

annual A plant that grows, flowers, produces seed, and then dies within one year or growing season.

aquatic plants A term given to plants that grow entirely covered by water, like water-milfoil, or at the surface, such as yellow water-lily. Some plants have both aquatic and emergent forms.

aquifer Water-bearing strata eg sandstone.

arboriculture The cultivation of trees or shrubs.

armour layer The coarse surface layer of stones overlying (and protecting) finer sediment in gravel-bed rivers.

arterial drainage Main part of river or drainage system.

ASPT Average score per taxon; an invertebrate survey score system.

backwater Aquatic or semi-aquatic areas of low velocity or stagnant water, most commonly of present or former river channel within the alluvial plain.

bank Permanent side to river, top marked by first major break in slope.

bankfull discharge Discharge that fills a channel without overtopping the banks. It is an intermediate discharge which is considered to be a critical or dominant channel-forming event in natural rivers.

bar An accumulation of sediment in a river, formed underwater in floods and subsequently exposed at lower flows.

baseflow The long-term response of a catchment to rainfall.

batter Slope of a bank, expressed either as a ratio of horizontal distance to vertical distance (eg 1:2) or as the angle of slope in degrees (eg 63°).

benthos Flora and fauna living on the bed of the river.

berm Shelf at the base of a bank that is at the level of normal flow and gives extra channel width in high flows.

bio-technical engineering The combination of engineering materials and vegetation to provide defence against erosion eg geotextiles/reeds.

biomass A quantitative estimate of animal and/or plant matter.

biotic Relating to living things.

blockstone Large pieces of natural stone, preferably of local origin, used in bank protection and current deflectors.

BMWP Biological Monitoring Working Party score; an invertebrate survey scoring system.

bole The trunk of a tree, especially the lower portion.

braided channel Formed by a constantly dividing river.

brashings Small branches trimmed from the sides and top of a main stem.

bryophyte Moss or liverwort; any member of the division Bryophyta.

buttress An exterior pier, often sloped, used to provide support against lateral forces, particularly for tall walls.

by-pass A channel built to divert water from a primary channel (main river).

callus A mass of plant cells that form around a wound on a plant.

capital works Initial capital outlay such as re-sectioning or widening (as opposed to maintenance works).

carr Wet woodland composed of trees such as willow and alder, which is a successional stage between open water and dry woodland.

channelisation Artificial modification of channels by widening, deepening, straightening, embanking or concrete lining for purposes of flood alleviation, drainage of agricultural land or stabilisation.

coarse fish Eg pike, chub, dace, roach. Not Salmonid species (eg salmon, trout).

cohesiveness A property of loose, fine-grained sediments whereby the particles stick together as a result of the surface forces (eg clay).

colonisation The successful occupation of a new habitat by a species not previously found in the area.

communities Groups of plants and/or animals living together under characteristic, recognisable conditions.

conveyance Flow capacity of a channel (degree to which discharge is dependent on cross-section properties and friction).

coppicing Traditional management of trees and shrubs for wood production by cutting stems close to the base and removing regrowth periodically.

corridor That part of the floodplain or land either side of the river extending from bankfull banktop to 50-m width.

crotch Forked crown of pollarded tree.

culverts Covered channels or pipelines under a structure.

detritus Fragments of decaying plant/animal matter.

diversity Relates to the number of species present and their abundance.

dormancy An inactive or quiescent period in winter during which plant growth ceases.

DWF Dry weather flow.

electrical conductivity Measure of the total ion content of river water.

embankments Man-made bank to raise natural bank level in order to reduce frequency of flooding of adjacent agricultural/urban land.

emergent vegetation Plants that grow in water but have leaf structures that emerge above the surface, eg bulrush.

enhancement Small-scale environmental improvements.

environmental impact assessment EU requirement for developers to assess the possible impact on the environment of any significant development project (refer to HMSO Environmental Assessment: A guide to procedures).

environmental stress A threat to an organism caused by changes in their environment eg pollution, increasing/decreasing flows, that is having a detrimental effect on its population.

epiphytes A plant that uses another plant (usually a tree) or non-living structures for support but not for nourishment.

EQI Index of Environmental Quality.

ESA Environmentally Sensitive Area; where the landscape, wildlife and historic interest are of national importance. Payments are made by Agriculture and Fisheries Departments for appropriate sensitive land management.

eutrophic Nutrient enriched.

evapo- Loss of water to the

transpiration atmosphere by evaporation and through leaves.

fabric pockets Mesh for bank protection with pockets into which rhizomes and ballast material can be placed.

faggoting Method of bank protection using bundles of long branches (faggots) placed along the water's edge and pegged down.

fascine Bundle of brushwood, eg willow.

fens A flat region of land that has developed from stretches of base-rich water that have silted up with a build-up of basic peat. Persistent wet marshy conditions prevent large trees growing.

fines Small particles.

flashes Small depression with shallow water, which may be natural or excavated.

floating-leaved plants Plants rooted in soil with their leaves floating on the water surface.

floodplain The low relief area of valley floor adjacent to a river that is periodically inundated by flood waters.

flow augmentation The 'topping up' of rivers/streams with stored or diverted water.

flow convergence/ divergence Alternating tendency of surface stream lines to converge over pools and diverge over riffles and bars. The opposite action occurs at the riverbed and controls patterns of sediment transport.

fluvial Pertaining to, or found in rivers.

fluvio-geomorph-ology
Study of the physical nature of the earth's surface as affected by rivers.

freeboard
Distance between the water surface and top of the bank.

friable
Describing soils that when either wet or dry can be easily crumbled between the fingers.

fyke nets
Fishing net designed to catch eels, consisting of a tube of netting supported by hoops with three or more internal funnels leading to a toe closed by a purse string.

gabion
Basket, usually made of galvanised wire or polymer mesh (traditionally made of wicker), filled with stones, crushed concrete or earth and used for bank reinforcement.

game fish
Eg salmon and trout, as opposed to coarse fish

geomorph-ology
The study of earth surface features and their formation.

geotextiles
Natural or synthetic permeable fabrics used in conjunction with soil for the function of erosion protection.

GIS
Geographical Information System.

grasslands (neutral/wet)
Neutral grasslands are found mainly on clay or loam and are used for grazing and/or hay production. There are different types, depending on management and water regime. Lowland wet grassland is managed grassland below 200 m, which is usually subject to periodic flooding by water eg washlands and floodplain grassland.

groynes
Structure built into riverbank to deflect current and protect the land from erosion.

hard-engineering
Collective term for bank protection with materials such as steel, concrete etc. as distinct from protection with natural "soft' materials such as vegetation. See also 'soft-engineering'.

hardness
Measure of calcium salts dissolved in water.

heavy metal
Metals such as mercury that may have a deleterious environmental impact.

herbicides
Any agent either organic or inorganic, used to kill unwanted vegetation.

higher plants
All plants excluding fungi, mosses, lichens and algae. See also macrophytes.

holt
Resting or breeding site of an otter, usually an underground in the roots of bankside trees, piles of logs, caves in rock falls or drains.

home range
An area of land or water where an animal normally lives. It is not actively defended as a territory would be.

hover
An above ground resting or breeding site for an otter, which may be a bed of vegetation, eg brambles, or flood debris.

hurdles
Panels made of woven coppice stems, usually hazel, and used as a traditional bank revetment.

hydraulic radius
Defined as the cross sectional area of a river divided by its wetted perimeter.

hydrograph   A graph showing stage (water height) or discharge, plotted against time.

hydro-geomorph-ology   The integrated study of hydrological and geomorphological processes.

hydrology   The study of water and its dynamics.

hyporheic zone   Saturated interface between surface water and ground water below riverbed.

imbricated   Well-graded gravel deposit with ordered structure.

incised   Where a river has cut downwards into its channel, producing raised banks.

indigenous   Native or occurring naturally in a particular area.

interstices   Spaces between substrate particles.

invertebrates   Animals without a backbone, eg insects, worms, spiders.

larvae   Young stage of aquatic organisms, especially insects.

levees   A raised bank along a river or riverine flood plain.

levels of service   Minimum standards of flood alleviation for various classes of land potential.

lichen   A group of lower plants consisting of a fungus which enfolds an alga, the two living together to their mutual benefit.

macrophyte   Another term for higher plants (q.v.).

main river   Rivers designated as 'Main' on a map held by MAFF; generally defined as a watercourse of strategic nature, carrying flows from an upland catchment of significant size to the sea.

maintenance works   Regular river maintenance such as desilting or weed control.

Manning equation $(V = {}^1\!/\mathrm{n}\, R^{2/3}\, S^{1/2})$ Formula relating steady velocity to cross-section properties, energy slope and Manning's friction coefficient 'n'.

margin   A term used to describe the junction of the water and the bank.

meander   Broad, looping bend in a stream channel.

metabolic rate   The rate at which the chemical and physical processes take place within a living organism.

micro-organisms   A general term for any microscopic organism, including algae, bacteria, fungi, protozoa and viruses.

micro-climate   The climate of a very small or confined area, influenced by local conditions.

micro-habitat   A component of a habitat differentiated from its surroundings. It may be extremely small but can be important for providing a specialised environment for particular plants or animals.

migrant   An organism that moves from one region to another, particularly birds.

mire   Area of peatland; includes bog (acid) and fen (alkaline).

morphology   Science of form and structure of, eg a river channel.

mulch A protective covering that is spread on the ground around plants to inhibit evaporation and weed growth, control soil temperature, and enrich the soil. Commonly of organic material such as leaves or bark.

multi-stage channels Most commonly two-stage, with berms cut above normal water level to contain flood waters, increasing channel capacity in times of flood.

niche Where a plant or animal lives within its community, which determines its activities and relationships with other organisms and its environment.

nickpoint Abrupt step in the long-profile of a stream channel, often present in a straightened reach which is downcutting.

nurse crop A crop that is planted to protect another crop by providing shade and preventing weed growth.

nursery grounds Fish spawning areas.

nutrient cycle The manner in which nutrients move through an ecosystem.

nutrient stripping The removal of nutrients by either biological or chemical processes.

offstream pond Flood storage pond with the dry weather flow by-passing the storage area.

O group Fish less than one year old.

on-stream pond Flood storage pond with the dry weather flow passing through the storage area.

oxbow Small lake formed in former riverbed, when a bend in a meandering river is cut off from the main stream.

parasite An animal or plant living in or on an organism of another species, from which it takes nourishment.

passerine Perching or songbird, including finches, larks, sparrows, thrushes and crows.

penned Artificially held water level.

pH A scale of 14 points indicating the degree of acidity or alkalinity of water; 7 is neutral.

photosynthesis Production, in green plants, of organic compounds from carbon dioxide and water using light energy from the sun.

PHABSIM Physical HABitat SIMulation - a suite of computer programs used to generate habitat *vs* discharge relationships.

phytoplankton Microscopic photosynthetic organisms adapted to live suspended in water (eg algae).

pioneer trees First trees to establish themselves as part of succession, eg willow, alder.

planform Layout as viewed from above.

poaching Trampling by livestock causing land to break up into wet muddy patches.

point bar Bar formed on the convex side of a channel bed.

pollarding Method of managing trees, particularly willows, by cutting the trunk at head

protective canopy   Cover of leaves, providing protection from climatic extremes.

rank species   Those which grow vigorously and profusely, out-competing other species.

reach   A length of channel.

regime equations   Empirically derived channel design equations that are used to describe discharge-channel form relationships.

regime theory   The empirical science concerned with the design of stable channels formed in natural sediments and carrying a load of those sediments.

regrading   Changes to the long profile or gradient of the riverbed.

rehabilitation   The partial return to a pristine state.

remote sensing   The gathering and analysis of data from an object physically removed from the sensing equipment eg aerial photography.

resectioning   Changes to the cross-section of a river involving excavation or infilling.

restoration   The return to a pristine state.

revetment   Facing built to support a bank.

rhizomes   Underground stems which produce shoots at a distance from the parent plant.

riffle–pool sequence   The system of bedforms associated with minimisation of energy expenditure whilst permitting sediment transport. The riffle–pool sequence is characteristic of gravel-bed rivers.

riparian   Relating to or situated on the bank of a river or stream.

river terrace(s)   Lateral bench between a river channel and its valley sides.

roughness   Frictional drag is exerted on water as it flows in contact with the bed and banks of a channel. This drag depends on roughness which is determined by characteristics of perimeter sediment, channel sinuosity, shape size and the amount of aquatic plant growth. See also Manning's eqn.

scats   Animal faeces, usually mink.

scrub   The collective term for small shrubs and trees.

secondary currents   Secondary currents in rivers are associated with longitudinal vortices and result from non-uniform distribution of shear-stress/turbulence. Secondary currents are locally important in sediment transport processes.

sequential cutting   Cutting of vegetation on a rotation.

shear-stress   The result of two perpendicular loads applied parallel to a surface. They themselves are perpendicular to the normal stress; units are in force per unit area.

sheet piling   Corrugated metal sheets used for vertical bank protection.

shoal   Exposed gravel/pebble-bar deposit

sill   A narrow ledge of hard material protruding from the river bank and deflecting the current.

sinuosity   Degree of meandering in channel.

soft-engineering   Opposite of hard protection – normally employing natural materials. See also hard-engineering.

spate   Flood of high magnitude and short duration characteristic of upland streams eg after heavy rains or melting snow.

species map   Map showing positions and records of birds seen or heard, allowing territories and numbers to be determined.

species richness   The relative number of different species in an area or community.

spiling   Willow twigs woven around winter-cut willow stakes and used to protect steep or vertical banks.

spoil   Material such as vegetation and silt removed during dredging or digging.

spraint   Otter faeces used as territory markers.

SSSI   Site of Special Scientific Interest.

storage   Retention, normally temporary, of flood water on floodplains.

stream power   The rate of potential energy expenditure per unit length of channel.

submerged vegetation   Plants rooted to the bed and either completely submerged or with only part of their shoots floating or emergent.

substrate   Material making up the bed of a river.

sward   Above-ground components of grass.

tanalised wood   Wood impregnated with preservative.

target plant species   Plant species that are desired and actively encouraged by selective management.

taxon (taxa)   Any defined unit (such as species, genus or family) used in the classification of living organisms.

tilth   The physical state of soil that determines its ability to grow plants, taking into account texture, structure, consistency and pore space.

toe   The base of a bank.

trapezoidal channel   An artificial channel with sloping sides and a flat bed.

tributary   A stream or river which feeds into a larger one.

turbidity   Reduced transparency caused, in water, by suspended solids, giving a murky appearance.

turf   Section of sward lifted complete with root system and a layer of soil.

turion   A small shoot or bud of a water plant that detaches and remains inert during the winter, giving rise to a

	new plant in the spring. Any scaly shoot or sucker developed from an underground bud.	**wet fences**	Ditches used for stock control.
undershot	A type of sluice gate that opens and closes vertically.	**wetlands**	Areas of marsh, fen, peatland or water, whether natural or artificial, permanent or temporary, with water that is static or flowing, fresh, brackish or salt including areas of marine water, the depth of which at low tide does not exceed 6 m. (RAMSAR definition)
vane	A type of current deflector.		
washland	Extensive semi-natural area adjacent to a river created as flood storage area, eg Ouse/Nene Washes.		
water stress	Physiological stress to plants caused by insufficient water.	**wetted perimeter**	Length of bed and banks across a section in contact with water.
water table	Level below which the soil/rock is permanently saturated.	**whips**	Tree transplants less than *c* 1 m.
weir	A device to control flows whereby flow occurs when flow depth is above a pre-set level.	**winter bourne**	An intermittent stream.

References

Adams, J (1988) Trawling to sample fish populations. *Proceedings of the Institute of Fisheries Management 19th Annual Study Course*, Southampton. pp107–110. Institute of Fisheries Management, Nottingham.

Alabaster, J S (ed.) (1985) *Habitat modification and freshwater fish*. 278pp. Butterworths.

Amoros, C, Roux, A L, Reygrobellet, J L, Bravard, J P and Pautou, G (1987) A method for applied ecological studies of fluvial hydrosystems. *Regulated Rivers* 1:17–36.

Andrews J and Kinsman D (1990) *Gravel Pit Restoration for Wildlife*. RSPB, Sandy.

Andrews, E and Crawford, A K (1986) *Otter Survey of Wales 1984–85*. Vincent Wildlife Trust, London.

Anon (1988) *Methods for sampling fish populations in shallow rivers and streams*. DoE Standing Committee of Analysts. HMSO.

Armitage, P D and Petts, G E (1992). Biotic score and prediction to assess the effects of water abstractions on river macroinvertebrates for conservation purposes. *Aquatic Conservation: Marine and Freshwater Ecosystems.* 2:1–17.

Armitage, P D, Furse, M T and Wright, J F (1992) Environmental quality and biological assessment in British rivers – past and future perspectives. *Direccion de Investigacion y Formacion Agropesqueras: Gobierno Vasco.*

Armitage, P D, Gunn, R J M, Furse, M T, Wright, J F and Moss, D (1987) The use of prediction to assess macroinvertebrate response to river regulation. *Hydrobiologia* 144:25–32.

Armitage, P D, Machale, A M and Crisp, D C (1974) A survey of stream invertebrates in the Cow Green (Upper Teesdale) before inundation. *Freshwater Biology* 4:368–398.

Armitage, P D, Moss, D, Wright, J F and Furse, M T (1983) The performance of a new biological water quality score system based on macroinvertebrates over a wide range of unpolluted running-water sites. *Water Research* 17:333–347.

Armitage, P D, Pardo, I, Furse, M T and Wright, J F (1990) Assessment and prediction of biological quality. A demonstration of a British macroinvertebrate-based method in two Spanish rivers. *Limnetica* 6:147–156.

Arnold, E N and Burton, J A (1978) *A field guide to the reptiles and amphibians of Britain and Europe*. Collins, London.

Ash, J R V and Woodcock, E P (1988) The operational use of river corridor surveys in management. *Journal of the Institute of Water and Environment Management* 2:423–428.

Axford, S N (1979) Angling returns in fisheries biology. *Proceedings of the First British Freshwater Fisheries Conference.* pp259–272. University of Liverpool.

Axford, S N (1991) Some factors affecting angling catches in Yorkshire rivers. In I G Cowx (ed.) *Catch effort sampling strategies.* pp143–153 Fishing News Books.

Baines, C and Smart, J (1984) *A guide to habitat creation.* GLC.

Banks, B (1990) Identification – Britain's Frogs and Toads. *British Wildlife* 1(3):157–160

Banks B (1991) Identification - British Newts. *British Wildlife* 2(6):362–365

Barnes, H H (1967) Roughness characteristics of natural channels. US *Geological Survey and Water Supply Paper* 1849.

Barrell, J (1993) Pre-planning tree surveys: safe useful life expectancy (SULE) is the natural progression.

Barrett, P R F and Murphy, K J (1982) The use of diquat-algimate for weed control in flowing waters. *Proceedings EWRS 6th Symposium on Aquatic Weeds*, pp200–208.

Barrett, P R F (1978) Aquatic Weed Control. Necessity and Methods. *Fish Management*, 9(3):93–101.

Barrett, P R F (1985) The efficacy of glyphosate in controlling aquatic weeds. In E Grossbard and D Atkinson (eds.) *The Herbicide Glyphosate.* Butterworths.

Barrett, P R F and Newman, J R (1993) The control of algae with barley straw. *PIRA Conference Proceedings: Straw – A Valuable Raw Material* 20–22 April 1993.

Batten, L, Bibby, C J, Clement, P, Elliott, G D and Porter, R F (1990) *Red Data Birds in Britain*. T and A D Poyser, London.

Bayley, P B (1990). Sampling strategies for fish populations. In K T O'Grady, A J B Butterworth, P B Spillett and J C J Domaniewski (eds.) *"Fisheries in the year 2000"*. pp 253–259. Proceedings of the 21st anniversary conference of the Institute of Fisheries Management, held at Royal Holloway College, Egham. Institute of Fisheries Management, Nottingham.

Bayley, P B (1991) The flood pulse advantage and the restoration of river floodplain systems. *Regulated Rivers* 6(2):75–86.

Beebee, T J C (1985) *Frogs and toads.* Whittet Books, London.

Bibby, C J, Burgess, N D and Hill, D A (1992) *Bird Census Techniques.* Academic Press, London.

Biggs, J (1993) River Restoration Project: Summary of Phase 1. Report to RRP.

Birks, J (1990) Feral mink and nature conservation. *British Wildlife.* 1(6):313–323.

Bohlin, T (1991) Estimation of population parameters using electric fishing: aspects of sampling design with emphasis upon salmonids in streams. In I G Cowx (ed.) *Developments in electric fishing.* pp156–173. Fishing News Books.

Bohlin, T, Hamrin, S, Heggberget, T G, Rasmussen, G and Saltveit, S J (1989) Electrofishing – theory and practice with special emphasis on salmonids. *Hydrobiologia* 173:9–43.

Brandon, T W (ed.) (1989) *River Engineering - Part II Structures and coastal defence works* Number 8 IWEM, London.

Bravard, J P, Roux, A L, Amoros, C and Reygrobellet, J L (1992) The Rhône River: a large alluvial temperate river. In P J Boon, and G E Petts (eds.) *The Rivers' Handbook*, Volume 1.pp 426–447, Blackwell, Oxford.

British Herpetological Society (undated) *Save our reptiles*. Leaflet.

British Herpetological Society (undated) *Surveying for amphibians*. Advisory Leaflet.

Brooker, M P (1974) The risk of deoxygenation of water in herbicide applications for aquatic weed control. *Journal of the Institute of Water Engineers* 28:206–210.

Brooker, M P (1975) The ecological effects of the use of aquatic herbicides in Essex. *Surveyor* 145:25–27.

Brooker, M P and Edwards, R W (1973) Effects of the herbicide paraquat on the ecology of a reservoir. I. Botanical and chemical aspects. *Freshwater Biology* 3:157–175.

Brooker, M P and Edwards, R W (1974) Effects of herbicide paraquat on the ecology of a reservoir. III. Fauna and general discussion. *Freshwater Biology* 4:311–335.

Brookes, A (1981). *Waterways and Wetlands*. British Trust for Conservation Volunteers.

Brookes, A (1985) River channelisation, traditional engineering methods, physical consequences and alternative practices. *Progress in Physical Geography*. 9:44–73.

Brookes, A (1988) *Channelised rivers, perspectives for environmental management*. John Wiley and Sons, Chichester.

Brookes, A (1990) Restoration and enhancement of engineered river channels: some European experiences. *Regulated Rivers Research and Management* 5:45–56.

Brookes, A (1991) Geomorphology. In J L Gardiner (ed.) *River Projects and Conservation: A Manual for Holistic Appraisal*. pp57–66. John Wiley and Sons, Chichester.

Brookes, A (1992) Recovery and restoration of some engineered British River Channels. In: P J Boon, P Calow and G E Petts (eds.) *River Conservation and Management*. pp 337–352. John Wiley and Sons, Chichester.

Brookes, A and Long, H J (In prep). A method for the geomorphological assessment of river channels at the catchment scale.

Bubb, N J (1980) A large buoyant net designed to catch coarse fish fry quantitatively from shallow weed free water. *Fisheries Management* 11:29–34.

Buisson, R and Williams, G (1991) RSPB Action for lowland wet grasslands. *RSPB Conservation Review* 5:60–64.

Bullock, A, Gustard, A and Grainger, E S (1990) *Instream flow requirements of aquatic ecology in two British rivers – application and assessment of Instream Flow Incremental Methodology using the PHABSIM system*. Institute of Hydrology Report September 1990.

Bussell, R B (1978). *Fish counting stations*. Central Water Planning Unit. DoE.

Butcher, R W (1933). Studies on the ecology of rivers I. On the description of macrophytic vegetation in the rivers of Britain. *Journal of Ecology* 21:58–91.

Carle, F L and Strub, M R (1978) A new method for estimating population size from removal data. *Biometrics* 34:621–630.

Chanin, P R F (1993) *Otters*. Whittet Books.

Chow, V T (1959) *Open channel hydraulics*. McGraw-Hill, New York.

Church, M (1992) Channel morphology and typology. In P Calow and G E Petts (eds.) *The Rivers Handbook*, Volume 1 pp126–143. Blackwell, Oxford.

Churchfield, S (1984) Dietary separation in three shrews inhabiting water-cress beds. *Journal of Zoology* (London) 204:211–228.

Churchfield, S (1985) The feeding ecology of the European water shrew. *Mammal Review* 15(1):13–21.

Churchfield, S (1988) *Shrews of the British Isles*. No 30 in the Shire Natural History Series. Shire Publications Ltd, Aylesbury.

Churchfield, S (1990) *The Natural History of Shrews*. A and C Black, London.

Construction Industry Research Information Association (1980) *Guide to the design of storage ponds for flood control in a partly urbanised catchment area*. CIRIA. Technical Note 100.

Coles, T F, Wortley, J S, and Noble, P (1985) Survey methodology for fish population assessment within Anglian Water. *Journal of Fish Biology* 27 (Supplement A): 175–186.

Cooper, M J and Wheatley, G A (1981) An examination of the fish populations of the River Trent, Nottinghamshire, using anglers' catches. *Journal of Fish Biology* 19:539–556.

Copp, G (1991) *Habitat diversity and natural fisheries*. Presentation at Conservation and water quality for anglers conference. Hatfield Polytechnic, 27 April 1991.

Coppin, N J and Richards, I G (1990) *Use of vegetation in civil engineering*. Construction Industry Research and Information Association.

Corbet, G B and Harris, S (1991). *The Handbook of British Mammals*. Blackwell Scientific Publications, London. 2nd edition.

Corbett, K (1989) *Conservation of European reptiles and amphibians*. Christopher Helm, London.

Cowx, I G (ed.) (1990) *Developments in electric fishing*. Fishing News Books. 358pp.

Cowx, I G (ed.) (1991) *Catch effort sampling strategies*. Fishing News Books. 420pp.

Cowx, I G and Broughton, N M (1986) Changes in the species composition of anglers' catches in the River Trent (England) between 1969 and 1984. *Journal of Fish Biology* 28: 625–636.

Cowx, I G, Wheatley, G A and Hickley, P (1988) Development of boom electric fishing equipment for use in large rivers and canals in the United Kingdom. *Aquaculture and Fisheries Management* 19:125–133.

Crisp, D T and Gledhill, T (1970) A quantitative description of the recovery of the bottom fauna in a muddy reach of a mill stream in Southern England after draining and dredging. *Archives of Hydrobiology* 67:502–541.

Crisp, D T, Mann, R H K and McCormack, J C (1978) The effects of impoundment and regulation upon the stomach contents of fish at Cow Green, Upper Teesdale. *Journal of Fisheries Biology* 12:287–301.

Cummins, K W (1973) Trophic relations of aquatic insects. *Annual Review of Entomology* 18:183–206.

Dawson, F H and Kern-Hansen, U (1979) The effect of natural and artificial shade on the macrophytes of lowland streams and the use of shade as a management technique. *Int. Revue ges. Hydrobiol.* 64:437–55.

Dawson, F H (1989) *Ecology and Management of Water Plants in Lowland Streams.* FBA Annual Report pp43–60, Windermere.

Dawson, F H, Griffiths, G H and Saunders, R M K (1992) *River Corridor Strategic Overview Feasibility Study.* National Rivers Authority, Bristol.

Dickinson, N M and Polwart, A (1982) The effect of mowing regime on an amenity grassland ecosystem: above- and below-ground components. *Journal of Applied Ecology* 19:569–77.

DoE (1987). *Methods for the Use of Aquatic Macrophytes for Assessing Water Quality 1985–86.* Methods for the Examination of Waters and Associated Materials. HMSO, London.

Dony, J G (1977) Changes in the flora of Bedfordshire, England from 1798 to 1976. *Biological Conservation.* 11:307–320.

Eaton, J W, Best, M A, Staples, J A, O'Hara, K (1992) *Grass carp for aquatic weed control – a user's manual.* R and D Note 53. National Rivers Authority, Bristol.

Emery, M (1986) *Promoting nature in cities and towns. A practical guide.* Croom Helm, London.

Erhardt, A (1985) Diurnal lepidoptera: sensitive indicators of cultivated and abandoned grassland. *Journal of Applied Ecology* 22:849–61.

Exton, D M and Crompton, J L (1990) The use of audit surveys in assessing river management. Paper given to Institute of Water and Environmental Management Meeting, 19th January, 1990.

Frazer, D (1983) *Reptiles and amphibians in Britain.* Collins New Naturalist Series, London.

Furse, M T, Wright, J F, Armitage, P D and Moss, D (1981) An appraisal of pond-net samples for biological monitoring of lotic macro-invertebrates. *Water Research* **15**: 679–689.

Gardiner, V and Dackombe, R (1983) *Geomorphological field manual.* Allen and Unwin, London.

Gibbons, D W, Reid, J B and Chapman, R A (1993) *The New Atlas of Breeding Birds in Britain and Ireland 1988–1991.* T and A D Poyser, London.

Giles, N (1992) *Wildlife after Gravel – Twenty years of practical research by the Game Conservancy and ARC.* Game Conservancy, Fordingbridge.

Gordon, N D, McMahon, T A and Finlayson, B L (1992) *Stream Hydrology, An Introduction for Ecologists.* John Wiley and Sons, Chichester.

Goriup, P D (1978) *A Survey and Preliminary Classification of Rivers and Streams in South England.* Nature Conservancy Council, South Region, Newbury.

Green, J and Green, R (1987) *Otter Survey of Scotland 1984–85.* Vincent Wildlife Trust, London.

Gregory, K J and Walling, D E (1973) *Drainage Basin Form and Process.* Edward Arnold, London.

Griffiths, R (1987) *How to begin the study of amphibians.* The Richmond Publishing Company.

Guiver, K (1976) The Ely Ouse to Essex transfer scheme. *Chemistry and Industry.* pp 132–135.

Halyk, L C and Balon, E K (1983) Structure and ecological production of fish taxocerose of a small floodplain system. *Canadian Journal of Zoology.* 61(11):2446–2464.

Haslam, S M (1978) *River Plants. The Macrophytic Vegetation of Water Courses.* Cambridge University Press.

Haslam, S M (1981) *River Vegetation: its Identification, Assessment and Management. A Field Guide to the Macrophytic Vegetation of British Watercourses.* Cambridge University Press.

Haslam, S M (1982) *Vegetation in British Rivers. Volumes I and II.* Nature Conservancy Council, London.

Haslam, S M (1987) *River Plants of Western Europe.* Cambridge University Press.

Hawkes, H A (1975) River Zonation and Classification.In B Whitton (ed.) *River Ecology.* pp312–374. Blackwell, Oxford.

Hawkins, C P, Murphy, M L and Anderson, N H (1982) Effects of canopy substrate composition and gradient on the structure of macroinvertebrate communities in Cascade Range streams of Oregon. *Ecology* 63:1840–1856.

Hey, R D (1990) River mechanics and habitat creation. In K T O'Grady, A J B Butterworth, P B Spillett and J C J Domanienski (eds.) *Fisheries in the year 2000.* Proceedings of the 21st anniversary conference of the Institute of Fisheries Management held in Eghan. pp271–285. Institute of Fisheries Management, Nottingham.

Hellawell, J M (1977) Biological surveillance and water quality monitoring. In J S Alabaster (ed.) *Biological monitoring of inland fisheries.* pp69–88. Applied Science Publishers, London.

Hellawell, J M (1978) *Biological surveillance of rivers – a biological monitoring handbook.* Water Research Centre, Medmenham. 332pp.

Hellawell, J M (1989) *Biological indicators of freshwater pollution and environmental management.* Elsevier Applied Science. London and New York. 546pp.

Hemphill, R W and Bramley, M E (1989) *The protection of river and canal banks.* A guide to selection and design. CIRIA. Butterworths.

Hickley, P and Milwood, B (1990) The UK safety guidelines for electric fishing: its relevance and application. In I G Cowx (ed.) *Developments in electric fishing.* pp311–323. Fishing News Books.

Hillborn, R and Walker, C J (1992) *Quantitative fish stock assessment: choices, dynamics and uncertainty.* Chapman and Hall, New York and London. 570pp.

Hilton-Brown, D and Oldham, R S (1991) The status of the widespread amphibians and reptiles in Britain, 1990, and changes during the 1980's. Contract Surveys No 131, NCC, Peterborough.

HMSO (1978) *Methods of Biological Sampling: Handnet Sampling of Aquatic Benthic Macroinvertebrates 1978.*

HMSO (1980) *Quantitative Samplers for Benthic Macroinvertebrates in Shallow Flowing Waters 1980.*

HMSO (1983) *Methods of Biological Sampling: Sampling of Benthic Macroinvertebrates in Deep Rivers 1983.*

Hodgetts, N (1993) Atlantic bryophytes on the western seaboard. *British Wildlife* 4(5):287–295.

Holcik, J and Bastl, I (1976) Ecological effects of water level fluctuations upon the fish populations in the Danube River floodplain in Czechoslovakia. *Acta. Sc. Nat. Brno.* 10 (9): 1–46.

Holisova, V (1965) The food of the water vole *Arvicola terrestris* in the Agrarian environment of South Moravia. *Zoologicke Listy* 14(3): 209–218.

Holmes, N T H (1983a) *Classification of British Rivers According to their Flora.* Focus on Nature Conservation No 3. NCC, Peterborough.

Holmes, N T H (1983b) *Typing Rivers According to their Macrophytic Flora.* Focus on Nature Conservation No 4. NCC, Peterborough.

Holmes, N T H (1986) Wildlife Surveys of Rivers in Relation to River Management. A report to Water Research Centre, Medmenham.

Holmes, N T H (1989) Typing British rivers – a working classification. *British Wildlife.* 1(1):20–36

Holmes, N T H (1991) *Post-project Appraisal of Conservation Enhancement of Flood Defence Works.* NRA R and D Project Report, Bristol.

Holmes, N T H (1993) River restoration as an integral part of river management in England and Wales. In *Contributions to the European Workshop.* Ecological Rehabilitation of river floodplains, Arnhem, The Netherlands, 22–24 September 1992. Report No 11-6 under the auspices of the CHR/KHR, pp165–172.

Holmes, N T H and Newbold, C (1989) Nature conservation (A) – Rivers as natural resources: and Nature Conservation (B). Sympathetic river management. In *River engineering – part II, structures and coastal defence works.* Water Number 8. Ed T W Brandon. IWGM London

Holmes, N T H and Rowell, T (1993) British Rivers According to their Flora – Update.

Research Contract Report to Scottish Natural Heritage.

Huet, M (1949) Aperçu des relations entre la pente et les populations piscicoles des eaux courantes. *Schweiz. Z. Hydrol.,* 11:332–351.

Hynes, H B N (1960) *The biology of polluted waters.* University Press, Liverpool. 202pp.

Hynes, H B N (1970) *The Ecology of Running Waters.* University of Toronto Press, Toronto.

Hynes, H B N (1972). *The ecology of running waters.* University Press, Liverpool.

Inns, H (1990) Looking for British reptiles. *British Wildlife* 1(5):261–265.

Inns, H (1992) *British Wildlife*: 27–31

Iversen, T M, Kronvang, B, Madsen, B L, Markmann, and Nielsen, M B (1993). Re-establishment of Danish Streams: restoration and maintenance measures. *Aquatic Conservation: Marine and Freshwater Ecosystems* 3:73–92

José, P V (1988) The hydrochemistry of backwaters and deadzones. Unpublished PhD thesis. Loughborough University of Technology.

José, P V and Self, M (1993). The management of lowland wet grassland for birds. In A Crofts and R Jefferson (eds.) *Grassland Management Handbook.* English Nature/Wildlife Trusts Partnership.

Junk, W J, Bayley, P B and Sparks, R E (1989) The flood pulse concept in river-floodplain systems. In D P Dodge, (ed.)*Proceedings of the International Large Rivers Symposium (LARS).* pp110–127, Canadian Special Publication on Fisheries and Aquatic Sciences 106.

Kellerhalls, R, Church, M and Bray, D I (1976) Classification and analysis of river processes. *American Society of Civil Engineers, Journal of the Hydraulics Division* 102:813–829.

Kennedy, C E J and Southwood, T R E (1984) The number of species of insects associated with British trees: a re-analysis. *Journal of Animal Ecology* 53:455–478.

Kennedy, G J A and Strange, C D (1981) Efficiency of electric fishing for salmonids in relation to river width. *Fisheries Management* 12:55–60.

Kitchell, J F, O'Neill, R V, Webb, D, Gallepp, G W, Bartell, S M, Koonee, J F and Ausmus, B S (1979) Consumer regulation of nutrient cycling. *Bioscience.* 29:28–34.

Kondolf, G M and Sales, M J (1985) Application of historical channel stability analysis to instream flow studies. *Proc. Symp. on small hydropower and Fisheries.* pp184–194. Colorado.

Kondolf, M G and Micheli, E R (1993) Evaluating Success of Stream Restoration Projects. *Journal of Environmental Management.*

Kubecka, J, Duncan, A and Butterworth, A J B (1992) Echocounting or echo–integration for fish biomass assessments in shallow waters. In M Weyderf (ed.) *European conference on underwater acoustics.* pp129–132 Elsevier Applied Science, London and New York.

Lackey, R T and Nielson, L A (eds.) (1980) *Fisheries Management.* Blackwell Scientific Publications. 422pp.

Lagler, K F (1968) Capture, sampling and examination of fishes. In W E Ricker (ed.) IBP handbook No. 3. *Method for the assessment of fish production in fresh waters.* pp7–45. Blackwell Scientific Publishing, Oxford.

Lane, E W (1955) *The importance of fluvial geomorphology in hydraulic engineering,* ASCE Proc., 81, No. 745.

Langton, T (1989) *Snakes and lizards.* Whittet Books, London.

Large, A R G and Petts, G E (1992) Restoration of floodplains: a UK perspective. In *Contributions to the European Workshop.* Ecological Rehabilitation of floodplains, Arnhem, The Netherlands, 22–24 September 1992. Report no. 11-6 under the auspices of the CHR/KHR. pp173–180.

Lewis, G (1981) Somerset Rivers Survey: a survey of the Rivers Tone, Yeo, Cary and Northmoor Main Drain, to map and describe their flora and fauna. Somerset Trust for Nature Conservation/Wessex Water Authority. Unpublished report.

Lewis, G and Williams, G (1984) *The Rivers and Wildlife Handbook.* RSPB/RSNC, Sandy/Lincoln.

Luff, M L (1966) The abundance and diversity of the beetle fauna of grass tussocks. *Journal of Animal Ecology* 35:189–208.

Macdonald, S M and Mason, C F (1983) Some factors affecting the distribution of otters (*Lutra lutra*). *Mammal Review* 13:1–10.

MAFF (1985) *Guidelines for the use of herbicides on weed in or near watercourses and lakes.* Booklet 2078.

Maitland, D and Lyle, A (1993) Freshwater fish conservation in the British Isles. *British Wildlife* 5(1):8–15.

Maitland, P S and Campbell, R N (1992) *Freshwater Fishes of the British Isles.* Harper Collins Publishers, London. 368pp.

Mann, R H K (1974) Observations on the age, growth, reproduction and food of the dace *Leuciscus leuciscus* (L.) in two rivers in southern England. *Journal of Fisheries Biology* 6:237–253.

Mann, R H K (1982) The annual food consumption and prey preference of pike (*Esox lucius*) in the River Frome, Dorset. *Journal of Animal Ecology* 51:81–90.

Mann, R H K and Mills, C A (1986) Biological and climatic influences on the Dace (*Leuciscus leuciscus*) in a southern chalk stream. In FBA, Annual Report, 1986. pp123–136.

Mann, R H K, Blackburn, J H and Beaumont, W R C (1989) The ecology of brown trout *Salmo trutta* in English chalk streams. *Freshwater Biology.* 21:57–70.

Marshall, E J P and Westlake, D F (1978) Recent Studies on the role of macrophytes in their ecosystem. *Proceedings of EWRS 5th Symposium on Aquatic Weeds.*

Mason, C F and Macdonald, S M (1982) The input of terrestrial invertebrates from tree canopies to a stream. *Freshwater Biology* 12:305–11.

Mason, C F and MacDonald, S M (1986) Otters: *Ecology and Conservation.* Cambridge University Press.

Mason, C F, Macdonald, S M and Hussey, A (1984) Structure, Management and Conservation Value of the Riparian Woody Plant Community. *Biological Conservation* 29:201–216.

Masterman, R and Thorne, C R (1992) Predicting Influence of Bank Vegetation on Channel Capacity. *Journal of Hydraulic Engineering* 118(7):1052–1058

Matthews, C P (1971) Contribution of young fish to total production of fish in the River Thames near Reading. *Journal of Fish Biology* 3:157–180

Merritt, R W and Cummins, K W (eds)(1984) *An introduction to the aquatic insects of North America (2nd edition).* Kendall/Hunt Publishing Company, Dubuque, Iowa. 722pp.

Merritt, R W, Cummins, K W and Burton, T M (1984) The role of aquatic insects in the processing and cycling of nutrients. In V H Resh and D M Rosenberg (eds.) *The ecology of aquatic insects.* pp134–163. Praeger Scientific, New York.

Mills, D (ed.)(1990) *Strategies for the rehabilitation of salmon rivers.* Atlantic Salmon Trust, The Institute of Fisheries Management and the Linnean Society of London. 210pp.

Milner, N J, Hemsworth, R J and Jones, B E (1985) Habitat evaluation as a fisheries management tool. *Journal of Fish Biology* 27 (Supplement A): 85–108.

Ministry of Agriculture, Fisheries and Food, English Nature and The National Rivers Authority (1992). *Environmental Procedures for Inland Flood Defence Works.*

Minshall, G W (1984) Aquatic insect-substratum relationships, In V M Resh and D M Rosenberg (eds.) *Ecology of Aquatic Insects* pp358–400. Praeger, New York.

Morris, M G (1979a) The response of grassland invertebrates to management by cutting. I. Species diversity of Hemiptera. *J Applied Ecology* 16:77–98.

Morris, M G (1979b) The responses of grassland invertebrates to management by cutting. II. Heteroptera. *Journal of Applied Ecology* 16:417–32.

Murphy, K J, Hanbury, R G and Eaton, J W (1981) The ecological effects of 2-methylthiotriazine herbicides used for aquatic weed control in navigable canals. 1. Effects of aquatic flora and water chemistry. *Archiv für Hydrobiologie* 91:294–331.

National Rivers Authority (1991) *Code of practice for electric fishing.* NRA, London.

National Rivers Authority (1992a) *A guide to bank restoration and river narrowing.* NRA, Southern Region.

National Rivers Authority (1992b) *River Corridor Surveys;* Methods and Procedures Conservation Technical Handbook No 1, NRA Bristol.

National Rivers Authority (1993a) *R and D Report on Bank Erosion on Navigable*

Waterways. Project 336, by Nottingham University (Thorne, C R *et al.*) NRA, Bristol.

National Rivers Authority (1993b) *River Management for Otters*. Conservation Technical Handbook, Number 3.

National Rivers Authority (1993c) *Draft guidelines for the design and restoration of flood alleviation schemes*. R & D Note 154. National Rivers Authority.

National Water Council (1981) *River quality. The 1980 survey and future outlook*. National Water Council, London.

Nature Conservancy Council (1984a) *River Corridor Survey: Draft Methodology*. NCC, Peterborough.

Nature Conservancy Council (1984b) *Nature Conservation in Great Britain*. NCC, Peterborough.

Nature Conservancy Council (1989) *Guidelines for selection of Biological SSSIs. Rationale, Operational Approach and Criteria*. NCC, Peterborough.

Newbold, C (1976) Herbicides in aquatic systems. *Biological Conservation* 7:97–118

Newbold, C (1981) The decline of aquatic plants and associated wetland wildlife in Britain – causes and perspectives on management techniques. *Proceedings of Aquatic Weeds and their Control*.

Newbold, C, Honnor, J and Buckley, K (1989) *Nature Conservation and the management of drainage channels*. NCC/ADA.

Newson, M D (1992a) River Conservation and catchment management, a UK Perspective. In P J Boon, P Calow and G E Petts (eds.) *River Conservation and Management*. pp385–396. John Wiley and Sons, Chichester.

Newson, M D (1992b) *Land, water and development*. Routledge, London.

Nielsen, M B (1992) *Re-creation of meanders and other examples of stream restoration in Southern Jutland, Denmark*. Sønderlyllands Amt.

Nixon, M (1966) Flood regulation and river training. In R B Thorn (ed.) *River Engineering and Water Conservation Works*.

National Research Council (1992) *Restoration of aquatic ecosystems: science, technology, and public policy*. Committee on Restoration of Aquatic Ecosystems: Science, Technology and Public Policy, Water Science and Technology Board, Commission on Geosciences, Environment, and Resources, NRC National Academy of Sciences, Washington, DC.

Nyholm, E S (1965) The ecology of *Myotis mysticinus* and *Myotis daubentoni. Annales Zoologica Fennica* 2:77–123.

Ormerod, F J and Tyler, S J (1987) Dippers *Cinclus cinclus* and Grey Wagtails *Motacilla cinerea* as indicators of stream acidity in upland Wales. In A W Diamond and F Filion (eds.) *The use of birds*. ICBP Technical Publication No 6, International Council for Bird Preservation, Cambridge.

Palmer, M and Newbold, C (1983) *Wetland and Riparian Plants in Great Britain. An assessment of their Status and Distribution in Relation to Water Authority, River Purification Board and Scottish Islands Areas*. Focus on Nature Conservation No 1. NCC, Peterborough.

Palmer, M (1989) *A botanical classification of standing waters in Great Britain*. NCC Research and Survey Series, No 19.

Parker, G and Andres, D (1976) Detrimental effects of stream channelisation, ASCE. *Rivers* 76:1248–1266.

Pearson, R G and Jones, N V (1975) The effects of dredging operations on the benthic community of chalk stream. *Biological Conservation*. 8:273–278.

Pearson, R G and Jones, N V (1978) The effects of weed-cutting on the macro-invertebrate fauna of a canalised section of the River Hull, a northern English chalk stream. *Journal of Environmental Management* 7:91–97.

Pelikan, J (1974) Dynamics and energetics of a reed swamp population of *Arvicola terrestris* (Linn). *Zoologicke Listy*. 23(4):334.

Penczak, T and O'Hara, K (1983) Catch-effort efficiency using three small seine nets. *Fisheries Management* 14. p83–92.

Perrow, M and Wightman, A S (1993) River Restoration Project Phase 1: Feasibility Study. Report to RRP.

Petts, G E (1980) Long term consequences of upstream impoundment *Environmental Conservation* 7:325–332.

Petts, G E (1983) *Rivers*. Butterworths Publications, London.

Petts, G E and Foster, I D L (1985) *Rivers*. Butterworths, London.

Philips, R and Rix, M (1985) *Freshwater Fish of Britain, Ireland and Europe*. Pan Books Limited, London. 144pp.

Pieterse, A H and Murphy, K J (1990) *Aquatic Weeds*.

Plachter, H (1986) Composition of the carabid fauna of natural riverbanks and man-made secondary habitats. In P J den Boer, M L Luff, D Mossakowski and F Weber (eds): *Carabid beetles: their adaptations and dynamics*. pp509–535. Gustav Fischer, Stuttgart.

Pugh, J C (1975) *Surveying for field scientists*. Methuen, London.

Raven, P J (1986a/b/c) Vegetation changes within the flood relief storage of two-stage channels excavated along a small rural clay river. *Journal of Applied Ecology* 23:1001–1011

Raven, P J (1986a) Changes of in-channel vegetation following two-stage channel construction on a small rural clay river. *Journal of Applied Ecology* 23: 333–345.

Raven, P J (1986b) Changes in waterside vegetation following two-stage channel construction on a small rural clay river. *Journal of Applied Ecology* 23: 989–1000.

Rheinalt, T ap (1990) River Corridor Surveys in Relation to the Nature Conservation Activities of the NRA. National Rivers Authority, Bristol, report produced by Water Research Centre, Medmenham.

Richards, K S (1982) *Rivers; Form and Process in Alluvial Channels*, Methuen, London

Richards, K S (ed.) (1987) *River Channels: Environment and Process*. Blackwell, Oxford.

RIZA (1992) *Contributions submitted to European Workshop: Ecological Rehabilitation of Floodplains*. Arnhem. Report No II-6, CHR.

Robson, T O and Barrett, P R F (1980) The concept of localised control of aquatic weeds. *ADAS Quarterly Review* 37:123–128.

Rodwell, J (ed.) (1992) *British Plant Communities. Volume 4 Swamps and Aquatic Communities*. Cambridge University Press.

Roux, A L (1982) (Ouvrage collectif public sous la direction de) Cartographic polythematique appliquée à la gestion ecologique des caus: étude d'un hydrosysteme fluvial: le Haut Rhône français, Ed. C N R S Centre Region. Publ. Lyon, 116pp.

Royal Society for the Protection of Birds (1978a) *A survey of the birds of the River Wye*. RSPB, Sandy.

Royal Society for the Protection of Birds (1978b) *A survey of the birds of the River Severn*. RSPB, Sandy.

Royal Society for the Protection of Birds (1979) *A survey of the birds of the Avon*. RSPB, Sandy.

Royal Society for the Protection of Birds (1983) *Land Drainage and Birds in England and Wales: An Interim Report*. RSPB, Sandy.

Sargent, G (1991) The importance of riverine habitats to bats in County Durham. MSc Thesis, University of Durham.

Schumm, S A (1977) *The Fluvial System*. Wiley Interscience, New York.

Seber, G A and LeCren, E D (1967) Estimating population parameters from catches large relative to the population. *Journal of Animal Ecology* 36:631–643.

Sellin, R J H and Giles, A (1988) *A two stage channel flow*. Department of Civil Engineering. Contract Reference. IRAB/ENG/13/7/E.

Shearer, W M (1988) Relating catch records to stock. In D Mills and D Piggins (eds.) *Atlantic Salmon: planning for its future*. pp256–274. Croom-Helm, London and Sydney.

Slater, F (1992) *The Common Toad*. Shire Natural History Series No 60, Aylesbury.

Smart, N and Andrews, J (1985) *Birds and broadleaves handbook*. RSPB, Sandy.

Smith, C D, Harper, D M and Barham, P J (1991) Physical environment for river invertebrate communities. Project Report, National Rivers Authority Anglian Region, Operational Investigation A13-38A. 101pp.

Smith, H and Drury, I (1990) Otter conservation in practice. A report to the Water Research Centre.

Soutar, R and Peterken, G F (1989) Regional lists of native trees and shrubs for use in afforestation schemes. *Arboricultural Journal* 13:33–44.

Stafford, P (1987) *The Adder*. Shire Natural History Series No 18, Aylesbury.

Stafford, P (1989) *Lizards of the British Isles*. Shire Natural History Series No 46, Aylesbury.

Statzner, B, Gore, J A and Resh, V H (1988) Hydraulic Stream Ecology: observed patterns and potential applications. *Journal of N American Benthological Society* 7:307–60.

Stebbings, R E and Jefferies, D J (1982) *Focus on bats: their conservation and the law*. Nature Conservancy Council, Peterborough.

Stoddart, D M (1970) Individual range, dispersion and dispersal in a population of water voles. *Journal of Animal Ecology* 39:403–425.

Strachan, R, Birks, J, Chanin, P and Jeffries, D J (1990) *Otter Survey of England, 1984–1986*. NCC, Peterborough.

Sports Turf Research Institute (1981) *Turfgrass seed*. STRI.

Swift, S M and Racey, P A (1983) Resource partitioning in two species of Vespertilionid bats (Chiroptera) occupying the same roost. *Journal of Zoology, London* 200:249–259.

Swift, S M, Racey, P A and Avery, M I (1985) Feeding ecology of *Pipistrellus pipistrellus* (Chiroptera: Vespertilionidae) during pregnancy and lactation II.Diet. *Journal of Animal Ecology* 54:217–225.

Taylor, K (1982) *Waterways Bird Survey Instructions*. British Trust for Ornithology, Tring.

Templeton, R G (1984) *Freshwater Fisheries Management*. pp83–96. Fishing News Books.

The Wildlife Trusts (1991) *Focus on otters – a guide to their natural history and conservation*. The Wildlife Trusts, Lincoln.

Thornton, D and Kite, D J (1990) *Changes in the extent of the Thames Estuary grazing marshes*. NCC.

Tickner, M and Evans, C (1991) *Management of lowland wet grassland*. RSPB unpublished internal report.

Tinkler, B (1993) *Working together*. ADA Gazette Summer 1993 p14.

Valdez, R A and Wick, E J (1983) Natural versus manmade backwaters as native fish habitat. In V D Adams and V A Lamarra (eds.), *Aquatic Resources and Management of the Colorado River Ecosystem*. pp519–536, Ann Arbor Science Publ. Ann Arbor, Mich.

Van Donk, E (1990) Necessity of aquatic plant management after restoration by biomanipulation. EWRS. *8th International Symposium on Aquatic Weeds*, pp91–96.

von Brandt, A (1984) *Fish catching methods of the world*. Third edition. Fishing News Books. 418pp.

Walker, K F, Thoms, M C and Sheldon, F (1992) Effects of weirs on the littoral environment of the River Murray, South Australia. In P J Boon, P Calow and G E Petts (eds.) *River Conservation and Management*. pp271–292. John Wiley and Sons, Chichester.

Ward, D (1992) (ed.) *Reedbeds for Wildlife*. Proceedings of a conference on creating and managing reedbeds with value to wildlife. RSPB/Univ. of Bristol.

Welch, I M, Barrett, P R F, Gibson, M T and Ridge, I (1990). Barley Straw as an indicator of algal growth In Studies on the Chesterfield Canal. *Journal of Applied Phycology* 2:231–239.

Welcomme, R L (1992) River Conservation Future Prospects. In P J Boon, P Calow and G E Petts (eds.) *River Conservation and*

Management. pp453–462. John Wiley and Sons, Chichester.

Welcomme, R L (1985) *River Fisheries*. FAO Fish. 1985, Technical Paper, 262, 330pp.

Wells, T, Bell, S and Frost, A (1981) *Creating attractive grasslands using native plant species*. NCC, Peterborough.

Wheeler, B (1980a) Plant Communities in Rich Fen Systems in England and Wales. I. Introduction. Tall Sedge and Reed Communities. *Journal of Ecology* 68:365–395.

Wheeler, B. (1980b) Plant Communities of Rich Fen Systems in England and Wales. II. Calcareous Mires. *Journal of Ecology* 68:405–20.

Wheeler, B (1980c) Plant Communities of Rich Fen Communities in England and Wales. III. Fen.

Williams, D D and Hynes, H B N (1974) The occurrence of benthos deep in the substratum of a stream. *Freshwater Biology*. 4:233–256.

Williams, D D and Hynes, H B N (1976) The recolonisation mechanisms of stream benthos. *Oikos* 27:265–272.

Williams, G, Newson, M and Browne, D (1988) Land Drainage and Birds in Northern Ireland. *RSPB Conservation Review* Volume 2, Chapter 16.

Williams, G and Hall, M (1987) The loss of coastal grazing marshes in south and east England with special reference to east Essex, England. *Biological Conservation* 39:243–253.

Wisniewski, P J (1989) *Newts of the British Isles*. Shire Natural History Series No 47, Aylesbury.

Wojcik, D F (1981) Flood Alleviation, Conservation and Fisheries – an experimental scheme on the River Roding. MSc Thesis, City University, London.

Woodall, P F (1977) Aspects of the ecology and nutrition of the water vole *Arvicola terrestris* (L). DPhil, University of Oxford.

Worthing, C R (ed.) (1983) The pesticide manual: a world compendium. 7th edition. British Crop Protection Council.

Wright, J F, Blackburn, J H, Armitage, P D, Dawson, F H and Winder, J.M (1991) An investigation of the relationship between the aquatic plant and animal communities of rivers. Report for the period April 1990 to March 1991. Report to the Nature Conservancy Council, 45pp.

Wright, J F, Blackburn, J H, Westlake, D F, Furse, M F and Armitage, P D (1992) Anticipating the consequences of river management for the conservation of macroinvertebrates. In P J Boon, P Calow and G E Petts (eds.) *River Conservation and Management*. pp137–150. John Wiley and Sons, Chichester.

Wright, J F, Hiley, P D, Ham, S F and Berrie, A D (1981) Comparison of three mapping procedures developed for river macrophytes. *Freshwater Biology* 11:369–379.

Zippin, C (1958) The removal method of population estimation. *Journal of Wildlife Management* 22: 82–90.

The Royal Society for the Protection of Birds
The Lodge, Sandy, Bedfordshire SG19 2DL.

National Rivers Authority
Rivers House, Waterside Drive, Aztec West, Almondsbury, Bristol BS12 4UD

The Wildlife Trusts
The Green, Witham Park, Lincoln OL5 7JR

RSPB Habitat Management Handbooks

Farming and Wildlife - A Practical Management Handbook by John Andrews and Michael Rebane, RSPB, 1994. ISBN 0 903138 67 0. £21.95

Gravel Pit Restoration for Wildlife by John Andrews, RSPB, 1990. ISBN 0 903138 60 3 £12.

Gravel Pit Restoration for Wildlife - Managers Summary, RSPB, 1990. £5

Habitat Management for Invertebrates - A Practical Handbook by Peter Kirby, RSPB and JNCC, 1992. ISBN 0 903138 55 7 £9.

Index

The alphabetical arrangement is letter by letter.
Numbers in *italics* refer to photographs.
Numbers in **bold** refer to case studies, figures and tables.

Hatfield Waste Drain (Notts) **370–1**
health and safety 379–81
hedge-laying **278**, 278
hemp agrimony *40*
herbicides 241–4, **242**, **243**, 244, 259, **259**
heron, grey 65
high energy stream/river **30**
holts *see under* otter
Hull, River (Humberside) 191, **191**, *192*
hurdles, woven hazel **286**, 287–8
hydro–acoustics, to survey fish 140
hydrographs **16**, 17, 18, **196**, **230**

Idle, River (Notts) *258*
in–channel management *see* channel
    management
invertebrates 86, **86**, **88**, 88
    data sources 93, 95, 153
    in floodplain wetlands 97
    functional trophic groups 91–2, **92**
        micro–habitats **87**, 88–91, **89**
    pollution tolerance 152, **152**; score
        systems 156–8, **157**
    population changes downstream **93**
    and river management 92–7, **94**
    sampling 153–6, **154**, **156**, 159
    and shingle/gravel bars 12, *90*, **91**
    surveys 152–3
islands 180–1, *180*, 228, 230, **296**, *297*, **302**,
    323
ivy 280

kingfisher 65, *65*

lapwing 66
larch poles
    deflectors 223, *224*
    retaining spoil *179*
    revetment *220*
lateral bar *13*
Leach, River (Glos) **364–5**
leats 191–2
leech, medicinal 390
Leptospirosis 379
levees *see* floodbanks
limestone
    placement on riverbed **304**, **305**, *305*
    use in channel narrowing 178–9, *179*
livestock
    access to banks and margins 189–90
    see also browsing; grazing
Loddon, River (Surrey/Hants), catchment
    358–9
Loddon pondweed **358**, **359**, *359*
logs and branches, as bank protection 286,
    286, **326**, *326*, *327*

Loughrans Weir Fish Pass **330–1**
low energy stream/river **30**
lowland rivers *12*, *60*
    birds 62, **63–4**, 64–5
    channel straightening: impact *190*
    fish zonation 72, **73**, **74**, 74–5
    hydrograph **16**
    invertebrates **87**
    plants *40*
Lugg, River (Herefordshire) 199, **199**, *230*,
    277, **320–1**, **334–5**
Lyde, River (Hants) **296–7**

machinery, and access to banks 169
macrophytes, surveying/mapping 120–1,
    121, **122**, 123–4, **123**
mammals
    requirements and distribution **48**
    see also under names of individual species
Manning's 'n' 109, 110
marginal/bankside plants **40–1**, *74*, *309*,
    311
    as bank protection 251–2
grass tussocks *256*
habitat creation **294**, **310**, **346**, *350*, **351**, *351*
    management **254**, 254–5
    planting *251*, **318**, **347**, *347*; for screening
        250, *251*, **356**, **357**, **362**, **363**, *363*
    recolonisation *237*, *303*
    transplantation **310**, **352**, **353**
    see also plants; trees; trees and shrubs
marigold, marsh *32*
martin, sand, and nest hole *65*
matting *179*, **180**
meanders *188*, 202
    see also bend reprofiling; realignment
Medway, River (Kent) 289, **372–3**, **374–5**
Meece Brook (Staffs) 249, 289
micro–habitats, use by invertebrates **87**,
    88–91, **89**
mill leats 191–2
Milton Keynes, flood storage 230–1, **231**
mink *52*, 52–3, **130**
    scats and footprints **126**
Monnow, River (Herefordshire) 216,
    316–17
moss, *Rhynchostegium riparioides* 39
mowing 257–8, *257*, **257**, *258*, **258**, **370**, *371*
multi–stage channels 195, **195**, *197*, **317**, *317*
    design **196**, 196–9, **198**, **199**
    maintenance **316**
    see also berms; reprofiling; two-stage
channels
mussel, pearl 391

narrowing channels 177–80, **178**, *179*, **300**,